CHILDREN FAMILIES & COMMUNITIES

Contexts and Consequences

Edited by

Third Edition

Jennifer Bowes

Rebekah Grace

OXFORD
UNIVERSITY PRESS
AUSTRALIA & NEW ZEALAND

OXFORD
UNIVERSITY PRESS
AUSTRALIA & NEW ZEALAND

253 Normanby Road, South Melbourne, Victoria 3205, Australia

Oxford University Press is a department of the University of Oxford.
It furthers the University's objective of excellence in research,
scholarship, and education by publishing worldwide in

Oxford New York

Auckland Cape Town Dar es Salaam Hong Kong Karachi
Kuala Lumpur Madrid Melbourne Mexico City Nairobi
New Delhi Shanghai Taipei Toronto

With offices in

Argentina Austria Brazil Chile Czech Republic France Greece
Guatemala Hungary Italy Japan Poland Portugal Singapore
South Korea Switzerland Thailand Turkey Ukraine Vietnam

OXFORD is a trademark of Oxford University Press
in the UK and in certain other countries

National Library of Australia Cataloguing-in-Publication data

Bowes, Jennifer.
Children, families and communities: contexts and consequences/Jennifer Bowes and Rebekah Grace.
3rd ed.
South Melbourne, Vic.: Oxford University Press, 2008.

9780195551549 (pbk.)

Includes index.
Bibliography.

Socialization—Australia.
Environment and children—Australia.
Parent and child—Australia.
Family—Australia—Psychological aspects.
Children and adults—Australia—Psychological aspects.

Grace, Rebekah.

303.320994

Edited by Josephene Duffy
Cover design by Stella Vassiliou
Text design by Rob Cowpe Design
Typeset by diacriTech
Proofread by Anne Mulvaney
Indexed by Jeanne Rudd
Printed in Hong Kong by Sheck Wah Tong Printing Press Ltd.

Contents

Part C: Face-to-face Influences: Families, Schools and Communities

Figure and Tables

Preface

This book is about the ways in which children, families and communities influence one another, and how different contexts can affect them all. Our interest stems from a concern with the well-being of children and their development into confident and competent members of society. Many contributors to the book come from a background of developmental psychology and wish to extend the growing focus in that field on development in context, moving away from past consideration of children as isolated individuals whose development proceeds regardless of context. The inclusion of authors from a variety of disciplinary backgrounds (including sociology, history, social work, education, health, geography and the law) has allowed us to explore this wider approach to the study of child development.

Development implies a process and some kind of desirable outcome. We see outcomes in a contextual way. Rather than focus on competently functioning individual children and individual families, we want to put the emphasis on successful interconnections among children, families and communities. An optimum outcome for individuals is to operate well and to contribute within their families and communities. A family's participation in the life of the wider community is seen as a goal for family development as well as an index of the conditions for development of children. Ultimately this can lead to a stronger social unit, one in which individuals provide support for one another and work well together. We hold a view of individuals as interdependent rather than entirely independent, and interconnections with others as fundamental to positive functioning in society.

In examining the role of context in children's development, we are not claiming that context is all that needs to be considered in human development or in the functioning of families and communities. We are also not concerned with exploring in this book the important question of the relative influence of environment and genetics on development. It is widely acknowledged that development is a function of both and behavioural genetics is adding rapidly to our knowledge of how genes interact with environmental influences.

Our claim is rather that children, families and communities cannot be considered apart from one another. Any attempt to analyse children's development or to consider policy that might enhance the well-being of children in our society must take into account the families of those children and the communities to which they belong. It is important to remember, however, that the effect is not one-way, with context affecting children only. Children are active participants in the daily lives of families and communities and influence and change their families and communities through their involvement. In doing so, they are part of the construction of the contexts that surround them. The third edition of this book develops the theoretical groundwork for exploring these mutual influences that was laid down in the previous editions.

The book examines contextual differences on several levels, beginning with the individual, exploring the contexts in which children and families are involved, and ending with issues of social policy. The introductory chapter explores the central concepts of context and consequences, and acquaints the reader with the theoretical framework used throughout the book. Chapter 2 provides an introduction to child development research that takes context into account by examining the design and methods used in several large international and Australian studies. Chapters 3, 4 and 5 present three examples of individual characteristics that can affect well-being and development in children, families and communities. The characteristics—disability, ethnicity and playfulness—were chosen to exemplify ways in which individual characteristics interact with contexts to produce a range of outcomes. This does not imply that other child characteristics such as age or temperament are less important. A range of individual characteristics could have been chosen for this kind of analysis. Equally, the characteristics of family and community members other than children also interact with contexts, resulting in consequences for children, families and communities.

Chapters 6, 7 and 8 examine the effects of three contexts that directly involve most children: families, educational settings and the local community. Community influences are highlighted by an examination of the consequences of isolation or diminished community connectedness for families and children. Chapter 9 takes a detailed look at the special case of refugee children and families in Australia and the effects of context on their development and well-being. Chapters 10, 11 and 12 look beyond face-to-face contexts to issues of social policy that are more distant from individual children and families but nevertheless exert a strong influence on their lives. The three areas explored—child protection policies in response to child neglect and abuse, the removal of Indigenous children from their families as a result of government policy, and the changes in provision of child care in Australia in relation to changes in social policy—illustrate the ways in which the wider society can intervene directly in the lives of children, families and communities. The final chapter looks at the implications of the analysis in this book for Australian policy. It considers current features of Australian society and social policy and the strengths and limitations of intervention and prevention approaches to strengthening children, families and communities.

Acknowledgments

We are grateful to all of the authors for their contribution to the third edition of this book. Many have contributed to all three editions and we are delighted that new authors have joined the book for this edition, contributing new ideas and chapters. We owe a special debt to three contributors. Jacqueline Goodnow and Ailsa Burns provided inspiration for the book with their *Children and Families in Australia* (published in 1985), and both encouraged its development, contributing generously with their ideas and experience. Alan Hayes co-edited the first edition and was a key contributor of ideas for the book as well as co-authoring several chapters in all three editions.

We are pleased to acknowledge also the excellent work done by Vijetta Bachraz and Margaret Bowes in preparation and checking of the manuscript and thank Josephene Duffy for her careful editing of the book for Oxford University Press. Our thanks go too to Debra James and Michelle Green of Oxford University Press for their encouragement and guidance as the third edition was prepared. We wish to acknowledge with thanks Brown & Benchmark for permission to reproduce a figure in this book. Table 1 on page 9 from the ABS *National Survey of Indigenous People*, 1994, cited in HREOC, 1997, p. 14, is copyright of the Commonwealth of Australia, reproduced with permission. Finally, we are both very grateful for the support and forbearance of our children, families and academic colleagues as we focused on the book's completion.

Jennifer Bowes and Rebekah Grace

Contributors

Jennifer Bowes is a Professorial Fellow at the Institute of Early Childhood, Macquarie University and founding Director of the Children and Families Research Centre, Macquarie University. She has a research background in educational and developmental psychology and is leader of two Child Care Choices research projects, a longitudinal investigation of the effects of multiple and changeable child care in the first three years of life on the development of young children and an investigation of the child care choices and attitudes of Indigenous families, both funded by the NSW Department of Community Services. She is also leading studies into the investigation of early childhood education for four groups: children with disabilities, children of recent arrivals in Australia, gifted children and Indigenous children, funded by the Australian government Department of Education, Employment and Workplace Relations.

Deborah Brennan is Professor in the Social Policy Research Centre, University of New South Wales. She specialises in Australian politics, gender and politics and the comparative study of welfare states. She was a founding member of the National Association of Community Based Children's Services and has served on government advisory committees at State and Commonwealth level as well as the boards of community organisations including ACOSS and Community Child Care NSW. Her publications include *The Politics of Australian Child Care: Philanthropy to Feminism and Beyond* (2nd edn, Cambridge University Press, 1998) and *'No Fit Place for Women': Women in NSW Politics, 1856–2006* (UNSW Press, 2006). She is the immediate past President of the Australasian Political Studies Association.

Anita Bundy is Professor and Chair of Occupational Therapy at the Faculty of Health Sciences, University of Sydney. Her teaching and research have emphasised occupational therapy, particularly the promotion and assessment of play in children with disabilities. Recently, she has become interested in using active outdoor play with children at risk of obesity or mental health problems. She is the author of two observational assessments of play: the *Test of Playfulness (ToP)* and the *Test of Environmental Supportiveness (TOES)*. She also is co-editor of *Sensory Integration: Theory and Practice* and a soon-to-be-published textbook: *Kids Can Be Kids: Supporting the Occupations and Activities of Childhood*. The latter captures a long-term interest in enabling children with disabilities to live ordinary lives.

Ailsa Burns is an Honorary Associate in the Department of Psychology, Macquarie University, Sydney. Her longstanding research interest in the changing nature of families in Australia has led to the publication of many articles and books, including *Children and Families in Australia* (with J. J. Goodnow, Allen & Unwin, 1985), *Australian Women: Contemporary Feminist Thought* (with N. Grieve, Oxford University Press, 1994), *Mother-headed Families and Why They Have Increased* (Erlbaum, 1994) and *Adopting Overseas* (with L. Burns, Rockpool, 2007). She is currently involved with refugee family issues.

Kate Burns is a lawyer with a background in human rights and international law. From 1991 until 1997 she worked with the Human Rights and Equal Opportunity Commission. While there, from April 1996 until April 1997, she was the senior researcher and writer with the Commission's National Inquiry into the Separation of Aboriginal and Torres Strait Islander Children from their Families. She is currently a Senior Solicitor in the Crown Solicitor's Office of New South Wales.

Judy Cashmore is an Associate Professor in the Faculty of Law, University of Sydney, adjunct Professor in the Division of Arts, Southern Cross University, and Honorary Research Associate at the Social Policy Research Centre, University of New South Wales. Her research has focused on children's involvement with and perceptions of legal and child welfare processes. This includes investigating children's roles as child witnesses; research into their participation in decisions concerning residence and contact following parental separation; reports on systems abuse (harm caused by the very systems that are set up to protect children) and on physical punishment; and a longitudinal study of wards leaving out-of-home care. She is a member of a number of government and non-government committees, including the New South Wales Judicial Commission, the Research Advisory Committees for the New South Wales and Queensland child welfare/safety departments, and Defence for Children International (Australia).

Pamela Coutts is an Associate Professor and Director of the Teacher Education Program in the School of Education, Macquarie University. Her research interests are in the area of social cognition as it applies to educational issues such as children's ideas about responsibility for homework as well as issues around assessment. Professor Coutts is responsible for both undergraduate and postgraduate courses in educational psychology within the School of Education.

Monica Cuskelly is a Senior Lecturer in the School of Education at the University of Queensland. Her research interests include the development of people with Down syndrome, the impact on families of having a child with a disability, and the development of self-regulation in normally developing children and those with an intellectual disability. Dr Cuskelly is Co-director of the Down Syndrome Research Project, which incorporates a longitudinal (thirty-year) study following the development of individuals with Down syndrome, among a range of other projects.

Maureen Fegan is Director of the Early Childhood Road Safety Education Program at Macquarie University. She has a longstanding involvement with community groups, including those in rural and remote areas of Australia, with particular emphasis on facilitating provision of innovative and flexible early childhood services that support families.

Jacqueline J. Goodnow is an Emeritus Professor at the Institute of Early Childhood, Macquarie University. She has a long-term interest in cross-generational relationships and the ways in which individuals and their social or cultural contexts influence one another. Books include *Development According to Parents* (with W.A. Collins, Lawrence Erlbaum, 1990), *Men, Women and Household Work* (with J.M. Bowes, Oxford University Press, 1994) and *Cultural Practices as Contexts for Development* (edited with P. Miller and F. Kessel, Jossey-Bass, 1995). In recognition of her work she has been made a Companion of the Order of Australia (AC) and, in the USA, received the G. Stanley Hall Award for Distinguished Contributions to Developmental Psychology.

Rebekah Grace is a Postdoctoral Research Fellow in the Children and Families Research Centre, Macquarie University. Her research background is in developmental psychology, health sciences and medical psychology. Her teaching and research have primarily centred on children with disabilities and their families. Dr Grace also has a research interest in the early childhood service and support needs of families who experience socio-economic disadvantage, as well as the including of young children's voices in research on issues that affect them. She has published within the disability and education field.

Linda Harrison is an Associate Professor in Early Childhood Education at Charles Sturt University. Her research and professional work are in the area of child development, specialising in the ways that provisions and practices in child care and the early years of school influence the quality of teaching and learning experiences for children. She is a principal investigator on three longitudinal research studies— the Sydney Family Development Project, Child Care Choices, and the Longitudinal Study of Australian Children—that are investigating the use and impact of early education and child care on children's health, development and well-being.

Alan Hayes took up his appointment as Director of the Australian Institute of Family Studies in September 2004. With qualifications in psychology, he has longstanding research and policy interests in the pathways children and their families take through life, and the role of families in supporting and sustaining development across life, from infancy and early childhood. The role of vulnerability and resilience in shaping developmental pathways has been a particular interest. Much of his work has focused on disadvantage, with a longstanding interest in prevention and early intervention as well as in the impacts of disabilities on families. The factors that impede access to opportunity continue to be a key focus. Professor Hayes holds a Chair of Early Childhood Studies at Macquarie University, where he was also foundation Dean and Head of Division at the Australian Centre for Education Studies (ACES). He has been the chair, deputy chair or a member of four Australian Government Ministerial Advisory Councils, including the Commonwealth Child Care Advisory Council (CCCAC), the Australian Council for Children and Parenting (ACCAP), the Stronger Families and Communities Strategy (SF&CS)

Partnership and the Australian Families and Children Council (AFCC). For the NSW Government he chaired the committee that successfully established the Institute of Teachers in 2004 and was a member of the NSW Child Protection Council. An Alexander von Humboldt Fellow, he has been a Visiting Professor at the Free University of Berlin and Pennsylvania State University.

Jeanette A. Lawrence is Associate Professor in the School of Behavioural Science, University of Melbourne. She is a developmental psychologist with longstanding interests in both developmental theory and its applications to social policy. Those interests have led to a series of projects and publications on topics ranging from concepts of justice to views on family obligations and the analysis of developmental pathways. Her current research is focused on the views held by refugee African children about their progress through Australian schools, on ways to facilitate their progress, and on methods that allow a separation of cultural effects from the effects of socio-economic disadvantage.

Tim Luckett is a Senior Research Assistant in the Discipline of Occupational Therapy at the Faculty of Health Sciences at the University of Sydney. He has a background in speech pathology and a research interest in developmental disabilities, especially autism spectrum disorders. He has co-authored several publications, most recently a journal article that reviewed the evidence for benefits of playfulness in children with autism taking part in behavioural therapy.

Karen Menzies is an Aboriginal woman from the Wonnarua people of the Hunter Valley, New South Wales. As an education and training consultant she has delivered seminars and workshops on child protection, cross-cultural issues, health, human rights, Indigenous issues, interpersonal skills, social policy and welfare-related issues to government departments and non-government agencies. She spent two years at the Human Rights and Equal Opportunity Commission working with the National Inquiry Team that produced the *Bringing Them Home* Report. She is currently a Conjoint Social Work Lecturer with the University of Newcastle.

Geraldine Naughton is Director of the Centre of Physical Activity Across the Lifespan at the Australian Catholic University. She is a paediatric exercise scientist with a background of projects aiming at improvements in health and well-being through physical activity. She has researched with a range of young populations from overweight and obese children to intensively training adolescents.

Cathrine Neilsen-Hewett is a Lecturer at the Institute of Early Childhood, Macquarie University. She has a research background in children's peer relationships in school and outside school. Her current research interests are family and child response to bullying at school and in early childhood settings.

Emma Pearson is a Lecturer at the Institute of Early Childhood, Macquarie University. She has a research background in cross-cultural perspectives on early childhood and socialisation. Her recent activities have involved work as a consultant to UNICEF on projects in Cambodia, Laos, the Democratic People's Republic of Korea and Vietnam.

Paul Tranter is a Senior Lecturer in the School of Physical, Environmental and Mathematical Sciences at UNSW@ADFA (the Australian Defence Force Academy) in Canberra. He lectures in social geography and transport geography. His research interests include the themes of child-friendly environments and sustainable cities. He has examined the geography of children's play and independent mobility at scales ranging from school grounds to cities. Paul is an author of several publications relating to child-friendly environments and has presented at numerous forums on child-friendly cities in Canberra, Brisbane, Melbourne and Sydney. His recent research includes the examination of the implications of 'peak oil' for children and child-friendly environments.

Judy Ungerer is an Associate Professor in the Department of Psychology, Macquarie University. She is a developmental psychologist with a research background in children's attachment relationships with their parents. Associate Professor Ungerer is a key researcher in the Longitudinal Study of Australian Children, particularly in issues of early childhood care and development.

Johanna Watson is Manager, Centre for Parenting and Research within the NSW Department of Community Services. Her research interests are in the area of developmental psychopathology, in particular the influence of the social context on children's life chances. This interest stems from her background in clinical child and family psychology. Her current research interests focus on child protection issues, particularly childhood neglect and the importance of early intervention programs aimed at preventing maltreatment and enhancing children's developmental well-being.

Shirley Wyver is a Senior Lecturer in child development at the Institute of Early Childhood, Macquarie University. Her main publications are in the area of play and cognitive development and early development of children who are blind or have low vision.

Part A

Contexts and Consequences

1

Contexts and Consequences: Impacts on Children, Families and Communities

Jennifer Bowes, Rebekah Grace and Alan Hayes

This chapter outlines the rise of interest in the interconnecting contexts of children, families and communities and the consequences of those interconnections. Families and communities can offer both opportunities and constraints for children's participation in the world and their general development. The impact of context varies with the child's age and other characteristics such as disability, ethnicity and playfulness. The interest in context has led to descriptions of 'the ecology of childhood', and explorations of 'the cultural nature' of children's development.[1] It has led also to the recognition that—for the analysis of child development, family life or social policy—we need studies on the ways in which children, families and communities are interconnected. The pathways that lead to negative and positive consequences for individual children, families and communities also need close examination as do the best opportunities for intervention to enable a turning point in life trajectories.

The chapter begins with the assumptions made in this book about the meaning of context, and discusses the ways in which contexts need to be described to allow a greater understanding of their consequences for children and families. It goes on to provide an account of some of the approaches to context in the lives of children and families, looking particularly at the social ecological model put forward by Urie Bronfenbrenner[2] and two models that have built on the foundation Brofenbrenner laid: the cultural development model proposed by Barbara Rogoff[3] and the Ecocultural theory developed by Ronald Gallimore, Thomas Weisner and colleagues.[4]

Within the broad model of contexts and consequences that has been used here as a framework for child–family–community interconnections, we argue for the importance of considering consequences on all three levels (children, families and communities). In the discussion of consequences for children, families and communities, the challenges facing each of these three elements are examined in relation to the resources available to deal with challenges. In doing so, the concepts of risk, vulnerability, protective factors, resilience and developmental pathways are introduced and discussed in the context of a strengths–based approach to working with individuals, families and communities. The importance of these concepts in understanding the consequences of different person–context interactions, and in planning policy and intervention programs, is explored in relation to issues raised in later chapters of the book.

The meaning of context

This first section of the chapter is concerned with what we mean by context, how context has been described, and the aspects of context that need to be considered when we talk about the interconnections among children, families and communities. It is useful to consider some concrete examples, such as the hypothetical cases of Nathan and Kylie.

NATHAN AND KYLIE

Nathan is three and a half years old, and is a healthy, active and engaging child. He lives with his parents in the outer suburbs of an Australian city. Both parents have paid jobs, have a happy marital relationship and have completed high school education. Nathan's two older sisters, aged eight and ten, attend the local primary school and include Nathan in their games at home whether they are playing school or practising soccer. Nathan attends a long day care centre for two days per week, and his grandmother looks after him on another day, while his mother goes to work part-time. When at home with his mother on the other two weekdays, and with both parents on the weekend, Nathan plays computer games, helps his mother cook, is read to by his parents and is taken to the local park. Sometimes his father takes him to his workplace to collect paperwork to be completed at home.

Kylie is four years old and is a quiet child, currently living with a foster family after being removed from her family a few weeks previously. State authorities placed her in temporary foster care after her parents were convicted of drug dealing from their home. The authorities are assessing her grandmother's suitability to provide foster care for her. For her first year of life Kylie lived with her grandmother while her parents battled their drug dependency. She returned to live with her parents but looked forward to seeing her grandmother on weekends. At her grandmother's house she would play with the dog and have meals at the kitchen table, talking to her grandmother. At home, Kylie's father watched TV with her and her mother had started to take her to a playgroup where she liked seeing the other children but felt shy about joining in their games.

What can we say about context from these examples? The first point is that context is a *multiple* rather than a unitary term. It is misleading to assume that children below school age have only one context, namely the home. Young children like Nathan and Kylie experience many contexts, inside and outside the home. Nathan and Kylie are cared for by a range of different people (see Chapter 7 for the current situation in Australia). Within the one setting they have many different kinds of interactions, such as playing with siblings and being read to by parents, or playing with a pet and eating a meal with a grandparent, with both children effectively experiencing multiple contexts.

Even at such an early age, children's lives include contexts in which they themselves are not directly involved, contexts such as Nathan's sisters' school and the jails where Kylie's parents currently live. We can see that context does not have to involve face-to-face contact. Nathan has learned about schoolwork from watching his sisters as they do their homework. Kylie has learned about the world of drugs from watching her parents and their clients. The decision of the local council to provide a park with playground equipment and the church to run a playgroup are also influencing the lives of Nathan and Kylie. Context, then, can be experienced indirectly and still have considerable impact on developing children.

These multiple contexts affect children's development through the opportunities they open up or the constraints they impose. Nathan is a fortunate child who is growing up in a context of high human and social capital (see Chapters 6 and 8 for more detail about these terms). He is offered many opportunities for learning. He knows a variety of contexts and his relationships with the people there are secure and non-threatening. He is a healthy and well-adjusted child—the kind of child that other people enjoy—so that his development is likely to be enhanced by interaction with a wide variety of people. Kylie has also had opportunities to interact with a variety of people. She has formed a strong relationship with her grandmother, spends time with her parents even though they are often not emotionally available to her, and has some play experiences with the other children at playgroup. She is a shy girl, often unsure about how other people will respond to her, and so is less likely than Nathan to have people initiating contact with her.

What are the features of context that might constrain rather than open up opportunities for children? First, there are personal characteristics such as shyness. As discussed in Chapter 6, family factors can also introduce constraints. Because of their characteristics or circumstances, some families restrict the opportunities available to their children through a lack of resources—psychological and social as well as financial—or through limited dealings with the world outside the family. Some communities, too, can be restrictive. Those that provide few resources to families and have impoverished social networks restrict the opportunities for children and families within them. (See Chapter 8 for an analysis of the role of communities and the effects of isolation.)

Descriptions of context

What is the best way to describe contexts? Let us look now at an example of context, a long day care centre set up especially to include disadvantaged children, and consider its features.

Jennifer Bowes, Rebekah Grace & Alan Hayes

A LONG DAY CARE SERVICE FOR DISADVANTAGED FAMILIES

The centre is located in a disadvantaged outer suburb of a major city. It has two large indoor spaces, one used as a play space for children, the other used for sessions in which parents are taught how to play with their children and strategies to deal with the challenges of parenting as well as their own lives. There is a small outside area with play equipment. Five staff and twenty-five children are present at any one time. Families are recruited to the centre by an outreach worker. Parents are offered free child care for their children so that they can attend parent education and support sessions on site. They are required to attend at least three sessions per week.

This description is plainly incomplete. It gives only an objective outline of the physical features of the context and some hints on the interactions that take place at the centre. It is also apparent from the description that this early childhood centre has been set up as part of a larger context in which society takes responsibility for the well-being of its children. In matters of child protection, the state intervenes in the family in a variety of ways (see Chapter 10). This centre is a clear representation of a set of wider social values and laws.

The other hidden aspect of this context, but one that is true of all contexts, is that it is always changing. From one day to the next, with different staff and different children and parents, and with different interactions occurring, the centre changes and keeps changing. Through their participation, the people involved are creating the context they also experience. For the people involved in the centre, it is not simply one context but multiple contexts. Staff, children and parents experience the centre in different ways: as a context for work, for social contact, for play, for learning or for multiple purposes. Each individual has a different emotional response to the centre, and this too is subject to change. One child, for example, may find it frightening; another may be fascinated by the new experiences. One parent may welcome the assistance and support available at the centre; another may find it threatening or humiliating. In this sense, contexts need to be seen subjectively in addition to being described objectively.

Our brief description of the centre did not contain many aspects of the context that might assist us in predicting consequences for children and families. We need to ask more questions. How do people interact in the centre, for example; how are values communicated through the everyday routines of the centre; and how in this context are the families' strengths taken into account? We might ask what the participants expect to happen, what they think they are learning, and whether they believe that the skills learnt can be transferred to another context. We need to ask about previous experiences that might be shaping the behavioural and emotional responses of parents, children and staff in this context.

Contexts can be described in terms of the practices, activities or events that take place within them.[5] Each context also carries with it a type of 'social contract', a set of obligations and beliefs about responsibilities and the actions that should take place.[6]

Contexts also have an emotional element. The responses of individuals to the setting and the relationships between individuals in the setting are of great importance when it comes to linking contexts with consequences.[7] Once these elements are included in descriptions of context, we can begin to make those connections.

In summary, contexts are more complex than they at first seem. Contexts are multiple, changing over time, as individuals themselves change. Perceptions of contexts are important, as are the expectations we hold about the opportunities and obligations associated with contexts. In addition, contexts come with a history and can be described in objective and subjective ways. Contexts often have predictable activities and routines that differentiate one from the other and through which values are expressed and learnt. Importantly, their influence on people is linked to emotional responses. These ideas about context come from a variety of theoretical models and research projects, and a brief review follows.

Models of context

Within studies of child development there are now widespread attempts to address the kind of criticism made by Oakley in 1994: 'the emphasis on childhood as an individual process unfolded from within has tended to neglect the impact on children and childhood of social and cultural contexts'.[8] Although there has always been interest in context in the past, increasing attention is now given to the contexts of development and how development and context interrelate.

A superficial view of context is seen in the 'social address' approach. This simplifies context by referring to an individual's membership of a broad social category such as socio-economic status or a particular ethnic group. Diversity within groups is not considered in this approach, nor is the possibility that people brought together under the same label may perceive their social group membership in a different way. In the discussion on ethnicity in Chapter 4, for example, we see that having an 'Aboriginal' or 'Chinese' identity is not a simple matter of social address. It involves people's perceptions of the meaning of the social group, their reasons for membership, and the constraints imposed by others on using the term.

Studies of context in child development have moved beyond this 'social address' model to consider the multiple influences of the social contexts in which most children are involved: family, school and the peer group. Early research studies documented the physical aspects of these contexts, and later studies looked at psychological aspects such as the nature of the interactions that occurred in these settings.[9]

While such studies are relevant and important, they do not account for all of the contextual influences on children's lives. It was the social ecological model put forward by Bronfenbrenner that moved thinking beyond the contexts in which children are immediately involved to consider also the effects of more distant contexts such as social policy and culture. In addition, Bronfenbrenner's model, influenced by Kurt Lewin's theory of dynamic psychology, extended Lewin's psychological 'life space' in order to 'confront the real world of interactions, relationships and contexts. Actions then lie at the adaptive interaction between the person and the environment'.[10]

Jennifer Bowes, Rebekah Grace & Alan Hayes

BRONFENBRENNER'S SOCIAL ECOLOGY MODEL

Figure 1 is a diagrammatic representation of Bronfenbrenner's model. Presented as an expanding set of contextual structures, his model has the developing child at its centre along with that child's particular characteristics such as age and gender. Each surrounding contextual layer is seen as nestled within the other 'like a set of Russian dolls',[11] and the relationship between child and setting is seen as a dynamic one. Bronfenbrenner explained it thus: 'The ecology of human development involves the scientific study of the progressive mutual accommodation between an active, growing human being and the changing properties of the immediate settings in which the developing person lives, as this process is affected by relations between these settings, and by the larger contexts in which the settings are embedded.'[12]

The system of contextual influences closest to the child is called the *microsystem*. The microsystem consists of the face-to-face settings with which children are involved such as the immediate family, the school or child care centre, the doctor or the church. Settings are seen to influence children not only through their physical features and activities but through the personality and belief systems of people in those settings, and the effect of the settings is modified by children's perception of the context and the people within them.

In addition, Bronfenbrenner included in his model the importance of emotion in the effect of context on the developing child. His definition of development includes the importance of emotional attachment with other people as a powerful element in the process by which the microsystem wields its influence: 'Learning and development are facilitated by the participation of the developing person in progressively more complex patterns of reciprocal activity with someone with whom the person has developed a strong and enduring emotional attachment, and when the balance of power gradually shifts in favour of the developing person.'[13]

The next layer of the model is called the *mesosystem*. The mesosystem refers to the interrelationships between settings in which the child actively participates. It refers to the degree of congruence or match between two settings in the microsystem. An example is the match between home and child care centre. If, for example, the styles, expectations and values of people working in a child care centre are similar to those that children have experienced at home, they and their parents will settle more readily into the routines of the centre.

Bronfenbrenner's model contains a further system, the *exosystem*, which refers to the linkages between two or more settings. It is represented as a step further removed from the child than the microsystem and mesosystem because in the exosystem the child is not directly involved in all settings but is nevertheless directly affected by them. The three exosystems most likely to influence children, through their influence on family members, are the parents' workplaces, parents' social networks, and community influences.

The outermost system shown in Figure 1, the *macrosystem*, refers to broad societal or cultural contexts. The macrosystem incorporates the sets of values or cultural belief systems around which life in a society is organised, and which are passed on through families, schools, churches and other social and government institutions. The influence of the outer layers of the model on the developing child can be illustrated by the 'trickle

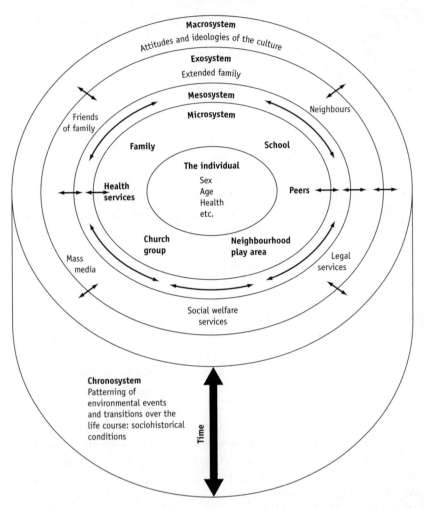

down' effect of changing societal attitudes and practices over the last twenty years in Australia concerning women's increasing involvement in the paid workforce. Many women in the workforce are also the mothers of young children, and their working outside the home has altered parenting practices and the patterns of child care that characterised previous generations of families.[14]

In response to the needs of mothers in the workforce, out-of-family child care has become part of the life of many families. While parents are at work, children below school age may be cared for in one or several of a range of formal and informal settings. Formal child care, as well as enriching children's knowledge of many school-like activities, presents a new setting of group care involving larger groups of children than would be present in a family. This kind of setting demands social skills of sharing, learning to play cooperatively with other children and forming relationships with adult carers as well as a degree of assertiveness and aggression in some children—all skills that children have been found to develop in child care centres.[15] This example shows how wider social influences such as changes in the patterns of work can affect families and children.

Jennifer Bowes, Rebekah Grace & Alan Hayes

Two additions made to his model by Bronfenbrenner are important in that they affect the way we think of context and how it influences individuals.[16] The first addition is the inclusion of the idea of individuals seeking their *developmental niche* or actively seeking contexts to match their own characteristics. Children in a child care centre, for example, who enjoy construction or who see other children building with blocks and think that those children are like them, may choose the 'block corner' over the 'book corner', finding for themselves a developmental niche—a setting that, in turn, will influence their future learning and activity choices.

The second addition to Bronfenbrenner's model is a time dimension, the *chronosystem*, as shown in Figure 1. This is important because it acknowledges that, just as individuals change over time, so too do contexts. Developmental and historical changes need to be taken into account in any model of the interrelationships between people and their context. An example of the effects of an individual's development on context can be seen in differing approaches to behaviour management in the education system according to the age of the student. Teachers use different methods of discipline with kindergarten children, for example, from those they use with high school students.

Historical time also changes the nature of contexts that affect children and families. An example is the changing attitudes towards immunisation of young children in Australia. The poliomyelitis epidemics during the late 1930s had an enormous impact on children and families of that time, with parents and children living in fear of the disease, obliged to deal with prolonged hospitalisation of children, and having education disrupted by the closure of schools. When immunisation against major infectious diseases became available, families who had witnessed the epidemic were more than anxious to have their children immunised. The impact of such historical events, however, weakens when several generations, protected by widespread immunisation from major infectious diseases, have not personally experienced the diseases or their social impact. This appears to have happened in Australia, which during the early 1990s had one of the lowest immunisation rates among developed countries.[17] The emergence of new diseases that threaten the health of children, such as meningoccocal septicaemia, as well as a concerted national campaign to encourage immunisation, have reversed this trend. In recent years, Australia has enjoyed a close to universal childhood immunisation rate.[18] Such historical changes in attitude have clear implications for the health of children and for the well-being of families and communities.

Bronfenbrenner's model of social ecology has had a great impact on thinking about the interaction between people and contexts (for details see Chapter 2). The model has influenced the structure of this book with its progression from individual through proximal to more distal contextual influences on child development.

ROGOFF'S ANALYSIS OF THE CULTURAL NATURE OF DEVELOPMENT

Another major influence on our thinking about context has been the work of Barbara Rogoff. Rogoff's theory was developed in reponse to Bronfenbrenner, as she was critical of some features of the model of contextual influences he proposed. One criticism was that in many parts of his writing (but not all) people are 'treated as products of their immediate settings and "larger" contexts'.[19] The diagrammatic representation of nested contexts presented in Bronfenbrenner's model is seen by Rogoff as unduly and even inadvertently separating 'person and culture into stand-alone entities'.[20] Her analysis places more emphasis both on the active nature of the developing child and on their lack of separation from context. She sees individuals not as responding to contexts or seeking contexts that fit their characteristics and interests, but as participants in contexts who by their participation help create and change those contexts. For example, Rogoff explains how this happens in relation to learning cultural norms through cultural participation:

> Some of the most dramatic issues of autonomy and interdependence have to do with social relations across generations, between adults and children. Through participation in those relationships and those with peers, the next generation learns about its community's models of how individuals and communities relate. In the process, each generation may question and revise the practices of its predecessors, particularly when distinct practices of different communities are juxtaposed in their lives.[21]

Rogoff's analysis is valuable in that it makes clear the changing nature of contexts. Families, for instance, are constantly changing contexts for children's development due to the changing membership of families (for example, the birth of a new baby or parental separation) and their own individual courses of development (parenting changes as parents gain more skills and confidence) as well as the involvement of that child in the family. Schools change constantly with different personnel and different cohorts of children and even government policy comes from a changing context according to the party in power and the people who occupy key positions in the government.

Another contribution Rogoff has made to our understanding of context in development is her close attention to the processes of learning that take place in cultural contexts. Rogoff has built on the work of Lev Vygotsky,[22] taking his idea that children learn though the assistance of more experienced members of their community, adult or child, operating with their assistance at a level of thinking that they would not be capable of alone at that stage (operating in what Vygotsky termed their 'zone of proximal development').[23] Her elaboration of the processes of 'guided participation' beyond the educational settings that were Vygotsky's focus, to everyday cultural contexts, is also a valuable contribution. It extends her earlier work on cognitive development in cultural context through the use of cultural tools and through an 'apprenticeship' with other cultural members,[24] and Lave and Wenger's model of how we develop through our participation in numerous communities of practice, moving from initial peripheral to central participation.[25]

Rogoff's cultural analysis is also important in reminding us that a range of practices and beliefs are found in different countries of the world and in different groups within our own communities. The danger of much research on child development deriving from European-American samples is that these research findings can be misinterpreted as representing developmental patterns and processes for all groups within the USA or even globally. The examples of different approaches to child rearing presented by Rogoff are a timely reminder of this danger and offer a critical lens for reassessment of our views about the norms of child development.

Jennifer Bowes, Rebekah Grace & Alan Hayes

ECOCULTURAL THEORY AND ACTIVITY SETTINGS AS THE CRITICAL UNIT OF ANALYSIS

Ecocultural theory, developed by Gallimore, Weisner and colleagues,[26] is derived from anthropological and cross-cultural psychology and takes families rather than individuals as its focus. This approach embraces Bronfenbrenner's notions of the interrelatedness and complexity of the social-ecological influences on a family. It shares with Rogoff a commitment to understanding cultural differences and both the individual and collective meanings people assign to the contexts in which they live. According to Thomas Weisner, a family's 'cultural place' is 'the single most important fact' for a researcher of families to know.[27]

Ecocultural theory explores the responses families make to their circumstances and constructed meanings. It acknowledges that there are forces outside the control of families (including social and economic forces), but it stresses their ability to take individual and collective action to modify and counteract these forces. Families are seen as proactive in shaping their contexts. From this balance of forces and actions comes the construction of a family's 'ecocultural niche'.

An important contribution of Ecocultural theory is that it provides a research approach for exploring difference and meaning within families. It is one thing to understand that families operate within their own context and that cultural difference must be acknowledged, and quite another to think about how to best observe, document and capture what makes one family different from another. Ecocultural theory argues that the mediation of forces that act upon the life of a family occurs through the activity settings of the family's daily routine. Activity settings are, then, the critical units of analysis for Ecocultural theory.

> Children's activity settings are the architecture of everyday life, not a deliberate curriculum; they are homely and familiar parts of a family's day: preparing meals, eating dinner, clearing up, and dozens of mundane settings in which adult-child interaction is embedded. They can also be deliberate teaching opportunities.[28]

Activity settings provide families with opportunities to influence the learning and development of the children through modelling, joint participation, task engagement and other forms of mediated social learning. It is the 'sustainability' of activity settings across time and multiple situations, rather than more conventional measures such as stimulation level or quality of home environment that is hypothesised to be the best predictor of child and family outcome. Activity settings are insightful units for analysis. They are a 'perceptible instantiation of ecology and culture',[29] and can be carefully explored through a variety of research methodologies, including ethnographic fieldwork, systematic observation and interviewing.[30]

In other words, Ecocultural theory answers the earlier question about how we examine the ways in which one family is different from another. It argues that we explore the routines and activity settings that make up their everyday lives, that we think about who is present during these activity settings, the values and goals that underline the activity, the tasks that are being performed, the motive and feelings surrounding the actions, and the scripts defining the appropriate way to engage in that activity. The everyday activities of the family are the windows to understanding each family and how family members respond to and interact with the world around them.

Consequences for children, families and communities

Until relatively recently, outcomes from or consequences of the interaction between individual characteristics and contexts have been considered mainly for individuals. Cowan, Cowan and Schulz[31] suggest that this reflects a research approach that sought to show, mainly with reference to individual characteristics, which people might be at risk of particular psychological disorders or undesirable behaviours such as depression or aggression.

These authors argue for an additional level of analysis of consequences, namely outcomes for families. Desirable outcomes for families might be demonstrated by the psychological and physical health of the individual members, the extent to which they feel empowered and capable in their roles, and by the ability of the family to continue as a well-functioning unit.[32] There is, of course, no single outcome, but an ever-changing series of outcomes that either go on to become part of the demands on families or a component of their resources.

We wish to argue that consequences for the community also need to be taken into account. The community level of analysis is particularly important for policy analysis and for the planning of prevention or intervention programs to circumvent or reduce negative consequences for individuals and families. Factors such as the availability of community resources and support have been shown to be linked with better outcomes for children and families (see Chapter 8). Policy changes and intervention programs need to be designed with a view to the 'social capital' they bring at a community level as well as the cultural and psychological capital they bring to the children, families and communities that they target.

Risk and resilience

Various studies[33] have led to consideration of resilience in the face of adversity and how protective factors can buffer children, families and communities from risk and vulnerability.[34] The concepts of resilience, risk, vulnerability and protective factors are worth examining in more detail, keeping in mind that risk is currently seen as a less useful concept than resilience. The more useful policy question at present is how might a balance be achieved in matching the challenges inevitably experienced in life with the resources to enable people to deal with those challenges in a way that has benefits rather than negative consequences for individuals, families and communities.

Jennifer Bowes, Rebekah Grace & Alan Hayes

RESILIENCE

Major adversity such as a death in the family, disease or chronic poverty can lead to a variety of responses in children, including delays in normal development or psychopathology. Many children, however, thrive or display resilience in conditions of adversity. Luthar, Suniya and Cicchetti have defined resilience as 'a dynamic process encompassing positive adaptation within the context of significant adversity'.[35] Masten and Powell have cautioned against the tendency to view resilience as a characteristic of an individual, protecting them against adversity.[36] Rather, they say, it needs to be seen as a pattern of adaptation that is evident throughout a person's life even though they may show resilience in the face of one set of stressors but be vulnerable to another. The experience of coping successfully in adversity teaches children a range of successful strategies, making it more likely that they will adapt successfully to later challenges.[37]

'AT RISK' FAMILIES AND RESILIENCE

A key study on resilience was conducted over three decades in Hawaii by Werner and Smith.[38] These researchers studied children who had experienced high risk in their first two years of life, due to low birth weight, complications during birth and living in families that through poverty, family conflict or parental psychopathology made them poor child-rearing contexts. Children growing up with such characteristics and in such adverse circumstances might be expected to have poor outcomes.

While this was true of many in the group, for a third of the children the consequences were the opposite of those expected. This subgroup of 'at risk' children became well-functioning, responsible adults who were caring, confident and competent in their adult activities. These children had several features in common. They showed distinctive personal characteristics such as an easy-going personality, high self-esteem, a sense of personal control over their lives, a tendency to plan and good reasoning and problem-solving. They came from families that were not very large (no more than four children) and that had clear rules in the home. They had at least one positive attachment to an adult who gave them a lot of attention in the early childhood years. External factors were also important. These individuals had received support from outside the family unit from teachers, classmates or others in the community. They had also had experiences during their lives that boosted their self-esteem and competence. These included 'continuing education at community colleges, educational and vocational skills acquired through voluntary service in the armed forces, marriage to a stable partner, conversion to a religion that required active participation in a "community of faith", recovery from a life threatening illness or accident that required a lengthy hospitalization and occasionally psychotherapy'.[39] These kinds of personal, family and external factors have also been linked to resilience in later research.[40]

Research has shown some of the different routes to resilience associated with various adverse events or stressful experiences. For example, the Christchurch longitudinal project in New Zealand showed that children found to have relatively good outcomes as adults despite multiple family adversity as children were more likely to have had personal resources to help them cope (higher intelligence as children and lower rates of novelty-seeking as adolescents) and were less likely to have had delinquent friends when they were growing up.[41]

The developing research emphasis on factors likely to boost resilience in children, families and communities mirrors a shift in focus by practitioners: from working from the deficiencies or 'at risk' status of individuals, families and communities to taking a strengths-based approach.[42] A strengths-based approach involves identifying and working with the strengths that individuals and families bring with them. For example, an otherwise chaotic family may show concern for the health of their children. This concern can form the basis for support provided by community agencies. Underlying the strengths-based approach is research on its effectiveness in boosting the self-esteem, parenting confidence and self-efficacy of parents—all factors that have been identified as associated with resilience in children.[43]

According to Rutter, paths to resilience relate to overall level of risk and sensitivity to risk as well as to opportunities to reduce the impact of stress or adversity, to reduce negative chain reactions and increase positive chain reactions, and to open up new opportunities.[44] All of these mechanisms are potentially open to efforts of intervention and prevention.

Community resilience in the face of risk is a less researched area. As seen in Chapter 8, however, the notion of social capital is useful in the prediction of factors that might buffer communities in times of risk or that might lead to community resilience. Just as in families, the level of physical, psychological and cultural resources of a community can either weaken its resilience or strengthen it in times of external threat such as high unemployment or prolonged drought.

RISK

It is common to see risk factors listed under the headings of child, family and community characteristics.[45] Some examples of risks associated with child characteristics are low birth weight, prenatal exposure to toxins or infections, chronic illness, difficult temperament and poor self-esteem. Family factors that have been shown to pose risks for children include poverty, violence, parents who use drugs or alcohol, and abusive or neglectful parenting. Some community risk factors are neighbourhood violence and crime, lack of support services for families, poor housing and social and cultural discrimination. Listing possible sources of risk for children, however, does not indicate the complexity of the way risk operates to affect people's lives.

Risk is really a probability statement about negative outcomes. We might say, for example, that a child born of drug-addicted parents or with a disability is at risk in terms of development. However, as Cowan, Cowan and Schulz[46] pointed out, not all individuals at risk develop the same negative outcomes, and some individuals at risk never develop a disorder. Equally, some individuals with no risk factors do go on to

Jennifer Bowes, Rebekah Grace & Alan Hayes

develop disorders. It is interesting, for example, to note that at the age of four, more children with disabilities actually come from the group considered normal at birth than from those considered 'at risk'.[47]

Risk factors are not clear-cut. Is poverty always a risk for children, for example? Think of the successful business people, motivated to succeed, who have emerged from childhood poverty. Is shyness always a risk for later development? Children who spend a lot of time on their own can develop into creative artists or writers. It depends on the person and his or her circumstances, what is seen as a positive or negative outcome, and the number of risks present at the same time. It may be that some experience of risk is necessary to develop resilience. There is little evidence that positive experiences by themselves are sufficient to develop resilience.[48]

The concept of risk is complex in other ways, as Cowan, Cowan and Schulz explain: 'In real life, people move in and out of risk status. Psychological risks may fluctuate as life circumstances change. As time goes on, individuals are increasingly likely to be faced with new risks, to develop new vulnerabilities, and to have new opportunities to develop resilience.'[49]

This dynamic view of risk is a useful one compared with the static category view of psychological pathology. It allows us to see development as a moving in and out of adaptation to the inevitable changes and challenges in life.[50] The extent to which people are susceptible to negative consequences depends on their vulnerability and resilience in those circumstances and at that time.

Despite these qualifications, it is unusual for risks to occur one at a time. It is far more common for children to experience multiple stressors or for adverse experiences to accumulate in life. The risk of child psychiatric disorder increases markedly with each new additional adverse or stressful experience. In their twenty-one-year longitudinal study of children in New Zealand, Fergusson and Horwood found that children exposed to six or more risk factors in childhood had a 2.4 times higher rate of aggression than other children and were 1.8 times more likely to be depressed.[51]

The adequacy of reference to risk factors in relation to Indigenous communities and other marginalised groups has been questioned by Homel and colleagues.[52] They argue that risk factors do offer some kind of indication of the probability of adverse outcomes, but do not encompass the lived reality of Indigenous people in Australia who have experienced forced removal of children from their families and the inter-generational effects of that removal (see Chapter 11).

VULNERABILITY

Vulnerability is characterised by a reduction in flexibility and capacity to cope in response to adverse experiences. If a similar stress has been managed successfully in the past, the result is likely to be resilience. On the other hand, vulnerability may stem from a genetic disposition or from characteristics that have developed through experience— low self-esteem or depression, for example, that predispose an individual to a negative outcome when risk is present. At other times, that characteristic may not make a difference to general functioning. Cowan, Cowan and Schulz explain this interaction of risk and vulnerability with the following analogy.

VULNERABILITY

A sailboat is returned to the water after a brief time in dry dock, during which a crack in the hull has been hurriedly patched. As long as the weather is reasonably good and the waves are moderate, the boat is fine and will probably remain so indefinitely. If a violent storm springs up, however, all sailboats in the vicinity are at risk of damage, but this sailboat is particularly vulnerable to severe damage as soon as the storm begins.[53]

In this way the prior experiences or characteristics of children, their families or their communities can make them vulnerable to risks. In a study of aggression in children, for example, Miller and colleagues[54] found that while parental depression was not associated in a direct way with children's aggression, the presence of depression in parents was a factor in making children more likely to be aggressive when there was conflict within the family. In this example, conflict was like a storm threatening all the children concerned. But those children who were vulnerable as a result of parental depression were more prone to aggressive reactions.

PROTECTIVE FACTORS

When risk is present, some children, some families and some communities are more resilient than others. There are factors operating to protect or buffer them in part or completely from the negative consequences that might be predicted in risk situations. Werner and Smith[55] suggest that risk and protective factors work together to achieve a balance between an individual's power and the power of the social or physical environment. For example, institutionalised racism is a risk factor for Indigenous children in Australia. Homel has identified what he calls cultural resilience and strong ties to family as protective factors.[56] Other examples of factors that increase resilience in the face of risk are the protective effects for children with divorced parents of a warm relationship with at least one of them (see Chapter 6), and the buffer provided by social support for families at risk of child abuse through poverty or unemployment. Several protective factors consistently linked to resilience in the face of multiple risk factors have been identified by Rutter: the person's overall level of cognitive functioning, a sense that it is possible to cope with challenges, the opportunity to make decisions and to learn from mistakes as well as successes, and warm, supportive relationships.[57]

BALANCE BETWEEN VULNERABILITY AND RESILIENCE

The balance between vulnerability and resilience depends on the demands being placed on individuals, their resources to cope, the support available to meet the demands, and appraisal of the balance of challenges versus resources. In turn, the resources available within any family are also dependent upon the extent of other, competing pressures. Access to support outside the family, for example, appears to be very important in ameliorating stress experienced by parents.[58]

Jennifer Bowes, Rebekah Grace & Alan Hayes

Appraisal is an important element of most current models of stress and coping, and accounts in part for individual differences in response to stress. As well as contributing to variation, appraisal is also important in explaining variability. Appraisal is ongoing so that one's response to an event may change over time. Reappraisal may even change the evaluation of events, such that a personal 'disaster' at one time may be reframed to become 'a growth point of my life' with the passage of time. What is most important in terms of outcome is how the stressor is perceived, and not the stressor in and of itself.

Consequences in terms of outcomes, processes and pathways

The concepts of resilience, risk, vulnerability and protective factors provide the building blocks for a dynamic model of the consequences for children, families and communities of the interplay between individual characteristics and contextual factors. Just as there is no single steady balance of vulnerability and resilience for individuals, it is misleading to search for a single developmental process to a particular outcome. Instead, a framework is needed to incorporate the range of developmental routes.

The consequences of different pathways are often presented in terms of probability. In his discussion of pathways to crime, for example, Kazdin[59] concluded that: 'influences can place a child on a trajectory or path. The trajectory or path is not a fixed or a determined course. Some outcomes become more probable (e.g., being arrested, bonding with delinquent peers) and other outcomes become less probable (e.g., graduating from high school, entering a monastery).'

The challenge is to identify the pathways generally followed on the road to crime or drug dependence, for example, and then to identify points along the pathway where intervention might have the greatest chance of success. Studies of resilience have indicated that there is often a distinct turning point that changes a life trajectory, whether that is joining the armed forces or forming a relationship with a supportive partner. It has been suggested that commonly experienced transition points in life, such as starting school or high school, or the birth of a first child, could be the optimal times for intervention and support programs to succeed in diverting trajectories in the direction of resilience rather than vulnerability in the face of stressful events.[60]

The model outlined in this chapter of the influence of personal and contextual factors on consequences for children, families and communities has implications for understanding development, predicting policy outcomes, and designing prevention and intervention programs. It is the model used throughout this book to analyse contexts and consequences of a range of issues for children, families and communities in Australia.

The concepts of risk and resilience and of different developmental pathways are central to any consideration of intervention in the lives of children, families or communities. They assist in identifying groups 'at risk', the protective factors that can be introduced or augmented by changes to context, and the opportune times for intervention during developmental pathways. Various models of intervention are presented throughout this book and examined in relation to the theoretical framework presented in this chapter.

STUDENT EXERCISES

1 Consider the impact of government initiatives and reforms, both positive and negative, for each level of Bronfenbrenner's model. For example: In 2006 the Australian Government implemented a new 'Welfare-to-Work' initiative. One part of this initiative required that all single parents find and participate in at least fifteen hours of paid employment per week once their youngest child reached six years old. Single parents who were not able to demonstrate active seeking of paid employment would be penalised in the financial support they received from the Government. Questions for discussion include:

   a) Macrosystem: How does this initiative reflect cultural beliefs about the role of adult community members? What cultural ideas around parenting underlie the choice of a minimum of fifteen hours of paid employment per week, and six years of age as the appropriate levels for this policy?

   b) Exosystem: How does this initiative impact on the Australian economy? How might workplaces need to change to accommodate the needs of this group of workers? What are the implications of this initiative for organisations involved in vocational training and job seeking? How might the policy affect a family's broader community and social networks?

   c) Mesosystem: What do you think the impact of this initiative might be for families in terms of their involvement with the school, establishing and maintaining a support network, accessing support services, and meeting the medical and care needs of their children?

   d) Microsystem: What are the implications for families in trying to meet this new requirement—including the potential need for vocational training, having to provide proof of job seeking, and securing a position that is compatible with the needs of all family members? What kinds of changes need to happen in the day-to-day running of a household to accommodate a single parent returning to work? What do these changes mean for children of different ages?

2 What are some of the risk and protective factors for child development in terms of:

   a) child characteristics

   b) family characteristics

   c) community characteristics?

3 Discuss some of the range of factors (personal, familial and community factors) associated with successful adaptation in conditions of adversity.

Notes

1   U. Bronfenbrenner, 'The Biological Model from a Life Course Perspective: Reflections of a Participant Observer', in *Examining Lives in Context*, eds, P. Moen, G.H. Elder Jr & K. Lüscher, American Psychological Association, Washington, DC, 1995a, pp. 599–618; B. Rogoff, *The Cultural Nature of Human Development*, Oxford University Press, New York, 2003, p. 45.

2   Bronfenbrenner, 1995a.

3   Rogoff, 2003.

4   R. Gallimore, T.S. Weisner, L.P. Bernheimer, D. Guthrie & K. Nihira, 'Family Responses to Young Children with Developmental Delays: Accommodation Activity in Ecological and Cultural Context', *American Journal on Mental Retardation*, 98, 1993, pp. 185–206.

Jennifer Bowes, Rebekah Grace & Alan Hayes

5   M. Cole, 'The Supra-individual Envelope of Development: Activity and Practice, Situation and Context', in *New Directions for Child Development*, no. 67, eds, J.J. Goodnow, P.J. Miller & F. Kessel, Jossey-Bass, San Francisco, 1995, pp. 105–18; P.J. Miller & J.J. Goodnow, 'Cultural Practices: Toward an Integration of Culture and Development', in Goodnow, Miller & Kessel, 1995, pp. 5–16.

6   J.J. Goodnow, 'Differentiating Among Social Contexts: By Spatial Features, Forms of Participation, and Social Contracts', in *Examining Lives in Context*, eds, P. Moen, G.H. Elder Jr & K. Lüscher, American Psychological Association, Washington, DC, 1995a, pp. 269–301.

7   Bronfenbrenner, 1995a.

8   A. Oakley, 'Women and Children First and Last: Parallels and Differences Between Children's and Women's Studies', in *Children's Childhoods: Observed and Experienced*, ed., B. Mayall, Falmer Press, London, 1994, p. 22.

9   See A.W. Wicker, *An Introduction to Ecological Psychology*, Cambridge University Press, Cambridge, 1979, and M. Bonnes & G. Secchaiaroli, *Environmental Psychology*, Sage, London, 1995, for historical accounts of ecological and environmental psychology.

10 R.B. Cairns & B.D. Cairns, 'Social Ecology Over Time and Space', in Moen, Elder & Lüscher, 1995, p. 403.

11 U. Bronfenbrenner, *The Ecology of Human Development*, Harvard University Press, Cambridge, MA, 1979, p. 3.

12 Bronfenbrenner, 1979, p. 21.

13 Bronfenbrenner, 1979, p. 60.

14 From 1986 to 2006 the percentage of couples with dependents who were both employed rose from 48.5 per cent to 59.9 per cent. Australian Bureau of Statistics, *Australian Social Trends 2007*, catalogue no. 4102.0, Australian Government Publishing Service, Canberra, 2007a.

15 National Institute of Child and Human Development (NICHD) Early Child Care Research Network, eds, *Child Care and Child Development: Results from the NICHD Study of Early Child Care and Youth Development*, Guilford Press, New York, 2005a.

16 U. Bronfenbrenner, 'Developmental Ecology Through Space and Time', in *Examining Lives in Context*, eds, Moen, Elder & Lüscher, 1995b, pp. 619–48.

17 P. Boss, S. Edwards & S. Pitman, *Profile of Young Australians: Facts, Figures and Issues*, Churchill Livingstone, Melbourne, 1995.

18 2007 statistics indicate that rates of full immunisation are 91.3 per cent of children aged 12 to 15 months, 92.4 per cent of children aged 24 to 37 months and 88.6 per cent of children aged 72 to 75 months. Australian Childhood Immunisation Register (ACIR) statistics can be found at <www.medicareaustralia.gov.au>, accessed 14 December 2007.

19 Rogoff, 2003, p. 45.

20 Rogoff, 2003, p. 49.

21 Rogoff, 2003, p. 195.

22 L. Vygotsky, *Mind in Society: The Development of Higher Psychological Processes*, Harvard University Press, Cambridge, MA, 1978.

23 Rogoff, 2003, p. 282 for Rogoff's account of her debt to Vygotsky's ideas.

24 B. Rogoff, *Apprenticeship in Thinking: Cognitive Development in a Social Context*, Oxford University Press, New York, 1990.

25 J. Lave & E. Wenger, *Situated Learning: Legitimate Peripheral Participation*, Cambridge University Press, Cambridge, 1999; E. Wenger, *Communities of Practice: Learning Meaning and Identity*, Cambridge University Press, New York, 1998.

26 Gallimore et al., 1993; R. Gallimore, T.S. Weisner, S.Z. Kaufman & L.P. Bernheimer, 'The Social Construction of Ecocultural Niches: Family Accommodation of Developmentally Delayed Children', *American Journal on Mental Retardation*, 94, 1989, pp. 216–30.

27 T. Weisner, 'Ethnographic and Ecocultural Perspectives on Sibling Relationships', in *The Effects of Mental Retardation, Disability, and Illness on Sibling Relationships*, eds, Z. Stoneman & P.W. Berman, Paul H. Brookes Publishing, Baltimore, 1993, pp. 51–83.

28 Gallimore et al., 1989, p. 217.

29 Gallimore et al., 1989, p. 217.

30 T.S. Weisner, 'Ecocultural Understanding of Children's Developmental Pathways', *Human Development*, 45, 2002, pp. 275–81.

31 P.A. Cowan, C.P. Cowan & M.S. Schulz, 'Thinking about Risk and Resilience in Families', in *Stress, Coping and Resiliency in Children and Families*, eds, E.M. Hetherington & E.A. Blechman, Lawrence Erlbaum, Mahwah, NJ, 1996.

32 C.J. Dunst & I. Dempsey, 'Family-professional Partnerships and Parenting Competence, Confidence, and Enjoyment', *International Journal of Disability, Development and Education*, 54, 3, 2007, pp. 305–18.

33 For a review, see S. Luthar & L. Zelazo, 'Research on Resilience: An Integrative Review' in *Resilience and Vulnerability: Adaptation in the Context of Childhood Adversities*, ed, S. Luthar, Cambridge University Press, Cambridge, 2003, pp. 510–49.

34 M.A. Zimmerman & R. Arunkumar, 'Resiliency Research: Implications for Schools and Policy', *Social Policy Report*, VIII, no. 4, Society for Research in Child Development, Ann Arbor, MI, 1994.

35 S. Luthar, S. Suniya & D. Cicchetti, 'The Construct of Resilience: A Critical Evaluation and Guidelines for Future Work', *Child Development*, 71, 2000, pp. 543–62, p. 543.

36 A. Masten & J. Powell, 'A Resilience Framework for Research, Policy and Practice' in *Resilience and Vulnerability: Adaptation in the Context of Childhood Adversities*, ed, S. Luthar, Cambridge University Press, Cambridge, 2003, pp. 2–25.

37 K. Deater-Deckard, L. Ivy & J. Smith, 'Resilience in Gene-environment Transactions' in *Handbook of Resilience in Childhood*, eds, S. Goldstein & R.B. Brooks, Springer, New York, 2006, pp. 49–63.

38 E.E. Werner & R.S. Smith, *Kauai's Children Come of Age*, University of Hawaii Press, Honolulu, HI, 1977.

39 E.E. Werner, 'Resilience Research: Past, Present and Future' in *Resilience in Children, Families and Communities: Linking Context to Practice*, eds, R.deV. Peters & R.J. MacMahon, Plenum, New York, 2005, pp. 3–11.

40 Luthar & Zelazo, 2003.

41 M. Rutter, 'Resilience Reconsidered: Conceptual Considerations, Empirical Findings, and Policy Considerations', in *Handbook of Early Childhood Intervention*, eds, J.A. Shonkoff & S.J. Meisels, Cambridge University Press, Cambridge, 2000, pp. 651–82.

42 C. Dunst, C. Trivette & A. Deal, *Supporting and Strengthening Families: Methods, Strategies and Practices*, Brookline Books, Cambridge, MA, 1994.

43 Dunst, Trivette & Deal, 1994.

44 Rutter, 2000.

45 See, for example: National Crime Prevention, *Pathways to Prevention: Developmental and Early Intervention Approaches to Crime in Australia*, Attorney General's Department, Barton, ACT, 1999; Australian Government Task Force on Child Development, Health and Wellbeing, *Towards the Development of a National Agenda for Early Childhood: Consultation Paper*, Commonwealth of Australia, Canberra, 2003.

46 Cowan, Cowan & Schulz, 1996.

47 G.P. Aylward, N. Gustafson, S.J. Verhulst & J.A. Colliver, 'Consistency in the Diagnosis of Cognitive, Motor and Neurologic Function over the First Three Years', *Journal of Pediatric Psychology*, 12, 1987, pp. 77–98.

48 M. Rutter, 2000.

49 Cowan, Cowan & Schulz, 1996, p. 7.

50 Cowan, Cowan & Schulz, 1996.

51 D.M. Fergusson & L.J. Horwood, 'Resilience to Childhood Adversity: Results of a 21-Year Study' in *Resilience and Vulnerability: Adaptation in the Context of Childhood Adversities*, ed, S.S. Luthar, Cambridge University Press, Cambridge, 2003, pp. 130–155.

52 R. Homel, C. Lamb & K. Freiberg, 'Working with the Indigenous Community in the Pathways to Prevention Program', *Family Matters*, 75, 2006, pp. 18–53.

53 Cowan, Cowan & Schulz, 1996, pp. 10–11.

54 N.B. Miller, P.A. Cowan, C.P. Cowan, E.M. Hetherington & G. Clingempeel, 'Externalising in Preschoolers and Early Adolescents: A Cross-study Replication of a Family Model', *Developmental Psychology*, 29, 1993, pp. 3–18.

55 Werner & Smith, 1992.

56 R. Homel, C. Lamb & K. Freiberg, 2006.

57 Rutter, 2000, pp. 661–2.

58 Rutter, 2000.

59 A.E. Kazdin, 'Conduct Disorder Across the Life-span', in *Developmental Psychopathology: Perspectives on Adjustment, Risk and Disorder*, eds, S.S. Luthar, J.A. Burack, D. Cicchetti & J.R. Weisz, Cambridge University Press, Cambridge, 1997, p. 257.

60 National Crime Prevention, 1999.

2

Research on Children, Families and Communities

Judy Ungerer and Linda Harrison

The main aim of this chapter is to demonstrate how Bronfenbrenner's[1] social ecology model has been used to guide the design of empirical research on children, families and communities. We will show how the model shapes the kinds of research questions that are asked and how it influences specifically *what* researchers measure and *when* assessments occur. The social ecology model has had a broad influence on developmental research. Its impact can be seen in the design of very large-scale, longitudinal studies as well as in smaller scale projects.

To demonstrate this influence, we will draw examples from four longitudinal studies that differ in the size and complexity of their designs. These include two Australian studies (the Longitudinal Study of Australian Children (LSAC) and Child Care Choices (CCC)), and one study from the USA (National Institute of Child Health and Human Development Study of Early Child Care and Youth Development (NICHD Study)). These three studies have included research questions regarding the impact of child care on the development of young children and we will focus on this domain when discussing these works. In addition, we draw on a study from the United Kingdom (Effective Provision of Preschool Education (EPPE)) that has investigated the impact of children's pre-school experiences on development. Although the starting age of children differs across these four studies, each has generated detailed records of children's experiences of early education and child care and has followed the children's development through to the early years of school.

Overview of the ecological model

Bronfenbrenner's social ecology model[2] provides a reference point for most major studies of child development today. One of its important contributions has been to move the study of child development from a narrow focus on characteristics of the child and the family to an appreciation of the broader contexts that impact on the development of children in diverse ways. Thus, an assessment of the 'child in context' includes not only a consideration of child characteristics likely to be important influences on development (for example, gender, temperament or birth order), but also consideration of the various contexts that children experience over time (for example, the family, child care, school and the neighbourhood) and the relationships they form within these contexts. These include not only those that directly impact on the child via the child's experience of the context, like the caregivers and peers in the child care setting they attend each week or the quality of the neighbourhood playgrounds, libraries or healthcare facilities they use, but also contexts where the impact may be more indirect. For example, changes in a parent's working conditions that result in greater stress at work or longer working hours may influence the child indirectly via their negative impact on the family environment. These workplace changes may lead to increased parent–parent conflict or less time for quality parent–child interaction, resulting in a less supportive home environment for the child. Alternatively, changes in child care policy leading to a reduction in the direct cost of child care for parents could lessen economic stress on the family and thereby positively influence not only relationships within the family but also the amount of family resources available to children.

The social ecology model also stresses that child–context relationships are bidirectional.[3] For example, when children experience greater conflict between their parents, they themselves may become more upset and express more anger and distress, which may then increase the stress levels of their parents. The active role of children in influencing their social environments is emphasised by Dunlop,[4] who adapted Bronfenbrenner's model to include 'the idea of the agency of the child' in her modelling of the process of school transition. Dunlop argues that a child's sense of agency affects their ability to function effectively across different contexts with different expectations, for example, one-to-one scaffolding of learning with an adult at home versus activity-based learning with adults and peers at school. Agency, like resilience, describes a 'collection of qualities that support adaptation and the capacity to manage change'.[5]

In seeking to develop comprehensive models of the interactive nature of children's development, it is important to remember that contexts not only present risks, but that they also contribute protective factors. For example, good nutrition at home or positive relationships with child care workers may enhance children's development directly, but they also serve to buffer children from the potential negative impact of risks of childhood illnesses or poor parent–child relationships. How these risk and protective factors influence development may vary depending on the specific outcomes that are assessed.[6] Therefore, it is also important to assess children's functioning across a wide range of domains (for example, cognitive, language, social-emotional, health and motor skills) if a broad understanding of the processes important in children's development is to be obtained.

Studies that are comprehensive also understand the importance of longitudinal designs, since the factors that influence children's development and the nature of child–context relationships will change over time. Longitudinal designs enable the identification of developmental trajectories that lead children towards positive or negative outcomes, as well as crucial transition points that may determine the specific pathways individual children follow. These could include, for example, children's experiences in commencing child care or making the transition to school. Longitudinal designs also enable the assessment of historical context, particularly when the development of children growing up in different time periods can be compared.

We will now look at four longitudinal studies of young children in order to provide specific examples of how researchers have attempted to operationalise the social ecology model in recent developmental research. We will begin with a relatively detailed description of the Longitudinal Study of Australian Children which will focus on how the *contexts of development* and child *outcomes* are assessed in this research. We will then provide brief descriptions of three other studies, highlighting aspects of their study designs and approaches to measurement that have been particularly useful in developmental research.

The Longitudinal Study of Australian Children (LSAC)

The Longitudinal Study of Australian Children is a nine-year study (2002–2010). It is funded as part of the Australian Government Department of Family and Community Services and Indigenous Affairs' *Stronger Families and Communities Strategy*, 'which aims to establish new partnerships to strengthen families and communities and develop and deliver solutions at a local level'.[7] The study, therefore, has a strong interest in policy-relevant outcomes that can be used to identify policies to help strengthen the family and community contexts in which Australian children develop.

The study design includes two nationally representative cohorts of children—5000 infants and 5000 four to five-year-olds—who were recruited and first assessed in 2004. Major follow-up assessments occur at two-year intervals, with shorter assessment contacts occurring in the intervening years. The major assessments involve face-to-face interviews in the home with the child's primary caregiver, typically the mother, and questionnaires that are completed by both parents, including parents living away from the child's home. Parents also complete a 24-hour Time-Use Diary that provides a full record of the child's activities for a weekday and weekend day. With parental consent, questionnaires are sent to the care provider (for infants) or teacher (for four- to five-year-olds) in the child care, pre-school or school setting that the child attends. In addition, direct assessments of the children are conducted during the home visit. As children reach the age of six years, these assessments include interviews with the child.

CONTEXT: HOW ARE FAMILY, COMMUNITY AND CHILD CARE/EARLY EDUCATION CONTEXTS MEASURED IN LSAC?

The interviews and questionnaires completed by the parents provide information about each member of the household and about the different contexts in which the child and family members live. The information collected is extensive, covering characteristics of parents and children, as well as of the family environment, neighbourhood, work, support services, and children's early education and child care contexts. In all areas

LSAC attempts to assess both risk and protective factors and to identify the resources available to families for supporting their children's development.

Basic demographic information collected on each family member includes age, sex, relationship to the study child, country of birth, language spoken at home and work status. In addition, broad information on the parents' levels of education, sources of income, languages spoken as a child and religious identities are obtained. Child health status is recorded through parent information concerning illness and disability as well as direct measurements of height, weight and girth. Health information on parents includes indices of physical and mental health (for example, medical conditions or disability, depression) and lifestyle activities that impact on health (for example, cigarette smoking, alcohol consumption, diet and exercise).

The family context is described in terms of the physical characteristics of the family home (for example, type and condition of the dwelling, overcrowding) and broad indices of family functioning and relationships that include both positive (protective) and negative (risk) characteristics (for example, support and conflict in the parents' relationship, parenting stress, coping, feelings of self-efficacy in the parenting role, discipline practices, agreement and/or conflict between parents about parenting). Each parent's work environment and how it affects the family is also assessed. Parents are asked to report on the hours they work, whether there is flexibility in their work arrangements and on issues regarding work and family balance (for example, whether work responsibilities make time spent with the family less enjoyable; whether work is perceived to have a positive impact on the child).

Community context is assessed by a range of questions on social relationships outside the family, community participation and characteristics of the neighbourhood in which the family lives. For example, parents are asked about the type and quality of support they receive from friends, whether they feel they can trust people in their neighbourhood, whether they are involved in community organisations such as church, school, arts groups or sporting clubs, whether they have access to the services they need, and whether they see their neighbourhood as safe, clean and a good place to bring up children.

The type of early childhood setting attended also forms part of the broader community context that may affect the child in various ways. LSAC collects detailed information on the child's current attendance patterns—type of child care, pre-school or school arrangements, and hours attended in each setting per week—as well as information on the child's first experience of child care, for example, age of first entry into care, type of arrangement and hours per week. Parents are also asked about the reasons the child is attending a child care/early education setting and their level of satisfaction with the arrangement. Through questionnaires completed by care providers and teachers, LSAC also attempts to assess the quality of the child care/early education setting and the nature of the child's experiences in that setting. For example, care providers in under-three-year-old care settings give information about the time they spend in different types of activities with the children, like singing, telling stories, reading books, active outdoor play, pretend play or routines. Teachers in pre-school and school settings provide ratings of the availability of space and resources (for example, for independent learning, art and writing, problem-solving, motor development) and time spent in teacher-directed, teacher-supported and child-centred activities. Determinants of quality also include care providers' and teachers' qualifications and experience, as well as the number and age range of the children in the group. Carers and teachers are also asked to report on positive and negative aspects of their relationship with the LSAC child, for example, whether the relationship is warm and affectionate or whether the child is often angry with or overly dependent on them. A further feature of LSAC is the inclusion of linked data provided by the National Childcare Accreditation Council[8] for long day care centres, family day care and outside school hours care services attended by the child.

LSAC also provides the opportunity to assess the impact of the historical time and cohort effects on children's development, because two different age groups of children are being studied. Thus, when the infant cohort is assessed at the same age as the four- to five-year-old cohort and the results are compared, it may be possible to determine whether differences in the two time periods (such as unemployment rates, availability and financial support for child care or pre-school) or in the two cohorts themselves (such as differences in average family size or financial hardship) have had any influence on the development of these Australian children.

OUTCOMES: WHAT MEASURES OF CHILDREN'S DEVELOPMENT ARE INCLUDED IN LSAC?

Outcomes for children are assessed across three broad domains: physical, social-emotional and learning.

- For infants, the physical domain is measured by parents' ratings of their infant's physical health and health care needs; the social-emotional domain is measured by parent ratings of their infant's temperament with respect to sociability, irritability and cooperativeness; the learning domain is measured by parent ratings of their infant's early vocal and gestural communication skills.
- At age two-to-three years, these domains are extended by including parents' and/ or child care providers' ratings of social-emotional competence and problems, vocabulary and grammar, and involvement in cooperative and pretend play.
- For four- to five-year-olds, the physical domain is measured by parent ratings of motor skills and physical health and by a direct assessment measure of the child's weight for height, the Body Mass Index; the social-emotional domain is measured by parent and teacher ratings of children's social competence with peers, and the presence of internalising (nervousness, worry) and externalising (hyperactivity, behaviour problems) behaviours; and the learning domain is measured by teacher ratings of the child's reading, writing and numeracy skills and by direct assessment of the child's receptive vocabulary and skills in early literacy and numeracy.
- At age six-to-seven years these domains are extended by including parent-reported abilities in speech and grammar, teachers' ratings of children's skills, knowledge and behaviours in language and literacy and mathematical understanding, as well as their ability to work independently, and an assessment of logical reasoning. At age six or seven children are also asked to rate how they feel about school and about themselves.

ANALYSING DEVELOPMENT-IN-CONTEXT: WHAT ARE SOME OF THE FINDINGS FROM LSAC?

An ecological research design such as LSAC enables researchers to analyse the independent effects of early education and child care on child outcomes by adjusting for the effects of child characteristics and important features of the family environment. Analysis of the first wave of data from the LSAC[9] has provided some results that support the social ecology model's emphasis on the importance of context in children's development.

For infants, the influence of non-parental child care was most clearly identified in the analyses of physical health outcomes. Just over one-third of infants were receiving regular child care. Those who experienced twenty-one hours or more of centre-based care were more than twice as likely to have poorer physical health and particularly more acute infections (for example, diarrhoea, colitis) than infants cared for by their parents or in home-based child care with relatives or other care providers. This finding is likely explained by the greater exposure to infectious diseases that occurs in settings containing large numbers of children and staff. However, poorer physical health was also predicted by family context (more children in the household) and child factors (being a male child or Indigenous). Poorer health was also more likely in infants with parents who perceived themselves as less effective, less warm and more hostile in interactions with their children.

For the four- to five-year-old cohort, experience of child care/early education was tested as a predictor of performance on the Peabody Picture Vocabulary Test,[10] which measures children's receptive vocabulary. The results suggested similar outcomes for the different types of care/early education when this was pre-school, long day care or a single school; however, the addition of other care arrangements (for example, long day care plus care by a neighbour) appeared to have a negative effect on children's performance. This was supported by evidence that children who attended care/education programs for long hours (that is, over thirty hours per week) had the lowest levels of receptive vocabulary. It is important to note that these effects were relatively small when compared with the more substantial negative effects on receptive vocabulary of child characteristics (being male or Indigenous) and family environment (three or more children in the household, one-parent family, low household income and mothers having a Year 10 or less education).

STRENGTHS AND LIMITATIONS OF THE LSAC DESIGN

Large, nationally representative studies like LSAC are important from a government policy perspective, since the results can be generalised to the Australian population. As noted above, following two cohorts of children (infants and four- to five-year-olds) longitudinally also allows for identification of developmental trajectories leading to positive or negative outcomes for children, as well as the identification of cohort and historical period effects. Such 'big picture' questions can only be effectively addressed by large, sample-size studies with considerable breadth of measurement. In contrast, the main disadvantage of large studies like LSAC is the trade-off that occurs between breadth and depth of measurement. A large number of variables are measured in LSAC,

Judy Ungerer & Linda Harrison

but these are typically collected using shortened assessment instruments that may not be as reliable as the longer measures on which they are based. Furthermore, except for information collected in direct assessment or provided by child care providers and teachers, most of the information collected by LSAC is reported by parents. While parents are often the most informed about family and child issues, it is always important to recognise the potential for bias in self-reports by any informants. This concern is being addressed in the design of future waves of LSAC where other sources of data, such as assessments by a trained interviewer, child self-report information and nationally collected test scores, are being included.

National Institute of Child Health and Human Development Study of Early Child Care and Youth Development (NICHD study)[11]

The USA's NICHD Study of Early Child Care and Youth Development has as its primary aim 'to examine how variations in nonmaternal care are related to children's social-emotional adjustment, cognitive and linguistic development, and physical growth and health'.[12] Similarly to LSAC, Bronfenbrenner's ecological framework guided the design of the study, enabling children's development to be investigated within the context of their family, child care and community contexts, and over time.

Rather than recruiting a nationally representative sample, the study design followed a single cohort of 1364 healthy newborns and their families who were recruited from ten study sites distributed broadly around the USA. The range of constructs measured in the NICHD study was similar to that assessed in LSAC. What distinguishes the NICHD study, however, is the frequency and depth of assessments conducted. Major face-to-face assessments of the children were conducted at 1, 6, 15, 24, 36 and 54 months of age, and when the children were in kindergarten and first grade. Constructs were assessed with a range of measurement techniques (such as questionnaire, interview and direct observation in home, child care and laboratory settings) and, where possible, were completed by different informants (such as mothers, child care workers, teachers and trained observers) to increase the reliability and validity of the findings. In addition, in between the major face-to-face assessments, information was collected using telephone interviews and questionnaires.

OBSERVATIONAL MEASURES OF SOCIAL-EMOTIONAL OUTCOMES IN THE NICHD STUDY

A major strength of the NICHD study was the use of observational assessments, including observations of the quality of mother–child interactions and of the security of the mother–child attachment relationship. Observations of mother–child interaction and mother–child attachment were conducted in well-controlled laboratory settings where the environment was similar for all participants. In addition, mother–child interaction was observed in the naturalistic home environment which was uniquely different for each family. For example, home environments vary in size, noise level, how child-friendly they are, whether other people or pets are present and so on, and each of these differences may influence how mothers and children behave with each other. However, the advantage of conducting observations in both laboratory and naturalistic home settings is that it makes it possible to look at similarities and differences in the ways mothers and children behave in different contexts. This leads to a better understanding of how characteristics of people and of contexts combine to influence children's development. In addition, observational assessments are typically conducted by researchers who are blind to the child's past history and behaviour, and thus these assessments are not biased by this past information as the reports of parents may be.

The results of analyses predicting attachment security versus insecurity (as assessed in the laboratory-based Strange Situation procedure[13]) indicated that children whose mothers were more sensitive and responsive in their interactions and whose mothers had better overall psychological adjustment were more likely to have secure mother–child attachment relationships. With respect to direct effects of child care, 'there were no significant differences in attachment security related to child care participation'.[14] However, various combinations of child care and either mother, care provider or child variables were shown to impact on mother–child attachment security. For example, children who received less sensitive and responsive care from both their mothers and their child care providers had the highest rates of insecure attachments. In addition, more time in child care was associated with higher rates of insecurity, but only for boys.[15] On the other hand, the results also suggested that high-quality child care compensated for less sensitive mothering. For children with less sensitive and responsive mothers, higher-quality care was linked to an increase in mother–child attachment security.

Child Care Choices: Effects of Multiple and Changeable Child Care on Children's Development (CCC)[16]

The Child Care Choices project differs from the other studies described in this chapter in that it was designed in response to a request by government, the Office of Child Care in the NSW Department of Community Services, to address the problem, identified by child care practitioners and policy makers, of an increasing trend for very young children to use multiple child care settings and for child care arrangements to be changed frequently.[17] One of the driving questions was to explore the extent to which families' use of 'patchwork' arrangements to meet their child care needs was due to choice or to financial barriers and poor accessibility of care.

As with LSAC and the NICHD study, the effects of multiple and changeable care were investigated within the wider context of family, child and other contextual factors that may have a direct or indirect influence on children's developmental outcomes. The study adopted a sequential design with cross-sectional, longitudinal and time-lag components. Three different age groups of children aged between one and three years were recruited and assessed at yearly intervals for seven years (2002–2008). The

Judy Ungerer & Linda Harrison

design allowed for an economical assessment of a broad age span of children as well as providing the potential for collapsing age groups to increase sample size across the age span of children. An urban and a rural area were selected for sampling in order to provide a wide range of service types and families. Recruitment of families took place in long day care and family day care settings.

CHILD CARE CONTEXT AND OUTCOMES IN THE CCC STUDY

Detailed information was collected about the child's care arrangements, including who provided the care, the number of hours attended each week, changes of care setting or care provider, and the reasons for choosing or changing care. Parents were also asked questions about their family circumstances. Directors of child care centres and the child's caregiver in the centre or family day care home also provided information about the service, the number and qualifications of staff and the number of children in the group. A trained research assistant visited the centre/family day care home to record observations of the quality of the care setting using well-established measures of care quality.

The findings from the first year of data collection indicated that the use of multiple care in this sample of children attending regulated child care settings was fairly common: more than one-quarter (29.4 per cent) of the 662 families were using multiple care. Of these, the most common additional arrangement was grandparent care (19.9 per cent). The remaining 10.2 per cent combined long day care or family day care, or both, or added care by an adult relative (other than grandparents), friend, babysitter or nanny.[18] Parents' satisfaction with their care arrangements was relatively high for all care settings (over 4.5 on a 1–5 scale), but tended to be highest for grandparents (average rating of 4.77) and lowest for centre-based programs (average rating of 4.51).

Children's language and communication skills were the first child development indicators to be examined for links to multiple child care. Results identified the following as predictors of language skills: age (older children had higher scores), gender (girls had higher scores), health (poor health predicted lower language scores), birth order (first-borns had higher scores) and mother's education (children of more highly educated mothers had higher scores). Having multiple child care arrangements, however, did not predict children's language and communication skills once the above factors were taken into account.[19]

Together, these results indicated that the use of multiple care arrangements involving regulated settings and informal home-based care may not be detrimental to children, and when involving care by a close relative such as a grandparent may be the type of child care that parents prefer.

Effective Provision of Pre-school Education (EPPE)

The United Kingdom's Effective Provision of Pre-school Education (EPPE)[20] was a national longitudinal study of young children's development that aimed to identify the benefits to children's developmental progress of attending an early childhood education setting. EPPE employed a Bronfenbrenner model to assess the 'value added' by pre-school education after taking account of a range of child, parent and home background factors. The EPPE design also included a qualitative component, Effective Pedagogy in the Early Years,[21] to more fully explore the characteristics of 'effective' educational programs.

Unlike the LSAC and the NICHD study's recruitment of birth cohorts, EPPE recruited children at age three years who were attending a range of pre-school settings. In order to cover the full range of pre-school provisions across a range of geographically, ethnically and economically diverse communities, the EPPE study recruited centres and families in five strategically chosen regions. Six main types of pre-school provision were included in each region—playgroups, local authority or voluntary day nurseries, private day nurseries, nursery schools, nursery classes and integrated centres (that combine care and education). Random selection was used to identify twenty to twenty-five centres within each type of provision, and to recruit twenty children and their families in each centre. This procedure generated a sample of approximately 2800 children and 141 centres. In addition, some 300 'home' children with no or minimal pre-school attendance were recruited from schools at age five years, bringing the total sample to 3171 children.

One of the major aims of the EPPE project was to identify the characteristics of pre-school programs that resulted in the best outcomes for children. The initial assessment of all the 141 participating programs was broad-based and sought to identify the ways that pre-school programs promoted the development of 'positive dispositions to learning, self-confidence and independence'.[22] Interviews with centre managers provided data on child–staff ratios, staff training, aims, policies, curriculum and parental involvement. Classroom observations by the research staff used the ECERS-R[23] to rate provisions for space and furnishings, personal care routines, language reasoning, activities, interaction with peers and adults and program structure, and the ECERS-Extension[24] to assess educational provision in the areas of language, mathematics, science and environment, and diversity. In addition, the Caregiver Interaction Scale[25] was used as a tool for rating the extent to which the teacher/main pre-school worker demonstrated positive relationships, permissiveness, detachment and punitiveness in interacting with children.

EPPE also asked parents to rate the home learning environment, for example, reading to the child, teaching nursery rhymes and songs, playing with letters and numbers, visiting the library, painting and drawing, emphasising the alphabet and watching television. This measure provided an important indicator of the ways that families support their children's learning.

A battery of cognitive tests such as verbal and non-verbal comprehension, naming vocabulary and spatial awareness tests was used to assess children's general developmental outcomes. Assessments of social and emotional adjustment and specific literacy and numeracy skills were also conducted. Overall, results supported the positive influence of pre-school experience, particularly for vulnerable groups, but background factors also remained powerfully predictive of children's attainment. The home learning environment was found to exert a significant and independent effect on outcomes at age three years and at the start of primary school, and on progress over the pre-school period.

In terms of the impact of quantity and quality of pre-school, results showed that the highest gains were seen in children who spent a longer time at pre-school (two years) and attended higher quality centres. Quality effects were similar across economically and educationally advantaged and disadvantaged groups.

Judy Ungerer & Linda Harrison

A CASE STUDY ANALYSIS OF EFFECTIVE PRE-SCHOOL PROGRAMS

Based on the child outcome data for the main study, the most effective pre-school centres, school classrooms and pre-school workers were identified. A detailed case study analysis of each centre was conducted to discover the most effective pedagogical strategies, that is, 'the instructional techniques and strategies which enable learning to take place'.[26]

Twelve pre-school centres and school classrooms and forty-six pre-school workers participated. Researchers attended each centre for a two-week period and collected 'naturalistic observations of staff pedagogy, and systematic structured observations of children's learning'.[27] Additional information was obtained through interviews with parents, staff and managers. The twelve case studies were then considered together, and the three centres whose children achieved the best outcomes across indices of cognitive and social skills and emotional adjustment were identified. Analyses then focused on identifying the pedagogical strategies and centre characteristics that differentiated these most effective centres from the rest.

The results indicated that the most effective centres were characterised by:[28]

1 Staff–child verbal interactions which involve *sustained shared thinking* (see below).
2 Staff who have a good understanding of curriculum content and appropriate strategies for promoting learning.
3 A balance of both staff-initiated (e.g. group teaching) and child-initiated (e.g. instructive free play) activities.
4 Discipline/behaviour policies 'in which staff supported children in being assertive, while simultaneously rationalising and talking through their conflicts'.[29]
5 The sharing of child-related information and educational aims between parents and staff.

WHAT IS SUSTAINED SHARED THINKING?

Sustained shared thinking occurs in interactions where an adult and a child '"work together" in an intellectual way to solve a problem, clarify a concept, evaluate an activity, extend a narrative, etc'.[30] Both the adult and child must be involved in attempting to understand the other's thinking, and an extension of the understanding must occur as a result. Observations of interactions in centres indicated that sustained shared thinking was most likely to occur when children were interacting one-to-one with an adult. The authors of the EPPE study cautioned that this finding should not be interpreted to mean that the majority of children's time should be in adult-directed activity, and particularly not in activities that are overly directed or didactic. In the most effective centres, children spent about half their time in free play activities, and sustained shared thinking was often observed when adults engaged with children in these less structured activities, for example, when adults were directly involved in children's play and stimulated their imagination by open questioning as in the example below.[31]

TEACHER 1 [Goes to home corner]: What's this?
CHILD: Teatime.
TEACHER 1: Can I join in?
CHILD: Yes.
TEACHER 1: What's for dinner?
CHILD: Spaghetti.
TEACHER 1: What kind, long or short? [Encouraging descriptive language]
CHILD: Short.
TEACHER 1: Well, I'll have a little bit.
CHILD: Would you like a yellow plate? What else would you like?
TEACHER 1: An egg please.

The contribution of ecological research

The four studies described in this chapter have provided some indication of the breadth of research that has been informed by Bronfenbrenner's modelling of development-in-context. Each has sought to address the complexities of children's development through the use of a highly sophisticated research design, which takes into account the interplay between the child's own attributes, family characteristics and the multiple contexts that directly or indirectly influence development. The research questions that have driven the four study designs centre on how children are growing up in today's modern society. The Longitudinal Study of Australian Children has covered a wide range of broad questions related to family functioning, health, child care and education, for example:

• How do family and neighbourhood circumstances interact?
• How do characteristics of parents' labour force participation affect child outcomes?
• What factors in early childhood ensure a positive 'fit' between child and school?[32]

The USA's NICHD Study of Early Child Care and Youth Development, in contrast, has focused on questions related specifically to child care, including:

• How are ethnicity, family size and income related to the age that an infant enters child care, the type of care selected, the quality of the care and the number of hours per week?
• How can parents and teachers judge the quality of child care?
• Is there a causal relation between child care quality and child outcomes?[33]

The UK's Effective Provision of Pre-School Education Project has been even more specific in its focus:

• What is the impact of pre-school on development?
• Can pre-school reduce social inequalities?[34]

Judy Ungerer & Linda Harrison

In each study, a rigorous methodology was employed to operationalise the research questions. Multiple sources of information (parents, caregivers and teachers, children, trained research assistants) and types of measures (interviews, questionnaires, observations, standardised procedures and tests, educational assessments, physical measurements, formal records, time-use diaries) were included to ensure that analysis of the research questions is based on data that are comprehensive and valid. As a result, the findings generated by these large-scale representative studies are having a considerable impact on social policy and professional practice. One area where this impact is clearly evident is the importance for children's development of quality experiences in early childhood and care. Findings from the NICHD study and EPPE have not only resulted in a greater appreciation of the need to provide such quality, they have also contributed to a clearer understanding of the factors that underpin quality.[35] These findings have direct implications for the decisions made by government policy makers, early childhood professional organisations, practitioners and parents.

STUDENT EXERCISES

1 Large-scale government-funded research studies, such as the Longitudinal Study of Australian Children (LSAC), the NICHD Study of Early Child Care and Youth Development (NICHD study), and the Effective Provision of Preschool Education (EPPE) and Effective Provision of Preschool and Primary Education 3-11 (EPPE 3-11) are accessible to policy makers, researchers, students and the public. Each has a website that provides detailed information about the design of the study, the instruments that are used to collect the data, technical papers, published reports, conferences and so on. In many cases, there are also provisions for approved researchers to access the data. In this first exercise, you should view and peruse the following websites:
    (a) LSAC: www.aifs.gov.au/growingup
    (b) NICHD study: www.nichd.nih.gov/research/supported/seccyd/overview.cfm or
        http://secc.rti.org for links to the study materials for each phase of the research
    (c) EPPE and EPPE 3-11: www.ioe.ac.uk/schools/ecpe/eppe/index.htm.
       The LSAC study has been complemented by a more detailed investigation of eleven Australian families and their one-year-old children in the *Life* documentary series. The first program, titled *Life at One*, was released in 2006; *Life at Three* was due for release in April 2008. Each child and family in the programs is described on the *Life Series* website: www.abc.net.au/life or http://blogs.abc.net.au/lifeat2/. The websites also present a series of research topics that report findings from the LSAC study. Open the Childcare link to read about patterns of care and the role of grandparents as caregivers.
2 Familiarise yourself with either the LSAC or NICHD study by viewing the instruments used to collect the data.
       For the LSAC website, open the Publications link and then the Survey Instruments link, and work your way through Wave 1 2004 Parent 1 (B) or Parent 1 (K) interview

and Teacher (K) questionnaire, and then Wave 2 2006. Download and read the documents. Identify the items designed to assess family relationships and parenting style. Then find and review the items that assess children's temperament, cognitive abilities, social competence and behaviour. Consider the different ways that children's development is assessed at the different ages (Wave 1: one and four years; Wave 2: three and six years).

For the NICHD study, materials are available for each of the four phases of the research on the RTI website. Open the Phase 1 Data Forms link and review the different types and sources of information that were collected about infants' child care (items 10A through 11X). Then open item 12B: Attitude Toward Maternal Employment. Read and complete the eleven-item questionnaire. Consider how mothers' ratings on this scale may be related to the information collected about their infants' child care experiences.

3 Based on your review of the LSAC or NICHD study instruments, reflect on the extent to which large-scale survey studies are able to implement Bronfenbrenner's ecological model in child and family research.

Notes

1 U. Bronfenbrenner, *The Ecology of Human Development*, Harvard University Press, Cambridge, MA, 1979.

2 Bronfenbrenner, 1979; U. Bronfenbrenner, 'Developmental Ecology through Space and Time: A Future Perspective', in *Examining Lives in Context*, eds, P. Moen, G.H. Elder Jr & K. Lüscher, American Psychological Association, Washington, DC, 1995, pp. 619–47; U. Bronfenbrenner, 'Environments in Developmental Perspective: Theoretical and Operational Models', in *Measuring Environment across the Life Span: Emerging Methods and Concepts*, eds, S.L. Friedman & T.D. Wachs, American Psychological Association, Washington, DC, 1999, pp. 3–28.

3 U. Bronfenbrenner, 'Recent Advances in the Research on Human Development', in *Development as Action in Context*, eds, R.K. Silbereisen, K. Eyforth & G. Rudinger, Springer-Verlag, Heidelberg, Germany, 1986, p. 288.

4 A.W. Dunlop, 'Bridging Early Educational Transitions in Learning Through Children's Agency', in *Transitions, European Early Childhood Education Research Journal Themed Monograph Series no. 1*, 2003, pp. 67–86.

5 Bernard, cited in Dunlop, 2003, p. 71; B. Bernard, *Fostering Resilience in Children*, ERIC Clearinghouse on Elementary and Early Childhood Education, EDO-PS-95-9, Illinois, 1995.

6 E.E. Werner & R.S. Smith, *Kauai's Children Come of Age*, University of Hawaii Press, Honolulu, HI, 1977.

7 The Consortium Advisory Group, *Introducing the Longitudinal Study of Australian Children, LSAC Discussion Paper no. 1*, Australian Institute of Family Studies, Melbourne, Australia, 2002, p. x.

8 The National Childcare Accreditation Council administers the Child Care Quality Assurance (CCQA) systems for children's services to facilitate and support continuous improvement to the quality of child care provided for children in Australia. See the NCAC website <www.ncac. gov.au> for details of the CCQA systems for long day care, family day care and outside school hours care.

9 L.J. Harrison & J.A. Ungerer, 'What Can the Longitudinal Study of Australian Children Tell Us about Infants and 4 to 5 Year Olds' Experiences of Early Childhood Education and Care?', *Family Matters*, 2006, 72, pp. 26–35; L.J. Harrison, J.A. Ungerer, G.J. Smith, S.R. Zubrick & S. Wise, with F. Press, M. Waniganayake and the LSAC Research Consortium, *Child Care in Australia: The Longitudinal Study of Australian Children, Wave 1 Thematic Paper*, Australian Government Department of Families, Community Services and Indigenous Affairs, Canberra, Australia, 2007.

10 L. Dunn & L. Dunn, *Peabody Picture Vocabulary Test-Revised*, American Guidance Service, Circle Pines, MN, 1981.

11 The NICHD Early Child Care Research Network, eds, *Child Care and Child Development: Results from the NICHD Study of Early Child Care and Youth Development*, Guilford Press, New York, 2005a.

12 The NICHD Early Child Care Research Network, 2005a, p. 4.

13 M.S. Ainsworth, M. Blehar, E. Waters & S. Wall, *Patterns of Attachment*, Erlbaum, Hillsdale, NJ, 1978.

14 The NICHD Early Child Care Research Network, 2005a, p. 205.

15 The NICHD Early Child Care Research Network, 2005a.

16 J. Bowes, L. Harrison, S. Wise, A. Sanson, J. Ungerer, J. Watson & T. Simpson, 'Child Care Choices: A Longitudinal Study of Children, Families and Child Care in Partnership with Policy Makers', *The Australian Educational Researcher*, 2004, 31, pp. 69–86.

17 J. Goodfellow, *Multicare Arrangement Patchworks: The Multiple Use of Formal and Informal Care in NSW*, report for the NSW Department of Community Services, Office of Child Care, Sydney, 1999.

18 J. Bowes & L. Harrison, 'Patterns of Care Involving Regulated Childcare Settings: Parent Perspectives', presented at the Australian Human Development Association Biennial Conference, Sydney, July 2007.

19 S. Wise, B. Edwards, J. Bowes, A. Sanson, J. Ungerer, L. Harrison & T. Simpson, 'The Relation of Multiple and Changeable Childcare Arrangements to Early Communication Skills', presented at the 9th Australian Institute of Family Studies Conference, Melbourne, February 2005, <www.aifs.gov.au/institute/afrc9/wise1.html>, accessed 8 January 2008.

20 K. Sylva, E. Melhuish, P. Sammons, I. Sirag-Blatchford & B. Taggart, *Technical Paper 12, The Final Report: Effective Pre-School Education*, University of London, Institute of Education, London, 2004.

21 I. Siraj-Blatchford, K. Sylva, S. Muttock, R. Gilden & D. Bell, *Research Report no. 356, Researching Effective Pedagogy in the Early Years*, University of London, Institute of Education/Department for Education and Skills, London, 2002.

22 Siraj-Blatchford et al., 2002, p. 10.

23 T. Harms, M. Clifford & D. Cryer, *Early Childhood Environment Rating Scale, Revised Edition (ECERS-R)*, Teachers College Press, New York, 1998.

24 K. Sylva, I. Siraj-Blatchford & B. Taggart, *The Early Childhood Environmental Rating Scale: 4 Curricular Subscales*, University of London, Institute of Education, London, 2003.

25 J. Arnett, 'Care-givers in Day-care Centers: Does Training Matter?', *Journal of Applied Developmental Psychology*, 10, 1989, pp. 541–52.

26 Siraj-Blatchford et al., 2002, p. 10.

27 Siraj-Blatchford et al., 2002, p. 10.

28 K. Sylva, E. Melhuish, P. Sammons, I. Siraj-Blatchford, B. Taggart & K. Elliot, *The Effective Provision of Pre-School Education (EPPE) Project: Findings from the Pre-school Period*, University of London, Institute of Education, London, 2003, pp. 3–4.

29 Sylva, Melhuish et al., 2003, p. 4.

30 Sylva, Melhuish et al., 2003, p. 3.

31 Siraj-Blatchford et al., 2002, p. 44.

32 A. Sanson, J. Nicholson, J. Ungerer, S. Zubrick, K. Wilson, J. Ainley, D. Berthelsen, M. Bittman, D. Broom, L. Harrison, B. Rodgers, M. Sawyer, S. Silburn, L. Strazdins, G. Vimpani & M. Wake, *Introducing the Longitudinal Study of Australian Children, LSAC Discussion Paper no. 1*, Australian Institute of Family Studies, Melbourne, 2002.

33 The NICHD Early Child Care Research Network, 2005a.

34 K. Sylva et al., 2003.

35 F. Press, *What about the Kids?: Policy Directions for Improving the Experiences of Infants and Young Children in a Changing World*, NSW Commission for Children & Young People, QLD Commission for Children and Young People and Child Guardian, National Investment for the Early Years (NIFTeY), Sydney, 2007.

Part B

Characteristics of Children: Effects of Disability, Ethnicity and Playfulness

3

Disability: Characteristics, Contexts and Consequences

Monica Cuskelly, Rebekah Grace and Alan Hayes

Disability affects a large number of individual Australians, their families and their communities. In 2003 there were 166,700 children below the age of 14 years with 'severe or profound core activity restrictions'.[1] Severe and profound core activity restrictions are labels used by the Australian Bureau of Statistics to refer to those individuals who sometimes (severe) or always (profound) need help with a core activity (self-care, mobility and communication). This may include people with intellectual, physical and sensory disabilities. Consistent with the focus of this book, this chapter examines aspects of the development of people with disabilities in the context of their families and communities.

The majority of children with a disability live with their family[2] and many individuals continue to live with their parents in adulthood, some into their old age.[3] This is, in part, a consequence of increased longevity in individuals with a disability[4] coupled with a move away from institutional care at all ages.

There are both positive and negative consequences for individuals, families and communities from children with disabilities remaining with their family, although it is clear from the research that having their child with them is the strong preference of most families.[5] Consistent with the ecological framework described in Chapter 1, both positive and negative consequences may follow from an event, and change in one part of a system may have unanticipated consequences for other parts. Before considering the consequences for children, families and communities, it is important to examine the nature of disability and how context affects perceptions of disability.

This chapter, then, addresses three questions:

- What kind of characteristic is disability and what impact does context have on its expression?
- Does context influence beliefs about and attitudes to disability?
- What are the consequences for children, families and communities?

Contexts

What kind of characteristic is disability?

Consistent with the framework proposed by the World Health Organization,[6] disability is understood as an umbrella term that incorporates the three components of impairments, activity limitations and participation restrictions. The framework reflects a biopsychosocial model of disability. It combines the medical model that views disability purely as a personal characteristic and the social model that views disability as a product of socially constructed barriers. The World Health Organization provides the following definitions:

- *Impairments* are problems in body functions (for example, mental, sensory, neuromusculoskeletal functions) or structures (for example, structure of the nervous, metabolic or endocrine systems) such as a significant deviation or loss. The degree of impairment may be mild, moderate, severe or complete.
- *Activity limitations* are difficulties an individual may have in executing activities such as learning and applying knowledge, mobility or self-care.
- *Participation restrictions* are problems an individual may experience in participating in life situations such as engaging in the life of their community and in interpersonal relationships.

Many individuals have more than one impairment, a situation likely to lead to increased activity limitations and restrictions on participation.[7] In addition, secondary conditions— that is, sequelae of the original disabling condition (for example, obesity resulting from the mobility restrictions of some physical disabilities)—may bring additional limitations and contribute to the barriers to full participation and inclusion within the community.[8]

These definitions make it clear that disability as a characteristic is inseparable from the context(s) in which the individual lives. To understand this interconnectedness, important distinctions between the terms need to be understood. Impairment is a personal attribute. The extent of the activity and participation restrictions that result from impairment can be reduced or increased by context. An impairment such as blindness, for example, may be less disabling in an appropriately supportive environment. Mobility aids (such as wheelchairs and walking frames), building access (such as ramps or lifts) and communication systems (such as Braille and sign language) all reduce the extent of restrictions experienced by people with a physical or sensory impairment. Societies vary, however, in the importance they place on ensuring that such measures are available to reduce the handicapping effects of impairment and disabilities.

MARTHA'S VINEYARD

The example of Martha's Vineyard aptly illustrates the point that impairment and context interact to determine the degree of handicap experienced. When the community in

Martha's Vineyard was first established in the seventeenth century it contained a large proportion of deaf members. Those with hearing and those who were deaf both used sign language as a natural language. In this context, deafness did not impede participation in community life and, as a result, was less of a handicap than it was in other communities.[9] Importantly, those in this community who were hearing-impaired were regarded as unique individuals in their own right. They were not defined by their disability as 'the deaf'.

It is not uncommon for people with disabilities to be inappropriately seen as members of a homogeneous group. In reality, as with all groups of human beings, individuals with disabilities are notable for their heterogeneity. There are numerous types, levels, causes and consequences of disability. Even within the various disabling conditions there is considerable variation in the characteristics associated with each.[10]

Does context influence beliefs about and attitudes to disability?

Disability provides an important insight into the ways in which the beliefs, perceptions and attitudes of any community or society alter the context for children and their families. Today the terms 'disability' and 'disabled' generally carry negative connotations. This has not always been the case. Across history, societies have varied considerably in the ways in which they defined disability and the value they placed upon people with disabilities.[11] For example, children with Down syndrome were regarded by the Olmecs of Ancient Mexico (1500 BC to 300 AD) as hybrids of humans and the gods. They were regarded as rare and special.[12]

The incidence and prevalence of disabilities have also changed over time. One of the most noticeable changes to occur is the increased survival rate of infants born with disabilities; and, at least for some conditions, life span has also increased.[13] Nevertheless, those with a disability are more likely to suffer ill health, receive poorer health care and die at earlier ages than are members of the general population.[14]

Improvements in the care provided have flowed from changes in attitude towards those with a disability. As one example, children with Down syndrome were denied access to heart surgery for a number of years, although the technology was available. Now that these children are given the necessary medical care, their survival rate has improved significantly.[15] These improvements may be related to economic factors, level of service and cultural beliefs and attitudes. In some parts of the world, infanticide is still practised when children are born with marked impairments or congenital defects, resulting in a greatly reduced prevalence of children with disabilities in these societies. In addition, our capacity to identify the genetic bases of conditions has increased, following improvements in gene technology. This means that conditions once regarded as of unknown aetiology have now been labelled and understood. As a further consequence, appropriate and timely medical care is more available, leading to the possibility of better outcomes. This genetic knowledge may also be used to prevent the births of children with certain characteristics, a consequence seen by some as reflecting a basic lack of acceptance in our society of those with disabilities.[16]

WAYS OF SEEING: FROM TYPES TO VARIANTS

Seeing individuals as a unitary group that is distinctly different, irrespective of context, and 'other than us' or an 'outgroup', is the first step in dehumanisation,[17] a process too often suffered by those with a disability and by their families. Valsiner identified this process as an example of typological thinking, which he defined as 'thinking in static categories that are ... context free'.[18]

Societies define disability in different ways. The definition of disability, and the community reaction to those labelled as 'disabled', says as much about the people who define the outgroup as it does about the group itself. In particular, it highlights the tendency to overlook the wide individual differences among people with any disability, and to overgeneralise core characteristics. For example, the communication difficulties of people with cerebral palsy may be mistakenly regarded as evidence of intellectual impairment. There may also be a tendency to focus only on the disability and overlook characteristics that are common to those who are disabled and the rest of the population.

This tendency highlights some important characteristics of human perception, cognition and communication. There would appear to be a restricted 'zone of difference' in which variation is permissible. Those whose characteristics place them outside this zone are in danger of rejection. This way of thinking can, however, lead to erroneous classifications, inaccurate typologies and distorted social evaluation.

STIGMA AND DISABILITY

People who are seen as different, such as those with disabilities, may be subjected to stigmatisation.[19] The person who is stigmatised is given a negative social identity by others, the consequence of which is often social isolation, and possibly even hostile interactions.

When considering concepts such as stigma it is important to recognise the central role of context. For example, in our society a premium is placed on formal education, and individuals who have difficulty acquiring reading or writing are seen as different from the mainstream. As Mercer observed,[20] some children are regarded as disabled only in the context of formal schooling, operating as 'normal' children in the world beyond the classroom.

Those who are members of groups that are negatively evaluated (or stigmatised) may attempt to change their status and join more acceptable groups. Tajfel labelled this process 'passing'.[21] Children with a disability usually have limited options for passing as members of the ingroup, as their outgroup status is often clearly apparent. Across cultures and historical eras, those with a disability have tended to be seen as a clear outgroup.[22]

In Western societies, some disabilities are more acceptable than others. Acceptability is likely to be influenced by the age of the affected person, by behaviour (with less troublesome children being more acceptable than those who are disruptive) and by developmental difference (with those who show average intellectual ability being more acceptable than those who are cognitively impaired).[23] Cultures may differ in the types of condition regarded as acceptable, and these judgments may be influenced by gender, religious affiliation or social status. Those whose conditions take potentially confronting forms (for example, those with epilepsy or schizophrenia) may be more likely to be seen as unacceptable and to be avoided. It is important to recognise that attitudes can be changed.[24] There is some research evidence of increasing acceptance of individuals with disabilities in our society[25] as well as changes to legislation, building codes and employment opportunities. Changing attitudes towards the *expression* of negative beliefs is also occurring and presents a challenge for researchers of attitudes towards those with a disability.[26] The discussions we are seeing in the media about 'wrongful life' (that is, families litigating against doctors for failing to identify a foetus as having a disability and therefore providing the opportunity to terminate the pregnancy) show that acceptance of those with a disability is still far from being achieved.

In summary, disability is part of the range of human variation. How people perceive those with disabilities has varied historically and culturally, and continues to change. The ways in which impairments are viewed reflect the influence of culture and context. In turn, views of disability affect the extent to which an impairment results in restrictions to full engagement in life's opportunities.

Consequences

What are the consequences for children, families and communities?

CONSEQUENCES FOR CHILDREN WITH DISABILITIES

In the research literature there has been an overwhelming concentration on the negative aspects and consequences of disability, with little consideration given to the other side of the balance sheet, although the recent emphasis on quality of life begins to deal with this aspect. In an effort to bring some balance, Allen Crocker edited a special issue of the *American Journal on Mental Retardation* devoted to the topic of happiness in individuals with intellectual disability.[27] Of course, people with disabilities have many of the same life experiences as those without disabilities. Having a disability is one of a number of individual characteristics that will shape life experiences.

Research indicates that most people with intellectual disabilities[28] and physical disabilities[29] have relatively good self-perceptions, especially during childhood and adolescence. The view one holds of oneself is not, of course, a product solely of the individual, or the impairment; it is the product of the interaction the individual has with his or her environment. As an example, Mrug and Wallander found that young people with physical disabilities had higher self-concepts when they attended an integrated school rather than being educated in a segregated setting.[30]

Monica Cuskelly, Rebekah Grace & Alan Hayes

Despite the negative view of disability in our society, there is evidence that some individuals with an impairment accept this aspect of themselves and do not wish to change to fit into the 'normal' mainstream. This can be seen in the rejection by some deaf people of cochlear implants to improve their hearing. In addition, there are reports available that make it clear that some individuals, at least, accept their impairment as integral to their understanding of self:

> 'For those of us with congenital conditions, disability shapes all we are. Those disabled later in life adapt. We take constraints no-one would choose and build rich and satisfying lives with them. We enjoy pleasures other people enjoy, and pleasures peculiarly our own. We have something the world needs'.[31]

Some individuals with disabilities adopt the negative views of disability held by those around them, thus undermining their capacity to develop a view of themselves that incorporates and accepts their impairment.[32] Low self-esteem may also flow from lack of opportunities for educational advancement, productive work, creative expression or social fulfilment.

As one example of the negative outcomes of disability, children with a disability are more likely to be victims of crime and subject to abuse than are those who are developing normally—another indicator of their marginal status in society.[33] The causes of their vulnerability to maltreatment are complex, and may be associated with the increased caregiving demands in a family with few resources (material or personal) to meet their needs. Maltreatment may also be associated with the perceived status of children with a disability in our society, so that predators may feel there will be no retribution for ill-treating them. Cooke and Standen also raised the issue of service providers failing to 'see' the abuse of children with a disability. The reasons for this may be conscious or subconscious, and reflect both a lack of knowledge and support for service providers, and a desire to avoid the complications of such a case that drains time and resources. The protection of children with disabilities may be seen as of lesser importance than the protection of their non–disabled peers.[34]

The following sections deal with some of the areas in which having an impairment is likely to have consequences for the individual.

Opportunities for and constraints on education and employment

In Australia and other developed countries there has been a significant improvement in educational opportunities and access to public life and spaces for people with disabilities. Nevertheless, limitations on access to experience and opportunity remain a defining feature of the participation restrictions that flow from impairment and disability. Increased opportunities and improvements in quality of life have occurred, largely as a function of recognition of the importance of context. Those involved with children who have a disability have come to understand that education and experience can have a substantial impact on the capacities of children, who previously had been left in unstimulating environments because little was expected of them. Policies of inclusion, intended to increase the access of children with disabilities to the life of their communities, may be difficult to implement in the face of prejudice and lack of acceptance.

INCLUSIVE EDUCATION: A CASE STUDY

Inadequate teacher training in inclusive practice and inflexible education models are reflections of the broader lack of acceptance of children with disabilities in our society. Nonetheless, it is important to acknowledge that there are some extraordinary teachers who rise above these barriers and provide a positive, stimulating and inclusive education experience for children with disabilities.

For example, Colin is a kindergarten teacher in a rural area. He became particularly interested in inclusive practice when Matthew, a boy with autism, was enrolled in his class. Colin established regular meetings with the family, often held in the family's own home. He attended meetings with the intervention professionals to better understand Matthew's needs and abilities and coordinated fund-raising activities to help the family meet the costs of Matthew's intervention program. Colin's classroom and teaching methods are sensitive to the needs of all of his pupils, including Matthew. His understanding, flexibility and patience have benefited Matthew and his family immeasurably. He has also provided a wonderful model of unconditional acceptance to the children in his class. Parents of other young children with disabilities have applied for enrolment at the school and requested Colin as their child's teacher.

Social changes can have positive or negative consequences for individuals with disabilities. New technologies that aid sensory acuity and communication, for example, have enhanced educational and employment prospects for those with sensory or physical impairments. On the other hand, a reduction in rural and unskilled work has reduced employment opportunities for those with intellectual disabilities. There are differences across cultures in employment of people with disabilities. In the USA, for example, many people with disabilities work, but because there is no regulation of wages there is also considerable opportunity for exploitation. In this case, the consequences are a complex mix of positive and negative for people with disabilities.

Opportunities for and constraints on relationships

People with disabilities often experience restrictions in their ability to form relationships and obtain emotional support. Their opportunities for self-expression and development may also be reduced. While policies of deinstitutionalisation may have been intended to enhance opportunities for contact with the community at large, in practice they may not lead to increased social inclusion, as individuals may live in a home within the community but engage with no one but their housemates and their paid carers.

Social engagement and companionship are basic human needs. One of the most important requirements for the development of social relationships is access, and another is the openness of possible partners. Friendships require reciprocity and for some children, despite having the desire and the competence required to form relationships, personal intent may be frustrated by social rejection.[35] Of course, many individuals with a disability experience very satisfying social relationships and deep friendships.

Monica Cuskelly, Rebekah Grace & Alan Hayes

Participation in youth disability sport is just one example of an avenue for children with disabilities to form quality friendships,[36] although some families may see this avenue as not acceptable because of its segregated nature.

The health problems associated with many disabling conditions may also have social consequences. In addition to the direct impact of illness on quality of life, increased social isolation may ensue as periods of hospitalisation interfere with the maintenance of friendships.

Social isolation may be the usual experience for individuals with a disability after they have completed schooling, particularly those with an intellectual disability or multiple disabilities. Although many individuals with these conditions remain living in the community, often residing within the family home, they are usually dependent on family members for their social networks and have little peer contact outside the home. [37]

The move from institutionalisation towards community participation is opening the way for people with disabilities to pursue the same dreams that many people have, including becoming a parent. This is a particularly controversial issue in the case of people with intellectual disabilities. For women with intellectual disability, sterilisation is still common practice.[38] When a woman with an intellectual disability does have a child, she faces considerable prejudice, stigma and constant scrutiny. It is apparent that within the legal system there is an assumption that these parents will inevitably put their children at risk, and this assumption is often used to justify the removal of children from parents with disabilities even in the absence of any evidence that there are child protection issues.[39] The importance of social networks and formal professional support cannot be understated for parents with intellectual disability. However, it is clear that when these supports are in place, and when these parents are provided with opportunities to learn good parenting strategies, many parents with intellectual disabilities are able to provide a loving, nuturing and effective family environment.[40]

Parents with physical disabilities may also experience the constant challenging of their ability to be a good parent, and are also at risk of social isolation. This group of parents may experience difficulties with access to services, appropriate transportation and housing, and there may also be barriers to child care and recreational activities. For parents with physical disabilities there is tremendous value in developing adaptive techniques and equipment.[41]

Social and personal outcomes for any individual will be the product of a complex interaction between individual characteristics and understanding, the opportunities that have been available, social support, societal views of disability and the sociopolitical and cultural contexts in which the individual lives.[42] All of these elements are changeable, so the process will be a dynamic one throughout the individual's life.

PARENTS WITH DISABILITIES: A CASE STUDY

Sandi is a competent and intelligent woman with a successful academic career. She has a physical disability and is unable to use her arms or hands. After having a baby, Sandi felt more stigmatised and unaccepted than at any other time in her life. Her frustration became even more acute when her little girl started at child care when she was twelve months old. When she arrived to collect her child, Sandi had to stand at the front door until another parent came because the doorbell was too high for her to reach and the centre refused to lower it. She was also asked not to continue coming to the centre to breastfeed her child because staff said it was distressing for the other children and parents to see her holding her child with her feet. Sandi offered to provide information, and run an information session in the evening for the other parents, but this offer was rejected. Offers to provide the centre with books about people who are different were also rejected. Eventually Sandi stopped going to the centre herself and hired a nanny who communicates with the centre.

CONSEQUENCES FOR FAMILIES AND THEIR MEMBERS

Although the birth of any child heralds many fundamental changes for families, the birth of a child with a disability is often unexpected and has a significant impact on the family as a unit and on its individual members. Disability is an example of an area of potential stress, strain and/or life problems over which individuals have limited control. There are, however, many aspects over which family members can have control, and individuals will vary in their openness to exploring these possibilities. The work of Gallimore and colleagues, as discussed in Chapter 1, has provided a framework for examining family life when there is a child with a disability.[43] They underscored the need to focus on the key issue confronting families of creating 'a sustainable and meaningful daily routine of family life', and labelled this process 'family accommodation'. They highlighted the importance of a model of family accommodation that 'takes account of *all* family members, not just the child with delays'. Families vary in the extent to which they can achieve this. Education, material resources, personality, prior experience, available social supports and general coping skills may all facilitate accommodation. Recent research focusing on family quality of life has provided a valuable complementary approach to examining effects on families and the ways in which they find balance and meaning.[44]

Parental response to disability

The personal response of parents to having a child with a disability will vary. One important consideration is time: early responses may differ markedly from those experienced later in the family's life. It is likely that the initial response to the birth of a child with an impairment will be more uniform than at any other time. Almost all parents go through a process of grieving,[45] and some experience denial as part of the process on their journey towards acceptance.[46] For many parents their child's disability is not known at birth or is acquired later in life. Over time, parents may come to see their child's disability very differently from their initial view, with some parents reporting that the experience of living with their child has changed them completely, and in ways they appreciate.[47] Parents of children with disabilities may be at greater risk of stress-related illnesses and

Monica Cuskelly, Rebekah Grace & Alan Hayes

psychological problems such as chronic anxiety.[48] However, as Emerson and colleagues have pointed out, a considerable proportion of these difficulties may be attributable to socio-economic factors related to additional expenses involved in the care of children with disabilities.[49] There can also be physical sequelae for parents, such as developing back problems as a consequence of lifting an immobile child or constant tiredness due to the sleep disturbance of the child.[50] Personal characteristics,[51] family characteristics[52] and community characteristics[53] will all play a part in assisting or undermining parental capacities to cope. Parental functioning is important, not only for the individual, but for all members of the family, including the child with the disability.[54]

Social support has been shown to be very important in assisting parents in the raising of a child with a disability.[55] The availability of such support will depend upon the acceptance by the community of the individual with a disability, the acknowledgment of the increased difficulties associated with parenting a child with a disability, and an acceptance of some community responsibility to support the family—all of which are clearly contextual issues. The importance of context has been particularly highlighted in cross-cultural research.[56]

Not all families are vulnerable, and many prove to be remarkably resilient.[57] Even in families who experience stress, many also report positive aspects of parenting a child with a disability.[58] In a longitudinal investigation of families of children with autism, Gray found that the majority of parents reported that their family was coping better than they had been a decade previously.[59] This improvement was attributed to a number of changes including a decrease in the difficult behaviour of the child with autism, an improvement in services and improvement in parents' coping strategies over time.

There is a danger in focusing only on the family as a unit, as this overlooks the fact that the family system is composed of individuals who all have unique experiences and perspectives. As noted earlier, most research investigating family and parental response to disability has been based on maternal reports, which may limit our understanding of the range of experiences within families. Those studies that have investigated differences in parental experiences and perceptions usually reported some differences between mothers' and fathers' responses. Mothers have often been found to experience more negative consequences[60] but in some studies, more positive experiences.[61] Both results may reflect the different roles mothers and fathers take with respect to the child with the disability.[62] Some aspects of family life that are important for psychological functioning appear to be different for mothers and fathers.[63] They use services differently,[64] and also use different strategies for coping.[65]

Consequences for other family members

Much of the literature that examines the issue of care provision across the life span of those with a disability focuses on the role of parents. However, many individuals with a disability outlive their parents, and care therefore needs to be provided by other family members or through government or non-government agencies. Siblings may provide direct care, for example by taking the individual to live with them, or indirect care by providing support and advocacy with respect to the agencies providing services to their brother or sister.[66]

The literature on the adjustment of siblings to having a brother or sister with a disability was initially very pessimistic about the consequences. More recently, research evidence suggests an improved outlook for brothers and sisters of a child with a disability.[67] This change may be due to a number of factors including parental awareness of the possibility of negative outcomes for their other children, and greater societal acceptance of children with disabilities.

Extended family members have generally been overlooked in research about families with a member with a disability; however grandparents, in particular, are often a great resource for families.[68] The particular needs of grandparents in dealing with this role are little understood.[69]

When a parent has a disability, children may be required to participate in caring activities that are not required of other children their age. These responsibilities include practical care as well as emotional care (particularly for those children of parents with mental health problems). If these responsibilities are inconsistent with a child's abilities and levels of maturity and understanding, a child's development and well-being may be adversely affected. It is essential that support services do not focus only on the parent, but adopt a family-centred approach, and address the support needs of all members of the family.[70]

It is important that families' experiences of living with a child with a disability are not characterised as always burdensome. An increasing number of researchers have begun to seek an understanding of the positive experiences of living with a family member with a disability. There is evidence, for example, that many brothers and sisters of a child with a disability have positive relationships with their siblings with a disability, with a number of reports finding more positive relationships in these families than in comparison families where all children are developing typically.[71] Siblings' social skills may also be improved by their experiences.[72] A number of researchers have now documented the personal and family benefits parents attribute to having a child with a disability.[73] These include increased self-knowledge, the development of self-confidence, pleasure in fulfilling a demanding parental role and improved family relationships. We have little understanding about what contributes to these long-term positive appraisals, and it is probable that different outcomes are influenced by different processes. As an example, relationships with support agencies are likely to contribute to parental confidence[74] while family relationships may be influenced more by personal characteristics of the members of the family. In many families, there is recognition of both the difficulties and the positive aspects of having a child with a disability.[75]

The interactive cycle between the functioning of individuals and the family as a system needs to be considered. There is a great deal of research examining the impact of the individual with a disability on family life. Adaptive behaviour, rather than overall level of severity of the disability, may have a greater influence on the stress experienced. Temperamental characteristics of the child with a disability and the level of behavioural problems also seem to have a stronger influence on family stress levels than the disability per se.[76] It is important to keep in mind that having a child with a disability does not protect families from the other vicissitudes of life and these families may also experience demands from other sources that strain their capacity to cope, such as sickness or death of other family members, mental health problems and loss of income.

Monica Cuskelly, Rebekah Grace & Alan Hayes

Family characteristics and response to disability

In any family, size and structure (nuclear, one-parent or blended) may have an influence on the impact of life events. There is some evidence that one-parent families may experience more stress when they include a child with a disability,[77] although the finding of increased stress is common to all one-parent families.[78] A review of marital status found that divorce and separation were no more common in families with a child with a disability than in comparison families.[79] There will be considerable variation across all family configurations, both in the type and number of problems encountered and in their coping resources.

Ethnicity and cultural background influence a family's daily life and value systems and are reflected in the beliefs parents hold about their role in the development of their children as well as the meaning they assign to their child's disability.[80] It is likely that cultural values related to children, achievement and parenting act to affect the family's appraisal of the situation.

Having a child with a disability brings with it extra costs for the family. However, many of the families with a child with a disability are already at an economic disadvantage; indeed, their poverty may be one of the factors contributing to their child's condition, particularly if the primary cause of the condition was related to inadequate health care.[81] Park, Turnbull and Turnbull[82] report that almost one-third of children with a disability living in the USA live in families whose income is below the poverty line. Poverty then brings additional limitations for the family and the child across at least five dimensions of family quality of life identified by Park and her colleagues: health, productivity, physical environment, emotional well-being and family interaction.

Characteristics of the family as a unit as well as those of individual members are also important in determining the well-being of families. Cohesiveness and good communication have been identified as contributing to effective family functioning[83] and characteristics such as these will vary between and within families across time. Approaches to dealing with stress are important contributors to individual and, therefore, family functioning. Use of problem-solving strategies rather than a focus on reducing the negative emotions associated with a situation has been found to contribute to family well-being, as has the capacity to find a positive meaning in meeting the demands of caring for the child with a disability.[84] Marital satisfaction has been found to be an important contributor to coping, particularly for fathers of a child with a disability.[85]

Stage of family life may be an important aspect to consider, with elevated potential for stress at transition points such as the initial diagnosis, or when parents recognise the faster developmental rate of younger siblings, or on entry to school, or at puberty, or when residential or other adult life issues become central. Transitions related to the lives of other members of the family may also be important, such as when a parent retires or a sibling marries. Failure to make a normative transition can be difficult for both the individual with a disability and the family.

Many of the problems encountered by families may reflect the mismatch between the life cycle in such families and community norms. The gap may become particularly marked when the person with a disability continues to behave in adulthood in ways that are usually associated with childhood, such as engaging in tantrums or aggressive outbursts. In later life, elderly parents may find that they lack the personal and physical resources to cope with these problems. Their situation may be exacerbated by the lack of respite care or residential placement options.

Links to the community for families of children with a disability

Parents of a child with a disability are more likely to report social isolation than are parents whose children are developing normally, as can be seen in this mother's words: 'I miss my friends. I miss my family. It is the camaraderie of people outside disabilities that I miss'.[86] The problem of limited friendships for families following the birth of a child with a disability may have several causes. It may not only be a matter of isolation or ostracism, but the withdrawal of families from their previous social networks. It can also be a matter of preoccupation with the demands of caring and maintaining other aspects of family life. Mothers of a child with a disability are less likely to be involved in work outside the home,[87] and this may have serious consequences for their capacity to form friendships.

Employment can be a protective mechanism for mothers in particular.[88] This protective effect may be due to release of tension, the sense of competence that may be associated with accomplishment, or to the social opportunities that work provides. Unfortunately, employment opportunities that are sufficiently flexible to cope with the increased time demands experienced by mothers of children with a disability are often not available,[89] with fathers' work also being affected in some families.[90] In the modern world when there is a social expectation, and often a financial need, for mothers to work, lack of employment opportunities will have consequences for other members of the family, as well as for the mother herself. Finding a solution to the lack of opportunities in this domain requires a concerted commitment from their community.

Consequences for families depend, on the one hand, upon the interplay of the characteristics of the children with the disability and their families. On the other hand, families are affected by the beliefs, attitudes, values and actions of members of their communities and the wider society. Just as people with disabilities vary greatly in their characteristics, attainments and life outcomes, so too do families.

Before viewing disability as the cause of particular patterns of functioning observed in such families, there is a need to consider the extent to which these patterns of functioning are similar to those that are the norm for the community to which a family belongs. A balanced perspective on the impact of having a child with a disability places the emphasis first on the person, rather than the disability, and next on the family, rather than only one of its members. As such, it moves away from the view that the child with the disability is central to all major family decisions, characteristics and outcomes.

For many families, the negative consequences of having a family member with a disability would be ameliorated if the community in which they lived valued those with a disability as equal members of society, and provided the necessary financial and service supports to allow families to meet their responsibilities to all members.[91]

Monica Cuskelly, Rebekah Grace & Alan Hayes

CONSEQUENCES FOR COMMUNITIES

Earlier in this chapter the historical and cultural differences in societal attitudes to people with disabilities were discussed. The emphasis was on the impact of beliefs, attitudes and values on those affected by disabilities. But beliefs, attitudes and values also have an effect on those who hold them. For example, tolerance and acceptance, as opposed to prejudice and rejection, are features of open societies. Openness to diversity can be seen as part of the 'adaptive fitness' of societies and an index of advancement of their moral, intellectual and social capital. Cultural differences lead to diversity of moral, intellectual and social norms, and economic factors in a society may further constrain the extent to which openness is possible.

Family and community responsibilities

We have recently seen more major changes to government policies for the disability sector.[92] Some have been positive while others may act to increase the burden on individual families; for example, recent changes to residential service provision for children with severe behavioural disturbances may make the situation for some parents even worse.[93]

While it is difficult to be sure of the exact statistics, and of the direction of the effects, it is evident from the numbers of children with a disability in foster care that caring for a child with a disability may be beyond the capacities of some families, due to a complex mix of personal and family difficulties, in concert with inadequate support from government.[94] In part, this is due to the lack of support such families experience—responsibility for the individual with a disability is seen almost entirely to be a family affair. There is a lack of options to family care, insufficient respite services (in both number and flexibility), too few specialised educational and therapy supports, and inadequate employment and living opportunities (independent of family) for adults with a disability. Governments have increased demands on agencies (including their own) to meet certain standards in the services they deliver, but have failed to make adequate provision for the level of need in the community.[95] The rhetoric is that the community cares, but the reality is that parents (and other family members) are left virtually alone to cope with the increased demands of caring for a child with a disability, often into the parents' old age.[96]

In Australia, services are not equally available to all citizens. Where one lives makes a big difference to one's daily experiences. Rural and remote communities have few services for children with disabilities and their families, and many families have made the decision to leave their homes and move to regional and metropolitan areas where they see more opportunities for their child with a disability.

While family characteristics and resources impact on their response to having a member with a disability, it is important to recognise the role society plays in supporting or increasing the burden on families, as well the direct impact on the individual with the disability. Governmental policy embodies the formal responses of society to disability in its citizens.

Bowman and Virtue wrote about experiences with their own daughters:

> Caring for our daughters was hard but it was made so much harder by lack of support, lack of information, lack of child care, inadequate housing, living on a low income

and struggling through the medical maze—all issues of public policy. Our experience was personal but it was also political. Nothing could have changed the disability but the circumstances of our lives and the lives of our children were shaped by social and economic policies.[97]

While disability has increasingly become visible to the community through events such as the Special Olympics and disability-focused advertising campaigns, there is still quite a way to go before tolerance and acceptance are widespread. Until that is achieved, community prejudice and rejection will continue to set the context for too many people with disabilities and their families.

STUDENT EXERCISES

1   What do you associate with the word 'disability'? Write down the thoughts that immediately come to mind and discuss these with a fellow student.
2   Take a tour of your community. Make a list of all the aspects that could increase the difficulty of living and access for people with disabilities (such as buildings that are difficult to enter in a wheelchair). Analyse your list to identify those features that could easily be modified and those that are more difficult to change.
3   In what ways can contexts alter the experiences and developmental opportunities for children with disabilities? How can professionals such as teachers, therapists or social workers change contexts to make children with disabilities and their families less vulnerable?
4   Consider how the various types of disability might exacerbate normative life stressors such as changing schools or having a seriously ill parent.
5   What factors may contribute to the increased vulnerability of children with a disability to abuse and how might these be addressed? Consider individual, community and policy changes that might contribute to an improvement in this area.

Notes

1   Australian Bureau of Statistics, *Disability, Ageing and Carers: Summary of Findings*, catalogue no. 4430.0, Australian Government Publishing Service, Canberra, 2003a. These were the most recent figures available at the time of the publication of this book. The ABS Survey of Disability, Ageing and Carers (SDAC) is conducted every six years, and so the next round of data collection will take place in 2009.
2   D. Braddock, E. Emerson, D. Felce & R.J. Stancliffe, 'Living Circumstances of Children and Adults with Mental Retardation or Developmental Disabilities in the United States, Canada, England and Wales, and Australia', *Mental Retardation and Developmental Disabilities Research Review*, 7, 2001, pp. 115–21.
3   C. Bigby, *Moving on Without Parents. Planning, Transitions, and Sources of Support for Middleaged and Older Adults with Intellectual Disability*, MacLennan & Petty, Sydney, 2000; Braddock et al., 2001.
4   M.P. Janicki, A.J. Dalton, C.M. Henderson & P.W. Davidson, 'Mortality and Morbidity among Older Adults with Intellectual Disability: Health Service Considerations', *Disability and Rehabilitation*, 21, 1999, pp. 284–94.
5   G. Llewellyn, P. Dunn, M. Fante, L. Turnbull & R. Grace, 'Family Factors Influencing Out-of-home Placement Decisions', *Journal of Intellectual Disability Research*, 43, 3, 1999, pp. 219–41.

Monica Cuskelly, Rebekah Grace & Alan Hayes

6   World Health Organization, 'International Classification of Functioning, Disability and Health', WHO, Geneva, 2001.

7   See, for example, M.A. Traci, T. Seekins, A. Szalda-Petree & C. Ravesloot, 'Assessing Secondary Conditioning Among Adults with Developmental Disabilities: A Preliminary Study', *Mental Retardation*, 40, 2002, pp. 119–31.

8   R.J. Simeonsson, J.S. McMillen & G.S. Huntington, 'Secondary Conditions in Children with Disabilities: Spina Bifida as a Case Example', *Mental Retardation and Developmental Disabilities Research Reviews*, 8, 2002, pp. 198–205.

9   N.E. Groce, *Everybody Here Spoke Sign Language: Hereditary Deafness on Martha's Vineyard*, Harvard University Press, Cambridge, MA, 1985.

10   See, for example, V. Lewis, *Development and Disability*, Blackwell Publishing, Malden, MA, 2003; C.L. Vash & N.M. Crewe, *Psychology of Disability* (2nd edn), Springer Publishing, New York, 2004.

11   A.B.D. Clarke & A.M. Clarke, 'The Historical Context', in *New Approaches to Down Syndrome*, eds, B. Stratford & P. Gunn, Cassell, London, 1996, pp. 12–22.

12   B. Stratford, 'In the Beginning', in Stratford & Gunn, 1996, pp. 3–11.

13   See E.J. Glasson, S.G. Sullivan, B.A. Patterson, P.D. Montgomery & A.H. Bittles, 'The Changing Survival Profile of People with Down's Syndrome: Implications for Genetic Counselling', *Clinical Genetics*, 62, 2002, pp. 390–3; L. Ouyang, S.D. Grosse, B.S. Armour & N.J. Waitzman, 'Health Care Expenditures of Children and Adults with Spina Bifida in a Privately Insured U.S. Population', *Birth Defects Research Part A: Clinical and Molecular Teratology*, 79, 2007, pp. 552–8.

14   K.E. Lavin, B.E. McGuire & M.J. Hogan, 'Age at Death of People with an Intellectual Disability in Ireland', *Journal of Intellectual Disability*, 10, 2006, pp. 155–64; A.H. Bittles, B.A. Patterson, S.G. Sullivan, R. Hussain, E.J. Glasson & P.D. Montgomery, 'The Influence of Intellectual Disability on Life Expectancy', *Journal of Gerontology: Series A: Biological Sciences and Medical Sciences*, 57A, 2002, M470–M472; D. Strauss, R. Shavelle, R. Reynolds, L. Rosenbloom & S. Day, 'Survival in Cerebral Palsy in the Last 20 Years: Signs of Improvement?', *Developmental Medicine and Child Neurology*, 49, 2, 2007, pp. 86–92.

15   K.A. Hallidie-Smith, 'The Heart', in Stratford & Gunn, 1996, pp. 84–99.

16   E. Parens & A. Ach, 'Disability Rights Critique of Parental Genetic Testing: Reflections and Recommendations', *Mental Retardation and Developmental Disabilities Research Reviews*, 9, 2003, pp. 40–7; M. Tankard Reist, *Defiant Births: Women who Resist Medical Eugenics*, Spinifex Press, Melbourne, 2006.

17   D. Thomas, *The Social Psychology of Childhood Disability*, Methuen, London, 1978.

18   J. Valsiner, 'Two Alternative Epistemological Frameworks in Psychology: The Typological and Variational Modes of Thinking', *Journal of Mind and Behavior*, 5, 1984, pp. 450–70.

19   E. Goffman, *Stigma*, Penguin, Harmondsworth, 1963.

20   J. Mercer, *Labelling the Mentally Retarded*, University of California Press, Berkeley, 1973.

21   H. Tajfel, *Human Groups and Social Categories*, Cambridge University Press, Cambridge, 1981.

22   M. Rosen, G. Clark & M. Kivitz, *The History of Mental Retardation: Collected Papers, vols. 1 & 2*, University Park Press, Baltimore, 1976; Clarke & Clarke, 1996.

23   E.A. Nowicki, 'A Cross-Sectional Multivariate Analysis of Children's Attitudes towards Disabilities', *Journal of Intellectual Disability Research*, 50, 2006, pp. 335–48; D.E. Most, D.J. Fidler, C. LaForce-Booth & J. Kelly, 'Stress Trajectories in Mothers of Young Children with Down Syndrome', *Journal of Intellectual Disability Research*, 50, 2006, pp. 501–14.

24   F. Rillotta & T. Nettelbeck, 'Effects of an Awareness Program on Attitudes of Students without an Intellectual Disability towards Persons with an Intellectual Disability', *Journal of Intellectual & Developmental Disability*, 32, 2007, pp. 19–27.

25   See M. Townsend & J. Hassell, 'Mainstream Students' Attitudes to Possible Inclusion in Unified Sports with Students Who Have an Intellectual Disability', *Journal of Applied Research in Intellectual Disabilities*, 20, 2007, pp. 265–73.

26   See N. Akrami, B. Ekehammar, M. Claesson & K. Sonnander, 'Classical and Modern Prejudice: Attitudes Toward People with Intellectual Disabilities', *Research in Developmental Disabilities*, 27, 2006, pp. 606–17.

27   A.C. Crocker, 'Introduction: The Happiness in All Our Lives', *American Journal on Mental Retardation*, 105, 2002, pp. 319–25.

28   C. Cunningham & S. Glenn, 'Self-awareness in Young Adults with Down Syndrome: I. Awareness of Down Syndrome and Disability', *International Journal of Disability, Development and Education*, 51, 2004, pp. 335–62; S. Glenn & C. Cunningham, 'Self-awareness in Young Adults with Down Syndrome: II. Self-understanding', *International Journal of Disability, Development and Education*, 51, 2004, pp. 363–82.

29   J.C. Manuel, R. Balkrishnan, F. Camacho, B.P. Smith & L.A. Koman, 'Factors Associated with Self-esteem in Pre-Adolescents and Adolescents with Cerebral Palsy', *Journal of Adolescent Health*, 32, 2003, pp. 456–58.

30   S. Mrug & J.L. Wallander, 'Self-Concept of Young People with Physical Disabilities: Does Integration Play a Role?', *International Journal of Disability, Development and Education*, 49, 2002, pp. 267–80.

31   H. McB. Johnson, 'My Right to Life', *Weekend Australian Magazine*, 3–4 May, 2003, p. 21. Also see N. Watson, 'Well, I Know This is Going to Sound Very Strange to You, But I Don't See Myself as a Disabled Person: Identity and Disability', *Disability and Society*, 17, 2002, pp. 509–27.

32   Vash & Crewe, 2004.

33   S. Vig & R. Kaminer, 'Maltreatment and Developmental Disabilities in Children', *Journal of Developmental and Physical Disabilities*, 14, 2002, pp. 371–86.

34   P. Cooke & P.J. Standen, 'Abuse and Disabled Children: Hidden Need …?', *Child Abuse Review*, 11, 2002, pp. 1–18.

35   G. Laws & E. Kelly, 'The Attitudes and Friendship Intentions of Children in United Kingdom Mainstream Schools Towards Peers with Physical or Intellectual Disabilities', *International Journal of Disability, Development and Education*, 52, 2005, pp. 79–99; J. Wiener & B.H. Schneider, 'A Multisource Exploration of the Friendship Patterns of Children with and without Learning Disabilities', *Journal of Abnormal Child Psychology*, 30, 2002, pp. 127–41.

36   C. Pottie & J. Sumarah, 'Friendships Between Persons with and without Developmental Disabilities', *Mental Retardation*, 42, 2004, pp. 55–66.

37   A. Jobling & M. Cuskelly, 'Life Styles of Adults with Down Syndrome Living at Home', in *Down Syndrome Across the Life Span*, eds, M. Cuskelly, A. Jobling & S. Buckley, Whurr Publishers, London, 2002, pp. 109–20.

38   L. Servais, 'Sexual Health Care in Persons with Intellectual Disabilities', *Mental Retardation and Developmental Disabilities Research Reviews*, 12, 1, 2006, pp. 48–56.

39   D. McConnell & G. Llewellyn, 'Stereotypes, Parents with Intellectual Disability and Child Protection', *Journal of Social Welfare and Family Law*, 24, 3, 2002, pp. 1–21.

40   T. Booth & W. Booth, *Parenting Under Pressure: Mothers and Fathers with Learning Difficulties*, Open University Press, Buckingham, 1997; J. Strike & D. McConnell, 'Parents with Intellectual Disability: Just the Same, Only Different', *Interaction*, 15, 4, 2002, pp. 11–15.

41   M. Krishbaum, 'A Disability Culture Perspective on Early Intervention with Parents with Physical or Cognitive Disabilities and their Infants', *Infants and Young Children*, 13, 2, 2000, pp. 9–20.

42   See B.M. Noonan, S.M. Gallor, N.F. Hensler-McGinnis, R.E. Fassinger, S. Wang & J. Goodman, 'Challenge and Success: A Qualitative Study of the Career Development of Highly Achieving Women with Physical and Sensory Disabilities', *Journal of Counselling Psychology*, 51, 2004, pp. 68–80.

43   See, for example, R.G. Gallimore, L.P. Bernheimer & T.S. Weisner, 'Family Life is More than Managing a Crisis: Broadening the Agenda of Research on Families Adapting to Childhood Disability', in *Developmental Perspectives on Children with High Incidence Disabilities*, eds, R. Gallimore, L.P. Bernheimer, D. MacMillan, D. Spence & S. Vaughn, Lawrence Erlbaum, Mahwah, NJ, 1999, pp. 40–80.

44   J.A. Summers, D.J. Poston, A.P. Turnbull, J. Marquis, L. Hoffman, H. Mannan & M. Wang, 'Conceptualizing and Measuring Family Quality of Life', *Journal of Intellectual Disability Research*, 49, 2005, pp. 777–83.

45   G.M. Foley, 'The Loss-Grief Cycle: Coming to Terms with the Birth of a Child with a Disability', in *Mental Health in Early Intervention: Achieving Unity in Principles and Practice*, eds, G.M. Foley & J.D. Hochman, Paul H Brookes, Baltimore, MD, 2006, pp. 227–43.

46   K.M. Ho & M.K. Keiley, 'Dealing with Denial: A Systems Approach for Family Professionals Working with Parents of Individuals with Multiple Disabilities', *The Family Journal*, 11, 2003, pp. 239–47.

47   See, for example, G.A. King, L. Zwaigenbaum, S. King, D. Baxter, P. Rosenbaum & A. Bates, 'A Qualitative Investigation of Changes in the Belief Systems of Families of Children with Autism or Down Syndrome', *Child: Care, Health & Development*, 32, 2006, pp. 353–69.

48   J. Manuel, M.J. Naughton, M.R. Balkrishnan, B.P. Smith & L.A. Koman, 'Stress and Adaptation in Mothers of Children with Cerebral Palsy', *Journal of Pediatric Psychology*, 28, 2003, pp. 197–201.

49   E. Emerson, C. Hatton, G. Llewellyn, J. Blacher & H. Graham, 'Socio-economic Position, Household Composition, Health Status and Indicators of the Well-Being of Mothers of Children with and without Intellectual Disabilities', *Journal of Intellectual Disability Research*, 50, 2006, pp. 862–73.

50 S. Magaña & M.J. Smith, 'Health Outcomes of Midlife and Older Latina and Black American Mothers of Children with Developmental Disabilities', *Mental Retardation*, 44, 2006, pp. 224–34; S. Cotton & A. Richdale, 'Brief Report: Parental Descriptions of Sleep Problems in Children with Autism, Down Syndrome, and Prader-Willi Syndrome', *Research in Developmental Disorders*, 27, 2006, pp.151–61.

51 See, for example, G. Hedov, G. Anneren & K. Wikblad, 'Swedish Parents of Children with Down's Syndrome', *Scandinavian Journal of Caring Sciences*, 16, 2002, pp. 424–30.

52 A. McCarthy, M. Cuskelly, C. van Kraayenoord & J. Cohen, 'Predictors of Stress in Mothers and Fathers of Children with Fragile X Syndrome', *Research in Developmental Disabilities*, 27, 2006, pp. 688–704; D.C. Lustig, 'Family Coping in Families with a Child with a Disability', *Education and Training in Mental Retardation and Developmental Disabilities*, 37, 2002, pp. 14–22.

53 See M. Azar & L.K. Badr, 'The Adaptation of Mothers of Children with Intellectual Disability in Lebanon', *Journal of Transcultural Nursing*, 17, 2006, pp. 375–80; D. Pelchat & H. Lefebvre, 'A Holistic Intervention Programme for Families with a Child with a Disability, *Journal of Advanced Nursing*, 48, 2004, pp. 124–31; M.B. Olsson & P.C. Hwang, 'Influence of Macrostructure of Society on the Life Situation of Families with a Child with Intellectual Disability: Sweden as an Example', *Journal of Intellectual Disability Research*, 47, 2003, pp. 328–41.

54 G. Llewellyn, K. Thompson & S. Whybrow, 'Out-of-home Placement of School Age Children with Disabilities', *Journal of Applied Research in Intellectual Disabilities*, 18, 2005, pp. 1–16.

55 See, for example, A. Taanila, L. Syjälä, J. Kokkonen & M.R. Järvelin, 'Coping of Parents with Physically and/or Mentally Disabled Children', *Child: Care, Health & Development*, 28, 2002, pp. 73–86.

56 See, for example, J.Y. Shin, 'Social Support for Families of Children with Mental Retardation: Comparison between Korea and the United States', *Mental Retardation*, 40, 2002, pp. 103–18.

57 P. Hauser-Cram, M.E. Warfgield, J. P. Shonkoff & M.W. Krauss, 'Children with Disabilities: A Longitudinal Study of Child Development and Parent Well-being', *Monographs of the Society for Research in Child Development*, 66, 2001, pp. 1–131.

58 R.P. Hastings & H.M. Taunt, 'Positive Perception in Families of Children with Developmental Disabilities', *American Journal on Mental Retardation*, 107, 2002, pp. 116–27.

59 D.E. Gray, 'Ten years on: A Longitudinal Study of Families of Children with Autism', *Journal of Intellectual & Developmental Disability*, 27, 2000, pp. 215–22.

60 L. Little, 'Differences in Stress and Coping for Mothers and Fathers of Children with Asperger's Syndrome and Nonverbal Learning Disorders', *Pediatric Nursing*, 28, 2002, pp. 565–70.

61 R.P. Hastings, H. Kovshoff, N.J. Ward, F. degli Espinosa, T. Brown & B. Remington, 'Systems Analysis of Stress and Positive Perceptions in Mothers and Fathers of Pre-school Children with Autism', *Journal of Autism and Developmental Disorders*, 35, 2005, pp. 635–44.

62 D.E. Gray, 'Gender and Coping: The Parents of Children with High Functioning Autism', *Social Science & Medicine*, 56, 2003, pp. 631–42.

63 McCarthy et al., 2006.

64 Little, 2002.

65 See P. Harland & M. Cuskelly, 'Patterns of Involvement: The Responsibilities and Concerns of Young Adult Siblings in Relation to their Brother/Sister with Vision and Hearing Disabilities', *International Journal of Development, Disability and Education*, 47, 2000, pp. 293–307; M.M. Seltzer, J.S. Greenberg, G.I. Orsmond & J. Lounds, 'Life Course Studies of Siblings of Individuals with Developmental Disabilities', *Mental Retardation*, 43, 2005, pp. 354–59.

66 A. Gath & D. Gumley, 'Family Background of Children with Down's Syndrome and of Children with a Similar Degree of Mental Retardation', *British Journal of Psychiatry*, 149, 1986, pp. 161–71; A. Bågenholm & C. Gillberg, 'Psychosocial Effects on Siblings of Children with Autism and Mental Retardation: A Population-based Study', *Journal of Mental Deficiency Research*, 35, 1991, pp. 291–307.

67 M. Cuskelly, 'Adjustment of Siblings of Children with a Disability: Methodological Issues', *International Journal for the Advancement of Counselling*, 21, 1999, pp. 111–24; B. Mandleco, S.F. Olsen, T. Dyches & E. Marshall, 'The Relationship Between Family and Sibling Functioning in Families Raising a Child with a Disability', *Journal of Family Nursing*, 9, 4, 2003, pp. 365–96.

68 B. Trute, 'Grandparents of Children with Developmental Disabilities: Intergenerational Support and Family Well-being. Families in Society', *The Journal of Contemporary Human Services*, 84, 2003, pp. 119–27.

69 W. Mitchell, 'Research Review: The Role of Grandparents in Intergenerational Support for Families with Disabled Children: A Review of the Literature', *Child and Family Social Work*, 12, 2007, pp. 94–101.

70 J. Aldridge, 'The Experiences of Children Living with and Caring for Parents with Mental Illness', *Child Abuse Review*, 15, 2006, pp. 79–88.

71 See, for example, M. Cuskelly & P. Gunn, 'Sibling Relationships of Children with Down Syndrome: Perspectives of Mothers, Fathers and Siblings', *American Journal on Mental Retardation*, 108, 2002, pp. 234–44.

72 Mandleco et al., 2003.

73 See, for example, S. Muirhead, 'An Appreciative Inquiry about Adults with Down Syndrome' in *Down Syndrome Across the Life Span*, eds, M. Cuskelly, A. Jobling & S. Buckley, 2002, pp. 149–58; T. Stainton & H. Besser, 'The Positive Impact of Children with an Intellectual Disability on the Family', *Journal of Intellectual & Developmental Disability*, 23, 1998, pp. 57–70; Hastings & Taunt, 2002; C. Schwartz, 'Parents of Children with Chronic Disabilities: The Gratification of Caregiving', *Families in Society*, 84, 2003, pp. 576–84.

74 G. Llewellyn, L. Gething, H. Kenndig & R. Cant, 'Older Parent Caregivers' Engagement with the Service System', *American Journal on Mental Retardation*, 109, 2004, pp. 379–96.

75 B. Trute, D. Hiebert-Murphy & K. Levine, 'Parental Appraisal of the Family Impact of Childhood Developmental Disability: Times of Sadness and Times of Joy', *Journal of Intellectual & Developmental Disability*, 32, 2007, pp. 1–9.

76 J. Blacher & L.L. McIntyre, 'Syndrome Specificity and Behavioural Disorders in Young Adults with Intellectual Disability: Cultural Differences in Family Impact', *Journal of Intellectual Disability Research*, 50, 2006, pp. 184–98; B.L. Baker, L.L. McIntyre, J. Blacher, K. Crnic, C. Edelbrock & C. Low, 'Pre-school Children with and without Developmental Delay: Behaviour Problems and Parenting Stress over Time', *Journal of Intellectual Disability Research*, 47, 2003, pp. 217–30; P. Minnes & L. Woodford, 'Well-being in Aging Parents Caring for an Adult with a Developmental Disability', *Journal on Developmental Disabilities*, 11, 2005, pp. 47–66.

77 McCarthy et al., 2006; J.B. Chan & J. Sigafoos, 'A Review of Child and Family Characteristics Related to the Use of Respite Care in Developmental Disability Services', *Child & Youth Care Forum*, 29, 2000, pp. 27–37.

78 A. Cunningham & C. Knoester, 'Marital Status, Gender, and Parents' Psychological Well-being', *Sociological Inquiry*, 77, 2007, pp. 264–87.

79 K. Scorgie & D. Sobsey, 'Transformational Outcomes Associated with Parenting Children who have Disabilities', *Mental Retardation*, 38, 2000, pp. 195–206.

80 See R. Littlewood, 'Mental Health and Intellectual Disability: Culture and Diversity', *Journal of Intellectual Disability Research*, 50, 2006, pp. 555–60.

81 A. Birenbaum, 'Poverty, Welfare Reform, and Disproportionate Rates of Disability among Children', *Mental Retardation*, 40, 2002, pp. 212–18.

82 J. Park, A.P. Turnbull & H.R. Turnbull III, 'Impact of Poverty on Quality of Life in Families of Children with Disabilities', *Exceptional Children*, 68, 2002, pp. 151–71.

83 J.M. Patterson, 'Understanding Family Resilience', *Journal of Clinical Psychology*, 58, 2002, pp. 233–46.

84 H.W. Kim, J.S. Greenberg, M.M. Seltzer & M.W. Krauss, 'The Role of Coping in Maintaining the Psychological Well-being of Mothers of Adults with Intellectual Disability and Mental Illness', *Journal of Intellectual Disability Research*, 47, 2003, pp. 313–27.

85 E.L. Essex, 'Mothers and Fathers of Adults with Mental Retardation: Feelings of Intergenerational Closeness', *Family Relations*, 51, 2002, pp. 156–65; L. Abbeduto, M.M. Seltzer, P. Shattuck, M.W. Krauss, G. Orsmond & M.M. Murphy, 'Psychological Well-being and Coping in Mothers of Youths with Autism, Down Syndrome, or Fragile X Syndrome', *American Journal on Mental Retardation*, 109, 2004, pp. 237–54.

86 'Peg', in D. Bowman & M. Virtue, *Public Policy, Private Lives*, Australian Institute of Intellectual Disability, Canberra, 1993, p. 127.

87 M. Gordon, L. Rosenman & M. Cuskelly, 'Maternal Employment: A Comparative Study of Paid Work Levels and the Desire to Work among Mothers with and without Dependent Children with Disabilities', *Journal of Applied Research on Intellectual Disabilities*, 20, 2007, pp. 236–46.

88 M.E. Warfield, 'Employment, Parenting, and Well-being among Mothers of Children with Disabilities', *Mental Retardation*, 39, 2001, pp. 297–309.

89 See, for example, S.E. Green, '"We're Tired, Not Sad": Benefits and Burdens of Mothering a Child with a Disability', *Social Science & Medicine*, 64, 2007, pp. 150–63.

90 M. Einam & M. Cuskelly, 'Paid Employment of Mothers and Fathers of an Adult Child with Multiple Disabilities', *Journal of Intellectual Disability Research*, 46, 2002, pp. 158–67.

91   Green, 2007; M. Wang, A.P. Turnbull, J.A. Summers, T.D. Little, D.J. Poston, H. Mannan & R. Turnbull, 'Severity of Disability and Income as Predictors of Parents' Satisfaction with Their Family Quality of Life During Early Childhood Years', *Research & Practice for Persons with Severe Disabilities*, 29, 2004, pp. 82–94.

92   See, for a discussion, C. Bigby & E. Ozanne, 'Shifts in the Model of Service Delivery in Intellectual Disability in Victoria', *Journal of Intellectual & Developmental Disability*, 26, 2001, pp. 177–90.

93   Gray, 2000.

94   P.M. Sullivan & J.F. Knutson, 'Maltreatment and Disabilities: A Population-based Epidemiological Study', *Child Abuse and Neglect*, 24, 2000, pp. 1257–273.

95   See <www.aph.gov.au/library/intguide/sp/disability.htm>, accessed 2 August 2007.

96   Bigby, 2000.

97   Bowman & Virtue, 1993, p. i.

4

Ethnicity: Spotlight on Person–context Interactions

Jacqueline J. Goodnow and Jeanette A. Lawrence

All of us use shorthand labels when we describe others and ourselves. Depending on the situation, we use words such as male/female; student/worker; tall/short; from Adelaide, Melbourne or Sydney; Mediterranean/Asian/African, and so on.

When do we use words like these? What do they mean? What do they imply? What consequences do they have?

These questions apply to any shorthand description, any social category or social box into which we put ourselves or others. In this chapter, we ask them in relation to 'ethnicity': descriptions that often refer to country of origin.

One reason for choosing ethnicity as a focus is because it often has educational, political and social significance. We choose it also because ethnicity provides a spotlight, an entry point, into understanding the nature of contexts and how people and contexts are intertwined. The first chapter used as a starting point a view of contexts as offering a mix of opportunities and constraints, of challenges and resources. Our emphasis falls on issues of identity: issues of how we see ourselves and others, what others call us or think about us, and—to use more formal terms—how identity labels are often fluid and often imposed, resented, resisted, corrected or 'negotiated'.

We start with a first feature of identity descriptions: they often have different meanings for different people. In this case, the term with variable meanings is 'ethnic'. The example is a conversation overheard at a wedding between Tony Mulcahy and Angela Petradopoulos (names fictional, family backgrounds unchanged). His great-great-grandfather came from Ireland; her parents arrived in Australia from Athens shortly before she was born. The people speaking are an uncle (A) and an aunt (B) of the groom:

A: You know, this is the family's first ethnic wedding.

B: What do you mean? Two have married Americans; one's married a Dubliner; and two have married Māoris.

A: You know what I mean. It's our first *ethnic* wedding.

B: Mmm. I gather her father's not too happy. He would have preferred her to marry a Greek. Probably feels Mulcahy's a strange name, too hard to pronounce.

People clearly do not always agree in the way they use the term 'ethnic'. The meanings of the term may vary from one person to another.

To reveal other features of categories such as 'ethnic', we need to look beyond the surface labels and their uses. We need, to be more specific, to look at the nature of:

- social categories—the boxes in which we place others or ourselves
- social contexts—our social worlds rather than the geographic areas we live in
- processes—the ways in which people and their contexts influence one another.

Why these areas? We need an understanding of *social categories* because grouping by ethnicity is just one example of what we do all the time. We always group people in some way or another: as short or tall, male or female, child or adult, fair or dark. We may add a rider ('not your usual Scandinavian type', for example), but grouping is still there. Grouping is present also in the ways we describe ourselves: 'I'm average in height' or 'I'm a bit on the skinny side', for example, are statements about boxes, as are the references we often see in newspapers to 'Mediterranean in appearance'.

We need a closer look at *social contexts* in order to specify the difference between one and another. We make little progress as long as we describe contexts in gross terms: describing some, for example, as more stimulating, more tolerant, more diverse or more rigid than another. Nor do we get far if the way we describe one context is of little use when we come to describe another. We need descriptions that are transferable. And, because all contexts change, we need descriptions that help us explain how they change.

We need to describe the *processes* that link the characteristics of contexts with the characteristics of individuals, because otherwise we stop only with correlations. It is one thing to establish correlations: to determine, for example, that people of Type X have trouble or do well in places that are Type Y. But that is only part of the story. The next step is to locate the processes that account for these interconnections. In doing so, we need also to give more than lip-service to the argument that processes need to be thought of as bidirectional. It is easy to say that people influence contexts and contexts influence people. Being more specific about those mutual influences is a more difficult matter.

The emphasis in this chapter on understanding categories, contexts and processes means that we shall give relatively little space to reports noting that people from some countries of origin do especially well at school, are overrepresented among the unemployed, tend to live in particular neighbourhoods, display more signs of family stress, have lower rates of divorce, or are more caring of their ageing parents than are people from other groups. Reports of this kind are valuable and there are now several available.[1] To help us generalise across groups and across chapters, however, we need to ask how these correlations come about.

We shall also use examples that may not at first sight fit a focus on ethnic groupings in Australia. Sometimes these examples refer to the position of Indigenous Australians, at other times to events or groupings in other countries. The reasons for using Indigenous examples are twofold. One is to bring out the variable meanings of ethnicity: from an Indigenous perspective, everyone who arrived after 1788 might be regarded as 'ethnic'. The other is to remind us that the points being made about person–context interconnections in relation to ethnicity apply also to other social categories. Whenever one group regards another as 'other', as 'different', many of the same processes swing into action. 'Ethnicity' and 'ethnic' grouping, then, are not issues that matter only to 'ethnics'. In fact, what we learn from considering ethnicity helps to illuminate the nature of all our lives.

The reason for occasionally looking outside Australia is that doing so often sharpens our understanding of the Australian scene. We become aware, for example, that Australian distinctions among ethnic groups often reflect recency of arrival. To use Gillian Bottomley's expression, the meaning is often that 'ethnics' have recently come 'from another place'.[2]

Distinctions based on country of origin, however, are often made in places where recent immigration is not the case. Examples are the distinctions between Serbs and Croats in what was Yugoslavia, between 'Afrikaners', 'blacks' and 'English' in South Africa, or within the USA between African-Americans and 'Caucasians' (a strange term, which in general means 'white' or, in some states, 'non-Hispanic white'). In effect, we are reminded that describing people in terms of their country or region of origin is not always a response to who came first or later. Country of origin is instead often a shorthand way of referring to perceived differences in lifestyle and social identity.[3]

Contexts

Social groupings as social categories

One old way of thinking about ethnicity sees it as a fixed characteristic, an unchangeable grouping: people either 'are' or 'are not' African, Chinese, German, Greek, Russian and so on. All that people do is to name these 'essences' or fixed characteristics. Children need only learn the names that go with those differences.

The wedding vignette, however, highlights the fact that the terms 'ethnicity' and 'ethnic' often vary in their meaning. One person's use of the term 'ethnic' is not the same as another's. One country's use of the term is also often not the same as another's. One person's self-identification is often not the same as the identity officially assigned. And all the meanings may vary from time to time.

These variations provide a base for an alternative to the usual assumption of fixed characteristics or 'natural kinds'. This is that *ethnicity is a social category*. It is a box in which we place people, or in which people place themselves.[4] This change of framing matter helps us to describe contexts and specify processes. It also helps us to understand the ways in which, in the course of everyday life, we make judgments, identify ourselves, share meanings and communicate with one another.

Jacqueline J. Goodnow & Jeanette A. Lawrence

CATEGORIES AND THEIR QUALITIES

Categories may vary in how broad or narrow they are ('Asian' is a broad category; Cantonese is narrower). Categories differ also in the labels and the meanings attached, and in the extent to which people see membership in one group as incompatible with belonging to another. Angela's father, for example, may not have been happy about the marriage. He did not, however, refuse to come to the wedding or declare that from this moment Angela was no longer a member of the family.

To bring out the nature and impact of category qualities in relation to ethnic groupings, we highlight three features:

• the extent to which categories and their meanings are shared
• the functions that social categories serve
• the ways in which categories change.

The extent to which categories and their meanings are shared

Anthropologists often describe the difference between one social context and another in terms of the extent to which people share meanings—the extent to which they take the same world view, interpret events in the same way, and work from the same 'cultural models'.[5]

Does this feature of categories matter? One impact, the argument runs, is on the extent to which we understand one another and have the sense that we are understood. Another impact is on the extent to which we feel that here is a person or a place with values possibly similar to our own, rather than awkwardly 'different' or 'foreign'.

When people emigrate or travel from one place to another, the likelihood increases that their sense of who they are will not be fully shared by those they encounter. Even identifying oneself by country of origin may not produce much in the way of shared meaning. It is difficult, for example, to convey the significance of identifying oneself as Macedonian to people who are unaware of a possible difference between Macedonian and Greek, as Hakka to people for whom 'Chinese' is a category with no further distinctions within it, or as Eritrean, Somali or Sudanese to people who know only the category 'African'.

Ethnic groupings also bring out the particular lack of agreement that may exist between an officially assigned category and the one in which we place ourselves. Take, for example, the demographer's or the statistician's grouping on the basis of 'country of origin'. The easiest way for bureaucracy to make ethnic groupings is by birthplace. But that grouping may not coincide with the way an individual or a family sees itself. I may regard myself, for example, as a Pole, a Ukrainian or an Assyrian even if political circumstances have meant that neither I nor my parents were born in Poland, the Ukraine or Assyria. I may be classed in Australia as 'Vietnamese', in the sense that this is where I and my parents were born, but regard myself as ethnically Chinese on the grounds that our earlier ancestors were from China, we speak a Chinese dialect at home, and no Vietnamese would ever think of us as 'Vietnamese' (that is, we maintain the distinction and so do the people around us).

This is not to say that the experience of unshared meanings is unique to immigrants. Think, for example, of what it is like trying to describe to someone else a time you have spent in another place, even on a holiday. Being an immigrant, an expatriate or a 'returnee' to one's own country simply heightens the likelihood that experiences and meanings will not be shared.

The functions that social categories serve

Dividing people into groups can serve several functions. Some of these functions are regarded, especially by psychologists, as 'cognitive'. Once we group people, once we decide that they belong to this or that type, we can make quick judgments about them. The judgments may be 'quick-and-dirty', but they will be quick. We also do not need to carry around with us a large number of possible types. The 'cognitive load' is lightened.

Categories may also provide a quickly available explanation for what we see. 'Ah', we say to ourselves, 'you do that because you are young, old, a student, an American'. Or: 'These people are having difficulty because they are Turks, Lebanese or "whingeing Poms"'. Our explanation for the difference is their ethnicity rather than that they are poor, hemmed in by local restrictions, or know that there is another way to live. We may then feel no further need to think about the matter.

Psychologists who are more socially oriented remind us that we also create new categories, or shuffle around old ones, to meet our changing social needs. We create new names, for example, in order to express a sense of change or difference. Some Australian names provide an example. After 1945, the Australian Government actively sought immigrants from a variety of countries. They entered Australia at a time when most of the people already in place referred to themselves generally as 'Australian' or 'British', with distinctions then often in terms of whether people were English, Irish or Scottish in background. English was for most people the only language spoken or heard. What then to call the incoming groups? Among the new names were words such as 'New Australians', 'reffos' and 'Balts'. These names may seem strange to us now, but they were attempts to create a feeling of order within variety and to put a finger on what the differences were. They were also, to note another social need or social function, groupings designed to keep at a distance people who were felt to be not exactly like 'us'.[6]

That last function—'distancing' other people—is especially well illustrated by the labels often used to place some people outside our usual concerns. Think, for example, about groupings such as the 'deserving' and the 'undeserving poor', or 'dole bludgers' and 'welfare cheats'. When people are thought of as 'undeserving', 'bludgers' or 'cheats', it is easy to see them as outside our need to give assistance or sympathy.

CHILDREN IN REFUGEE DETENTION CENTRES

The debate over children in refugee detention centres is an example of how social categories are used to distance people. In some descriptions, they were called the children of 'boat people', the children of parents who care so little about their children that they 'throw them overboard'. They are held in detention because their parents are

Jacqueline J. Goodnow & Jeanette A. Lawrence

'illegals' and the responsibility for what happens to them rests with their parents. In contrasting descriptions, these are first of all 'children' and they should be treated with the care we normally extend to the young, regardless of what their parents have done. Their placement 'behind barbed wire', without schooling and without protection from various types of threat for periods that can extend to years, is 'inhumane'. It undermines the sense we have of ourselves as 'Australian', with its implication of commitment to 'decency' and 'a fair go'. It is also, in a reverse use of legal categorisations, in itself 'illegal', in violation of both national and international agreements about the treatment of children.

In effect, we can see all around us the way social categories are a standard part of debates and decisions about action. We cannot simply say 'no categories', because categories are intrinsic to the way we think and describe everything around us. Nor can we avoid distinctions having moral overtones. What we can do, however, is to think about the distinctions that are important to us and the grounds for their being important. What we can avoid also is being persuaded without thought by labels that seem to justify giving up principles that are important to us.

SELF-DESCRIPTIONS AS CATEGORIES

It is easy to think of social categories as terms that are tacked on by others. What about the other side of the picture? Where do we place ourselves? Why in some boxes rather than others? How do our descriptions of ourselves and others vary from one situation to another?

The ways in which categories change

We have noted that categories can change from time to time. Now we need to ask: what gives rise to change?

We have already partly answered this question. The groupings change as our needs to make particular distinctions change. In the early days of post-1945 immigration, for example, the main concern was to distinguish between European groups: to separate, for example, the northern Europeans (for example, the 'Balts' or the 'Poles') from people who came from further south (the 'Mediterranean' group). Since that time, Australia has taken in more immigrants from countries known as 'Asian'. The contrasts that now seem to stand out for the people who are 'already in place' are between 'Asian' and 'non-Asian', and between various subgroups within that very broad category, 'Asian'.

For an example of the changing functions that distinctions serve, consider the distinctions we make between restaurants. Few Australians would speak of going to eat at an 'ethnic' restaurant. Especially in urban areas, they would feel the need to specify whether the food was Cambodian, Chinese, Japanese, Korean, Thai or Vietnamese. They may even differentiate within the 'Chinese' group, specifying the region. In effect, the groupings shift to meet our changing purposes and our changing awareness of differences.

The example of restaurants, however, leaves out two important components of change. One of these is the extent to which a social category is officially assigned or is open to self-description. On Australian census forms, for example, people can decide whether they identify themselves as Indigenous or not. When it comes to issuing passports, however, most societies are not willing to accept an individual's own description of a particular identity or a particular ancestry. Now the category is one that is officially determined.

Self-description clearly allows for change more easily than does official assignment. With Aboriginality emerging now as a point of pride, the incidence of self-categorisation as Indigenous is increasing, making the Australian context now seem demographically different from what it was even a short while ago.

SPECIFYING PROCESSES

What processes are highlighted by framing ethnicity and ethnic groupings as social categories rather than as 'essences' or fixed characteristics? We single out two:

- the way in which categories tend to wipe out attention to individual differences
- the extent to which people accept, resist, transform or question a category and its basis.

Categories and the nature of attention

The moment we place people in a category by virtue of one characteristic, the way in which we perceive other characteristics shifts. I place you in a particular ethnic group, for example, by virtue of your name, and immediately become more likely to assume that you will have some other characteristics: that you will be, for example, more rather than less industrious, bookish, frugal, interested in sport, easy to understand.

The effect on attention that is especially highlighted by considering ethnic groupings is one that is called 'the outgroup homogeneity effect'.[7] One of the effects of any social grouping is that we quickly lose sight of differences among the people within the group. The members of any group that we see as 'them' tend to be seen as like one another. In contrast, we see 'us' as made up of obviously diverse individuals. We may, in fact, have difficulty perceiving even physical differences among other groups. 'All Chinese look alike' is an old saying, but to the Chinese the differences among themselves are obvious. To them, it may be the 'Europeans' who all look alike.

The end result is not only galling to the person whose individuality has just been wiped out. We also lose sight of dimensions that cut across groups. There may, for example, be more similarity in values between a middle-class Lebanese from Beirut and a middle-class locally born Australian than there is between the Beirut-born person and a Lebanese person who grew up in a small village. Between the latter two can be a shared knowledge of place, of history and of language. Their views with regard to education or parenting, however, may be far apart.

Once again, the tendency to overlook differences within a group is not restricted to the lives of immigrants. We all become alert to outgroup homogeneity effects, for example, when we are overseas. 'I know some Australians', say some of the people we meet. They then expect that we will be like these other Australians, often to our dismay.

Jacqueline J. Goodnow & Jeanette A. Lawrence

Acceptance, resistance, transformation and questioning

In one-way descriptions of contextual effects, social contexts may be regarded as simply imposing categories. These groupings are seen as already present in the culture. People, as they become socialised or acculturated, are then seen as simply taking over the established or pre-packaged categories. The only thing children need to do is to absorb and accept the groupings presented to them by their parents, their peers or their communities. The reality highlighted by ethnic groupings is more dynamic. People may publicly object to a label such as 'New Australian' or 'African'.

A diabetes clinic in Melbourne, for example, set aside 'a special day' for 'Africans' from 'the Horn of Africa'. Staff were then surprised by the arguments that broke out among these 'Africans' and by their general refusal to be regarded as like one another or even at peace with one another. The clinic quickly learned to make some narrower 'ethnic' descriptions and to schedule different times for particular groups to attend.

More gently, people may invent or propose new categories: 'Anglo-Celtic', for example. They may, in a second or third generation, relabel themselves and reidentify with a parent's or grandparent's country of origin.

How far are such transformations or resistances possible? Clearly there are circumstances under which we raise no questions. At other times, however, even officially assigned categories may come to be questioned. An example is the recent and continuing debate over 'the stolen generations' of Indigenous children (see Chapter 11). Until recently, few people questioned the right of various welfare agencies or government departments to make decisions as to whether children were of 'mixed blood' and, on that basis, could legitimately remove them from their families. Now the motives, legalities and consequences of those categorisation policies are being broadly questioned.

There are also limits, other than legal limits, to the freedom with which people may happily change their category descriptions of themselves. During 1996, for example, heated debate took place in Australia over the legitimacy of an author presenting herself as Ukrainian and her novel as written 'from the inside' of a history of persecution (the 'Demidenko debate'). In the same year there were also arguments about the ethics of a non-Aboriginal artist (Elizabeth Durack) representing her paintings as being by an Aboriginal (under the name of Eddie Durrup). In neither case was the law broken. There was, however, strong social disapproval and a sense of inappropriateness, making us aware that there is still a great deal to be understood about the ways we respond to what we see as 'wrongful' claims to membership of a particular group.[8]

Variations in context

Our overheard (wedding) conversation at the beginning of this chapter introduced the ways in which we group people by country or region of origin. It pointed to differences between contexts in terms of the kinds of groupings that are made. It also introduced the need to understand the process of grouping in itself. To demonstrate some further ways of delineating contexts and processes, we start again with a concrete example, categorising by name.

CATEGORISING BY NAME

On the current or recent Australian scene, some 'visible' people have a variety of surnames: Tony Albanese, Victor Chang, Ernie Dingo, Cathy Freeman, Yasmine Gooneratne, Mary Kostakides, Indira Naidoo, Mark Phillippoussis, Aiden Ridgeway, Richard Tognetti, Penny Wong, John Yu.

Who are these people? What are they known for? Can you pronounce these names? Can you identify the countries where these names originate? What names would you add to illustrate the diverse images of 'Australians'? What areas of visibility or achievement do these names involve? Are there some groups that tend to be 'invisible', or for which the popular image seems especially inaccurate? Do people passively accept the images that others have of them?

THE NATURE OF CONTEXTS: PATHWAYS AND OPPORTUNITIES

One of the reasons for examining that list of names is to highlight the need to think about the areas in which people achieve success or become visible. It is not simply that people from various groups differ in their overall levels of achievement. Instead, they tend to become visible in specific fields and to be thought of as associated with those fields, for example, the arts, media, medicine, politics, sport and so on.

Anthropologists and sociologists use such differences to point out one useful way to differentiate one social context from another. This is in terms of 'structure and opportunity'. Psychologists more often use terms such as 'pathways' or 'lifelines'.[9] In both cases the general notion is that people follow a variety of paths and that societies make it harder or easier for people from various groups to make a sound initial choice, to recover from an error, or to shift from one path to another. People from various ethnic groups, then, may differ not only in the kinds of achievement they value. They may differ also in the information they have about what is possible, and in the extent to which they encounter doors that are open or closed, and people who are able and willing to provide the information they need.

THE NATURE OF CONTEXTS: IMAGES AND MULTIPLE GROUP MEMBERSHIPS

It is easy to see that contexts differ in their demographics, for example, in the number of people who are locally born or born overseas. The list of names helps us see that they differ as well in the visibility of people from various social groups and in the images (positive or negative, accurate or inaccurate) that go with the distinctions.

Do these differences matter? Suppose we anchor that question in comments on a phrase often used in discussions about ethnic groupings. This is the phrase 'multicultural context' or 'multicultural society'. Australia, it is often said, is a 'multicultural society'. What does this phrase mean?

Jacqueline J. Goodnow & Jeanette A. Lawrence

At one level, the term simply refers to the presence of people who were born in different countries and who possibly follow lifestyles different from those of the main-stream culture.

Most anthropologists would add another level. All societies, they propose, are made up of several groups and contain more than one lifestyle. Even among 'Anglo' groups, for example, there is formal medicine and 'alternative' medicine. There is also conventional schooling and 'alternative' schooling. What matters, anthropologists propose, is not the simple presence of these alternatives but the ways in which the community perceives them and the people who endorse them. People may, for example, regard formal approaches and alternative approaches as being impossible to combine. They may consider the people who endorse one approach rather than the other to be narrow-minded or gullible. Between the two groups there may be various degrees of tolerance, scorn, competition or attempts at suppression.

This general line of argument is often summarised by the phrase 'multiplicity and contest'. No society, the proposal runs, operates with a single, neatly organised set of rules or values. Instead, to take a 1992 comment from the anthropologist Claudia Strauss, we need to recognise 'conflict, contradiction, ambiguity, and change in cultural understandings—the way cultural understandings are "contested" or "negotiated" in current jargon'.[10]

From this point of view, a truly multicultural or 'pluralist' society is one where people from different cultural groups can negotiate, maintain or change lifestyles from positions of equal power, visibility and respect. Australia has not reached that ideal state, although it could be described as moving towards it.

Is the definition of multiculturalism purely an academic matter? The answer is no, for reasons that are best brought out by taking a look at the term 'bicultural identity'. It used to be said that the immigrant child in Australia was inevitably 'torn between two worlds'. Being 'torn', however, occurs only in contexts where membership in one social group (for example, being a properly Australian schoolchild) is seen as being incompatible with another (for example, being of the Spanish-speaking community, or being a Muslim and following an Islamic dress code). The perceived incompatibility, it should be noted, may exist on both sides. That is, either group may see a child, an adolescent or an adult as having ceased to be 'one of us' by virtue of having become 'one of them'.

In most lives, however, as Parke and Buriel have demonstrated, we manage to be members of several groups, involving family, schools, friendships, leisure or religion, for example.[11] Most of the time we are also able to combine those memberships, altering our ways of acting and speaking as we shift groups. The difficulties start only when we are short on navigating skills, when the shifts violate our own sense of what we are or of what is right, or when the shifts are seen not as adjustments to necessity but as signs of insincerity, disloyalty or betrayal. Those conditions are not unique to immigrant experience, as many a person who has changed 'class' or religion would point out. They may, however, be more likely to occur as families emigrate and come to terms with a new country.

A PARTICULAR PROCESS: SOCIAL REFLECTION OR IMAGE-MAKING?

A frequent proposal within analyses of contexts is that contexts exert their effects by a process of 'mirroring' or 'social reflection'. The general argument is that we tend to see ourselves as others see us, to develop in some respects a 'looking-glass self'.[12]

Obviously we do not always see ourselves in simple mirror-like fashion. Nor are we totally dependent on others agreeing with what we say or finding it at least meaningful. Nonetheless we have to work a little harder or find new ways of establishing who we are and what we mean in situations where, to use the mirror metaphor, we are invisible or the reflected picture is superficial, a caricature or a negative image. To be an immigrant, or to be classed as 'an ethnic', carries all those hazards.

To speak only of hazards, however, is to ignore the extent to which people make an active effort to control the images that others have of them, to make or transform the image rather than simply accept it or try to come to terms with it. The general argument here comes especially from the work of Henri Tajfel on ways of responding to prejudice.[13]

All of us, Tajfel pointed out, wish to maintain a positive self-image. When we are members of a group that has a poor image in the eyes of a more established or prestigious group, we may make several strategic moves. We may attempt to 'pass': to become accepted as members of the more privileged group, to be seen as 'just like them'. We may also seek to change the image that others have of us, or to take control of that image and turn it into one of our own making.

Taking control of the name applied to us provides an example. You, the established group, may originally construct the category and the label 'wog'. I may object to it. Later, when you have learnt not to use it, I may then claim it as my own and use it deliberately (as is the case for members of the Australian comedy team who describe themselves as 'wogs'). Terms such as 'black' and 'queer' may show a similar pattern. The preference of some Indigenous groups for the application to them of terms such as 'Koori' (terms of their choosing) is part of a similar pattern. It is also an example that invites an interesting contrast with the situation in New Zealand, where the names used for the main ethnic groupings ('Māori' and 'Pākehā', with the latter referring to 'whites') are Māori terms, used by both Māori and Pākehā. In all such cases we need to ask: who has the power to give a name or to change one? And when do people seek to do so?[14]

That 'Pākehā' example highlights also a particular aspect of research into social categories. We know most about the categories and labels used by the established or dominant group to describe 'others'. We know comparatively little about the categories and labels used by those groups to refer to the people they see as 'others'. An Italian mother, for example, says to a child 'you are becoming a kangarooni'. What is meant by that term? How is it understood by the child? What other terms are there like this? How, for example, does a second-generation 'Australian' refer to parents they may now see as 'different' from them?

Jacqueline J. Goodnow & Jeanette A. Lawrence

Consequences

Social categories have more than academic meaning. They have consequences for the way we feel about others and ourselves and for what we do. To start bringing out some of those consequences, we take one that particularly involves the interplay of children, families and communities. This has to do with the way parents prepare their children for life outside the family.

Parents preparing children for life outside the family

All parents take some steps towards preparing children for encounters and experiences outside the family. They may do so by way of advice about what is to come and what will be needed: 'you won't be able to do that in school' or 'in high school you'll have to work harder', for example. Before the first transition to school, parents may introduce children to books, to reading or to some familiarity with numbers. They may also send their children to child care settings, to pre-school or to kindergarten, either for some advance academic skills or 'so they will be used to other children'.

Like-minded people may be sought via parents' choices of where to live. That choice may also be influenced by the need to find people who will be helpful sources of information or support—one factor contributing to what have been called 'ethnic concentrations' in particular areas, especially after first arriving in a new country.[15] When an area is more 'mixed', parents may need to take special steps. To take one interesting study, African-American parents are more likely to talk to their children about racial differences when the neighbourhood is 'mixed' rather than 'all-of-one-kind'.[16]

Another study of African-American families makes it clear that parents use more than one strategy to prepare their children for misunderstanding and prejudice. They may teach children the history of their own group. They may teach children what to do or say when they experience prejudice: 'Think of yourself as a tennis ball. The harder they throw you down, the higher you bounce back!' They may also promote distrust of the outgroup. The strategies they use are often related to the age of the child and to the parents' own experiences of racial bias.[17] This type of research, however, and the kinds of findings reported, are clearly relevant also to person–context interconnections in Australia with its diversity of family backgrounds. We know comparatively little, however, about parents' perceptions of what is needed and about the kinds of strategies they use.

Considering immigrant or ethnic families also highlights the need to ask which members of the family we are talking about. 'The family' suggests that here is a group that functions like a single, solid unit. An emphasis on 'parents' may lead us to ignore the *differential* contributions that each parent may make, or that siblings may make. The reality is that each parent, or each older sibling, is likely to play a different role in the introduction of a child to the world outside the family.

A differential role for parents is likely to be the case in most families. It especially needs to be considered, however, when we are looking at immigrant groups. Take, for example, the increasing occurrence of marriage across ethnic groupings.[18] Within marriages of this kind it is all the more likely that each parent will play a different part, varying with their knowledge of the world outside the family and with what they value. To take a comment made to us by an immigrant father who had married an 'Anglo' Australian: 'I teach them the need to do well, to work hard, and to recognise that there is a world and a history outside Australia. My wife has the local knowledge. She knows what happens in schools and how to approach teachers. It's a very effective combination'.

A second prompt towards the notion of differential input comes from the special role of older siblings within immigrant families. They are, for instance, the more likely sources of information about the way that Australian schools and Australian peer groups work than the parents may be. Nguyen and Ho made the insightful comment that this situation may not hold when an older child comes into the country after a younger child does, a phenomenon not unknown among refugee Vietnamese families, where members of the family may leave the country of origin at different times or be admitted to Australia at different times. The older child may then be in the awkward situation of having the younger one offering to be the guide or map-maker.[19]

These comments may make immigrant families seem different from all other families. Parents may in fact point out some particular differences among people and offer different names for them. They and their children may also have particular needs for information about opportunities and about what to expect when a transition is made (the transition to primary or secondary school, for example).

In related fashion, we may well ask when and how immigrant parents indicate to their children that they find acceptable or unacceptable a child's adopting new ways of speaking, dressing, achieving or spending time. There may be some special features to the comments that immigrant parents make when their children begin to be different from their parents' positions. We need to remember, however, that all parents face some differences across generations, and that only some of these differences will be disagreeable or unacceptable. Children achieving at a higher educational level than their parents did, for example, may be highly acceptable, and in fact hoped for.[20]

One-way assimilation or mutual accommodation?

We start again with some concrete examples. The first of these has to do with the outside wall of a central hospital in Melbourne. On this wall is a sign that says the equivalent of 'casualty/emergency' in English, Greek and Italian. This is not a painted sign. The letters are large and plastered onto the wall as part of the building. We are immediately prompted to ask: When did this signposting occur? What gave rise to it?

The second example is the emergence of a swimwear design that has been called 'the burquini'. In a Sydney beach area, there occurred some much publicised conflict between those who regarded themselves as 'locals' and those seen as 'outsiders' and 'Muslim'. In the wake of that conflict, two moves occurred. The local surf club took active steps to recruit and train some of the 'outsiders' so they could become members of the volunteer life-saving patrols on the beach. This move was aimed at recruiting both young men and young women. The other move came from within the Islamic group. A designer, herself Islamic in faith, developed a swimsuit that effectively covers all skin and all hair. This close-fitting 'skin' respects the local Islamic dress code for girls while being functional for the demands of life saving. To the wearers, it is all the more acceptable because a close-fitting, all-over 'skin suit' has been used by some Olympic swimmers.

Why do examples like these matter? They highlight a major issue in analyses of ethnicity and immigration. Some of these analyses suggest that change occurs, or should occur, in 'sudden switch' fashion. People can move quickly, for example, from being 'Greek' or 'Iraqi' to being 'Australian'. Others suggest that the move may or should occur over time, with variable rates for different people.

The examples we chose, however, highlight a different view of change, some-times called 'segmented assimilation'—that is, changes occur in some areas but not in others.[21] The best fit to the Australian scene, however, comes from analyses that highlight the occurrence of 'accommodation'—accommodation that is both 'mutual' and 'selective'.[22]

The term comes from analyses of cross-group interactions of all kinds and is not confined to interactions across ethnic groups. The general argument is that people or groups, when they need to interact with one another, engage in some forms of accom-modation to the other's status, competence, needs or values. Accommodation, the argu-ment runs, is almost always mutual, although it may be asymmetrical (that is, one person accommodates more than the other does). Accommodation is also usually selective; that is, a change is more readily made in some situations and some areas than in others. To take an Australian example, English-speaking professionals are more likely to make some language accommodations in emergency hospital situations than they are in schools.

Contexts may now be seen as varying from one another in the extent to which accommodation is asymmetrical and in the areas where accommodation occurs or is pushed for with strong feeling. Australia is quite different from Quebec, for example, where the language used in official documents and street signs has swung from all-English to a mixture of French and English, and then to French alone, with bitter and public fighting over each change.

Varying also are *the forms of pressure or persuasion* that people see as appropriate to use in the course of seeking change on the part of another group. Australia has a history of distinguishing among people with English, Irish and Scottish backgrounds (weaker distinctions than they once were, but still present). Towards each other, these groups would often engage in tactics of exclusion from prized positions or resources, but shoot-ing, bombing or arson were not widely regarded as reasonable forms of contest. To use a phrase that is more often heard in discussions of police actions or domestic violence, negative actions were expected to stay within a 'reasonable use of force'.

In contrast, the record between 'black' and 'white' in Australia was often one of dealing with differences by physical removal: by direct wiping out in earlier times, and later by formally restricting where Indigenous people could live, by excluding them from participation as citizens (denying them, until 1967, the right to vote, for example), or by removing children from their parents. One suspects that part of the fear that some immigrant groups inspire derives from the apprehension that they will use forms of pressure and persuasion no longer regarded as acceptable between 'civilised' groups.

The two previous examples highlight the *selectivity of accommodation*. Food, for example, is an area where accommodations often occur. Within Australia there have been changes in food habits on the part of both the 'Anglos', who formed the majority of the population in the 1950s, and the immigrants themselves. By contrast, accommodations in an area such as law—in deference to Aboriginal law or Islamic law, for example—have been minimal.

What distinguishes such areas? One difference proposed has to do with the extent to which there is already a 'niche' in the existing social context. Australians, for example, already had the habit of eating either 'Chinese' or 'Italian' in restaurants. All they needed to do was to expand their definition of 'something different'.

In contrast, there is no available 'niche' that would allow a different legal system to take precedence. There is instead a tradition of 'one law', and a sense that this is the way things should be. A sense of 'the way things should be' is probably the important condition. There appears to be the least accommodation when people see an issue as part of a 'basic' social contract, as part of some 'natural' pattern of rights and obligations, as what God or nature surely intended. The greater the number of areas then that are felt to be part of the moral or natural order (for example, when the moral order unexpectedly covers not only aspects of religion but also touches on food, drink or clothing), the more there will be a sense of a 'different' group.

Implications for the lives of all people

You do not need to be a 'foreigner' or an 'ethnic' or to belong to any special group in order to benefit from considering how life is influenced by differences in social contexts in combination with differences among individuals. The ideas are transferable to the nature of everyone's life.

All of us, as children or adults, need to learn how to participate in more than one social group. All of us encounter labels, expectations and assigned identities that we may welcome, resist, modify or transform. All of us move into some areas of activity rather than others—sometimes based on tradition or stereotypes, sometimes on active choice, sometimes because of what is available. And all of us can benefit from the help of others who know how things are done, who can act as guides or mentors.

Those several aspects of participation in a social context become clearer, and take some special forms, whenever we try to create or modify a path rather than follow one that is already established. In this situation it is more likely that we will encounter other people's labels, with their distinctions between 'us' and 'them' and their ideas about what we are like or what we should do. There is likely to be a mixture of open and closed doors in front of us, of willingness and unwillingness to meet our particular needs or interests. The path will also call for navigating skills, for a more active search for information on how to proceed, and for people who can act as guides. All those aspects of living become clearer when we consider the implications of being placed, or of placing oneself, in a group with an 'ethnic' label.

Jacqueline J. Goodnow & Jeanette A. Lawrence

STUDENT EXERCISES

1 Discuss what the following concepts mean:
   a) ethnic identity.
   b) social categories.
   c) person-by-context interactions.
   d) accommodation.

2 In an advanced undergraduate course at an Australian university, the lecturers wanted to know the cultural composition of the student body. They asked students to nominate their own cultural group. The students gave twenty-seven different self-description categories (Australian Vietnamese, Anglo-European, Anglo, Chinese Australian, Lebanese Australian, Australian, for example).
   a) If you were asked to do that spontaneously, how would you describe yourself?
   b) Discuss whether these self-descriptions are ways of saying something to oneself or to others, or both.

3 A teacher at a local primary school finds that the ethnic mix of the Grade 6 class causes some clashes, especially when the children are playing sport. The mix includes Serbian and Croatian, Somalian and Sudanese, Greek and Turkish, Vietnamese and Cambodian. Some of these groups have traditional antagonisms and doubts about 'others'. The teacher wants to help the children to work together. She considers three strategies:
   a) Ignore the ethnic differences and say, 'We're all Australians here. Let's forget everything else'.
   b) Ask children to tell the whole class the story of their family's experience: the experience of leaving their country and of coming to Australia.
   c) Give a brief lesson on ethnicity (at the appropriate level for Grade 6), put the children into ethnically mixed discussion groups and ask them to work out a way forward.
      i) Discuss whether each of these strategies is likely to be productive.
      ii) Rank them, with reasons for your ranking.

4 The significance of advice and information when it comes to transition points is not unique to immigrant families. Take a look at your own life. What kinds of anticipatory advice were helpful when you faced transitions and change? Who offered advice? Were there people whom you could ask and who would also be well informed? What influenced the kind of advice or preparation offered to you, and its usefulness?

Notes

1   R. Hartley, ed., *Families and Cultural Diversity in Australia*, Australian Institute of Family Studies, Melbourne, 1995. Each chapter describes a particular group of immigrants (since 1945) to Australia, and is written by a member of that group.
2   G. Bottomley, ed., *From Another Place: Migration and the Politics of Culture*, Cambridge University Press, Cambridge, 1992.
3   Hartley, 1995, p. 3, makes a similar point in commenting on self-identification as belonging to a particular group.
4   Jean Martin, in an early and influential analysis of immigration in Australia, called ethnic groupings a 'social construction': J.I. Martin, *The Migrant Presence*, Allen & Unwin, Sydney, 1979. This chapter

takes the term 'social category' from the work of several social psychologists who have been concerned with the nature of social grouping in general, without specific reference to immigration or ethnicity. See, for example, the work of Penelope Oakes, Peter Robinson, Henri Tajfel and John Turner, with a first introduction to these to be found in a useful general text: K. Durkin, *Developmental Social Psychology*, Blackwell, Oxford, 1995. See also L.A. Hirschfield, *Race in the Making: The Child's Construction of Human Kinds*, MIT Press, Cambridge, MA, 1996.

5   R.G. D'Andrade & C. Strauss, eds, *Human Motivation and Cultural Models*, Cambridge University Press, New York, 1992.

6   For a summary account of some of the labels that arose, see the chapter on inequality and disadvantage in A. Burns & J.J. Goodnow, *Children and Families in Australia*, Allen & Unwin, Sydney, 1985.

7   For a general review of studies on ingroup and outgroup perceptions, see P.W. Linville, P. Salovey & G.W. Fischer, 'Stereotyping and Perceived Distributions of Social Characteristics: An Application of Ingroup–outgroup Perception', in *Prejudice, Discrimination, and Racism*, eds, J.F. Davidio & S.L. Gaertner, Academic Press, San Diego, CA, 1986, pp. 165–208.

8   See also the autobiographical account of a change in self-identification by the artist and writer Sally Morgan: S. Morgan, *My Place*, Fremantle Arts Centre Press, Fremantle, 1987.

9   See R.B. Cairns & B.D. Cairns, *Lifelines and Risks: Pathways of Youth in Our Time*, Cambridge University Press, New York, 1994.

10 C. Strauss, 'Motives and Models', in *Human Motivation and Cultural Models*, eds, R.G. D'Andrade & C. Strauss, Cambridge University Press, New York, 1992, pp. 1–20. See also J.J. Goodnow, 'Parenting and the "Transmission" and "Internalization" of Values: From Social-cultural Perspectives to Within-family Analyses', in *Parenting Strategies and Children's Internalization of Values*, eds, J. Grusec & L. Kuczynski, Wiley, New York, 1997, pp. 333–61.

11 R.D. Parke & R. Buriel, 'Socialization in the Family: Ethnic and Ecological Perspectives', in *Handbook of Child Psychology*, ed., W. Damon, Wiley, New York, 1997, pp. 463–552.

12 The term 'looking-glass self' is from C.H. Cooley, *Human Nature and the Social Order*, Scribners, New York, 1902. For a careful analysis of this concept, see F.E. Aboud, *Children and Prejudice*, Blackwell, Oxford, 1988.

13 H. Tajfel, *Human Groups and Social Categories*, Cambridge University Press, Cambridge, 1981.

14 Within New Zealand most official functions now start with some statements in the Māori language, regardless of whether the speaker is 'Māori' or 'Pākehā'. See G.M. Vaughan, 'A Social Psychological Model of Ethnic Identity and Development', in *Children's Ethnic Socialization: Pluralism and Development*, eds, J.S. Phinney & M.J. Rotheran, Sage, Newbury Park, CA, 1987, pp. 73–91.

15 R. Birrell, 'Ethnic Concentrations: The Vietnamese Experience', *People and Place*, 1, 1993, pp. 26–32.

16 M.C. Thornton, L.M. Chatters, R.J. Taylor & W.R. Allen, 'Sociodemographic and Environmental Correlates of Racial Socialization by Black Parents', *Child Development*, 61, 1990, pp. 401–9.

17 D. Hughes & L. Chen, 'When and What Parents Tell Their Children About Race: An Examination of Race-related Socialization in African–American Families', *Applied Developmental Science*, 1, 1997, pp. 200–14.

18 See V. Carrington, 'The Interethnic Family in 1990's Australia', paper presented at the Australian Family Research Conference, Brisbane, 1996. See also C. Price, 'Ethnic Intermixture in Australia', *People and Place*, 2, 1993, pp. 8–10.

19 V. Nguyen & M. Ho, 'Vietnamese–Australian Families', in Hartley, 1995, pp. 216–40.

20 For a discussion of this way of framing cross-generation differences, see J.J. Goodnow, 'Acceptable Disagreement Across Generations', in *Beliefs About Parenting*, ed., J.G. Smetana, Jossey-Bass, San Francisco, 1995a, pp. 51–64. For a broad discussion of 'ethnic families' in relation to the contexts they encounter, see Parke & Buriel, 1997, or A.O. Harrison, M.N. Wilson, C.J. Pine, S.Q. Chan & R. Buriel, 'Family Ecologies of Ethnic Minority Children', *Child Development*, 61, 1990, pp. 347–62.

21 For an effective account of these several approaches, see K. Deaux, *To Be An Immigrant*, Russell Sage Foundation, New York, 2006.

22 H. Giles, N. Coupland & J. Coupland, 'Accommodation Theory: Communication, Context, and Consequence', in *Contexts of Accommodation*, eds, H. Giles, N. Coupland & J. Coupland, Cambridge University Press, Cambridge, 1991, pp. 1–68.

5

Playfulness: Interactions between Play Contexts and Child Development

Anita Bundy, Paul Tranter, Geraldine Naughton, Shirley Wyver and Tim Luckett

Playfulness is a characteristic of young children[1] and has been argued to have a critical role in all major areas of children's development,[2] particularly the acquisition of early academic skills.[3] Opportunities to engage in play can therefore have long-term quality of life consequences for children. In this chapter we examine how attempts to increase children's safety, undertaken to promote their growth and well-being, have paradoxically had an adverse impact on their opportunities for play and limited this important avenue for children's learning.

Contexts

We use Bronfenbrenner's social ecology model[4] to demonstrate the multilayered nature of what has been termed 'surplus safety' and how it impacts on the lives of children and families. The criticisms of Bronfenbrenner's model raised in Chapter 1 are as valid for playfulness as for any other child characteristic; no child is separate from his or her context. Nonetheless, Bronfenbrenner's model provides a useful tool to demonstrate how small but significant changes within each layer of the system can have a profound impact on children's lives. It is also a useful tool to demonstrate how small but significant changes can be made by parents and professionals to enhance children's opportunities to engage in play. In discussing the general reduction in children's playfulness, both in their school grounds and in their playful exploration of their neighbourhoods and cities, we use the term surplus safety. Surplus safety refers to the tendency to engage in extreme measures to promote safety.[5]

In this chapter we differentiate between two types of risk: excessive risk and healthy risk. Excessive risk places children at unnecessary and potentially harmful risk (for example, a two-year-old left to mind an infant while their mother visits friends). In contrast, healthy risk is an essential part of development; it is characterised by stretching the boundaries a little in order to test or develop skills. When a child slides in order to kick a ball and score a goal, tests her skill in controlling a wheelchair on an incline or tries climbing up a slide for the first time, there is a risk of physical injury and possible social embarrassment. However, in each case, the risk taking represents healthy risk. Taking the risk is essential for the child's individual development and for building resilience.

Throughout this chapter, we consider examples from a case study of a primary school based intervention to counteract surplus safety known as the Bubblewrap Project.[6] In this multifaceted project, we placed 'scrounge materials' or 'loose parts' (for example, hay bales, car tyres, cardboard boxes) in a school playground. We also conducted a 'risk reframing' intervention with parents, in which we helped them to consider the difference between excessive risk and healthy risk and to examine the consequences of taking no risks. We hoped to increase children's playfulness as well as their activity levels and social interactions.

There were several relevant microsystems in the Bubblewrap Project, the most obvious of which was the school playground. Teachers and parents also served as microsystems. We placed scrounge materials on the playground over two school terms, and the children received no instruction about the materials and were allowed to use them in any way they liked. Teachers were asked not to intervene unless they really felt a child was at excessive risk. The results of the study were that children played with the loose materials in ways that increased their physical activity as well as their level of creative and cooperative play.

Playfulness: an individual trait

Playfulness is a way of approaching play transactions that suggests the transaction is 'not for real' or at least that it is not 'life and death serious'. A playful approach has a way of spilling over into life itself. Playful children approach life adaptively and flexibly. They seem to understand that there are multiple ways to solve any problem and that there is rarely only one correct answer. Playful children tend to be fun-loving.[7]

Playful children share several important traits. They are intrinsically motivated. That is, they do things simply because they want to—not primarily for external gain. They become very engaged in what they are doing. In fact, they may be so involved that they fail to notice the passing of time or other things going on around them. When they encounter a barrier, they don't give up.[8]

Children who are playful are internally controlled. They are in charge of what they are doing but they are not bossy. They have good skills for playing with others. They share easily and do things to ensure that playmates have a good time. They like challenges and modify their actions and the things they are doing in order to create a challenge. They know when an activity has run its course and they should move on. At the same time, they stay with an activity as long as it is meeting their needs.[9]

Playful children are not bound by unnecessary rules or constraints. They may stretch the boundaries a little bit; in so doing, they develop and learn about their skills. They are often creative. They have a way of engaging others and including them in their play.[10]

Anita Bundy, Paul Tranter, Geraldine Naughton, Shirley Wyver & Tim Luckett

Playful children are able to use their voices, their bodies and their actions to convey a message about how they want others to interact with them. A child who is pretending to be an elegant lady at a tea party may sit very straight with knees together and with little finger extended while drinking from a pretend teacup. Similarly, playful children are good at reading the cues of others. They may notice that another child needs a friend to sit quietly beside her or that another child is posturing for a running race.[11]

Clearly, playfulness is a prominent characteristic in children. Not surprisingly, playful children are known to cope well with their lives in general.[12] Thus, playfulness is also a desirable characteristic. While it seems to be an inborn trait, day-to-day events and the environment, the varying contexts expressed in Bronfenbrenner's model, can have a big effect, positive or negative, on how readily and fully playfulness is expressed. As we show below, it is possible to systematically manipulate some of those contexts to have a positive effect on playfulness and activity, enhancing children's opportunities for learning and development.

The importance of playfulness for children's activity and well-being

The impact of play on child development cannot be understated. Other sections in this chapter show the value of play in childhood on physical, cognitive, emotional and social development. Without play, children would not learn to interact with their environment, explore their physical capacities and learn about problem solving, risk taking, leadership and cooperation. In this section, the value of play as a means of energy expenditure is framed in the context of preventing children from becoming overweight and obese. However, energy expenditure is acknowledged as just one aspect of the multiple layers of child development on which play can have an influence.

Becoming overweight and obese in childhood occurs as a result of long-term exposure to environments lacking in energy balance. More specifically, imbalance occurs when energy intake from food and drink exceeds energy output from physical activity and everyday tasks. Sound nutrition and physical activity provide major health-related benefits to early childhood development.

The disquieting increase in children becoming overweight and obese in the preschool years in Australia[13] highlights the importance of play as a means of developmentally appropriate energy output. Physical activity has a major role in the prevention of the problem. Inactive infants and toddlers can become overweight children[14] and be at risk of a number of serious conditions such as type 2 diabetes.[15] The harsh reality is that overweight children are also at risk of social exclusion and teasing. Parents of overweight and obese children report that the condition has a significant effect on the quality of their children's day-to-day lives.[16] While structured physical activity (for example, swimming, dance classes or sport) can help in weight management, organised sessions should complement and not replace time available for free, creative, outdoor play. The non-competitive nature of play may further appeal to children who do not particularly enjoy the competitive aspects of sport.

As well as the threats posed to physical health, low levels of fitness can also compromise skill development in children.[17] Through play, children develop and master fundamental movement skills such as running, jumping, hopping, throwing and kicking. The best time to practise skills is during free play. Skill mastery brings confidence and empowerment in new tasks and children can be better prepared to make the most of play opportunities.

OBESITY PREVENTION IN THE PRE-SCHOOL SETTING

- Pre-school policies and practices should recognise the need to accumulate thirty minutes of structured activity (for example, dance, or ball play), and a minimum of sixty minutes of unstructured activity per day.
- Set limits to sedentary time for children in the pre-school years to sixty minutes, with the exception of sleep.
- Outdoor play offers the best opportunities for young children to develop motor skills.
- Link families to low-cost and local options for physical activity.
- For less active children, consider the use of play buddies.
- Prevention (not treatment) is the role of the pre-school setting.
- Weight management is a family responsibility requiring a 'whole of family' approach and 'community-based support'.

Contextual factors limiting playfulness

As noted in our introduction, attempts to increase children's safety, and therefore promote children's growth and well-being, have paradoxically had an adverse impact on opportunities for play. In this chapter, we use the term 'surplus safety' to refer to excessive efforts to minimise or eliminate risk in children's environments even when the consequences are minor or statistically remote. A range of short-term motives such as avoidance of litigation or blame when injury occurs seems to underlie surplus safety.[18] And while fear of being sued may be valid, we do not believe that surplus safety is in the best interest of children. Exposure to healthy risks and the experience of minor injuries is a universal part of childhood. Learning the consequences of one's actions in the context of a safe environment is a positive benefit of play.[19]

Adult attempts to minimise risk sometimes lead to a vicious cycle where children attempt to increase risk, in order to compensate for the boredom that follows from the adults' actions.[20] Children may compensate by increasing physical risks or by engaging in antisocial behaviours such as bullying.[21] Thus, the unwitting outcome of surplus safety is that children are redirected from healthy risk taking to excessive risk taking.

Anita Bundy, Paul Tranter, Geraldine Naughton, Shirley Wyver & Tim Luckett

Playfulness and surplus safety considered within Bronfenbrenner's social ecology model

At this point, it is useful to consider surplus safety in the context of Bronfenbrenner's social ecology model.[22] The child is in the centre of the model along with his or her individual characteristics. In this case, we have focused on a single child characteristic: playfulness. Numerous other traits also occupy the central space, for example, temperament and intelligence. The surrounding layers represent varying contexts, in this case sources of surplus safety. Surplus safety arises from the fears of individuals or agencies that interact with or influence a child; it is also enshrined in legislation and other regulatory requirements. The elements of surplus safety interact with one another and with the characteristics of individual children such that they have a greater or lesser influence on the children's environments and on the children themselves.

ESCALATION OF PLAYGROUND SAFETY: THE MESOSYSTEM

The mesosystem, or degree of match between the microsystems influencing children, may also make important contributions to surplus safety. In the Bubblewrap Project, we learned that teachers thought parents had unreasonable expectations of their responsibilities to keep children safe at school. Teachers feared that parents would sue them if a child was hurt—whether or not injury prevention had been within the teachers' control. One teacher reported the experience of a parent threatening the school with legal action when her child required hospital treatment after an insect flew into her child's eye. However, most of the teachers' worries regarding litigation seemed to be based more on a 'climate of fear' than on evidence that such a risk was real. Teachers saw themselves as highly vulnerable in the event that a child became injured—in the words of one, 'guilty until proven innocent'. They also felt insufficiently protected by exosystem and mesosystem elements: policies within the school, their professional body, and the expectations of society in general. As a result, teachers tended to restrict the play of children at school in ways that exceeded precautions they would take to protect their own children at home. In these circumstances, surplus safety arose from teachers' desires to protect themselves rather than from any perceived benefit to the children in their care.

This finding provides an example of how a lack of shared agreement between two microsystem contexts—home and school—can give rise to surplus safety, impacting adversely on children's participation in activities they need to grow and learn. It also shows how perceptions about the macrosystem and exosystem can have important effects on the ways that children's everyday contexts are organised, whether or not these perceptions are based in fact. In this case, an obvious way forward in the Bubblewrap Project would have been to extend the risk-reframing intervention we ran with parents to include teachers and those with authority over the school more generally. Collective reframing of the risk of playground injury within the broader context of risks to children's health may have given teachers the information and support they needed to allow children to play actively in the playground and to allow more healthy risk.

CHILD CARE AND SCHOOL AS DANGEROUS PLACES: THE EXOSYSTEM

The exosystem refers to influences on the child's development that do not have a direct impact on the child, but do have an impact on the interactions between children and parents, teachers or others involved in their care and education. Through institutions such as media and community service organisations, as well as neighbours and extended family, parents and other individuals with direct responsibility for the care of children can feel pressured to take extreme measures to minimise risk and maximise physical safety. In this section, we examine government and community service influences that can lead to the introduction of extreme safety measures, which ultimately lead to fewer and poorer quality opportunities for play in child care and at school. This does not mean that these are the only, or the most significant, exosystem influences on playfulness. Many other examples could be provided; for instance, a concern expressed by parents in the Bubblewrap Project was that, while they would support greater risk taking in their child's play, they did not wish to be perceived by neighbours and extended family as being 'bad parents' by not being highly vigilant in terms of safety.

Regulations introduced through community services and other government organisations are part of the exosystem. The impact on children and their playfulness is mainly in terms of influencing the child's physical environment and shaping interactions between teachers and children. There is clear evidence that regulations enhance the quality of child care (see Chapter 7), but regulations can also introduce unintended consequences that accompany frameworks developed for the benefit of children.[23] In many cases, these unintended consequences can include surplus safety. Little has argued that early childhood teachers are well-equipped to provide environments that foster the positive risk taking that is essential to children's development.[24] However, her analysis of current regulatory requirements within New South Wales indicates that the emphasis is on removing all risk (even positive risk). This is problematic when it comes to providing for individual differences in children's risk taking during play.

Two recent Australian studies are particularly relevant. Both Bown and Sumsion and Fenech, Sumsion and Goodfellow interviewed early childhood educators who, while recognising the value of regulations, felt that lack of trust between staff and families and an overemphasis on safety had overall negative impacts.[25] Comments from three participants in Fenech, Sumsion and Goodfellow's study illustrated their concerns about surplus safety: 'we have to provide a cotton wool environment … the kids aren't allowed to be kids', 'all the equipment has become so supersafe that the children don't have any risk-taking activities' and 'we are so restricted by things like safety … it really restricts your pedagogy'.[26]

Interpreted within Bronfenbrenner's model, these findings are a clear indication of how the regulatory framework (exosystem), which was perceived by these teachers as advocating surplus safety, impacts on interactions between teachers and families (mesosystem) and children (microsystem) and ultimately results in an environment for children where risk is minimised and the teacher's insights and creativity in planning for children's learning are compromised, thus impacting on playfulness. The surplus safety concerns raised by early childhood teachers in these studies have some similarities to those raised by primary school teachers participating in the Bubblewrap Project.

Anita Bundy, Paul Tranter, Geraldine Naughton, Shirley Wyver & Tim Luckett

Eroding children's right to play: the macrosystem and chronosystem

Many of the principles of surplus safety discussed above in relation to playgrounds also apply at neighbourhood and city levels. In this section we examine the opportunities for play experiences provided in children's mobility within their own neighbourhoods and cities. The discussion here is relevant mainly to children in modern Western cities.

Recognising that children's play experiences cannot be understood independently of the context, it is important to briefly review changes to the lived experience of neighbourhoods and cities for children. Perhaps the most important part of this context is the growth in the dominance of private cars as the preferred mode of transporting children to school. Children are taking more trips by car than children did ten or fifteen years ago.[27] Many of these car trips are replacing trips that were once taken by walking or cycling. This may affect both physical and emotional well-being.

When Australian parents are asked to reflect on their childhoods, they usually remember having far more freedom than their own children have today.[28] A generation ago, children were far more likely to play independently in their own neighbourhoods. Children now have less time available to play outside because they are engaged in more indoor and adult-organised activities such as sport and music. Children are also more likely to be driven to these activities, partly because of the greater distances involved and partly because of the increased fear of traffic and 'stranger' danger. Other reasons for the loss of children's freedom include: the erosion of natural or wild spaces;[29] increased social pressure to be 'good parents' (for example, by driving their children rather than allowing them to walk or cycle);[30] the increasing choice of the 'best' schools and child care centres that require children to be transported by car; and the trend to 'over-occupy' and 'over-organise' children's lives.[31]

The parental response to traffic and 'stranger' danger is usually focused on an individualistic response to protect their own child or children. Typically, parents 'protect' their child from these dangers by driving them to destinations, rather than letting them travel independently. The collective impact of many individual decisions to protect children in this way unwittingly leads to a situation in which all children (and adults) may be worse off. Traffic danger is increased, particularly around schools. Fears of stranger danger may also be increased, because there are fewer people (adults and children) on the streets as pedestrians to provide passive surveillance for children. Not only are children worse off in terms of traffic dangers (and stranger danger) but when children are protected in this way, they are deprived of important play experiences. This in turn exposes children to a range of risks that are damaging to their health and well-being.

Children who are driven everywhere can miss out on the regular exercise that is so important for optimal physical development and easily attained by walking or cycling to school, their friends' houses or the local park. Medical experts describe increased levels of obesity as epidemic in Australia.[32] The extra traffic created by ferrying children to and from school, sport, music lessons and their friends' houses also contributes to higher levels of air pollution, including 'in-car pollution', which is usually much higher than levels at the side of the road.[33] Children are more susceptible to pollution because they breathe more air per unit of body weight than adults.[34]

Consequences

An often overlooked part of this 'bubble-wrapping' of children is that they miss out on the joy and wonder that comes from exploring the world at their own pace. Sport and other adult-organised activities have benefits for children, but they are not a substitute for spontaneous play.[35] Not only is it important that children be able to get to local play areas by themselves, but walking or cycling to school and other destinations provides vital play and learning experiences for children. Recent studies with children indicate that happiness is integral to their experience of walking to school.[36] Cunningham and colleagues found that when children are taken to school by car instead of walking, 'there were no opportunities for kicking rocks or toads, looking for dead birds, making friends with animals, playing, or simply dawdling along with friends—all activities unremarkable in adult eyes but part of the experience and development of childhood'.[37]

There seems to be a lack of awareness of the value of free play for children in their neighbourhoods and cities. (If the awareness was greater, it is unlikely that children would have been so effectively deprived of their play experiences.) However, when adults are asked to reflect on their own childhood they often recount playful experiences during their walks home from school or around their neighbourhood. They can remember transport as a play experience during their own childhoods.

LIVING IN THE 'NOWSCAPE'

Think of a time that you walked to a local shop with a child. As an adult, you might have been hurrying to get to the shop, to buy the bread, milk and paper and get back home so that you could get on with the next task. In contrast, the child with you is more likely to have been in the 'nowscape', living the moment in a sense of playful adventure: counting the trees, collecting autumn leaves, running their hands over the picket fence, listening to a bird calling or talking with a neighbour. For adults, the next task always seems more important than the present.

Promoting activity: the walking school bus

One initiative that has successfully enhanced playful experiences in children's everyday transport is the walking school bus (WSB).[38] This refers to a group of children who walk to and/or from school on a set route, with two or more adult supervisors (usually parents). Walking school buses have been implemented in several cities in Australia, New Zealand, the United Kingdom and Canada. They achieve the simultaneous benefits of assuaging parental fears about their children's safety, while at the same time providing some freedom and playful experiences for children on their journey to school.

Anita Bundy, Paul Tranter, Geraldine Naughton, Shirley Wyver & Tim Luckett

Research by Rooney on walking school buses in Canberra found that the things children valued most from the walking school buses were 'fun, engagement, empowerment, and [doing] the "right thing"'.[39] These were the same factors identified by children who were not yet on the WSBs, but who wanted to join. The negative comments made by children about driving included that it was 'bad for the environment, stressful, disempowering, anti-social'.[40]

Apart from the constant references to having 'fun', one comment in particular from a child shows how involvement in the WSB had an impact on their happiness: 'I like walking, I don't worry about anything, I don't even know I'm walking, it's better'.[41]

Both the children and the parents involved with the walking school buses in Rooney's research identified some key advantages of the WSBs that relate to key aspects of happiness: connection and belonging, empowerment and a sense of making a positive contribution to the environment. As Rooney explained: 'Belonging helps to establish a sense of wellbeing and is thus considered a motivator for participation'.[42] One parent explained the impact of her involvement in the WSB on her own happiness, when she explained that without community 'I'd be a very depressed person'. Parents also saw the 'belonging' aspect as important to their children: 'I think that's the biggest benefit [of the WSB] that sense of being a part of something'.[43]

Parents and children have an intuitive awareness of the value of playful experiences, of exploring their world at their own pace. Allowing parents to escape the social traps that force them to drive their children everywhere will increase children's access to valuable play experiences during their own journeys within their neighbourhoods and cities.

Interventions to promote childhood activity

In general, children, parents and teachers understand how to manage the physical environment, their social interactions and other behaviours to achieve a positive balance between healthy and excessive risk, with the former being encouraged and the latter minimised. Surplus safety, however, blurs the boundaries between healthy and excessive risk and leads to individual loss of confidence in promoting healthy risk taking. This in turn stifles playfulness and resilience. Through the Bubblewrap Project we introduced microsystem interventions that resulted in increased playfulness of the child participants. Ultimately, inexpensive interventions of this nature should result in mesosystem changes, in this case a better shared understanding of the roles of parents and teachers in promoting healthy risk taking in children. We have demonstrated in this chapter how surplus safety has invaded all systems as described by Bronfenbrenner. Nonetheless, we remain optimistic that well-targeted, low-cost interventions such as the Bubblewrap Project—that are based on an understanding of the importance of play in children's development and take into account local contexts and resources—can lead to significant changes throughout each system and restore children's healthy risk taking. Although, as a research project, implementation of the Bubblewrap Project has been top-down, the real-world application of the project should be bottom-up, with decisions about play space contexts and content determined largely by the users, especially children, teachers and parents.

STUDENT EXERCISES

1   Think of a risky outdoor physical activity you enjoyed as a child. Remember, what each person considers to be a risky activity varies considerably, so don't be concerned if your risky activity was not typical of early childhood risk taking. Try to remember the events in as much detail as possible, including who was there (or perhaps more importantly, who was not there) at the time. When you have recalled the activity in detail, consider the following questions.

a) How did this activity benefit you (physically, socially and emotionally)?

b) What risks were you aware of when you were engaged in the activity?

c) Would your answer to the above be the same or different now? If different, what has changed?

d) Overall, do you consider the benefits of engaging in the activity to have outweighed any potentially negative outcomes?

e) Assume you are on an outing with a friend's child. The child is the same age as you were when you enjoyed the risky outdoor activity. You are the only adult with the child.

   i)   Would you allow the child to engage in the activity you enjoyed as a child? Why or why not?

   ii) Would your answer to this question depend on the child's gender?

f) Assume you are the parent of a child who is the same age you were when you enjoyed the risky outdoor activity.

   i)   Would you allow your child to engage in the activity you enjoyed as a child? Why or why not?

   ii) Would your answer to this question depend on the child's gender?

   iii) Would your answer to this question depend on who is supervising (for example, s/he could engage in the activity under your supervision, but not with a teacher)?

2   Take a short trip in a car, not as a driver, but as a passenger in the back seat (young children are usually back seat passengers). Take the same trip, but this time walking. Include the person who was the driver of the car on your walking trip. Consider the following questions.

a) What did you observe as a passenger in the car that you did not observe when walking? In particular, what did you see, hear, smell and feel?

b) What did you observe when you were walking that you did not observe when you were a passenger in the car? In particular, what did you see, hear, smell and feel?

   If you are completing this exercise in a class or at a time that is not convenient to take two short trips (drive and walk), try to imagine a short familiar trip instead. This will be effective in helping you with some of the information. However, if you do complete the exercise this way, try to remember to think about the differences in experience next time you go for a walk or you are a passenger in a car.

Anita Bundy, Paul Tranter, Geraldine Naughton, Shirley Wyver & Tim Luckett

Notes

1   A.D. Pellegrini & D.F. Bjorklund, 'The Ontogeny and Phylogeny of Children's Object and Fantasy Play', *Human Nature*, 15, 1, 2004, pp. 23–43; A.D. Pellegrini & P.K. Smith, 'Physical Activity Play: The Nature and Function of a Neglected Aspect of Play', *Child Development*, 69, 3, 1998, pp. 577–98.

2   R.M. Golinkoff, K. Hirsh-Pasek & D.G. Singer, 'Play = Learning: A Challenge for Parents and Educators', in *Play = Learning: How Play Motivates and Enhances Children's Cognitive and Social-emotional Growth*, eds, D.G. Singer, R.M. Golinkoff & K. Hirsh-Pasek, Oxford University Press, Oxford, 2006, pp. 3–20.

3   J.K. Christie & K.A. Roskos, 'Standards, Science and the Role of Play in Early Literacy Education', in *Play = Learning: How Play Motivates and Enhances Children's Cognitive and Social-emotional Growth*, eds, D.G. Singer, R.M. Golinkoff & K. Hirsh-Pasek, Oxford University Press, Oxford, 2006, pp. 57–73.

4   See Chapter 1.

5   C. Buchanan, 'Building Better Playgrounds: A Project for Parents?', *UAB Magazine (University of Alabama)*, 19, 3, 1999, <http://main.uab.edu/show.asp?durki=25353>, accessed 12 July 2006.

6   A. Bundy, P. Tranter, T. Luckett, G. Naughton, S. Wyver, G. Spies & J.A. Ragen, (in press), 'Playful Interaction: Occupational Therapy for "All" Children on the Playground', *American Journal of Occupational Therapy*.

7   L.A. Barnett, 'Characterizing Playfulness: Correlates with Individual Attributes and Personality Traits', *Play & Culture*, 4, 4, 1991, pp. 371–93; L.A. Barnett, 'Playfulness: Definition, Design, and Measurement', *Play & Culture*, 3, 1990, pp. 319–36.

8   E.A. Neumann, *The Elements of Play, MSS Information*, New York, 1971; G. Skard & A.C. Bundy, 'Play and Playfulness: What to Look For', in *Play in Occupational Therapy for Children* (2nd edn), eds, L.D. Parham & L.S. Fazio, Mosby, St. Louis, in press.

9   Neumann, 1971; Skard & Bundy, in press.

10   Neumann, 1971; Skard & Bundy, in press.

11   G. Bateson, 'The Message, "This is Play"', in *Child's Play*, eds, R.E. Herron & B. Sutton-Smith, Wiley & Sons, New York, pp. 261–69; Skard & Bundy, in press.

12   L. Hess & A.C. Bundy, 'The Association Between Playfulness and Coping Adolescents', *Physical and Occupational Therapy in Pediatrics*, 23, 1, 2003, pp. 5–17; M. Moore & S.W. Russ, 'Pretend Play as a Resource for Children: Implications for Pediatricians and Health Professionals', *Developmental and Behavioral Pediatrics*, 27, 3, 2006, pp. 237–48.

13   Y. Zuo, M. Norberg, L.M. Wen & C. Risel, 'Estimates of Overweight and Obesity among Samples of Preschool-aged Children in Melbourne and Sydney', *Nutrition & Dietetics*, 63, 2006, pp. 179–82.

14   L.L. Moore, D. Gao, M.L. Bradlee, L.A. Cupples, A. Sundarajan-Ramamurti & M.H. Proctor, 'Does Early Physical Activity Predict Body Fat Change Throughout Childhood?', *Preventative Medicine*, 37, 2003, pp. 10–17.

15   American Academy of Pediatrics, 'Prevention of Pediatric Overweight and Obesity Committee on Nutrition (Policy Statement)', *Pediatrics*, 112, 2, 2003, pp. 424–29; P. Lewis & S. Ker, *The Relationship Between Australian Transport Systems and Public Health*, proceedings of the 28th Australasian Transport Research Forum, Sydney, 28–30 September 2005, <www.patrec.org/atrf/papers/2005/Lewis %20&%20Ker %20S %20(2005).pdf>, accessed 21 December 2007.

16   J. Williams, M. Wake, K. Hesketh, E. Maher & E. Waters, 'Health-related Quality of Life of Overweight and Obese Children—A Population Study', *Journal of the American Medical Association*, 293, 1, 2005, pp. 70–6.

17   M.J. Booth, A.D. Oakley, E. Denney-Wilson, L. Hardy, B. Yang & T. Dobbins, *NSW Schools Physical Activity and Nutrition Survey (SPANS) 2004: Summary Report*, NSW Department of Health, Sydney, 2006.

18   Children's Play Council, *Managing Risk in Play Provision: A Position Statement*, National Children's Bureau, London, 2002, <www.childfriendlycities.org/cgi-bin/cfc/main.sql?file=search_simple_result.sql&lunga=Yes&ProductID=426>, accessed 11 April 2006.

19   Children's Play Council, 2002.

20   A. Stephenson, 'Physical Risk-taking: Dangerous or Endangered', *Early Years: An International Journal of Research and Development*, 23, 1, 2003, pp. 35–43.

21   P. Walsh, 'Fixed Equipment: A Time for Change', *Australian Journal of Early Childhood*, 18, 2, 1993, pp. 23–9.

22   See Chapter 1, Figure 1.

23   M. Fenech, 'The Impact of Regulatory Environments on Early Childhood Professional Practice and Job Satisfaction: A Review of Conflicting Discourses', *Australian Journal of Early Childhood*, 31, 2, 2006, pp. 49–52.

24   H. Little, 'Children's Risk-taking Behaviour: Implications for Early Childhood Policy and Practice', *International Journal of Early Years Education*, 14, 2, 2006, pp. 141–54.

25   K. Bown & J. Sumsion, 'Voices from the Other Side of the Fence: Early Childhood Teachers' Experiences with Mandatory Regulatory Requirements', *Contemporary Issues in Early Childhood*, 8, 1, 2007, pp. 30–49; M. Fenech, J. Sumsion & J. Goodfellow, 'The Regulatory Environment in Long Day Care: A "Double Edged Sword" for Early Childhood Professional Practice', *Australian Journal of Early Childhood*, 31, 3, 2006, pp. 49–56.

26   Fenech et al., 2006, p. 55.

27   R. Gilbert & C. O'Brien, *Child- and Youth-friendly Land-use and Transport Planning Guidelines*, The Centre for Sustainable Transportation, Toronto, 2005; P.J. Tranter, 'Overcoming Social Traps: A Key to Creating Child Friendly Cities', in *Creating Child Friendly Cities: Reinstating Kids in the City*, eds, B. Gleeson & N. Sipe, Routledge, New York, 2006, pp. 121–35.

28   J. Cadzow, 'The Bubble-wrap Generation', *Sydney Morning Herald Good Weekend Magazine*, 17 January, 2004, pp. 18–21.

29   C. Cunningham, M. Jones & M. Barlow, *Town Planning and Children: A Case Study of Lismore, New South Wales, Australia*, Department of Geography and Planning, University of New England, Armidale, 1996; C. Cunningham, M. Jones & N. Taylor, 'The Child-friendly Neighbourhood: Some Questions and Tentative Answers from Australian Research', *International Play Journal*, 2, 1994, pp. 79–95.

30   P.J. Tranter & E. Pawson, 'Children's Access to Local Environments: A Case-study of Christchurch, New Zealand', *Local Environment*, 6, 1, 2001, pp. 27–48.

31   C. Honore, *In Praise of Slow: How a Worldwide Movement is Challenging the Cult of Speed*, Orion, London, 2004; F. Stanley, S. Richardson & M. Prior, *Children of the Lucky Country? How Australian Society Has Turned its Back on Children and Why Children Matter*, Macmillan, Sydney, 2005.

32   C.O. Stubbs & A.J. Lee, 'The Obesity Epidemic: Both Energy Intake and Physical Activity Contribute', *Medical Journal of Australia*, 181, 2004, pp. 489–91; E.B. Waters & L.A. Baur, 'Childhood Obesity: Modernity's Scourge', *Medical Journal of Australia*, 178, 9, 2003, pp. 422–23.

33   International Center for Technology Assessment, *In-car Air Pollution*, CTA, 2000, <www.icta.org/doc/In-car %20pollution%20report.pdf>, accessed 19 March 2008; J. Rank, J. Folke & P.H. Jespersen, 'Differences in Cyclists and Car Drivers Exposure to Air Pollution from Traffic in the City of Copenhagen', *The Science of the Total Environment*, 279, 2001, pp. 131–36.

34   C. O'Brien, 'Transportation that's Actually Good for the Soul', *National Center for Bicycling and Walking (NCBW) Forum (Canada)*, 54, 2003, pp. 1–13.

35   Honore, 2004.

36   O'Brien, 2003.

37   Cunningham et al., 1996, p. 37.

38   R.A. Kearns, D.C.A. Collins & P.M. Neuwelt, 'The Walking School Bus: Extending Children's Geographies?', *Area*, 35, 3, 2003, pp. 285–92; M. Rooney, '"Oh You're Just up the Street!" Discovering Community as an Agent of Change', BA Honours Thesis, Human Ecology Program, School of Resources, Environment and Society, Australian National University, Canberra, 2006; YWCA, *Walking School Bus Output and Performance Report*, YWCA, Canberra, 2006.

39   Rooney, 2006, p. 21.

40   Rooney, 2006, p. 21.

41   Rooney, 2006, p. 40.

42   Rooney, 2006, p. 48.

43   Rooney, 2006, p. 49.

Anita Bundy, Paul Tranter, Geraldine Naughton, Shirley Wyver & Tim Luckett

Part C

Face-to-face Influences: Families, Schools and Communities

6

Families as a Context for Children

Jennifer Bowes, Johanna Watson and Emma Pearson

Families are a primary context for child development. Most children grow up in families and, in their early years especially, families have a major impact on children's lives, influencing their developing patterns of thinking, feeling and behaviour. Families also have a critical role in instilling fundamental values in children, which in the vast majority of cases enables them to become ethical and law-abiding citizens. Although children may spend a lot of their time in contexts other than their family, the emotional intensity of families and the durability of kinship ties mean that learning in this context is likely to be extensive and long lasting.

In most Western contexts, families tend to operate as self-contained systems, in that they develop their own ways of dealing with problems, of allocating resources of time and affection, and of maintaining patterns of harmony or discord. Such patterns are learnt by children living within families, whether these patterns are subsequently accepted or rejected.

However, families are complex. They influence children's development in a number of direct and indirect ways. Parents, siblings and members of the extended family can exert an individual influence on any one child, but that influence is likely to be modified by the nature of multiple interactions within and outside the family. Any learning within a family is magnified by reinforcement from and the involvement of other family members. Not only are relationships among family members and their impact on individual children fluid, but so are families themselves.[1]

Families respond and adapt to circumstances that are within and beyond their control. An example of the first is marriage break-up and of the second changes in government policy on family and child care benefits. In the same way that individuals need to be seen in terms of their connections with other family members, families themselves cannot be understood in isolation from their community and cultural contexts. Even the question of what a family *is* remains subject to cultural interpretation. When Anglo-Australians refer to family, for example, they are likely to be referring to their immediate nuclear family whereas Indigenous Australians use the term 'family' to refer to an extended kin network.[2] Children are likely to include family pets as well as people in their depictions of family.

The influence of families in their community contexts on the development of children is the focus of this chapter. In exploring the nature of families as a context for children's development, we begin by considering two theoretical models of family functioning: family systems theory and the family life cycle approach. While we have seen substantial debate about the value of such approaches to understanding families, it is worth including them here in order to appreciate some of the ways in which families are believed to shape children and their development.

In the second part of the chapter, we present statistics and highlight social trends that provide support for arguments that the 'traditional' notions of family upon which family systems theory is built are no longer appropriate for a substantial proportion of Australian families.

In the final part of the chapter, we highlight further the need to move beyond the predominantly self-contained approach to families offered by family systems theory to consider in more detail how external factors beyond the family unit play a part in the well-being and socialisation of children. It is argued that families cope or fail to cope with the stresses of daily living and with the inevitable crises of family life through a combination of resources from within and outside the family unit. We discuss just what it is that makes some families more resilient and others more vulnerable.

When considering families it is easy to lose sight of the individuals within them. Our concern here is with children and the effects on their development of growing up in a family. Families stand between children and the wider society. They can operate to protect children from risks outside the family. It is also worth noting, however, that negative social influences can filter down to children through the family, in the form of parental alcoholism, drug use and poverty, for example. Equally, families can assist their children to gain access to aspects of the wider society that are beneficial for their development, or they can overprotect their children by preventing them from useful contact with the world outside.

Contexts

How do families operate?

FAMILY SYSTEMS APPROACH

Tolstoy in the first sentence of Anna Karenina wrote, 'All happy families resemble one another, but each unhappy family is unhappy in its own way'.[3] Family systems theory attempts to isolate the dimensions of life within families that make them happy or unhappy, although most research and clinical attention has focused on unhappy families.

A number of theories about the family as a system have been proposed. Generally, whichever systems theory one examines, the basic premises are the same.[4] First, the context for the child is seen as part of an interactional system whereby behaviours of individual members are influenced and maintained by the interactions between all family members.

These interactions are seen as circular in nature rather than in one direction only (as from parent to child, or from child to parent). For instance, cheerful gurgling babies will attract positive attention and elicit smiles from their parents. This in turn reinforces the happy response of the child, further encouraging positive responses from the parents. Second, each family has its own unique style of interacting, bound by the implicit family rules and accepted roles of each member. When two households combine in a step or blended family, the differences in these implicit rules and expectations can lead to some misunderstandings.[5]

In most accounts of family systems theory, healthy families are seen to be ones where communication is open and the 'rules' of family are flexible and can adapt to changing demands. If there are too many submessages, such as tight-lipped agreement that really means 'No', the communication is not so open and successful negotiation becomes more difficult. Families also need to be able to adapt to developmental changes in their children: the parental demands and expectations placed on a five-year-old will be quite different from those placed on a fifteen-year-old.

According to the family systems approach, a final premise of systems theory is that well-functioning families are expected to be in some kind of balance. As long as the implicit rules are followed, the feedback from other family members is fairly positive. If, however, rules are flouted, the feedback becomes negative and the family tips out of balance. This happens in all families, and can usually be dealt with within the family without undue distress (such as when children do not come home until after the curfew or leave a mess for others to clean up). In some families, however, the flouting of the rules is more serious and contravenes not only implicit family rules but also societal ones. For instance, when the person flouting the rules is a parent who is unable to function effectively due to drug abuse, or when parents abuse their children, the levels of distress are proportionally greater. Often the relative powerlessness of children within a family means they are the members most likely to become distressed.

Systems concepts are most commonly applied in therapeutic settings, and they may assist therapists and counsellors in working out strategies to help families to understand how they can function more effectively. However, the family systems model is strongly based on the cultural norms that existed when it was first developed. For example, it tends to assume that children are being raised in nuclear families, which does not apply to a large number of children in Australia, as the statistics presented later in this chapter indicate.

The model is also deficit based and seeks cause in 'dysfunction'. It was developed primarily to enable so-called 'dysfunctional' families to become 'functional'. For example, in the same way that the family life cycle model described below sees 'marriage' as normal, the family systems model emphasises the importance of a strong marital relationship. By implication, single parent families are seen as deficient because they lack a marital subsystem despite the research evidence suggesting it is not crucial to the adjustment of children. If a strong marital relationship is positively associated with positive outcomes, but not an essential component, the research question then becomes: What

Jennifer Bowes, Johanna Watson & Emma Pearson

is it about the marital relationship that contributes to positive child outcomes? If the essential element is support provided by a close and caring relationship, could strong supportive extended family or friends be as effective in providing this support? These are important questions, given the decline in two-parent families in Australia.

Family systems theory also implies fine-tuning to keep the family in balance. It seems underpinned by the notion of a comfortably middle class, reasonably well-adjusted family, where children may test family limits but go no further. Although family systems theory provides us with a useful lens through which to consider family relationships and their impact on individual children, it is insufficient as a model to deal with such community-based and wider social issues as poverty, alcoholism or drug use, all of which impact on families and their ability to function effectively.[6]

LIFE CYCLE APPROACH

In attempting to understand the ways in which families function and develop, the life cycle approach to families has focused on common changes in families over time and the responses of family members to these changes. Early models[7] put forward a simple life course for families: marriage, the birth of children, the moving away from the family home by the children ('empty nest') and finally the death of partners. Each point of transition was seen to be a major and predictable point of stress for families. Later writers have criticised the simplicity and inflexibility of this approach to family life cycle, arguing that the birth of children can occur before marriage or indeed without marriage and that partnerships can be dissolved not only by the death of one partner but by divorce or separation.[8] In addition, it is no longer certain that children will leave home when they reach adulthood. For financial reasons and because many young people are dependent on their parents owing to unemployment or further study, children may still be living at home into middle adulthood. This model also implies that any digression from the 'normal' timetable is abnormal, stigmatising the families and children concerned, and pays no attention to extended family. Recent developments of the family life cycle approach have incorporated a focus on transitions and their associated stress for families, and a view of families as multigenerational.[9]

In considering times of major stress for families it is important to keep in mind that families may perceive seemingly identical events as more or less stressful, and that the way family members cope with such stresses also varies according to the characteristics of individuals in the family and their relationships with one another.[10] Dunlop[11] found in a longitudinal study of the effects of divorce on Australian children that a key feature of children who were well adjusted three years after their parents' divorce was a good and continuing relationship with at least one of their parents. This is not to deny that divorce is a source of stress in the lives of children at the time, and a source of enduring unhappiness for some. The example is raised to show that the same event can affect families and individuals within families quite differently.

We have seen that families can be viewed in many different ways and that they differ over time, both historically and during a family's life cycle. Families are similar, however, in that for most children they are the most influential and immediate context for development. As a way of understanding how families operate and respond to change, the combination of these two theories offers an approach that goes beyond the mother–child focus that characterised most research on family influences until recent years.

During the first decade of the twenty-first century, we have seen renewed interest in the role of families as agents of children's development and socialisation among a range of professionals, including psychologists, sociologists, anthropologists and even political scientists. Social phenomena such as globalisation, which has led to migration and rapid growth in cultural diversity for countries such as Australia, and consumerism, widely associated with individualistic approaches to life and achievement, have led to widespread discussions on the changing nature of 'family' and its role.[12] Among the most challenging questions posed and addressed in recent literature on families are: What do we mean by 'family'? and: What is the nature of the family's impact on children? In the following sections we address these questions in the context of Australian families, first by examining current statistics on the structure of Australian families, and second by considering the impact of recent social changes upon families and parents.

What are families like?

Despite changes in the definition of family and the decline of the traditional, nuclear family type, most Australian children grow up in families. Improved contraception, the legalisation of abortion and the widely publicised detrimental effects of institution-alisation have resulted in nearly all children growing up in a family even if it is not their biological family. There are now only 200 children growing up in institutions in Australia and 500 in correctional centres.[13]

Fears expressed in the media that the family as an institution is in decline are not supported by statistics. According to census data 87 per cent of Australians lived in families in 2004.[14] What is slowly changing is the public perception of what defines 'family'. The traditional stereotype of most households in Australia consisting of a nuclear family with a father-breadwinner married to a mother who is at home caring for dependent children is misleading. In fact, this group makes up only a small and decreasing proportion of families.[15]

The assumption that children have to be present for a household to be seen as a family is also under question. Couple families with children are forming a decreasing proportion of all families (45 per cent in 2006).[16] There are increasing numbers of couples without dependent children who still consider themselves to be a family (now 37 per cent of all families).[17] Many of these are older couples whose children no longer live at home or are no longer dependent on them. It is not difficult to agree that such couples fall within the definition of family. If couples whose children have left home are still families, the term may then apply equally to other couples who do not have children (either because they have not had them yet or because they have chosen not to, or cannot have, children).

Traditionally, Western societies have tended to attach considerable importance to blood ties when considering family. For example, parenting someone else's biologi-cal child has long been challenging, in terms of both emotional and practical issues.[18] However, the line between what constitutes a family and what does not is increasingly blurred in today's society. Although they may not be married, a young man living with his girlfriend and her child from a previous relationship would still fall within the currently accepted definition of family. If two young people were renting a house together, however, but had stronger emotional ties to other people, this would probably be seen as sharing accommodation. The definition of family, while certainly applying to people with a blood tie, also increasingly applies to those with an emotional tie to each other.

In this case, we might ask, does a couple have to consist of a male and a female to count as a family? In the 1996 census, for the first time, homosexual couples with or without dependent children were counted as families. Again there is assumed to be a strong emotional tie or some kind of joint commitment. Definitions of family, then, refer consistently to personal relationships formed through kinship and residence, although definitions are fluid, changing over time and in different cultural groups. The Australian Bureau of Statistics defines family as comprising 'two or more persons, one of whom is at least 15 years of age, who are related by blood, marriage (registered or de facto), adoption, step or fostering, and who are usually resident in the same household. The basis of family is formed by identifying the presence of a couple relationship, lone parent–child relationship or other blood relationship. Some households will therefore contain one or more family'.[19]

CULTURAL DIVERSITY IN AUSTRALIAN FAMILIES

Australia is a country characterised by the migration of a diverse range of people. The British colonised Australia during the eighteenth century and this is reflected in the population today. The four most common ancestries reported in the 2006 census were Australian (people born in Australia of various ancestries including Indigenous people), English, Irish and Scottish. Immediately following World War II, migrants were principally from Europe (with the largest groups from Italy, Germany and Greece). More recently, many people of Chinese, Indian, Lebanese, Vietnamese and numerous other ancestries (250 in all) have joined the Australian population. In the 2006 census, just over half of children aged less than fifteen were reported as having Australian ancestry, with most having been born in Australia and having at least one Australian-born parent.[20] Within some ancestry groups many families speak a language other than English in the home, most notably Italian, Greek, Cantonese, Arabic or Mandarin. The diversity of languages and cultures in Australia adds to our social wealth as well as challenging the English-language and Anglo-Saxon cultural dominance of many services for children and families in Australia.

INDIGENOUS FAMILIES

In the 2006 census, 455,000 people, comprising 2.3 per cent of Australia's population, answered that they were of Aboriginal or Torres Strait origin.[21] Between 2001 and 2006 the percentage of people who identified as Indigenous increased by 11 per cent, possibly as a result of adjustments in recording processes.[22] While most live in major cities or in regional centres, proportionally more Indigenous than non-Indigenous people live in remote areas of Australia.

The multiple disadvantages that Aboriginal and Torres Strait Islander families have faced due to paternalistic and discriminatory policies are detailed in Chapter 11. We referred briefly above to the impact (both positive and negative) that communities and context can exert on families. In the case of Indigenous families, circumstances such as cultural displacement and lack of access to medical and social welfare services in remote communities have led to a range of challenges and burdens including poor health, a higher rate of infant mortality, a reduced life expectancy compared to non-Indigenous Australians, lower rates of employment, lower rates of educational achievement, higher rates of incarceration, and high incidences of domestic violence and child abuse and neglect.[23]

THE IMPORTANCE OF 'STRENGTHS-BASED' INTERVENTIONS FOR INDIGENOUS COMMUNITIES

Recent media reports reflect longstanding public contention over how to support Indigenous children, families and communities according to their needs and best interests.[24] In her discussion of intergenerational trauma caused by the removal of children from Indigenous families, Atkinson recommended that interventions adopt a strengths-based approach to local communities and incorporate a focus on facilitating local leadership, as well as attending to the physical and cultural well-being of young children.[25] Higgins' report on community development models also highlighted the need for intervention programs to empower families by including them in the process, rather than imposing restrictions and penalties. He cited Burchill who suggested that 'a positive Indigenous community development model must incorporate "yarning up not down"', so that community members can begin to feel a sense of agency in their development.[26]

Efforts to understand and work effectively with Indigenous communities are much-needed in order to achieve positive outcomes for families and, particularly, children. While forecasts for the general Australian population over the next few decades indicate there will be more older people than children, the reverse is true for the Indigenous population. The current population proportion of children aged four years or younger, for example, is 14 per cent for the Indigenous population and 6 per cent for other Australians.[27] This has implications for services for Indigenous and Torres Strait Islanders, particularly health and education, as there are a large number of dependents and relatively few adults to provide for them. In addition, Indigenous parents show several characteristics, related to their socio-economic circumstances, that point to a need for parenting support.[28] High levels of family violence and abuse also create an unpredictable and sometimes dangerous backdrop for Indigenous children.[29]

This need for support is counteracted to some extent by the strong sense of family and community in Indigenous culture, which leads to a lesser sense of isolation than might be experienced by non-Indigenous families in the same circumstances. For example, many grandparents are raising grandchildren whose parents are affected by drug use. The life expectancy of Indigenous Australians, however, is about twenty years

Jennifer Bowes, Johanna Watson & Emma Pearson

less than for non-Indigenous Australians,[30] so that grandparents are often not available to support Indigenous families and children. Given the age distribution of the Indigenous population, the geographic remoteness of many communities, their poor access to fresh food and their high rates of injury and illness, it is not surprising that there is a high need for health and social services for families.

Diversity in socio-economic circumstances

In 2004, a paper published by UNICEF's Innocenti Research Centre reported that 13 per cent of children in Australia live in circumstances of poverty.[31] The gap between the rich and the poor in Australia contributes to a corresponding difference in the experience of childhood depending on the material and social resources of the family.

The expectation of health and good health care, combined with a low birth rate[32] and a greater use of prenatal testing, has led to an assumption by more affluent women that they will have one or two 'perfect' children. The emphasis for these children is no longer just on surviving. They are encouraged to 'fulfil their potential', with many families who can afford to do so investing resources in private education and extra tuition fees for their children. Academic and sporting achievements are not only hoped for but expected in these families, and anything merely average may be regarded as a disappointment. These expectations for children have led to less emphasis on children's useful contributions to the family in terms of work in the home or of money.

At the other end of the spectrum, for children from more disadvantaged families, opportunities are fewer, and there seems to be an increasing sense of social alienation as they struggle to find money for books and school excursions. One particularly moving account of the impact of poverty on children is described in a Senate Committee Report that documents an outbreak of head lice in a public housing estate. For some children this resulted in them having their heads shaved because their parents could not afford treatment.[33] University education, which is often seen as a useful indicator of relative advantage, is increasingly out of reach for children of poor families in Australia. As tuition fees rise, the proportion of students from lower socio-economic-group families completing the more expensive university courses is decreasing.[34]

Changes in Australian families

Structural diversity of families

The definition of 'family' may be changing generally but, even within an individual family group, family membership alters as children are born, parents divorce and remarry and grandparents die. It is predicted that 29 per cent of newborns in 2000–2002 will never marry and 33 per cent could be expected to divorce.[35] There is a declining number of people remarrying after either the death or divorce of their spouse.[36] As a result of marriage breakdown, the increase in births outside marriage and, to a lesser extent, the death of a spouse, 22 per cent of children in Australia are living in a one-parent family, and more have experienced or will experience this at some stage in their lives.[37] Most couple families with children include the natural or adopted children of both parents.

In addition, about three-quarters of couples in Australia now live together before they marry, in contrast to patterns of the mid 1980s.[38] De facto relationships are now recognised by law, and many couples are choosing not to marry. This trend not to marry may partly explain why close to a third of children in Australia are now born outside a formal marriage.[39]

Changing patterns of work

Several additional factors have contributed to the decline of the 'traditional' family type. The most obvious area of change has been in the work patterns of men and women and, in particular, the increased participation of women with dependent children in the paid workforce. In the last two decades there has been an increase in the number of families where both parents work, an increase in the number where only the mother works and a decreasing number where only the father works.[40] While overall trends show that mothers and fathers are more likely to work part-time[41] and be in casual employment,[42] another group of high-income-earning parents has increased their commitment to work and work long hours each week.[43]

With the increasing involvement in paid work of women in Australia over the past two decades,[44] part of parenting involves managing work and family responsibilities. This has been made more difficult for dual-earner and single-earner families by a shift in Australia away from standard working hours to longer hours of work and to 'flexible' but 'unsocial' working hours involving early mornings, evenings and weekends. In addition, there has been a trend towards more casual work, with one in three positions now offered on a casual basis. This has led to greater financial insecurity, which has a detrimental effect on family well-being.

In general, mothers have coped with competing demands of work and family by adjusting their involvement in paid work, by either not working or working part-time when their children are young.[45] Some fathers have taken on the role of primary caregiver for their children or have reduced their working hours in order to be more involved with their children, although workplaces tend to be less understanding of such work adjustments by fathers than by mothers.[46] Some employers have responded to the family responsibilities of their workers by instituting family-friendly policies such as opportunities for leave, working reduced hours or job sharing.[47] Informal cultural pressures at work, however, often mean there is a reluctance by workers to take advantage of these provisions.

Consequences

Influence of parenting on children

Throughout this chapter, we have considered contexts in which families operate. We have also touched on consequences of context for young children. Here, we focus more closely on the impact that various family members may have in shaping young children's lives and experiences.

Jennifer Bowes, Johanna Watson & Emma Pearson

Although there is a wide range of parenting behaviours worldwide and within the different cultural groups in Australian society, a great deal of research on child-rearing behaviours has been conducted in Western developed countries, and this needs to be kept in mind when reading about child rearing in the following sections of the chapter. Recent literature acknowledges that parenting behaviour, for example, needs to be seen in historical and cultural contexts.[48] In many ways, parents and other family members are influenced by cultural traditions as well as current societal values and conditions, such as those described above in the section on working patterns.

PARENTING STYLE

There can be no question that parents shape the development of their children. There is a great deal of evidence that supports the idea that parental influence is critical in children's language, social and emotional development. Even in communities where child rearing is shared by extended family and non-family members, children's experiences are influenced by inherited traits such as personality and temperament. In most societies, parents are expected to take responsibility for raising their children and there is a substantial body of research that has worked on identifying parenting techniques that are likely to lead to positive outcomes for young children. One of the most influential parenting experts of our time has been Diana Baumrind.[49] Warmth and control were identified by Baumrind as the two dimensions that underlie parenting styles. In her early studies of parenting, Baumrind observed that children of parents who were authoritative (high in warmth but also consistent in applying rules and regulations) tended to have the most well-adjusted children. Children of parents who used permissive (high in warmth with little control) or authoritarian (low in warmth and high in control) styles showed less positive outcomes, particularly in terms of achievement motivation, and authoritarian parents (who appeared to show little warmth and high levels of control) tended to have children less skilled in social interactions.

For many years, Baumrind's research has guided our ideas about what constitutes 'good' parenting. However, recent research has acknowledged the role of a wide range of factors in shaping what makes a 'good' parent. For example, cultural expectations about children's behaviour exert a powerful influence over the methods that parents use to teach and socialise their children. Even the meaning attached to, and interpretations of, control over children's behaviour differs substantially across cultures. That parents are the most influential caregivers in the lives of all young children is itself an ethnocentric assumption.

The characteristics of children themselves can elicit differing styles of parenting. An authoritative style, for example, may be the parental response to an already competent child with an 'easy' temperament. A more authoritarian style might be adopted with a child who has a more 'difficult' temperament or with an 'easy' child who is behaving badly in public or when the parent is tired.[50] The static notions of warm or restrictive have been replaced by a recognition that parenting is complex and that 'good' parenting (parenting that leads to positive outcomes for children) is largely a function of social, economic and cultural factors.[51] Parents adjust in response to the unique needs and characteristics of their children as well as to the circumstances of their own lives.

FATHERS AND PARENTING

The inclusion of fathers in accounts of parenting is a relatively new phenomenon. Research on fathering has shown that fathers differ from mothers in the amount of time they spend with their children and in the ways they interact with their children. Fathers spend more time in play with their children, particularly outdoor and rough-and-tumble play, whereas mothers are more involved in caretaking activities and play indoors with their children, using toys and books.[52] Research on father–child interactions has suggested that fathers' unique approaches to interacting with children can lead to a range of positive outcomes for children. For example, fathers are more likely than mothers to encourage their children to participate in risk taking, problem solving and more active and autonomous behaviours.[53]

It has been suggested that it is how fathers take responsibility for children that is important. Being involved beyond financial responsibilities, and taking an interest in day-to-day responsibilities such as taking children to appointments and lessons, and transporting them to school or child care, is associated with more positive developmental outcomes.[54] It should be noted that a great deal of research on fathering has been conducted in two-parent families. Many fathers living apart from their children have no contact or less regular contact with their children and need to negotiate a new kind of father–child relationship and set of behaviours. Researchers in the field are still in the process of studying fathering under these circumstances.[55]

PARENT–CHILD RELATIONSHIPS

Whether a child's primary caregiver is his or her mother or father, parent–child relationships are usually defined on two dimensions: closeness (also called warmth, affection, affiliation or acceptance) and flexibility (also called adaptability, power or control).[56] Of these two dimensions, closeness is the most important. Shonkoff and Phillips argue that 'from birth to death, intimate and caring relationships are fundamental to successful human adaptation' and the relationships in the early years are the building blocks upon which 'fragile' or 'sturdy' foundations for future relationships are built.[57] Children need at least one warm and caring relationship where their caregiver can read the child's emotional cues and respond to them in a timely manner. Maternal negativity in responding to young children, for example, seems particularly damaging.[58] This finding underlines the fact that when it comes down to it, the most important thing that parents can give children is the unconditional and irrational positive regard that Bronfenbrenner listed in his summary of what every child needs.[59]

In the section on changes in Australian families (above), we referred to alterations in working patterns among Australian parents. There has been considerable concern over the impact that changes in the lives of family members (such as increased working hours among parents) could be having on parents and their relationships with their children and each other.[60] Reports on the impact of mothers' increased working hours upon children convey equivocal findings. On the one hand, large-scale community surveys indicate that parental employment does not significantly reduce time spent with children.[61] Children with working mothers are as equally likely as children with non–working mothers to share activities such as reading with their mothers.[62] However, physical and emotional well-being among non-working or part-time working mothers (both single and couple) is reportedly better than it is among full-time working mothers. This may impact on mothers' relationships with their young children. Work-related demands have also been found to influence parents' knowledge about their children's lives and their involvement in monitoring their children's activities.[63]

Among fathers, full-time work appears to offer significant health benefits, but many full-time working fathers do report personal and marital strain resulting from their work, which is also likely to impact on parent–child relationships.[64] These results indicate that most parents, working and non-working, place a premium on time spent with children. However, the impact of working arrangements on families and children is moderated by a range of other factors such as extended family support, financial circumstances and values regarding female and male roles within the family. For example, in some families, having an unemployed parent may be seen as beneficial. If there are financial difficulties, however, and if a father feels duty-bound to earn a full-time wage, unemployment will be viewed negatively.

One of the challenges faced by many working parents is availability of quality child care. Research has consistently shown that children who attend formal care settings outside the home from an early age are more likely to experience positive outcomes if they attend quality settings, where well-trained staff provide warm, respectful and consistent responses.[65] In many cases, child care is difficult for parents to organise as places and trained staff are insufficient in formal settings such as long day care centres and family day care schemes, especially for children under two years, and child care hours are generally structured around a standard working day.

Influence of siblings

A great deal of children's social understanding, including how to share and how to fight and resolve disputes, comes from their interactions with siblings. Older brothers and sisters, for example, often act as tutors to younger children, teaching them games, what to expect at school and skills such as how to skip or climb trees. They can also act as gatekeepers for their younger siblings, managing their access to, or protecting them from, children outside the family. In turn, older children can learn how to be prosocial from their interactions with younger children.

An indirect way in which children are influenced by siblings is through observing their parents with brothers and sisters. Watching their siblings get into trouble with parents, for example, can teach children about acceptable behaviour and legitimate excuses. Listening to the explanations given by parents to misbehaving siblings can teach children reasons for avoiding such misdeeds themselves.[66] With current trends towards smaller families in Australia, these benefits of growing up with siblings may be available to fewer children in the future, with children learning how to interact with peers in more formal contexts such as child care and school (see Chapter 7).

Influence of the extended family

Support from within the extended family is a crucial resource for families. Without support in the form of information, and financial and practical help such as grandparents' assistance in the care of young children, families become isolated and their children suffer. It is unusual in Australia for members of the extended family to live in the household of 'nuclear' families, although this is more likely in Aboriginal and Torres Strait Islander households, reflecting a wider kinship system.[67] Nevertheless, families in Australia tend to keep in touch with extended family by telephone, through visits and email. Although members of the extended family can be a source of great support for families, they are not always willing to act in that role and, where help is provided, there may be emotional costs.[68] In some family circumstances, such as domestic violence or chronic illness, or where family members undermine more than they help, external support from agencies other than extended family is more appropriate.

The role of grandparents in the lives of children has been of increasing interest to researchers and policy makers. On average, grandparents are living longer and having a longer period of shared lives with their grandchildren.[69] When grandchildren are of pre-school age and their parents are in the workforce, many grandparents act as regular part-time caregivers and increasingly are awarded custodial care of their grandchildren when parents are unable to care for them. In this way, they often take on shared parenting roles in the care of their grandchildren.[70]

GRANDPARENTS AS CARERS

In 2003 there were 22,500 Australian families in which a grandparent or grandparents were guardians of their grandchildren. These families are raising children in difficult circumstances. In two-thirds of these families neither grandparent is employed and they face considerable financial and legal burdens with little support.[71] There is also a social cost, with some grandparents reporting social isolation, feeling overwhelmed and at risk of 'granny burn-out'.[72] In addition, in 2003 grandparents also cared for 660,000 children informally, mostly to assist their own children who were in work. Most of this (97 per cent) was provided at no cost to the parents.[73]

Issues of family obligations within the extended family can vary according to cultural group. This is particularly so in the care of elderly parents. A higher sense of filial responsibility is felt for parents born in southern or eastern Europe and Asia than for Australian-born 'Anglo' parents.[74]

Resources and support beyond the family

So far in this chapter we have considered what families look like, how they are defined, and how they impact on the lives of young children. We have also touched on social

Jennifer Bowes, Johanna Watson & Emma Pearson

changes that have been seen to impact on family life in Australia. Indeed, although the family is the most powerful influence on children's lives, it does not operate in a vacuum. Families are influenced by the neighbourhood in which they live and the material resources and social support available to them from their local community. Families can be assisted by practical, emotional and informational support from informal sources in the community such as friends and neighbours, and from formal sources such as health and educational services provided by local councils or governments. In recent years there has been a shift in research towards understanding the influence of community on family functioning, and towards providing services at community level to improve child and family well-being. These issues are discussed in more detail in Chapters 8 and 13. In this section, we briefly introduce three concepts that have gained increasing importance in the literature on families and communities, particularly in discussions that focus on building communities that provide appropriate support services for families and young children: human, financial and social capital.

HUMAN CAPITAL

We referred earlier in the chapter to the issues of access to support services, such as medical and educational, and to the impact of working patterns on families and children. The term 'human capital' refers to parents' skills and knowledge, indicated particularly by their education level and employment status. Well-educated parents confer educational advantages on their children not only in what they can teach them but in their familiarity with educational institutions, their procedures and expectations. When parents, particularly mothers, have little education, this is seen as a risk factor for children, affecting the resources available to children and their aspirations.[75] A similar situation holds for parental employment. Employed parents bring home information to their children about the world of work. At the same time, children learn from employed parents about the work ethic and are influenced in their aspirations for employment and for further education.[76]

FINANCIAL CAPITAL

Amato includes income and the goods and experiences purchased with income in his definition of financial capital.[77] An adequate income for families can mean greater choice and opportunity, and family functioning that is not subject to the unrelenting financial stress that poverty brings. A family's income determines the resources available to children. Resources include material goods such as clothing, food and housing. In addition, parents can open up or restrict opportunities for their children by their choice (or their lack of choice in the matter) of where they live, and the resources of that community such as public transport and educational, cultural and recreational facilities; by their choice of child care and the schools the children attend; and by the friends they allow or encourage their children to make. Such choice is governed very much by income.

Poverty and low income are risk factors for children. Apart from restricting material resources and educational opportunities, poverty affects children through the stress it places on parents and the parental 'irritability and anger [that] may fester in chronic conditions'.[78] In a USA study, Brooks-Gunn found family functioning to be quite different for poor, near-poor, middle-income and affluent families, with poorer families having less predictable and stable family patterns of operation.[79] According to Radke-Yarrow, Richters and Wilson, 'the context of family chaos ... alters the quality of relationships in the family, the ways in which networks of relationships are organised in the family, and the factors that are critical influences on the child'.[80]

SOCIAL CAPITAL

Social capital relates to the relationships between people. This includes the relationships within the family and extended family as well as relationships with community members. An important resource in the development and maintenance of relationships is time spent with other people. Parents who build up relationships with neighbours, chat to other parents at school activities and welcome friends to their home provide children with an outward-looking and trusting model of social relationships, and a sense of being embedded in their community. When communities are high in social capital, there are better outcomes for children and for their parents as parents feel more supported and less stressed.

When children have two parents living with them, the co-parenting relationship is an additional source of social capital for children. Children can learn skills such as conflict resolution, open communication and how to provide emotional support to others by observing a strong co-parenting relationship. Conversely, children who observe parents engaged in conflict, hostility or violence do not have access to the social capital from parents that enables them to learn more positive patterns of behaviour, and their emotional security is likely to be compromised.[81]

Social capital available to children is also influenced by the psychological and physical health of parents, their parenting style and behaviours, and the support provided within the family, including the extended family. As we have seen, parenting style is important for child outcomes. In addition, particular parenting practices have been linked to children's cognitive development. These include parents' sensitive structuring of learning experiences based on their monitoring of children's current level of development. Children's progress in learning to read, for example, has been improved by intervention programs that teach parents to read more responsively to their children, to read more often, and to use the method of paired reading as their child progresses through school.[82]

Responsive parenting is less likely to be present when parents are not attentive to their children's signals—at times when, for example, they are depressed, abusive, or suffering from multiple stresses so overwhelming that they are unable to attend to the needs of others. It is also less likely when the children's signals are difficult to interpret—in cases where children, for example, have disabilities that make it difficult for them to communicate, or have received very little stimulation from birth. Parents also find it difficult to respond sensitively to children who are defiant, aggressive or hard to manage.[83]

Preparing children for life beyond the family

In addition to providing resources for children and protecting them from risks, families socialise children, teaching them cultural values and acceptable ways of behaving. Families transmit cultural values, often through everyday practices. In urban middle-class Anglo-Australian families, for example, it is acceptable for children to argue that they should not have to clean up all the mess if another child helped to create it. By contrast, such negotiation is not acceptable in comparable Chinese families.[84] Through this kind of everyday parental request to clean up at home, and from the negotiation that sometimes follows, children learn about cultural values and their relative importance.

Another important aspect of families as a context for children is the degree of fit between families and other contexts in which the child participates. Families can be seen as training grounds for children's participation in the wider society. In families, for example, children learn about relationships with others, the importance of literacy and education, and ways to work or avoid work. There are, however, important differences between the 'social contract' in the home and that in other settings such as the workplace. Whereas contexts outside the home often operate on an exchange model—a model of reciprocal obligations and rewards—relationships at home are generally assumed to operate under a more communal model, where the contribution of each family member is seen to benefit the family as a whole, and reciprocity, at least in the short term, is not a central expectation.[85]

Families as contexts for children

In summary, families may differ greatly in their structure and functioning but they are central contexts in the lives of children, offering them support and protection and preparing them for life beyond the family. The ability of families to perform these roles is determined by their resources: human, financial and social. Even in the most advantaged families, however, support and assistance are needed from outside the family for coping with the stresses of family life and child rearing. Families cannot be seen as standing alone in children's lives. They are tied to other social systems and institutions such as schools, and to their local communities. These issues are explored in the following chapters.

STUDENT EXERCISES

1   If current demographic trends continue, especially in terms of smaller numbers of children born in Australia, what do you see as the consequences in the future for children, their families and communities?

2   Discuss the impact of the birth of a first baby on families. What are the features of the family itself that may impact on their adaptation to this life event? What are the contextual influences beyond the immediate family that might affect the impact of this event on family members?

3 Do you think that the intrusion of society into the home by way of electronic media such as television, internet access and computer games is potentially harmful to children's development? In what ways do you think it could affect children and their parents? Is it the responsibility of parents to restrict and monitor children's use of these media, especially within the family, or should this be a responsibility of society?

4 Much of children's learning about aspects of the world, relationships and behaviour occurs in the context of the family. Discuss the nature of what children learn from family life and how that learning can transfer, appropriately or inappropriately, to other contexts such as child care, school and work.

Notes

1   L. McKie & S. Cunningham-Burley, eds, *Families and Relationships: Families in Society, Boundaries and Relationships*, Policy Press, Bristol, 2005.

2   B. Hunter & M. Gray, 'Family and Social Factors Underlying the Labour Force Status of Indigenous Australians', *Family Matters*, 62, 2002, pp. 18–25.

3   L. Tolstoy, *Anna Karenina*, trans. A. & L. Maude, Penguin Books, Harmondsworth, 1954, p. 3.

4   D.H. Olson, 'Circumplex Model of Marital and Family Systems: Assessing Family Functioning', in *Normal Family Processes*, ed., F. Walsh, The Guilford Press, New York, 1993.

5   M.A. Mason, 'The Modern American Stepfamily: Problems and Possibilities', in *Family in Transition* (14th edn), eds, A. Skolnick & J. Solnick, 2007, pp. 201–23.

6   A. Franks, *Indigenous Services in the Northern Rivers Region of NSW*, NSW Health, Sydney, 2001.

7   For an account of early models and a suggested alternative, see D.T. Rowland, 'Family Diversity and the Life Cycle', *Journal of Comparative Family Studies*, 12, 1991, pp. 1–14.

8   T.A. Laszloffy, 'Rethinking Family Development Theory: Teaching with the Systemic Family Development (SFD) Model', *Family Relations*, 51, 2002, pp. 206–14.

9   Laszloffy, 2002.

10   E.M. Cummings & P. Davies, *Children and Marital Conflict: The Impact of Family Dispute and Resolution*, The Guilford Press, New York, 1994.

11   R. Dunlop, 'Family Processes: Towards a Theoretical Framework', in *Images of Australian Families*, ed., K. Funder, Longman Cheshire, Melbourne, 1991, pp. 122–35.

12   D. Edgar, 'Globalization and Western Bias in Family Sociology', in *The Blackwell Companion to the Sociology of Families*, eds, J. Scott, J. Treas & M. Richards, Blackwell Publishing, Maldon, MA, 2004, pp. 3–16.

13   Australian Bureau of Statistics, *Population Characteristics: People Living in Institutions*, catalogue no. 4102.0, Australian Government Publishing Service, Canberra, 2003b, <www.abs.gov.au/AUSSTATS/abs@.nsf/7d12b0f6763c78caca257061001cc588/9c1dc93dd9a137daca2570eb0082e463!OpenDocument>, accessed 5 February 2008.

14   Australian Bureau of Statistics, *Year Book Australia, 2006*, catalogue no; 3101.0, Australian Government Publishing Service, Canberra, 2007a, <www.abs.gov.au/ausstats/abs@.nsf/Previousproducts/1301.0Feature%20Article92006?opendocument&tabname=Summary&prodno=1301.0&issue=2006&num=&view=>, accessed 5 February 2008.

15   There are now only 10 per cent of families who fit this stereotype. See Australian Bureau of Statistics, *Australian Social Trends, 2007*, catalogue no. 4102.0, Australian Government Publishing Service, Canberra, 2007b, <www.abs.gov.au/ausstats/abs@.nsf/mf/4102.0?OpenDocument>, accessed 4 February 2008.

16   Australian Bureau of Statistics, 2006, *Census Quickstats: Australia*, Australian Government Publishing Service, 2007c, <www.censusdata.abs.gov.au/ABSNavigation/prenav/ViewData?subaction=1&producttype=QuickStats&areacode=0&action=401&collection=Census&textversion=false&breadcrumb=PL&period=2006&javascript=true&navmapdisplayed=true&>, accessed 4 February 2008.

17   Australian Bureau of Statistics, 2007c.

18 R. Burr & H. Montgomery, 'Family, Kinship and Beyond', in *Childhoods in Context*, eds, J. Maybin and M. Woodhead, Wiley/Open University Press, Chichester, UK, 2003, pp. 39–80.

19 Australian Bureau of Statistics, *Family, Household and Income Unit Variables*, catalogue no. 1286, Australian Government Publishing Service, Canberra, 2005.

20 Australian Bureau of Statistics, 2007b.

21 Australian Bureau of Statistics, 2007c.

22 Australian Bureau of Statistics, *Population Distribution: Aboriginal and Torres Strait Islander Australians*, catalogue no. 4705, Australian Government Publishing Service, Canberra, 2007d.

23 R. W. Edwards & R. Madden, *The Health and Welfare of Australia's Aboriginal and Torres Strait Islander Peoples 2001*, catalogue no. 4704.0, ABS, Canberra, 2001.

24 R. Stuart, 'Ideology Drove Intervention', *The Australian*, 11 December 2007, p. 2.

25 J. Atkinson, *Trauma Trails Recreating Song Lines: The Transgenerational Effects of Trauma in Indigenous Australia*, Spinifex Press, North Melbourne, 2002.

26 D. Higgins, *Early Learnings: Indigenous Community Development Projects*, vol. 2, Telstra Foundation Research Report, Australian Institute of Family Studies, Melbourne, 2005.

27 NSW Aboriginal Education Consultative Group and New South Wales Department of Education and Training, *The Report of the Review of Aboriginal Education*, NSW Department of Education and Training, Darlinghurst, 2004.

28 J. Watson, 'Determined to be Self-Determined', paper presented at the Frozen Futures Conference, Sydney, November 2002.

29 Board of Enquiry into the Protection of Aboriginal Children from Sexual Abuse, *Little Children Are Sacred*, Northern Territory Government, Darwin, 2007.

30 Edwards & Madden, 2001.

31 J. Micklewright, *Child Poverty in English-Speaking Countries: Innocenti Working*, Paper no. 94, UNICEF Innocenti Research Centre, Florence, 2003.

32 An average of 1.81 children was born to each woman of child-bearing age in 2006. Australian Bureau of Statistics, *Births Australia 2006*, catalogue no. 3301, Australian Government Publishing Service, Canberra, 2007e.

33 Senate Community Affairs References Committee, *A Hand Up Not a Hand Out: Renewing the Fight against Poverty*, Report on Poverty and Financial Hardship, Senate Printing Unit, Parliament House, Canberra, 2004.

34 Commonwealth Department of Education, Science and Training, *Higher Education: Report for 2003 to 2005 Triennium*, Australian Government Publishing Service, Canberra, 2003.

35 Australian Bureau of Statistics, *Australian Social Trends, 2007: Lifetime Marriage and Divorce Trends*, catalogue no. 4102.0, Australian Government Publishing Service, Canberra, 2007f, <www.abs.gov.au/AUSSTATS/abs@.nsf/Latestproducts/26D94B4C9A4769E6CA25732C00207644?opendocument>, accessed 5 February 2008.

36 Australian Bureau of Statistics, 2007f.

37 Australian Bureau of Statistics, *Australian Social Trends 2003*, catalogue no. 4102.0, Australian Government Publishing Service, Canberra, 2003c, <www.abs.gov.au/AUSSTATS/abs@.nsf/46d1bc47ac9d0c7bca256c470025ff87/12a1c7480a30c138ca256d39001bc331!OpenDocument>, accessed 19 March 2008.

38 Australian Bureau of Statistics, *Marriages and Divorces, Australia, 2002*, catalogue no. 3310.0, Australian Government Publishing Service, Canberra, 2003d, <www.abs.gov.au/AUSSTATS/abs@.nsf/ProductsbyCatalogue/893C1288678FD232CA2568A90013939C?OpenDocument>, accessed 5 February 2008. See also D. de Vaus, L. Qu & R. Weston, 'Changing Patterns of Partnering', *Family Matters*, 64, 2003, pp. 10–15.

39 Australian Bureau of Statistics, 2003c.

40 In 2003, 59 per cent of children aged fifteen years or under had both parents in paid employment, compared with 51 per cent in 1993 (with increasing numbers of families where only the mother is employed from 2.8 to 3.3 per cent and decreasing numbers of families where only the father is employed from 36 per cent to 32 per cent). Australian Bureau of Statistics, *Trends in Women's Employment 2006*, catalogue no. 4201.0, Australian Government Publishing Service, Canberra, 2007g.

41 The labour force has also been restructured, with an increase in the number of people who are working part-time rather than full-time. Over the past twenty years the number of men working full-time hours has decreased from 94 per cent to 85 per cent and for women it has decreased from 63 per cent to 54 per cent. Australian Bureau of Statistics, *Australian Social Trends, 2006: Trends in Hours Worked 2006*, catalogue no. 4102.0, Australian Government Publishing Service, 2007h.

42   Australian Bureau of Statistics, *Special Article: Casual Employment*, Australian Government Publishing Service, Canberra, 2002a.

43   Australian Bureau of Statistics, 2007h.

44   J. Buchanan & L. Thornwaite, 'Paid Work and Parenting: Charting a New Course for Australian Families', report prepared for the Chifley Foundation, University of Sydney, Sydney, 2001; L. Strazdins, R.J. Korda, L.L.-Y. Lim, D.H. Broom, R.M. D'Souza, 'Around-the-clock: Parent Non-standard Work Times and Children's Wellbeing in a 24-hour Economy', *Journal of Mariage and Family*, 68, 2, 2006, pp. 394–410; R. Weston, L. Qu & G. Soriano, 'Implications of Men's Extended Work Hours', *Family Matters*, 61, 2002, pp. 18–25.

45   Buchanan & Thornwaite, 2001.

46   K. Hand & V. Lewis, 'Fathers' Views on Family Life and Paid Work', *Family Matters*, 61, 2002, pp. 26–9.

47   J. Earle, 'Family-friendly Workplaces: A Tale of Two Sectors', *Family Matters*, 61, 2002, pp. 12–17.

48   B. Rogoff, *The Cultural Nature of Human Development*, Oxford University Press, New York, 2003; S. Harkness & C. Super, eds, *Parents' Cultural Belief Systems*, The Guilford Press, New York, 1996.

49   D. Baumrind, 'Child Care Practices Anteceding Three Patterns of Preschool Behavior', *Genetic Psychology Monographs no. 75*, 1967, pp. 43–88; D. Baumrind, 'Current Patterns of Parental Authority', *Developmental Psychology Monograph*, Part 2, 4, 1, 1971, pp. 1–103.

50   L.K. Mekertichian & J.M. Bowes, 'Does Parenting Matter?: The Challenge of the Behaviour Geneticists', *Journal of Family Studies*, 2, 1996, pp. 131–45.

51   Royal Children's Hospital, *Parenting Young Children*, Policy Brief no. 9, Centre for Community Child Health, Royal Children's Hospital, Melbourne, 2007.

52   M.E. Lamb, 'Fathers and Child Development: An Introductory Overview and Guide', in *The Role of the Father in Child Development*, ed., M.E. Lamb, John Wiley & Sons, New York, 1997, pp. 1–18; L. Craig, *Caring Differently: A Time Use Analysis of the Type and Social Context of Child Care Performed by Fathers and Mothers*, Discussion Paper no. 116, Social Policy Research Centre, University of New South Wales, Sydney, 2002.

53   D. Paquette, 'Theorizing the Father-Child Relationship: Mechanisms and Developmental Outcomes', *Human Development*, 47, 2004, pp. 193–219.

54   Lamb, 1997.

55   Lamb, 1997; R.D. Parke, 'Fathers and Families', in *Handbook of Parenting*, vol. 3, ed., M.H. Bornstein, Lawrence Erlbaum, Mahwah, NJ, 1995.

56   H. Bee, *The Developing Child*, Harper Collins, New York, 1992.

57   J. Shonkoff & D. Phillips, *From Neurons to Neighbourhoods: The Science of Early Childhood Development*, National Academy Press, Washington, 2000, p. 27.

58   K. Deater-Deckard & J. Dunn, 'Multiple Risks and Adjustments of Young Children Growing Up in Different Family Settings', in *Coping with Divorce, Single Parenthood and Remarriage: A Risk and Resiliency Perspective*, ed., E.M. Hetherington, Lawrence Erlbaum, Mahwah, NJ, 1999, pp. 47–64.

59   U. Bronfenbrenner, 'Principles for the Healthy Growth and Development of Children', in *Marriage and Family in a Changing Society*, ed., J.M. Henslin, The Free Press, New York, 1989, pp. 235–41.

60   I. La Valle, S. Arthur, C. Millward, J. Scott & M. Clayden, *Happy Families?: Atypical Work and Its Influence on Family Life*, The Policy Press, Bristol, UK, 2002.

61   L. Craig, *How Do They Do It?: A Time-diary Analysis of How Working Mothers Find Time for the Kids*, Social Policy Research Centre, UNSW, Sydney, 2005; Australian Institute of Family Studies, *A Snapshot of How Australian Families Spend Their Time*, AIFS, Canberra, 2007, <www.aifs.gov.au/institute/pubs/snapshots/familytime.html>, accessed 9 January 2008.

62   Australian Institute of Family Studies, 2007.

63   J. Bowes, 'Emphasizing the Family in Work–Family Research: A Review of Current Research and Recommendations for Future Directions', in *Work and Family: An International Perspective*, ed., S.A.Y. Poelmans, Lawrence Erlbaum Associates, Mahwah, NJ, 2005, pp. 415–38.

64   J. Baxter, M. Gray, M. Alexander, L. Strazdins & M. Bittman, *Mothers and Fathers with Young Children: Paid Employment, Caring and Well-being*, Department of Families, Community Services and Indigenous Affairs, Canberra, 2007.

65   E.S. Peisner-Feinberg, M.R. Burchinal, R.M. Clifford, M.L. Culkin, C. Howes, S.L. Kagan & N. Yazejian, 'The Relation of Preschool Child-Care Quality to Children's Cognitive and Social Developmental Trajectories through Second Grade', *Child Development*, 72, 2001, pp. 1534–53.

66   J. Dunn, *The Beginnings of Social Understanding*, Harvard University Press, Cambridge, MA, 1988; C. Herrara & J. Dunn, 'Early Experiences with Family Conflict: Implications for Arguments with a Close Friend', *Developmental Psychology*, 33, 5, 1997, pp. 869–81.

67 Only 2 per cent of Australian households in 2001 contained extended family members. See D. de Vaus, *Diversity and Change in Australian Families: Statistical Profiles*, Australian Institute of Family Studies, Melbourne, 2004.

68 C. Millward, 'Intergenerational Family Support', *Family Matters*, 39, 1994, pp. 10–13.

69 P.K. Smith & L.M. Drew, 'Grandparenthood', in *Handbook on Parenting: Becoming a Parent*, vol. 3, ed., M.H. Bornstein, Lawrence Erlbaum, Mahwah, NJ, 2002, pp. 141–73.

70 V.L. Bengston, 'Beyond the Nuclear Family: The Increasing Importance of Multigenerational Bonds', *Journal of Marriage and the Family*, 63, 2001, pp. 1–16; J. Goodfellow, 'Grandparents as Regular Child Care Providers: Unrecognised, Under-valued and Under-resourced', *Australian Journal of Early Childhood*, 28, 2003, pp. 7–17; J. Laverty, *The Experience of Grandparents Providing Regular Child Care for their Grandchildren*, unpublished MEd (Hons) thesis, University of Western Sydney, Sydney, 2003.

71 Australian Institute of Health and Welfare, *Australia's Welfare*, AIHW catalogue no. AUS 65, Australian Institute of Health and Welfare, Canberra, 2005a.

72 Australian Institute of Health and Welfare, 2005a.

73 Australian Bureau of Statistics, *Family Characteristics, Australia, 2003*, catalogue no. 4442.0, Australian Government Publishing Service, Canberra, 2004a.

74 D. de Vaus & I. Wolcott, *Australian Family Profiles: Social and Demographic Patterns*, Australian Institute of Family Studies, Melbourne, 1997.

75 C. Flanagan, 'Families and Schools in Hard Times', in *New Directions for Child Development*, no. 46, eds, V.C. McLoyd & C.A. Flanagan, Jossey-Bass, San Francisco, 1990, pp. 7–26.

76 J.M. Bowes & J.J. Goodnow, 'Work for Home, School or Labor Force: The Nature and Sources of Children's Understanding', *Psychological Bulletin*, 119, 1996, pp. 300–21; Flanagan, 1990.

77 P.A. Amato, 'More than Money?: Men's Contributions to their Children's Lives', in *Men in Families*, eds, A. Booth & A.C. Crouter, Lawrence Erlbaum, Mahwah, NJ, 1998, pp. 241–78.

78 M. Radke-Yarrow, J. Richters & W.E. Wilson, 'Child Development in a Network of Relationships', in *Relationships within Families: Mutual Influences*, eds, R.A. Hinde & J. Stevenson-Hinde, Clarendon, Oxford, 1988, p. 56.

79 J. Brooks-Gunn, 'Children in Families in Communities: Risk and Intervention in the Bronfenbrenner Tradition', in *Examining Lives in Context*, eds, P. Moen, G.H. Elder Jr & K. Lüscher, American Psychological Association, Washington, DC, 1995, pp. 467–519.

80 Radke-Yarrow, Richters & Wilson, 1988, p. 63.

81 P.T. Davies, G.T. Harold, M.C. Goeke-Morey & E.M. Cummings, 'Child Emotional Security and Interparental Conflict', *Monographs of the Society for Research in Child Development*, Serial no. 270, 67, 3, 2002.

82 S. Meadows, *Parenting Behaviour and Children's Cognitive Development*, Psychology Press, Hove, 1996.

83 K.E. Barnard & L.K. Martell, 'Mothering', in *Handbook of Parenting*, vol. 3, ed., M.H. Bornstein, Lawrence Erlbaum, Mahwah, NJ, 1995, pp. 3–26.

84 J.M. Bowes, M-J. Chen, Q.S. Li & Y. Li, 'Reasoning and Negotiation about Child Responsibility in Urban Chinese Families: Reports from Mothers, Fathers and Children', *International Journal of Behavioral Development*, 28, 2004, pp. 48–58.

85 J.J. Goodnow, 'Differentiating Among Social Contexts: By Spatial Features, Forms of Participation, and Social Contracts', in *Examining Lives in Context*, eds, P. Moen, G.H. Elder Jr & K. Lüscher, American Psychological Association, Washington, DC, 1995b, pp. 269–301.

7

From Home to the World Beyond: The Interconnections among Family, Care and Educational Contexts

Cathrine Neilsen-Hewett and Pamela Coutts

The historical changes in families, as described in Chapter 6, have clear consequences for children, families and communities. This chapter explores the links between families and the contexts beyond them, focusing particularly on child care and, to a lesser extent, school. This brings into relief some of the processes that socialise children for life in the wider community. It illustrates the ways in which contexts are interconnected, and demonstrates how specific developmental consequences for children depend on the combination of their individual characteristics and the experiences they have at home and in the wider context of child care and school. The quality of experiences in each context is seen as the key determinant of developmental outcomes.

This chapter examines the following:

- the contemporary context of child care
- the influence of culture, beliefs and values on care and educational settings
- some of the sources of variation, such as child and family characteristics, social class, ethnicity and system differences
- the evidence of differential effects on children's development of group size, quality and duration of time in care and, particularly related to school, the effect of culture on academic achievement.

Contexts

The context of contemporary Australian child care

In contemporary Australia, men and women are frequently faced with the challenge of having to balance both family and paid work. Today, more than half (57.1 per cent) of all couple families with children under fifteen years have both parents in paid employment.[1] Further, the proportion of women who are employed has increased dramatically in recent years, with 70 per cent of those aged twenty-five to thirty-four now being employed outside the home. This has meant an increased demand for child care. Many families have unmet needs for child care,[2] and workplaces vary in the extent to which they accommodate the family responsibilities of their employees.[3] Taken together, these changes have direct implications for children, their families and the communities in which they live.

Over 1.5 million Australian children under twelve years of age, or almost half of their age group, experience some type of formal or informal child care. Twenty-five per cent of children under the age of three years use formal care arrangements and this increases to 73 per cent when children are aged four years.[4] Approximately one-third of children use informal care arrangements[5] and a significant proportion of families make child care arrangements that involve a mixture of formal and informal child care.[6] For many families with both parents in the workforce, non-parental care is their only option; child care is not a luxury but a necessity. As such, child care has multiple roles and functions. It serves care and educational needs, as well as the economy of families and the wider society, and enables opportunities for equal employment of women.[7] The prevalence of child care, in some form, has led Silverstein[8] to suggest that the key focus of concern should not be on the possible adverse effects of child care, but rather on the consequences of not providing children with quality care.

The most striking characteristic of existing child care provisions is its diversity. 'In Australia, the provision of early childhood education cuts across a number of jurisdictional boundaries. As a result there are variations in the way early childhood education is defined and in the types of settings that are considered to offer early childhood education.'[9] Child care takes a variety of forms, from informal care provided by family members, friends and neighbours to formal long day care, after-school care and occasional care. Irrespective of the type of care, child care experiences need to be seen in the context of those available in the home. Experiences across the two types of context—home and care—may complement each other,[10] or one may compensate for the lack of particular experiences in the other.[11] The degree of responsiveness to the needs of individual children is an essential aspect of the different care contexts.[12]

The outcomes of child care are related to the quality of care received, and how care settings link with the other contexts in which children develop.[13] The diversity of services to choose from means that children's care experiences vary markedly in terms of content and quality. High-quality care can enhance socio-emotional functioning, cognitive abilities and school performance.[14]

The importance of context

Three phases of child care research have been identified.[15] The first wave was characterised by simple contrasts between children reared at home and children enrolled in centre-based care. It had a strong focus on social-emotional development using attachment theory to frame the questions asked and the measures employed. In the second wave, the research focus shifted to identification of specific features of care environments that were related to the different developmental outcomes for children. More recently, a third wave has taken into account the impact of wider social influences on children's experiences in child care, and the influences of child and family characteristics on developmental outcomes. The research in this wave has sought to evaluate children's experiences within their social, economic and political context.

Progressively, child care research has moved beyond a narrow definition of the influences of particular types of care on children. The focus has turned increasingly to the interplay of program processes, staff experiences, family experiences and child characteristics. Of particular importance are the quality of the child care environment, the characteristics of children and families, and the social context in which child care programs operate.

Child characteristics, family factors and child care

Children's experiences at home and in the child care setting are related. Cumulatively and independently, they influence children's development. As such, development is multiply determined: by characteristics of the child, such as temperament, age, neurological integrity and impairment; by environmental factors, such as quality of relationships and interactions with parents and siblings and peers, and quality of non-parental care; and by factors in the child's larger social environment, including the immediate neighbourhood, social policy and the broader culture. These factors operate in a complex and integrated fashion to influence children's development.

Individual characteristics of children such as temperament and gender need to be considered in understanding the effects of non-parental care. Research by Watamura and colleagues[16] has suggested that not all children are similarly affected by the amount of time spent in non-parental care. The authors examined the cortisol levels of infants and toddlers enrolled in full-day centre-based child care as an indicator of child stress. They found that teacher ratings of children's social fearfulness were associated with larger cortisol increases over the day for those children. Watamura and colleagues suggested that infants and toddlers who are more temperamentally fearful show greater stress responses to full-time centre-based care and as such may find the child care environment particularly challenging. Differences in vulnerability to the child care environment have also emerged between boys and girls. The NICHD study[17] reported that among children who experienced more than thirty hours per week in non-parental care, boys were more likely than girls to be insecurely attached at age fifteen months. Age of entry may also shape child outcomes with recent research showing extensive group care in the first year of life may increase antisocial behaviour among children; similar patterns have not been detected for children entering centre-based care from two years of age.[18]

Findings from the study conducted by Watamura and his colleagues draw our attention towards the role of peers in shaping children's day care experience. Centre-based care, in particular, brings children into contact with many same-age peers and provides opportunities for interaction and play, which may otherwise be absent for children from the smaller families that are characteristic of Australia today. The importance of other children for children's social, emotional and cognitive development has been clearly underscored in research on children's peer relationships,[19] yet researchers have failed to account sufficiently for the role of peers in understanding the effects of child care.

Developmental outcomes of care also reflect the interrelationships among children's home environments, their individual differences and non–parental care. Richters and Zahn-Waxler[20] suggested that family background factors directly affect outcomes. In examining the relationship between children's attachment security, child care and home experiences, Howes and colleagues[21] found that the social behaviour of toddlers reflected their experiences both at home and in the child care setting. Toddlers with insecure attachments to their mothers and caregivers demonstrated the least ability to engage in interactions with caregivers while in care. Children with insecure attachments to their mothers but secure attachments to caregivers exhibited more socially competent behaviours than those children who were deprived of secure relationships in both settings.

Further, Ahnert and Lamb[22] found mothers of German children enrolled in child care compensated for the time away from their children by increasing the intensity and regularity in which they interacted with their children at home. The amount of attention children received was comparable to what they would have received had they not been in centre-based care. Similar results have been found in Australian research on mothers working full-time.[23] Research findings from the Competent Children Project[24] found that early child care services and home resources play complementary roles with regard to children's competency levels.

Experience in early childhood education appears to nourish children's social, communicative and problem-solving competencies in particular, while family resources may be important for children's cognitive competencies as well as their social skills. Home activities that were educational were also associated with higher levels of cognitive competencies.[25]

In the NICHD study,[26] similar associations were found between family, economic and psychological factors and child care experiences. Economic factors were most consistently associated with the amount and nature of non-parental care.

Recent research by Sylva and colleagues[27] in the United Kingdom showed family socio-demographic background (education, occupation and income level) and maternal beliefs to be the most consistent predictors of the amount and type of non-parental care infants received. Disadvantaged families were more likely to start infants in care with a family member rather than in centre-based care. Beliefs about the consequences of child care were related to the type and amount of care used; mothers who believed their employment benefited their child and had fewer negative consequences for them were more likely to choose centre-based care and to use it for more hours.

Child care occurs in the context of family circumstances and events as well as beyond them.[28] Each context affects the other and can only be understood in relation to the other. Previous approaches to understanding child care outcomes have underestimated the complexity of developmental processes. Children are not only influenced by their social and physical environments, but they also shape them.[29] Issues related to quality of care, amount of care, attachment security, and socio-emotional, linguistic and cognitive development can be more clearly understood within an ecological model of child care.

The importance of quality of care

The quality of care has been viewed as an important variable influencing children's development, particularly in the case of economically disadvantaged children attending high-quality programs.[30]

In linking quality care to child outcomes it is necessary to consider what constitutes quality of care and how this can be measured. The quality of non-parental care is a multidimensional construct[31] encompassing the physical environment, social policy, educational curriculum, staff training, child–staff ratios, group sizes and interpersonal relations.[32] Measurement typically involves global measures of program features (for example, ratings of program environmental features) and measures of dynamic processes (for example, caregivers' interactions with children). Proper assessment of care quality involves both specifying the goals of care and understanding the specific indicators of quality. In examining the quality of the child care experience, researchers have focused on structural and philosophical characteristics of early child care as well as on the quality of programs.

The National Day Care Study (NDCS)[33] proposed that the debate on child care quality focus on three variables: group size, caregiver-to-child ratio and caregiver quali-fications. Findings from the study suggested that, of the three, group size had the most consistent and pervasive effects on teacher and child behaviour and on later cognitive performance. In this study, caregiver-to-child ratio had less effect on pre-schoolers' functioning than on that of 'toddlers' and infants. Higher caregiver-to-child ratios were associated with less distress in infants and toddlers. Better caregiver qualifications were associated with more social interaction between caregivers and children, with more cooperation and task persistence among children, and with increased involvement of children in activities. While much of the subsequent research has focused primarily on these three features, a number of additional structural characteristics have been considered, including staff turnover, caregiver stability, programming, health and safety provisions, and available space and equipment.

High-quality care has been associated with short- and long-term cognitive, social and emotional benefits for children's development. A study conducted by Helburn and colleagues[34] found that children in higher-quality settings exhibited more advanced language development and pre-maths skills, displayed more advanced social skills, were more positive towards their child care experiences and had warmer relationships with their teachers. In examining the relationship between child care quality and social development, Phillips, McCartney and Scarr[35] found that children from better-quality programs were more sociable, more considerate, less anxious and more task oriented than children who were exposed to lower-quality care. Similar links have emerged from the NICHD study, where high-quality care, increases in the quality of care and experience in centre-type arrangements were associated with better pre-academic skills and language abilities in four-year-olds.[36]

Cathrine Neilsen-Hewett & Pamela Coutts

ARE THE EFFECTS OF CHILD CARE QUALITY SHORT-LIVED OR DO THEY HAVE LONGER-TERM IMPLICATIONS FOR CHILDREN'S DEVELOPMENT?

While some researchers contend the effects of child care are largely short-lived and do not extend beyond the pre-school or early school years,[37] others suggest the effects are more lasting, extending well into the later primary years.[38] Recent findings from the NICHD study show that better-quality care continues to be linked to enhanced performance on standardised tests of maths, memory at age eight years, and vocabulary skills at age eight and twelve years, while more time spent in care is associated with lowered social competence and more behavioural problems at age eight and twelve years, and poorer academic work habits at age eight.[39]

Similar long-term links have been noted in the EPPE study that compared pre-school aged children from six types of providers and a home sample on a range of school performance measures. Children who attended higher-quality pre-school settings performed better in maths and reading in kindergarten and again in Year 5 (age eleven), while the children who attended poorer-quality centres showed no cognitive benefits in Year 5 and did not differ in any way from the children who did not attend pre-school.[40] Interestingly, early social and behavioural differences that emerged between the pre-school and home groups were no longer significant at Year 2 (age seven) except for the children who attended high-quality care. This pattern of findings suggests that the impact of child care is more long-lasting with respect to intellectual development, while long-term social developmental outcomes may continue to be shaped by experiences with school-age peers or variations in classroom climate.[41]

AMOUNT OF TIME IN CARE

Along with the quality of care, the amount of time children spend in non-parental care has emerged as an important predictor of adjustment outcomes among children. Findings from a body of research suggest that a history of extensive and continuous non-parental care is associated with poorer socio-emotional outcomes.[42] Amount of time in care has also been linked with poorer mother–infant interactions. Evidence from the NICHD study[43] showed that more time in care was associated with less sensitive mothering and less harmonious mother–infant interactions at six, fifteen, twenty-four and thirty-six months. The ongoing study has shown that time spent in child care through the first four-and-a-half years of life was important in predicting children's social competence. More hours in child care were associated with more behaviour problems in pre-school and kindergarten, lower levels of social competence and more conflict with teachers. This relationship held after controlling for variations in family background factors, maternal sensitivity and child care quality. While some evidence pointed to more hours during infancy predicting later maladjustment, other findings suggested that it was the amount of care experienced in the third and fourth years that best predicted poor outcomes for children.

Several studies, however, have found that quality and type of care are factors that are as important, or more so, in predicting outcomes for children than time spent in care. Crockenberg[44] concluded that: 'given that most of the variance in child behaviour that is associated with amount of care is shared with quality and type of care, it appears that negative effects occur primarily when children spend long hours in poor quality, centre-based care'.[45] Findings from the Sydney Family Development Project support this contention, finding no significant correlation between quantity of care and behaviour problems, attachment, school social adjustment, and teacher–child conflict,[46] with quality of care emerging as the most important predictor of child outcomes. Love and colleagues[47] have argued that child care research needs to be interpreted in its cultural context. In countries such as Australia, where quality of centre-based care is monitored through an accreditation system, time in care is less likely to have the detrimental effects found in research in the USA, where quality of child care is more variable.

Congruence between home and care setting

Child care and family characteristics are linked. A problem in examining quality care in isolation from the influences of other contexts is the possibility that group differences do not result solely from the quality of the child care experiences, but reflect the complex interplay of child care, familial and individual differences in the child. More recently researchers have focused on variations in both the quality of non-parental care and the child's home environment and family circumstances.[48] Notably, children from advantaged families as well as those from impoverished families in the USA are more likely to experience centre-based care as well as higher-quality care, reflecting the widespread availability of Early Headstart for poor families.[49]

Researchers adopting a more ecological approach to understanding the effects of child care have begun to examine the quality of care that children receive at home (for example, in the NICHD and Thomas Coram Child Care projects). In examining the protective role of child care for children from disadvantaged backgrounds, Caughy, DiPietro and Strobino[50] found heightened reading and mathematical ability in children from low-income homes who entered care earlier and/or had more years in care. In contrast, children whose home environments promoted cognitive development and socialisation actually had lower scores if they had been cared for outside their homes. These results are echoed in recent publications emerging from the EPPE longitudinal study of pre-school education in the United Kingdom, where for disadvantaged groups, high-quality childcare promotes development and reduces the influence of social class and poverty on entry to school.[51] Further, the quality of the home environment coupled with parental educational levels were important factors relating to both mathematical and reading ability at school entry and Year 5. These findings underscore the complex relationship between the individual child, the environment and the processes of development.

Cathrine Neilsen-Hewett & Pamela Coutts

Consequences

Key outcomes of exposure to child care

ATTACHMENT SECURITY

As discussed earlier, initial research examining the outcomes of child care focused on the potential negative effects on mother–child relationships and children's socialisation, reflecting concerns that young children might not fare as well emotionally in large groups as they do in the more intimate surroundings of their homes.[52] Initial evaluations of early child care programs were greatly influenced by the debate about attachment, with researchers claiming that extensive non-maternal care in infancy was associated with an insecure attachment to the significant adults in children's lives.[53] A key assumption of attachment theory is that early social experiences, particularly the mother–infant relationship, play a key role in later development.[54] In a review examining early research on the effects of non-maternal care on children's attachment and development, Belsky and Steinberg[55] concluded that children were not harmed by the child care experience, and that children's relationships with their mothers were not in jeopardy. While this review represented a 'change in perspective', it was criticised on methodological grounds, in that many of the studies examined only high-quality centres and did not consider other important variables such as family background.[56]

The NICHD study[57] indicates that the effects of child care on attachment depend on the complex interplay of the characteristics of the child care setting, the duration of exposure, the gender of the child and the child's prior relationships outside the context of child care. In a later report, associations between child care and attachment were reported to occur under conditions of insensitive mothering.[58] The results showed that less sensitive mothering in combination with long hours per week in care increased the risk of children being classified as insecurely attached to their mothers. The authors argued that more hours in care served as an additional risk factor for children already experiencing poor mother–child interactions.

SOCIO-EMOTIONAL DEVELOPMENT

There have been mixed results from research into the short- and long-term effects of early child care experiences on children's social and emotional development. Measures of children's socio-emotional development have involved conflict resolution,[59] interactions with peers,[60] social self-perceptions and self-concept,[61] teacher–child relationships,[62] sociometric status[63] and externalising behaviours such as child hostility.[64]

A recent review of findings emerging from the NICHD study[65] suggests that both quality and quantity of care as well as the type of care children are exposed to make distinct and independent contributions to children's socio-emotional development, both in child care and the school setting. Data collected from children, classmates, teachers and mothers provide multiple perspectives on children's socio-emotional adjustment.

Loan Receipt
Liverpool John Moores University
Library and Student Support

Borrower ID: 21111119737120

Loan Date: 07/12/2009

Loan Time: 12:51 pm

Children, families & communities :
31111012927479

Due Date: 15/01/2010 23:59

Please keep your receipt
in case of dispute

Children who spent more time in quality care were seen to be more prosocial and displayed fewer negative behaviours in interactions with peers. Additionally, children who spent more time in care (irrespective of the type) were rated by caregivers as displaying more problem behaviours at thirty-six and fifty-four months through to sixth grade,[66] and more teacher–child conflict at fifty-four months as well as more negative interactions with friends at that age.

In examining the long-term impact of care on child outcomes it is essential that researchers consider and control for the significant link between family and child characteristics,[67] to ensure that behavioural outcomes are not a result of concurrent family factors. Hagekull and Bohlin[68] assessed the effects of child care quality on children's socio-emotional development with reference to child and family characteristics. Quality of child care was systematically related to children's socio-emotional behaviours both concurrently and over time, with those exposed to high-quality care showing more positive emotions at home, independent of family and child characteristics. In a study of the social competencies of New Zealand children, Wylie and colleagues[69] showed that family income and the mother's educational qualifications were the strongest predictors of children's social adjustment. Children from lower socio-economic groups had lower scores on measures of social skills and social interaction with peers. Again it is clear that, in evaluating children's socio-emotional adjustment, it is important for researchers to include variables related to both the family and non-parental care settings.

COGNITIVE AND LANGUAGE DEVELOPMENT

A number of studies have assessed the short- and long-term effects of exposure to child care on cognitive and language development and have found small but detectable gains in children's academic performance,[70] from infancy through to the high school years.[71]

Social class is an important variable in understanding the findings for cognitive and language development of children in care. Studies of at-risk and economically disadvantaged samples in high-quality care interventions show heightened cognitive performance in children exposed to early childhood education compared with children who did not have this experience.[72] In examining the protective role of day care participation for the cognitive development of low-income children, Caughy, DiPietro and Strobino[73] found day care participation during the first three years of life to be positively related to subsequent development of mathematical and reading skills. For mathematics, centre-based care in particular exerted a strong protective influence over the developmental effects of an impoverished environment.[74] These findings demonstrate the compensatory role that child care can play in children's cognitive development.

The relationship between duration of care and measures of academic achievement was examined in a thirteen-year longitudinal study conducted by Fergusson, Horwood and Lynskey in New Zealand.[75] The researchers found that high levels of exposure (two to three years) to early education were associated with small improvements in school achievement at thirteen years. This occurred even when confounding factors were controlled for, factors such as parental education, socio-economic status, position in family, child ethnicity, infant feeding methods, early mother–child interactions and child's birth weight.

Cathrine Neilsen-Hewett & Pamela Coutts

The ongoing Gotenburg Child Care Study[76] has shown that while the type of early child care experienced was important in predicting German children's cognitive performance at the age of eight, measures of cognitive abilities taken at forty months were the best predictors of later development. This study highlights the importance of adopting an ecological model in understanding children's development. Characteristics of children and their child care settings were related to later cognitive performance. Children who spent more months in centre-based care before they were forty months showed higher cognitive ability than children who started later and/or spent less time in care. The quality of non-parental care was predictive of verbal abilities in later years.

From home and care to school

Children usually begin their formal schooling by joining a same-age coeducational classroom of approximately twenty children, with a female teacher. The trend towards the feminisation of the Australian teaching profession is continuing, according to recent Australian Bureau of Statistics figures. In 2006, only 29.8 per cent of all teaching staff in Australia were male, compared to 33.6 per cent a decade ago, with the decline more pronounced in the government sector (a decrease of 4.7 per cent over this time period, including a reduction in the absolute numbers of male teaching staff).[77] Many students complete primary school with little, if any, direct experience of male teachers, given that four out of five primary teachers are female, and in the company of a set of classmates with whom they have been placed for the previous six years of schooling. This stability of the peer group is not, however, consistent across the sector, with some areas of disadvantage in New South Wales, for example, having an annual student mobility rate in excess of 25 per cent.[78] At a school level, a constant change in the student population makes it difficult for staff to perform the welfare function society increasingly expects of them. At a student level, this dislocation of schooling and lack of continuity is yet another contributing factor to potential disadvantage, and in terms of the focus of this chapter, adds to the likelihood of increased peer difficulties.

Secondary school presents many students with major challenges. Most change schools between the primary and secondary years, since there remain relatively few middle (grades 5–8) or kindergarten-to-grade-12 schools across Australia, although numbers are increasing.[79] In addition, many children change from the public to the non-government sector at this point. Regardless of school type, students are likely to join a larger school community, experience a variety of teachers each year, mix with a different group of peers according to each subject, and have a choice (albeit a limited one) of subject options. Moreover, the emphasis in the secondary system across Australia remains on an academic, competitive curriculum, and much of the focus, especially in the latter years of schooling, is directed towards performance in the final credentialling examination. Most schools at the beginning of the twenty-first century also continue to emphasise the importance of attendance, punctuality, conformity to uniform and routines. As Preston and Symes[80] have argued, these features encourage socialisation to the work ethic. In these respects school organisations, structures and bureaucracy have altered little since the 1970s.

Such a picture makes it easy to underestimate the diversity of experiences available across the educational sector. A number of factors make for increasing diversity of experience in current Australian schools. Not the least of these is the impact of technology, to be discussed shortly, but structural features are also important. For example, not all children enter same-age classrooms. Across Australia there are many one- and two-teacher schools, especially in remote rural areas. In such circumstances the structural parallels between the school setting and an extended family are far closer than in a primary school of 800 age-stratified students, and the transition from home to school is presumably a less daunting one.

Schools also vary according to whether they are in a government secular system or set up by a private group or organisation to follow a particular charter, based on religious or philosophical beliefs. Cutting across all these variations is the extent to which schools are linked to their immediate community or neighbourhood. An interesting example is in the Northern Territory, where Aboriginal community schools provide a curriculum designed by the local community and taught in the local language. The differences in experience between children in such settings and those taught in a large urban school, following a centrally prescribed curriculum, are marked.

There is also great diversity in the ethnic mix of classrooms, with some schools, particularly in certain areas of large cities, having a majority of students from recent-migrant, non-English-speaking backgrounds, whereas others in more established or country areas tend to have a higher proportion of children from Anglo-Australian backgrounds.

The greatest diversity in the educational system, however, is exhibited in the more subjective features of school and schooling and in the values held about schooling. The following section examines some of the variations in school culture across the Australian educational system, and the sources of these variations.

Culture, beliefs and values

From the point of view of critical theorists, no school curriculum is value-neutral as all knowledge is socially constructed. It is not surprising, therefore, that there are systematic differences across settings in terms of beliefs and values held. Some of these are a result of school types, others a consequence of family characteristics. The most obvious difference is between government and non-government school systems. By definition, government schools are secular and do not see any part of their role as transmitting or encouraging values and beliefs that are linked to particular religious viewpoints. Rather, they emphasise general values encapsulated in relevant state or Commonwealth policies. This restriction does not hold for schools in the private sector. As a consequence, for example, children in some fundamentalist Christian private schools have restricted student access to technology and the internet and teach a version of science—creationist 'science'—that is consistent with the religious views of those schools but is disputed by the majority of science researchers. In this case the values are to do with the primacy of certain forms of information (here, a literal interpretation of the Scriptures) rather than so-called scientific evidence.

Cathrine Neilsen-Hewett & Pamela Coutts

As is the case for child care, the factors most commonly considered to influence values about schooling are family characteristics such as socio-economic status (SES), gender and ethnicity. The evidence has been largely indirect and comes from a research base that has considered the link between family backgrounds and school success in terms of educational outcomes. Traditionally, a deficit model has been used whereby certain 'inadequacies' in family backgrounds (for example, low socio-economic status) have been linked to lower educational benchmarks such as school completion rates, university entry and performance on achievement measures. Governments have attempted to compensate for these factors by providing greater resources for certain schools and certain groups, for example, through initiatives such as the Disadvantaged Schools Program. Such models target 'at-risk' groups rather than individuals, assuming that the general societal factors are the principal determinants of success or failure.

In contrast, reproduction theorists argue that school success relates to the extent to which the beliefs, values and overall culture of the school correspond with those of the students.[81] In this viewpoint the notion of cultural capital, or the extent to which the contexts of child development ultimately enrich the whole culture of a society, plays a key role.

INTERCONNECTIONS BETWEEN FAMILIES AND SCHOOLS

The most direct and obvious link between a school and its community is through its parent body. During the 1970s, when it was commonly argued that the role of schools should be as an agent for social change, the emphasis was on a school-based curriculum. The argument was that children would be best served by curricula that reflected the needs of the local community. It was subsequently argued that such an approach advantaged those middle-class children from families of high social capital whose values most closely matched those of their teachers. Nevertheless, the movement foundered for far more pragmatic reasons, namely the recognition by teachers that to create school-based programs within staffing constraints verged on the impossible.

The shift more recently has been to centrally based curriculum structures, but the emphasis on links with parents has changed to an emphasis on their participation. In New South Wales, for example, schools are expected to have school councils with parent representation. It is widely accepted that parent participation is a good indicator not only of parental interest but of how directly parents assist the learning and development of their children. A publication by the Australian Parents Council espouses this viewpoint, arguing that 'parent participation has the potential to break a cycle of failure and set in motion a cycle of success'.[82]

This viewpoint seems consistent with the 'reproduction' view of education but appears to overlook several features of Australia's multicultural society. Within Australia, parental participation varies according to class and ethnicity. In contrast, teachers are predominantly from Anglo-Australian middle-class backgrounds. As Duchesne's research suggests (see case study below) there may be more than one successful developmental path in a multicultural society, and we should be cautious about interpreting parental actions without some understanding of their underlying beliefs and values.

PARENTAL PARTICIPATION IN SCHOOLS

A teacher notices that not all parents of her Grade 1 students appear equally involved with the school community and rarely attend school functions and programs. Indeed, there were many parents whom she had never met. Should she be concerned about the lack of parental participation?

Research reported in the doctoral thesis of Duchesne[83] strongly suggests that teachers should be very cautious about interpreting patterns of parental involvement according to their own value systems. In her case study Duchesne found that, while teachers thought the Vietnamese parents were less committed to their children's schooling because they did not participate in school-based activities as most Anglo-Australian families did, their children did well at school. Duchesne argued that this was largely a consequence of a congruence between the values held about the importance of education and the practices within the families, rather than a lack of interest in the schooling process. Vietnamese parents viewed education as providing the opportunity to change their children's lives and so encouraged them at every step. In contrast, while many of the Anglo-Australian parents participated as teachers expected them to, it was as often in an effort to monitor the school and express discontent as to actively assist in their children's learning.

POLICY INFLUENCES

One recent change in society's perceptions of the role of schools has had great impact. The rhetoric of the market economy is now used by policy makers and parents alike. Education is seen by many as a commodity, not a right. The emphasis is on schools performing a 'value-adding' function, and of being accountable to their 'customers'. This philosophic shift has implications for the ways that schools are seen as settings for the development of young children.

To take a simple example: since 1989 there has been deregulation of the 'zoning' system for New South Wales government schools. In effect this means that parents are not required to send their children to the local government school but can approach any school that has room and staff available. Parents now 'shop around' for the school they feel best suits the needs of their child. In principle this freedom of choice and the resultant accountability are admirable, but they may have unintended implications for the education of young children. If, for example, families take the opportunity for their children to attend a school near the parents' workplace rather than near their home, and especially if after-school care is located at the school, children have limited opportunities to establish friendship networks based on their neighbourhoods. There is a discontinuity and isolation between school and home communities. For young children in particular, friendships are established from the neighbourhood and from the circle of children with whom they are in close contact. Out-of-area schooling, particularly for children who are too young to use public transport without supervision and so are reliant on parents for their travel, means that the parents increasingly act as

Cathrine Neilsen-Hewett & Pamela Coutts

gatekeepers for the children's access to age mates. Given that Garbarino[84] considers that both schools and neighbourhoods have the potential to provide a supportive community to foster resilience, we may be unwittingly reducing the possible support networks for our children.

TECHNOLOGICAL CHANGE AND ITS CONSEQUENCES

The most obvious change facing education is to do with technology. Technology is causing us to rethink some of the traditional ways of teaching, learning and communicating. School websites are commonplace, with many schools using the internet as the prime method of communication with parents and the broader school community. Within the classroom, technology is moving from a role that supports traditional instruction to one that affords opportunities to change classroom pedagogies. Interactive whiteboard technology provides the clearest example, especially with its use in primary schools. Educational systems across Australia are investing, or have invested, vast resources into new technologies in the belief that student engagement and learning outcomes will be improved.[85] We may finally have reached the point where the classrooms of the next generation may be different to those of their parents.

But the implications go beyond this. Technology causes us to reconsider our definition of what it means to be educated and literate in the twenty-first century. Who is more literate: the fifty-year-old who can read and discuss a complex novel but avoids and cannot take advantage of information technology, or the fifteen-year-old who uses the internet for assignments, has an avatar in a virtual world, communicates hourly with friends using digital technologies, creates and accesses blogs and wikis but has never read a complete book and is poor at text-based comprehension and writing? Technology is also causing a redefinition of what it means to interact socially. For many adolescents in particular, Facebook, MySpace, YouTube and similar social and communication networks are replacing much face-to-face interaction. It is unlikely that we will ever return to a society where such digitally based communication is not central to the lives of young people.

The question that is most relevant to the present chapter is the extent to which these technologies, and the opportunities and threats they bring, will alter the traditional relationships between parents, teachers and children and between peers. They have the possibility of redefining class differences, not so much in terms of traditional socio-economic measures but in terms of access to and knowledge of technology. In rural and remote areas of Australia, for example, technology, especially the internet, has come some way to redressing traditional disadvantage in terms of resourcing. The proviso is there must be reliable and fast broadband access at both home and school in addition to classroom teachers who are proficient in technology use. These conditions are not always in place throughout Australia at present.

Technology also has the capacity to help us redefine the school community, and parent involvement reconceptualised within that community. Schooling acting *in loco parentis* has always played an important role in supporting and encouraging the social aspects of children's development. The challenge of the increasing role played by technology is to ensure that the interpersonal support so necessary for resilience in children is not diminished, and that school settings remain a positive context for development, whether as a physical or a virtual presence.

STUDENT EXERCISES

1 Reflect on your own transition to child care or to primary school. What were the factors that determined your experience of this change of context?

2 Another major transition is from primary to secondary school. In what respects are the same issues important? What additional factors impact on a student's experience of this change of context?

3 Briefly describe some of the programs in your local area that are designed to assist children to make the transition to school.

4 Which factors are particularly important in determining the degree of match between the home and care contexts?

5 In what ways might the cultural backgrounds of children influence their experience of child care or school?

6 Choose one of the pre-school, primary or secondary sectors. In what ways will the increasing dependence on technologies change the traditional relationships between parents and children or teachers and students?

Notes

1   Australian Bureau of Statistics, *Australian Social Trends*, catalogue no. 4102, Australian Government Publishing Service, Canberra, 2003.

2   J. Baxter, M. Gray, M. Alexander, L. Strazdins & M. Bittman, 'Mothers and Fathers with Young Children: Paid Employment, Caring and Well Being', Social Policy Research Paper no. 30, Department of Families, Community Services and Indigenous Affairs, Canberra, 2007.

3   C. Kilmartin, 'Working Mothers Throughout the Decade', *Family Matters*, 26, 1990, p. 49; G. Russell, 'Sharing the Pleasures and Pain of Family Life', *Family Matters*, 37, 1994, pp. 13–19.

4   Australian Bureau of Statistics, 2003c.

5   Australian Bureau of Statistics, 2003c.

6   J. Bowes, S. Wise, L. Harrison, A. Sanson, J. Ungerer, J. Watson & T. Simpson, 'Continuity of Care in the Early Years?: Multiple and Changeable Childcare in Australia', *Family Matters*, 64, 2003, pp. 30–5.

7   M. Sims & T. Hutchins, 'The Many Faces of Child Care: Roles and Functions', *Australian Journal of Early Childhood*, 21, 1996, pp. 21–46.

8   I. Silverstein, 'Transforming the Debate About Child Care and Maternal Employment', *American Psychologist*, 46, 1991, pp. 1025–32.

9   A. Rice & F. Press, *Early Childhood Education in New South Wales: A Comparative Report*, report for the NSW Department of Education and Training commissioned by the Strategic Research Directorate, Sydney, 2003.

10   K. Deater-Deckard, R. Pinkerton & S. Scarr, 'Child Care Quality and Children's Behavioral Adjustment: A Four-year Longitudinal Study', *Journal of Child Psychology and Psychiatry*, 37, 1996, pp. 937–48.

11   H. McGurk, M. Caplan, E. Hennessy & P. Moss, 'Controversy, Theory and Social Context in Contemporary Child Care Research', *Journal of Child Psychology and Psychiatry*, 34, 1993, pp. 3–23; L.J. Schweinhart & D.P. Weikart, 'A Summary of Significant Benefits: The High/ Scope Perry Pre-School Study Through Age 27', in *Start Right: The Importance of Early Learning*, ed., C. Ball, Royal Society for the Encouragement of Arts, Manufacture & Commerce, London, 1994, pp. 97–102.

Cathrine Neilsen-Hewett & Pamela Coutts

12 S. Scarr, *Mother Care/Other Care*, Basic Books, New York, 1984; S. Scarr & M. Eisenberg, 'Child Care Research: Issues, Perspectives, and Results', *Annual Review of Psychology*, 44, 1993, pp. 613–44.

13 National Institute of Child Health and Human Development Early Child Care Research Network, 'Characteristics of Infant Childcare: Factors Contributing to Positive Caregiving', *Early Childhood Research Quarterly*, 11, 1996, pp. 267–306.

14 National Institute of Child Health and Human Development (NICHD) Early Child Care Research Network, 'Child-care Structure Process Outcome: Direct and Indirect Effects of Child Care Quality on Young Children's Development', *Psychological Science*, 13, 2002a, pp. 199–206; J. Belsky, D. Lowe Vandell, M. Burchinal, K.A. Clarke-Stewart, K. McCartney & M. Tresch Owen & NICHD Early Child Care Research Network, 'Are there Long-term Effects of Early Child Care?', *Child Development*, 78, 2007, pp. 681–701.

15 J. Belsky, 'Two Waves of Day-care Research: Developmental Effects and Conditions of Quality', in *The Child and Day-care Setting*, ed., R. Ainslie, Praeger, New York, 1984, pp. 1–34; J. Belsky, 'Parental and Nonparental Child Care and Children's Socioemotional Development: A Decade in Review', *Journal of Marriage and the Family*, 52, 1990, pp. 885–903.

16 S.E. Watamura, B. Donzella, J. Alwin & M.R. Gunnar, 'Morning-to-Afternoon Increases in Cortisol Concentrations for Infants and Toddlers at Child Care: Age Differences and Behavioural Correlates', *Child Development*, 74, 2003, pp. 1006–20.

17 National Institute of Child Health and Human Development Early Child Care Research Network, 'The Effects of Infant Child Care on Infant-Mother Attachment Security', *Child Development*, 68, 1997, pp. 860–79.

18 K. Sylva, E.C. Melhuish, P. Sammons, I. Siraj-Blatchford & B. Taggart, *The Effective Provision of Pre-School Education (EPPE) Project: Final Report*, London: DfES/Institute of Education, University of London, 2004.

19 C. Howes, 'The Earliest Friendships', in *The Company They Keep*, eds, W.M. Bukowski, A.F. Newcomb & W.W. Hartup, Cambridge University Press, New York, 1996, pp. 66–86; G. Ladd, 'Peer Relationships and Social Competence During Early and Middle Childhood', *Annual Review of Psychology*, 50, 1999, pp. 333–59; C.M. Neilsen-Hewett, *Children's Peer Relations and School Adjustment: Looking Beyond the Classroom Walls*, unpublished PhD thesis, Institute of Early Childhood, Macquarie University, Sydney, 2001.

20 J.E. Richters & C. Zahn-Waxler, 'The Infant Day Care Controversy: Current Status and Future Directions', *Early Childhood Research Quarterly*, 3, 1988, pp. 319–36.

21 C. Howes, C. Rodning, D.C. Galluzzo & L. Myers, 'Attachment and Child Care: Relationships with Mother and Caregiver', *Early Childhood Research Quarterly*, 3, 1988, pp. 403–16.

22 L. Ahnert & M.E. Lamb, 'Shared Care: Establishing a Balance Between Home and Child Care Settings', *Child Development*, 74, 2003, pp. 1044–9.

23 M. Bittman, S. Hoffman & D. Thompson, 'Men's Uptake of Family-Friendly Employment Provisions', Social Policy Research Centre, University of New South Wales, Sydney, 2002.

24 C. Wylie, J. Thompson & A.K. Hendricks, *Competent Children at 5: Families and Early Education*, NZCER, Wellington, 1997.

25 Wylie et al., 1997, p. xiii.

26 National Institute of Child Health and Human Development Early Child Care Research Network, 'Child Care and Child Development: The NICHD Study of Early Child Care', in *Developmental Follow-up: Concepts, Domains and Methods*, eds, S.L. Friedman & H.C. Haywood, Academic Press, San Diego, CA, 1994, pp. 377–96.

27 K. Sylva, A. Stein, P. Leach, J. Barnes, L.-E. Malmberg & FCCC Team, 'Family and Child Factors Related to the Use of Non-maternal Infant Care: An English Study', *Early Childhood Research Quarterly*, 22, 2007, pp. 118–36.

28 National Institute of Child Health and Human Development Early Child Care Research Network, 1994.

29 C.D. Hayes, J.L. Palmer & M.J. Zaslow, *Who Cares for America's Children?: Child Care Policy for the 1990's*, National Academy Press, Washington, DC, 1990.

30 F.A. Campbell, E.P. Pungello, S. Miller-Johnson, M.R. Burchinal & C. Ramey, 'The Development of Cognitive and Academic Abilities: Growth Curves from an Early Intervention Educational Experiment', *Developmental Psychology*, 37, 2001, pp. 231–42.

31 B. Hagekull & G. Bohlin, 'Child Care Quality, Family and Child Characteristics and Socioemotional Development', *Early Childhood Research Quarterly*, 10, 1995, pp. 505–26.

32 Belsky et al., 2007; Sylva et al., 2004.

33   R. Ruopp, J. Travers, F. Glantz & C. Coelen, *Children at the Centre: Final Report of the National Day Care Study*, Abt Associates, Cambridge, MA, 1979.

34   S. Helburn, ed., *Cost, Quality and Child Outcomes in Child Care Centers*, University of Colorado, Denver, CO, 1995.

35   D.A. Phillips, K. McCartney & S. Scarr, 'Child Care Quality and Children's Social Development', *Developmental Psychology*, 23, 1987, pp. 537–43.

36   National Institute of Child Health and Human Development Early Child Care Research Network, 'Early Child Care and Children's Development Prior to School Entry: Results from the NICHD Study of Early Child Care', *American Educational Research Journal*, 39, 2002b, pp. 367–87.

37   M. Colwell, G. Petit, D. Meece, J.E. Bates & K.A. Dodge, 'Cumulative Risk and Continuity in Nonparental Care from Infancy to Early Adolescence', *Merrill-Palmer Quarterly*, 47, 2001, pp. 207–34.

38   Belsky et al., 2007.

39   Belsky et al., 2007; NICHD Early Child Care Research Network, 'Early Child Care and Children's Development in the Primary Grades: Results from the NICHD Study of Early Child Care', *American Educational Research Journal*, 43, 2005b, pp. 537–70.

40   P. Sammons, K. Sylva, E.C. Melhuish, I. Siraj-Blatchford, B. Taggart & Y. Grabbe, *The Effective Provision of Pre-School and Primary Education 3-11 Project (EPPE 3-11): Influences on Children's Attainment and Progress in Key Stage 2: Cognitive Outcomes in Year 5, Full Report*, London: DfES/ Institute of Education, University of London, 2007, <www.ioe.ac.uk/schools/ecpe/eppe/eppe3-11/eppe3-11%20pdfs/eppepapers/Tier%202%20full%20report%20-%20Final.pdf>, accessed 24 March 2008.

41   Sylva et al., 2004.

42   J. Belsky, 'Developmental Risks (still) Associated with Early Child Care', *Journal of Child Psychology and Psychiatry*, 42, 2001, pp. 845–59; National Institute of Child Health and Human Development, 2003.

43   National Institute of Child Health and Human Development Early Child Care Research Network, 'Childcare and Mother–child Interaction in the First 3 Years of Life', *Developmental Psychology*, 35, 1999, pp. 1399–413.

44   S.C. Crockenberg, 'Rescuing the Baby from the Bathwater: How Gender and Temperament (may) Influence how Child Care Affects Child Development', *Child Development*, 74, 2003, pp. 1034–8.

45   Crockenberg, 2003, p. 1034.

46   L.J. Harrison & J.A. Ungerer, 'The Sydney Family Development Project: Family and Child Care Predictors at Age Six', paper presented at the symposium on Longitudinal Studies of Early Childhood in Australia, Australian Association for Research in Education Conference, Brisbane, December 2002; J.M. Love, L. Harrison, A. Sagi-Schwartz, M.H. van Ijzendoorn, C. Ross, J.A. Ungerer, H. Raikes, C. Brady-Smith, K. Boller, J. Brooks-Gunn, J. Constantine, E.E. Kisker, D. Paulsell & R. Chazan-Cohen, 'Child Care Quality Matters: How Conclusions May Vary with Context', *Child Development*, 74, 2003, pp. 1021–33.

47   Love et al., 2003.

48   NICHD Early Child Care Research Network, 'Families Matter—Even for Kids in Child Care', *Journal of Developmental and Behavioural Pediatrics*, 24, 2003, pp. 58–62.

49   NICHD Early Child Care Research Network, 'Child Care Effect Sizes for the NICHD Study of Early Child Care and Youth Development', *American Psychologist*, 61, 2006, pp. 99–116.

50   M.O. Caughy, J. DiPietro & M. Strobino, 'Day-care Participation as a Protective Factor in the Cognitive Development of Low-income Children', *Child Development*, 65, 1994, pp. 457–71.

51   Sammons et al., 2007.

52   W.S. Barnett, 'Long-term Effects of Early Childhood Programs on Cognitive and School Outcomes', *The Future of Children*, 5, 1995, pp. 25–50; D.S. Gomby, M.B. Larner, C.S. Stevenson, E.M. Lewitt & R.E. Behrman, 'Long-term Outcomes of Early Childhood Programs: Analysis and Recommendations', *The Future of Children*, 5, 1995, pp. 6–24.

53   J. Bowlby, *Maternal Care and Mental Health*, World Health Organization, London, 1951; M. Rutter, *Maternal Deprivation Re-assessed*, Penguin, New York, 1981.

54   G. Ochiltree, *Effects of Child Care on Young Children: Forty Years of Research*, AIFS Early Childhood Study, paper no. 5, Australian Institute of Family Studies, Melbourne, 1994.

55   J. Belsky & L. Steinberg, 'The Effects of Day Care: A Critical Review', *Child Development*, 49, 1978, pp. 929–49.

56   D. Phillips & C. Howes, 'Indicators of Quality in Child Care: Review of Research', in *Quality in Child Care: What Does Research Tell Us?*, ed., D. Phillips, National Association for the Education of Young Children, Washington, DC, 1987, pp. 1–19.

57   National Institute of Child Health and Human Development, 1996; National Institute of Child Health and Human Development Early Child Care Research Network, 1997.

58   National Institute of Child Health and Human Development Early Child Care Research Network, 'Child Care and Child Development, Childcare and Family Predictors of Preschool Attachment and Stability from Infancy', *Developmental Psychology*, 37, 2001, pp. 847–62.

59   D.L. Vandell, V.K. Henderson & K. Wilson, 'A Longitudinal Study of Children with Child Care Experiences of Varying Quality', *Child Development*, 59, 1988, pp. 1286–92.

60   Helburn, 1995; C. Howes, 'Relations Between Early Child Care and Schooling', *Developmental Psychology*, 24, 1988, pp. 53–7; National Institute of Child Health and Human Development, 1994; Wylie et al., 1997; National Institute of Child Health and Human Development, 2003.

61   Helburn, 1995; NICHD Study, 1994 (see note 31); M. Whitebrook, C. Howes & D. Phillips, *Who Cares? Child Care Teachers and the Quality of Care in America*, final report of the National Child Care Staffing Study, Child Care Employee Project, Oaklands, CA, 1990.

62   Helburn, 1995; National Institute of Child Health and Human Development, 2003; NICHD, 'Early Child Care and Children's Development Prior to School Entry: Results from the NICHD Study of Early Child Care', *American Educational Research Journal*, 39, 2002, pp. 133–64.

63   M. Lerner, L. Gunnarsson, M. Cochran & S. Haggund, 'The Peer Relations of Children Reared in Child Care Centres or Home Settings: A Longitudinal Analysis', paper presented to the Biennial Meeting of the Society for Research in Child Development, Kansas City, MO, 1989.

64   Howes, 1990.

65   NICHD Early Child Care Research Network, 2006.

66   Belsky et al., 2007; NICHD, 2006.

67   Belsky et al., 2007.

68   B. Hagekull & G. Bohlin, 'Quality of Care and Problem Behaviors in Early Childhood', paper presented at the Biennial Meeting of the Society for Research in Child Development, New Orleans, LA, 1993; B. Hagekull & G. Bohlin, 'Child Care Quality, Family and Child Characteristics and Socioemotional Development', *Early Childhood Research Quarterly*, 10, 1995, pp. 505–26.

69   Wylie et al., 1997.

70   For example, Belsky et al., 2007.

71   For example, B. Andersson, 'Effects of Day-care on Cognitive and Socioemotional Competence of Thirteen-year-old Swedish School Children', *Child Development*, 63, 1992, pp. 20–36; National Institute of Child Health and Human Development, 2003.

72   J.R. Berrueta-Clement, L.J. Schweinhart, W.S. Barnett, A.S. Epstein & D.P. Weikart, *Changed Lives: The Effects of the Perry Preschool Program on Youths through Age 19*, Monograph 8, High/Scope Press, Ypsilanti, Michigan, 1984.

73   Caughy, DiPietro & Strobino, 1994.

74   Caughy, DiPietro & Strobino, 1994, p. 466.

75   D.M. Fergusson, L.J. Horwood & M.T. Lynskey, 'A Longitudinal Study of Early Childhood Education and Subsequent Academic Achievement', *Australian Psychologist*, July 1994, pp. 110–15.

76   A.G. Broberg, H. Wessels, M.E. Lamb & C.P. Hwang, 'Effects of Child Care on the Development of Cognitive Abilities in 8-year-olds: A Longitudinal Study', *Developmental Psychology*, 33, 1997, pp. 62–9.

77   Australian Bureau of Statistics, *Schools, Australia*, 2006, catalogue no. 4221.0, Australian Government Publishing Service, Canberra, 2006, <www.ausstats.abs.gov.au/ausstats/subscriber.nsf/0/9DDA83611950C66FCA25728B000CFC92/$File/42210_2006.pdf>, accessed 5 February 2008.

78   T. Vinson, *Reports of the Inquiry into the Provision of Public Education in New South Wales*, NSW Teachers Federation and Federation of P & C Associations of NSW, Sydney, 2002, p. 22.

79   ABS, Schools Australia, 2006.

80   N. Preston & C. Symes, *Schools and Classrooms: A Cultural Studies Analysis of Education*, Longman, Melbourne, 1997.

81   See, for example, P. McLaren, *Life in Schools*, White Plains, NY, 1989.

82   Australian Parents Council, *Children's Learning: The Parent Factor*, Australian Government Publishing Service, Canberra, 1996, p. 31.

83   S. Duchesne, *Parental Beliefs and Behaviours in Relation to Schooling*, unpublished PhD thesis, School of Education, Macquarie University, Sydney, 1996.

84   J. Garbarino, *Raising Children in a Socially Toxic Environment*, Jossey-Bass, San Francisco, 1995.

85   A. Davies, 'Classroom Revolution As Schools Connected to the World', *Sydney Morning Herald*, 17 March 2007, <www.smh.com.au/news/schools/classroom-revolution-as-schools-connected-to-world/2007/03/16/1173722745511.html>, accessed 31 January 2008.

8

Isolation in Rural, Remote and Urban Communities

Maureen Fegan and Jennifer Bowes

In this chapter we consider the role of communities in the support of families and children. To illustrate the importance of community influences, we discuss the benefits of well-functioning and adequate community links, then highlight difficulties encountered by families who are cut off from their communities, or who live in communities that are themselves isolated. We examine links between families and communities, discuss the impact of social change on the extent and form of isolation, and consider what it can mean for children and families to be excluded from community support. We conclude by identifying strategies and examples of innovative, ongoing and effective service models that have been used successfully in the Australian context to combat the negative effects of isolation. The first task, however, is to clarify how we are using the term 'community'.

Contexts

What is a community?

'Community' has been a widely discussed term in recent years and has been interpreted in multiple ways.[1] Definitions vary in terms of emphasis but most refer to non-familial social ties among a group of people with common perspectives or interests.[2]

The rise of virtual communities challenges definitions of 'community' that refer only to physical or geographical boundaries. Rheingold defined virtual communities as 'social aggregations that emerge from the Net when enough people carry on those public discussions long enough, with sufficient human feeling, to form webs of personal relationships in cyberspace'.[3] Several writers have suggested that Information and Communication Technology (ICT) is changing not only the nature and physical range of communities[4] but also the ways people interact within communities.[5]

However they are sustained, all communities have a common purpose of mutual support and all function to build 'social capital',[6] a concept that will be explored in the next section of the chapter. In brief, social capital is built on social networks, and when people are part of social networks they are more involved in community life, they provide more informal care for others, do more volunteer work and are more active in all kinds of social organisations.[7]

People's perceptions of their community also matter. We return to a recurring theme in the book that a crucial component of context is 'in the eye of the beholder'. If families perceive their local area as a community of which they are a part, despite distance from neighbours or lack of facilities, then they will behave as if it is a community. This perception will lead to behaviour that has benefits for the families and children within it. Parents and children will also be more likely to believe that they have something to contribute to the community themselves.

If, on the other hand, individuals or families believe that they are isolated from their community, even if they do have a network of family and friends, they will behave in ways that reflect their perceptions of isolation. They will be disadvantaged in relation to other families by not making use of the resources that communities can provide.

How can communities support families and children?

Communities provide families and children with infrastructure and the social links that have been referred to as social capital. Community investment in children enables neighbourhoods to bring direct benefits to their lives through provision of a variety of contexts such as children's services, schools, playgrounds, libraries, cinemas and theatres, community groups and venues where peer groups can play or gather safely. Access to wider societal contexts through transport or communication links may also be offered.

Affluent neighbourhoods can offer more of these resources to families and children. These resources, along with more positive parental behaviours and greater community regulation, have been found to influence the higher verbal skills, intelligence scores and school achievement found in more affluent neighbourhoods in Canada and the USA.[8] Research on a social policy initiative, Moving to Opportunity, in which families were assisted to move residence to higher-income areas in several cities in the USA, showed that changing neighbourhoods had large beneficial effects for the physical and mental health of children and for school achievement, especially in boys.[9] In contrast, research from the USA and the United Kingdom has found families in lower-income neighbourhoods are more likely than families in higher-income areas to have more mental health problems (in children), more criminal and delinquent behaviour and earlier and riskier sexual behaviour and child bearing (in adolescents)[10] as well as greater risks for future poverty and unemployment.[11]

Although less difference has been found in incomes between neighbourhoods in Australia than in the USA or Canada, an increasing differentiation between neighbourhoods in all three countries is evident over a thirty-year period.[12] In Australia, Vinson[13] has found that a small number of postcode areas show significant multiple indicators of disadvantage, similar to those found in much of the neighbourhood research from the USA, Canada and the United Kingdom. However, the conclusion of a recent review of the literature on social exclusion among Australia's children concluded that neighbourhood effects are less important than individual and family factors in determining disadvantage.[14] This point has been acknowledged by other researchers who, nevertheless, note that living in a low-income neighbourhood has a significant and additional effect.[15]

In terms of the less tangible social links through which communities confer benefits on families and children, the idea of social capital is a useful one. There is an increasing recognition that accounts of Australia's wealth and well-being need to include assessment of our 'social capital' as well as our 'economic capital'. 'Social capital refers to the processes between people which establish networks, norms and social trust and facilitate coordination and cooperation for mutual benefit'.[16] As part of his social capital theory, Coleman[17] has outlined several dimensions of community resources. Communities high in social capital, according to Coleman, had the following characteristics: relationships that were dense and complex, information networks that were seen as accessible and helpful, relatively clear-cut norms and sanctions about parental and child behaviour, perceived opportunities for advancement (for example, good schools, job opportunities, the chance to be a valued community member) and perceptions of stability of residence in the area. There is considerable research evidence that a strong network of social ties is associated with good physical and mental health, and isolation with poor health outcomes.[18]

Research on neighbourhood effects on children's development has led to the suggestion of a 'norms and collective efficacy' model to explain how neighbourhoods have their effect on children. The model suggests that neighbourhood influences depend upon the extent to which communities have 'mechanisms for social control in formal and informal social organisations that monitor residents' behaviour with the goal of maintaining public order'.[19] This involves the willingness of residents to intervene on behalf of children, which in turn depends on mutual trust rather than mistrust or fear of others in the neighbourhood.

Following a meta-analysis of forty studies of neighbourhood effects, Sampson, Morenoff and Gannon-Rowley suggested four possible mechanisms for neighbourhood effects: social ties/interaction (social capital), norms and collective efficacy, institutional resources such as libraries, schools, child care, medical facilities and employment opportunities, and routine activities or social activity patterns that affect children's well-being.[20] An example of the latter is the location of schools. If children are able to walk safely to school, for example, this can have many benefits for their health and enjoyment of life (see also Chapter 5).

When families are isolated from the community, the benefits of community resources, social supports and sanctions are less readily available to them. The next section of the chapter will examine the forms that isolation can take and some of the effects of isolation on families and children.

Maureen Fegan & Jennifer Bowes

Rethinking isolation

The first point to make is that isolation is not the same as solitude. Being alone, braving the elements, functioning independently, enjoying solitary endeavours and demonstrating resilience can all be positive experiences for individuals and for families. Certainly such attributes characterise many of the positive aspects of life in urban, rural and remote Australia. Kingwill noted the positive as well as negative aspects of solitude when she wrote: 'It is difficult to capture the richness of some forms of "isolation" or the despair of others'.[21]

Our concern in this chapter, however, is with those families, and the children within those families, who suffer as a result of their isolation.

FORMS OF ISOLATION

While geographic or physical isolation is perhaps the most easily recognised form in Australia, isolation has many causes, and children and families experience it in different ways. They may be isolated because they live in very remote areas, in valleys or mountains with difficult access or where there are particularly harsh climatic conditions, such as dust, floods or snow. They may be cut off from their local neighbourhood by a six-lane highway, or they may be isolated because of poor health, disability or special needs. They can be culturally isolated because they speak a different language, or have different-coloured skin or different traditions from the families around them. They may be 'the newcomer' in an established neighbourhood, or the last of a town's 'original' inhabitants. They may be isolated through lack of money to buy food or clothing, to reciprocate hospitality, to pay for a school uniform or to provide a child's birthday party.[22] They may be housebound due to illness, loss of a child or partner, frailty or disability,[23] or their isolation may be due to lack of paid employment, long working hours, shiftwork, juggling a number of part-time or casual jobs, or multiple family responsibilities. Alternatively, families and children can be isolated due to lack of education, telephone, internet access or transport.

For many Indigenous Australians, isolation from traditional lands and forced family separation have meant isolation from cultural and individual identity, with intergenerational effects on health and social breakdown.[24] During times of war or other international conflict, some families may become socially isolated because of their ethnicity or because their religious customs are seen as suspicious.

Sometimes communities make informed choices to deliberately embrace selected types of isolation from mainstream values and customs. Examples include gated communities, alcohol-free or 'dry' communities and communities grounded in common ethnic, religious or sexual identity. Yet this does not necessarily protect them from suffering the negative effects of isolation from other mainstream benefits such as reduced access to health services, schooling or social standing and respect.

Even in the most densely populated cities, people who live in close physical proximity to one another can still suffer from a lack of connection with their neighbours or with other community networks. Many families experience more than one form of isolation, often simultaneously, and this compounds their risk of suffering negative outcomes. One-parent families, for example, can be isolated within their families (no partner to assist with child rearing) as well as from connections to the community. As numbers of one-parent families increase in Australia, particularly in regional areas, this source of isolation for families is of particular concern.[25]

SOCIAL CHANGE AND ISOLATION

Several writers have voiced concern that society is changing in ways that make it increasingly difficult for people to establish or to maintain social links, even in the same local community. As Pocock has written of Australia: 'A generation ago, community was frequently locality and street based, with the extended family at its core. While this form of community has not disappeared, our research amongst women with domestic and caring responsibilities suggests that our streets are increasingly dormitories to a growing number of women and men who work'.[26]

In Australia, another factor is the high mobility of families within and between states.[27] Frequent moves have been shown to have a negative impact on children's school achievement and recent studies of highly mobile families in Australia have started to consider how schooling might need to change to accommodate these children's needs.[28]

Another factor affecting community links is the high cost and insufficient availability of housing that has led to an increase in the number of families living in apparent segregation from the wider community, in concentrations of public housing or in mobile homes within caravan parks. In addition, the numbers of people who are homeless continue to rise with a trend to homeless families, particularly teenage girls with babies.[29] Options for the homeless are limited and bleak: to move between the houses of relatives or friends, to live in cars, to sleep rough or, as is happening increasingly in Australia, to use the refuges for homeless people that used to mainly house homeless men.[30] These individuals and families, often cut off from the support of their extended families, live on the fringes of society, unable to make the social ties that are available to established families in a neighbourhood.

Within the wider society of Australia at present, there is disturbing evidence of a growing economic and social divide between rich and poor. Many Australians are living below the poverty line and being 'left behind despite a period of sustained economic growth'.[31] Vinson has highlighted areas within our largest cities with high concentrations of poverty, unemployment, violence and social distress that are manifested in crime, delinquency, domestic violence, child abuse and suicide.[32] At the same time more affluent areas are developing a fortress mentality, putting up physical and psychological walls to ward off perceived dangers from 'outsiders' within their own wider community.[33]

A further social change in Australia is the growing proportion of older people in the population. There is considerable concern about a growing social isolation among the elderly and the need for appropriate intervention programs to address this isolation.[34]

ISOLATION HAS MANY GUISES

The pressures of school life, too, can be isolating for both children and families. Children from some neighbourhoods have to travel long distances daily to reach their nearest school. Others do so as part of an increasing drift of students away from local state schools to selective or private schools, frequently located outside the student's home neighbourhood. Increased travel time reduces the time for 'play' in the local context. In some country towns in Australia, loss of student numbers has led to closure of schools, leaving communities without any local history of shared school networks and forcing children to board in the nearest town at a hostel, to be home schooled or to undertake distance education.[35] This decreases opportunities for frequent, incidental contact centred around school and neighbourhood activities between family members and neighbours. Schools themselves can represent a different cultural and social world for children, with truancy being one manifestation of feelings of isolation.[36]

Changes in work patterns also militate against the formation and maintenance of social relationships beyond families. Unemployment leads to increased social isolation by reducing opportunities to meet others in the workplace and by restricting the financial capacity of the unemployed to participate in wider society. Unemployment in rural areas often means relocation to the larger regional centres or to the cities to find work, making it more difficult to maintain family and community ties. Many people who are in employment are now working longer hours, a pattern that leaves little time for family relationships and less for friends outside the workplace.[37]

Social changes that affect community living and involvement are also taking place in rural Australia. National and international trends and prolonged drought have contributed to a downturn in the rural economy that has seen widescale rural restructure, rural incomes drop and many small towns suffer.[38] Centralisation of services in larger towns or cities has led to many small towns experiencing the closing of schools, hospitals and other essential services, a reduction in railway services and fewer jobs—including those in areas of public service and public utility such as electricity and water delivery.[39] Such reduced social infrastructure can increase the isolation of whole communities and change the age profile of small towns and regional centres as young people leave to seek further education or employment.[40]

As regional towns become larger and more like cities, and the infrastructure of smaller rural towns diminishes, informal social interaction at the local bank, supermarket or government agency is less likely. Travel to regional centres often involves high costs in travel and work time, fuel and convenience. Such factors can make the development of community social ties difficult for rural or remote families, make it difficult to attract and retain workers such as teachers and doctors, and can result in considerable stress for children.

Periods of prolonged drought can also have a devastating effect on families, especially in many parts of rural and remote Australia. Families can lose crops, breeding stock and livelihoods. Some are forced to sell up and move away, leaving local or itinerant workers such as shearers, station hands or fruit pickers with reduced job opportunities. As casual labour becomes less available or less affordable, the extra farm labour needed during drought for carting water or feeding stock is supplied from within the family to keep costs down. Sometimes children miss school as a result of assisting with farm labour.[41] To help their families cope with loss of farm productivity and income during drought, many more women are working for wages in nearby towns,[42] while many other women and men continue to look, often unsuccessfully, for employment outside their farms. At the same time, mothers often take on the duties of home tutor for their children, a task that can make them feel overwhelmed and isolated.[43] All of this adds to the daily pressure on men, women and children and can increase their isolation as their time for personal endeavour and social interaction beyond the family is eroded further. Recent drought in Australia has been linked to increased unemployment in rural areas as well as increased suicide rates, especially among men.[44]

The general social trends we have described do tend to increase the pressures on families and the risk of social isolation. The frequency of families changing place of residence, the intensity of modern living and the effects of economic trends, especially in rural areas, all militate against the establishment and maintenance of close and enduring local social networks for families and their children.

GEOGRAPHIC ISOLATION

While families who experience isolation, irrespective of cause, have much in common, physical or geographic isolation presents particular challenges and can magnify the collective impact of other negative aspects of isolation. This is particularly true in the Australian context.

Australia is a large country with a relatively small population. It is one of the most highly urbanised countries in the world, with the majority of the population of each state or territory living in or around large cities mostly located near the coast. Those living in areas classified as rural tend to cluster around large regional towns. Consequently, Australia has considerable areas of remote, sparsely populated outback land frequently characterised by harsh, hot and dry climatic conditions. This has usually meant that planning models used by governments often bypass the particular needs of very small communities, particularly those in remote areas.

In a country such as Australia, with its vast distances, families can live hundreds of kilometres from the next family or the nearest town, and this has implications for children and their parents. Young children who live in rural and remote isolated circumstances often have limited choices and opportunities to be with children of their own age for social interaction or for educational activities. This is equally true for their parents. Lack of opportunity to see their child interacting with other children, or to talk with other parents and professionals, can erode parents' confidence in their ability to monitor progress in their child's development and learning.

Parents in rural and remote areas often live long distances from most, if not all, of their extended families. Outside the larger cities transport costs are high and public transport frequently non-existent, particularly in remote areas. While some families can and do use telephones to stay in touch over long distances, physical separation from family members, especially grandparents, can limit access to this source of regular interpersonal support. The internet has the potential to make access to others easier and less expensive for isolated families.[45] However, this will only work if families have access to computers plus reliable and affordable internet access and the knowledge of how to use them, a situation that is less likely in rural than urban centres, particularly among low-income, less educated and Indigenous families.[46]

Maureen Fegan & Jennifer Bowes

The challenges of geographic isolation can be seen clearly in times of emergency or ill health. The nearest hospital may be more than a day's journey away by car, and childhood illness can be a time of extreme stress for families. When a child is hospitalised there may be no close neighbour or family member to help care for other children in the family. The range of health professionals such as doctors, physiotherapists, dentists and psychologists that is available in cities and often in regional centres does not exist in geographically isolated towns. An extreme indicator of the effects of geographical isolation on children is seen in child death rates that are three times higher in the most remote areas of New South Wales than in all other areas of the state.[47]

SOCIAL ISOLATION

Communities do not need to be geographically isolated to experience threats to social cohesion. Many newer suburbs on the outer rims of Australian cities, for example, are depleted in social capital. Such areas often have high levels of unemployment and little community infrastructure. When few residents have access to cars or cannot afford the rising costs of petrol, and there is little or no public transport, residents are effectively isolated in their homes. Financial concerns also mean that parents are so drained by their efforts to look after themselves and their families that they have no emotional resources left to provide help or support for their neighbours.[48]

Families in such neighbourhoods frequently do not know where to turn when they need help. They often cannot even contact the relevant societal agencies because they are unaware of the procedures for obtaining assistance from them. Gaining access to information is made even more difficult for parents with low levels of literacy or education or who are from culturally and linguistically diverse backgrounds. When social disadvantage and social isolation become entrenched within a locality, 'a disabling social climate can develop ... and the prospect is increased of disadvantage being passed from one generation to the next'.[49]

Consequences

How does isolation affect children and families?

Irrespective of how isolation has come about, lack of access to the resources that community links provide can result in non-involvement in the community, alienation, loneliness, low self-esteem, boredom, intolerance, lack of motivation, depression, vulnerability and even suicide for adult family members. Isolation can also have a negative impact on family functioning and disadvantage or impair children's development.

For some, the negative effects of isolation may be temporary, while for others they may seem almost insurmountable. The adolescent who has no choice but to leave the support of family and friends and the familiarity of the local community to attend boarding school or university, for example, may experience considerable disruption at least in the short term. So too may the few remaining adolescents in a small town when most other young people have moved to the city for employment. Yet their long-term prospects for social support are quite different from those of an elderly widow in the country forced to move hundreds of kilometres away from her community to the only available nursing home. Government policies, economic priorities and town planning all interact with an individual's own realities, perceptions and life chances to determine the experience of isolation at different points in the life cycle.

SOCIAL ISOLATION AND CHILD ABUSE

One of the most extreme negative outcomes of isolation has been found in the well-documented links between socially isolated families and child maltreatment. Social isolation increases the risk of all forms of domestic violence, including child abuse. Child abuse is one of the most serious possible outcomes of social isolation, and it has clear costs to children, families and communities.

When areas are low in physical and social capital and families are socially isolated, collective efficacy may be low.[50] In this type of situation, families and children are at risk of violence and abuse resulting from the stresses of few resources and the lack of contact with others who might act to curb this behaviour. This is a conclusion drawn by researchers into child abuse in the USA[51] and Australia,[52] who have found geographic pockets of high levels of child abuse within neighbourhoods. The feature distinguishing these areas from others close by that did not have such high levels of abuse was the social isolation of the families.

There are, however, structural differences between communities, and sometimes between urban and rural communities, that can affect the likelihood of violence. In a report analysing police statistics from different parts of Australia, Lievore found that geographic isolation was a powerful predictor of sexual assault, especially for Indigenous women. Regional areas of New South Wales, for example, had sexual assault rates around four times higher than metropolitan areas.[53] Hornosty noted that women in rural areas of Canada found it difficult to report abuse or to leave violent relationships because of lack of access to transport and support services, as well as conservative cultural beliefs about women, marriage and the family.[54] Attention to community infrastructure and attitudes is important for approaches to the prevention of such violence.

Successful interventions for isolated families

In these times of social and economic change, families living in all forms of isolated circumstances are increasingly at risk of disadvantage and sometimes despair. Their social and economic circumstances make the delivery of services to address their needs more difficult, but at the same time more necessary than ever. The challenges of providing support for families and alleviating the negative effects of isolation need to be met in a variety of creative and innovative ways.

Some service and community development strategies used to combat isolation and to support the emergence of community resilience have been particularly effective

Maureen Fegan & Jennifer Bowes

in the Australian context. The examples that follow illustrate interventions involving 'outsiders', those begun by parents to address a particular need, and interventions that attempt to coordinate the services of several government departments. In addition, a case study provides an example of a community initiated intervention that brought in outsiders with particular skills to strengthen an Indigenous community.

CONTACT INCORPORATED

Particularly in rural and remote areas, communities have to be very resourceful to help families establish social ties and gain access to the health and educational services of the wider society. In many cases, individuals or organisations from outside these communities are needed as a catalyst if such resourcefulness is to emerge and be sustained.

One example of the use of such a strategy is the CONTACT program, launched as an ongoing project for the International Year of the Child in 1979. CONTACT Incorporated is a community-managed program for isolated children, families and communities. The program's charter is to provide information, resources and support for people caring for young children in isolated circumstances. It acts to break down isolation by bringing information to isolated children, their families and communities, and to the professionals working with them. While working extensively across urban, rural and remote communities in New South Wales, CONTACT Incorporated is also proactive in initiating and influencing policies, service models and practices that address isolation across Australia.

The CONTACT experience suggests that strengthening the capacity of the communication, information and support networks that surround families is the most effective long-term strategy for addressing the challenges of isolation. The program works to achieve this in a number of ways. CONTACT staff provide regular support and resources to the parents, children's services, early childhood nurses, teachers and others who are involved in the care of young children. Staff also work closely with local communities to identify local needs and priorities, and to facilitate policy changes to address those needs.

In addition, CONTACT produces and disseminates information about children's development, parenting, community arts and crafts and community services. Resources are designed to assist in building caregiver competence and confidence to combat isolation and to interact effectively with young children. To assist individuals and local communities to locate other relevant services, CONTACT also prepares and distributes a list of community services and organisations of particular relevance for carers of children with disabilities. Material from CONTACT resources is often disseminated more widely by local and regional support agencies or community groups.

As well as providing information, CONTACT encourages people out of their isolation through 'Contact Days'. These days provide discussion groups for local families, access to visiting professionals, storytelling, arts and craft activities and early childhood programs. Invitations are extended to all in the community and, although families are involved in the various activities provided, parents may also choose to have private discussions with visiting professionals such as teachers, psychologists and health workers. CONTACT recognises the role of fun and the importance of providing social opportunities, especially in the context of stressed communities where these may be rare.

CONTACT is also actively involved in supporting innovative models of service delivery for children, including mobile children's services, which are designed to offer more regular and ongoing support for child–adult interactions in remote and disadvantaged areas. A mobile service reaches isolated communities by car, bus, plane or train, and provides staff with an appropriate range of equipment to support the educational programs offered.

WORKING IN A MOBILE CHILDREN'S SERVICE

Vicki Olds, Coordinator of the Outback Mobile Resources Unit at Broken Hill, explains why she enjoys working in a mobile children's service.

> What I like about being a mobiler is going somewhere different every day, to different places and seeing different faces. We go somewhere different each week. For example, we might go south and take the mobile to a property on Monday, a school in one town on Tuesday, a pre-school in a different town on Wednesday and another property on Thursday. We usually come back to Broken Hill on Fridays. When the gymkhana is on we often go along and provide play sessions and do other fun things with the kids.
>
> We take all the equipment we need for the week in the mobile, plus toys, resources, books and DVDs. Sometimes families ask us to bring groceries and other 'little things' with us—once this 'little thing' was a hot water tank!
>
> There's always been a strong support network in the outback. Someone's always there at the other end of the phone or the internet, as long as you know how to access it. There's another reason mobile visits mean so much to remote families: they get a chance to share their problems with someone first hand, have the opportunity to cry on your shoulder if they need to.
>
> More early childhood staff should try being mobilers. It's a terrific lifestyle, different every day. It's anything but a cushy office job and you learn very quickly how to change a tyre and where to put the oil. You learn a lot about yourself as well.

Education and professional qualifications can provide young people with a career pathway that encourages them to leave rural Australia in search of education and employment. CONTACT and growing numbers of community organisations are strong advocates for supporting lifelong learning within communities, including the provision of professional development, networking and support for those in the 'front line' of service delivery so they themselves avoid the risk of personal and professional isolation.[55] Macquarie University, for example, offers a program for Indigenous workers in children's services that enables them to become qualified early childhood teachers, and to remain in their communities working in local services after graduation.[56]

Maureen Fegan & Jennifer Bowes

THE ISOLATED CHILDREN'S PARENTS' ASSOCIATION

The formation of community groups around 'tasks in common', and the new social networks that often emerge as outcomes from parents' joint endeavours, all play a part in establishing community 'protection' against the effects of isolation. Shared recognition of their children's needs, and their own actions to have these needs met, unite parent groups at the local level. Many established early childhood services, playgroups, schools, hospitals and early intervention programs for children with special needs, for example, have benefited from the advocacy and voluntary support of families.

An example of such a parent-initiated group is the Isolated Children's Parents' Association of Australia (ICPA). Gaining access to education, including early childhood education, for their children is an ongoing challenge for families living in isolated rural and remote areas, and educational disadvantage has long been a feature of rural life. ICPA is a voluntary national parent body formed in 1971 and dedicated to ensuring that all geographically isolated students have equality of access to an appropriate education with their non-isolated peers.

ICPA brings together parents from around Australia who together are influential advocates for the educational needs of geographically isolated children. Although ICPA is run by volunteers, the organisation maintains highly effective infrastructure at both state and national levels. Over the years its repeated representations to government have helped bring about changes in government awareness of and responses to the needs of children living in rural and remote areas. For example, ICPA Australia has advocated strongly for the implementation of mobile children's services, including in-home child care for families that do not have access to any other child care services.

At state level, ICPA NSW has successfully lobbied for an effective school travel scheme as well as for improved access to correspondence lessons via distance education. Distance education has been revolutionised by the establishment of distance education centres, decentralised schools of the air, and by the use of new communication technology. Rapid advances in information technology now offer exciting opportunities for geographically isolated children who learn at home to interact more with peers. However, the limitations of technology in this regard are expressed eloquently by Alston and Kent: 'Computers won't play in your football team or marry your son or daughter'.[57]

SCHOOLS AS COMMUNITY CENTRES

Government responsibility is organised in terms of multiple tiers (local, regional, state and national levels) and of separately managed departments in areas such as health, education, community services and housing. Family needs and community needs, however, do not work in this fragmented way. It is difficult, for example, to separate the needs of a family living in a geographically isolated region into children's issues, education issues, or broader family or health issues, just as it is in urban areas.

Joint departmental projects can overcome artificial legislative or administrative barriers that hinder service delivery, and can increase the responsiveness of departmental programs and procedures to community needs. An example of such an interdepartmental project is the Schools as Community Centres program. This program commenced in 1995 as a pilot project in four disadvantaged communities in New South Wales. The project was a joint venture between the state government departments of Health, Community Services, and Education and Training. The Department of Housing joined the venture in 1998. By 2007, the Schools as Community Centres program was operating in fifty-one schools across New South Wales as an initiative of Families NSW (formerly Families First), the New South Wales Government's 'prevention and early intervention strategy that helps parents give their children a good start in life'.[58]

The program's aim is to influence the planning and integration of service delivery to meet the needs of disadvantaged families. It is targeted at families with children aged from birth to eight years, with a priority on children in the first five years, to promote the health, well-being and school readiness of those children. The objectives of the program and the strategies designed to meet them recognise both the commonality and the uniqueness of local social contexts as well as family and community needs.

The use of a local facilitator to connect families, service agencies and communities is a feature of the Schools as Community Centres program that has contributed to its success. Another key feature of the program is the use of a local school as a base for work with the community. Making the school a site for activities with pre-school-aged children and their families has had many benefits in terms of children's successful school transition and for the schools themselves in terms of greater parental involvement once children have started school. Parental involvement assists not only children's education but also their health outcomes, such as increased immunisation rates. Communities can also benefit. For example, on one site of the inter-agency pilot program, parents mobilised parental and local council assistance to build a path through a neighbouring swamp to assist children walking to the school.

CONNECTING COMMUNITIES

The Strong and Smart Digital Project is an example of a local community and an outside group (university department) joining together to improve school engagement in Indigenous children and to build cultural identity and pride in the children and their community. Cherberg State School in northern Queensland invited the Queensland University of Technology Department of Film and Television to work with its students in years 5 to 7 to develop a DVD as part of their multimedia training. Their work included a short film, *Strong and Smart*, based on children's activities in the school. The DVD has been used widely in the local community and in other schools to revitalise community pride and to present a positive image of Indigenous communities. As part of the project, digital technologies have been used to record culture and language and the children's positive engagement in the project has led to improved school retention and literacy rates.[59]

Maureen Fegan & Jennifer Bowes

Implementation of strategies such as Families NSW demonstrates evolving recognition by policy makers of the many benefits the whole-of-government approach offers for the planning and delivery of community services. At national level, too, there is increasing recognition that 'effective support for families and communities requires partnerships and governance arrangements that involve all levels of government, the community sector, non-government organisations, business and the research and academic sectors'.[60] The Australian Government's Communities for Children initiative, for example, uses a non-government lead agency to work with other community and government organisations to strengthen the social capital and services of communities to support families with young children. Following a review of fourteen projects to strengthen Indigenous communities in Australia, the following key themes were identified: building trust through relationships, using established community networks for flexibility and leverage, the need for Indigenous leadership and building sustainability.[61]

Our review of isolation problems has highlighted several additional issues specific to isolation to guide those who work with isolated children, families and communities. In general terms, policy makers, teachers, health professionals and community workers need to be aware that:

- There are special challenges posed by all forms of isolation and, in particular, by geographic and social isolation.
- While some of the problems caused by isolation are common across communities, others can only be understood and addressed at the local level.
- Strategies that involve communities in the identification of, and solutions to, their own local problems are more likely to be effective for both individuals and communities.
- We need to recognise the contradiction that sometimes strong group identity within communities can prevent inclusion of those deemed to be 'outsiders'.
- The processes used to prevent or address isolation can increase community resilience, social infrastructure and social capital.
- If we are to avoid 'blaming the victim', we cannot assume that all people and all communities can be equally resilient, innovative or resourceful in addressing the negative effects of isolation.
- While external intervention including professional staff can support communities, staff must be careful not to undermine existing support agencies, including the voluntary sector.
- Communities, families and individuals are best supported when all tiers of government commit to long-term inclusive strategies that promote partnerships and respond quickly to changes in local circumstances.

In conclusion, there is no single intervention model that can alleviate all forms of isolation, support all children and strengthen all families and all communities. There are, however, some tried and true characteristics of flexible model-building that have emerged from community development programs around the world. Ruth Cohen from the Bernard van Leer Foundation writes that many specifically targeted early childhood education programs, for example, can and do become catalysts for wider community development. Such programs reflect a 'model' for sustaining processes of individual and community growth. Cohen described this model as:

> a marvellously fluid, continually adapting combination of individuals of all ages, races, classes who listen to others, adapt what they learn to their own environments, then alter what they do as circumstances and people change. These are individuals who know what they want for their communities and their children and who have a vision for the future. They live in rural and urban areas all over the world and, even though they speak different languages, they understand each other.[62]

At times, in some neighbourhoods, community resilience is too depleted to nurture grassroots solutions. It is incumbent on governments to intervene in socially and culturally responsive ways to bring about community renewal and reduce the isolation of neighbourhoods and individuals.

With wise government and a shared language of individual endeavour, advocacy, social policy and just practice we can 'rethink' isolation, combat its negative outcomes and, in so doing, strengthen those 'buffers' of community capital and infrastructure that best protect children and strengthen their families and communities.

STUDENT EXERCISES

1   Think about the community in which you live. First, look up the statistical descriptors of your neighbourhood. This information can be found in publications of the Australian Bureau of Statistics or from its website at www.abs.gov.au. Consider such factors as:
    - local employment patterns (including unemployment rates, shift work, casual or seasonal employment)
    - socio-economic status
    - demographic composition (for example, proportions of young and old; married, partnered or living alone)
    - family composition and household size
    - accomodation types (houses, flats, farms, nursing homes, caravan parks)
    - where children go to school and how they get there
    - languages spoken in the community (and the availability of interpreters)
    - rates of car ownership (also who has a driving licence and who has access to a car)
    - costs of living (rent, petrol, public transport, food, child care, schooling, before and after school and vacation care and so on).
    a) Now walk around your local neighbourhood, observe closely, and think about the possible work, play and friendship patterns of the people who live there. You might consider public transport (is it available, how accessible is it, how often does it run and how much does it cost?), roads and their impact on people, or the availability of community resources such as shops, banks, schools, medical support, housing stock and population density.
    b) Identify community meeting places or other resources that provide opportunities for contact between people such as children's services, schools, parks, halls, churches and clubs.

Maureen Fegan & Jennifer Bowes

c) Consider how town planning contributes to or inhibits interactions between people. Some questions you might ask include: Where are the roads? Are they easy to cross safely? Are there footpaths? Where can children play or ride a bicycle safely? Are there opportunities for incidental contact between neighbours? Are there gated housing estates or other areas considered 'off limits' to the general public? Where do young children spend their days and who are they with? Where can teenagers and young adults gather? What leisure alternatives are available to them? Is internet access readily available to all (for example, in a public library)?

d) Find out whether there are any family support programs available in the local area. Are there playgroups or meetings for members of other self-help associations such as the Nursing Mothers Association or the Country Women's Association? Are family support programs available locally such as Good Beginnings, Parents as Teachers and Schools as Community Centres? Who can provide local families with accurate advice on how to choose properly fitting child restraints for their children? Who is authorised and available locally to make certain they are correctly fitted in cars and other vehicles? Are early intervention services available for families whose children have additional needs and how easy are they to access? Where are the nearest doctors and other health services? Where is the nearest hospital and how easy would it be for families to visit any patient admitted there?

e) How easy was it for you to access this information? How would families who are experiencing isolation find out about these networks?

2   Consider the various types of social networks and community supports that may or may not be available to the people who live in your community. Who might be experiencing isolation? What sorts of isolation? What could be done to alleviate the negative effects of isolation? Would you rate your local community as high or low in social capital? Why?

3   Think about yourself and the people and places that are important to you.

a) Have you ever experienced feelings of isolation? If so, write down how it felt. Then describe any influences you think may have contributed to the experience of isolation and identify any factors that may have alleviated its negative aspects.

b) What strategies have you (or might you) put in place to prevent yourself becoming personally or professionally isolated?

c) What contributions do you make (or might you make in the future) to the social capital of your community?

4   Find examples of innovative programs that strengthen families and communities and compare their characteristics to the programs described in this chapter. Use the following websites as starting points for your search.

- Australian Institute of Criminology: www.aic.gov.au
- Australian Institute of Family Studies: www.aifs.org.au
- CommunityBuilders: www.communitybuilders.nsw.gov.au
- CommunityBuilding: www.communitybuilding.vic.gov.au
- Department of Families, Housing, Community Services and Indigenous Affairs (FaHCSIA): www.facsia.gov.au

- Family Action Centre: www.newcastle.edu.au/centre/fac
- FamiliesNSW: www.community.nsw.gov.au/DOCS/STANDARD/PC_100941.html

Notes

1   S. Encel & H. Strudecki, *Partnership: A Review*, University of NSW Social Policy Research Centre, Sydney, 2000.
2   K.M. MacQueen, E. McLellan, D.S. Metzger, S. Kegeles, R.P. Strauss, R. Scotti, L. Blanchard & R.T. Trotter, 'What is Community? An Evidence-based Definition for Participatory Public Health', *American Journal of Public Health*, 91, 2001, pp. 1929–38; F. Biddulph, J. Biddulph & C. Biddulph, *The Complexity of Community and Family Influences on Children's Achievement in New Zealand*, New Zealand Ministry of Education, Wellington, New Zealand, 2003.
3   H. Rheingold, *The Virtual Community: Homesteading on the Electronic Frontier*, MIT Press, Cambridge, MA, 2000, p. 5.
4   An example is an online group for fathers of children with spina bifida that operated over a six-month period in Canada, bringing together geographically isolated men to share their experiences and offer information and support to one another. See D.B. Nicholas, T. McNeill, G. Montgomery, C. Stapleford & M. McClure, 'Communication Features in an Online Group for Fathers of Children with Spina Bifida: Considerations for Group Development Among Men', *Social Work with Groups*, 26, 2003, pp. 65–80.
5   M. Merkes, 'Is Social Capital Moving Online?', *Opinion Online*, posted 15 January 2002, <www.onlineopinion.com.au/view.asp?article=1471>, accessed 15 July 2007.
6   Australian Department of Communications, Infotech and the Arts, *The Role of ICT in Building Communities and Social Capital: A Discussion Paper*, Australian Department of Communications, Infotech and the Arts, Canberra, 2005, <www.dbcde.gov.au/communications_for_consumers/ funding_programs__and__support/community_connectivity/the_role_of_ict_in_building_ communities_and_social_capital_a_discussion_paper >, accessed 24 March 2008.
7   Merkes, 2002.
8   R. Hortulanus, 'Social Environment and Social Isolation', in *Social Isolation in Modern Society*, eds, R. Hortulanus, A. Machielse & L. Meeuwesen, Routledge, Oxford, UK, 2006a, pp. 156–75.
9   T. Leventhal & J. Brooks-Gunn, 'The Neighbourhoods They Live In: The Effects of Neighbourhood Residence Upon Child and Adolescent Outcomes', *Psychological Bulletin*, 126, 2000, pp. 309–37; T. Leventhal & J. Brooks-Gunn, 'Children and Youth in Neighbourhood Contexts', *Current Directions in Psychological Science*, 12, 2003, pp. 27–31; T. Leventhal & J. Brooks-Gunn, 'A Randomized Study of Neighbourhood Effects on Low-Income Children's Educational Outcomes', *Developmental Psychology*, 40, 2004, pp. 488–507.
10   Leventhal & Brooks-Gunn, 2000, 2003, 2004.
11   Leventhal & Brooks-Gunn, 2000; S. Gibbons, A. Green, P. Gregg & S. Machin, *Is Britain Pulling Apart? Area Disparities in Employment, Education and Crime*, University of Bristol Working Paper No. 05/120, The Centre for Market and Public Organisation, University of Bristol, Bristol, UK, 2005, <www.bris.ac.uk/Depts/CMPO/workingpapers/wp120.pdf>, accessed 2 December 2007.
12   B.H. Hunter, 'Trends in Neighbourhood Inequality of Australian, Canadian and US Cities Since the 1970s', *The Australian Economic History Review*, 43, 2003, pp. 22–44.
13   T. Vinson, *Dropping Off The Edge: The Distribution of Disadvantage in Australia*, Catholic Social Services Australia, Canberra, 2007.
14   A. Daly, *Social Inclusion and Exclusion Among Australia's Children: A Review of the Literature*, National Centre for Social and Economic Modelling Discussion Paper No. 62, National Centre for Social and Economic Modelling, University of Canberra, Canberra, 2006. Social exclusion refers to children being unable to participate fully in society due to multiple disadvantage.
15   A. McCollough & H. Joshi, *Neighbourhood and Family Influences on the Cognitive Ability of Children in the British National Child Development Study*, Institute for Social and Economic Research, University of Essex, Colchester, 2000, <www.iser.essex.ac.uk/pubs/workpaps/pdf/2000-24.pdf>, accessed 25 July 2007; R.W. Edwards, *Measuring Social Capital: An Australian Framework and Indicators*, Australian Bureau of Statistics, Canberra, 2004, <www.ausstats.abs.gov.au/ausstats/free.nsf/Lookup/13C0688 F6B98DD45CA256E360077D526/$File/13780_2004.pdf>, accessed 14 August 2007; B. Edwards, 'Does It Take a Village? An Investigation of Neighbourhood Effects on Australian Children's Development', *Family Matters*, 72, 2005, pp. 36–43.

Maureen Fegan & Jennifer Bowes

16   E. Cox, *A Truly Civil Society: 1995 Boyer Lectures*, ABC Books, Sydney, 1995, p. 15.

17   J.S. Coleman, 'Social Capital in the Creation of Human Capital', *American Journal of Sociology*, 94, 1988, pp. 94–120.

18   McCollough & Joshi, 2000.

19   R.J. Sampson, S.W. Raudenbush & F. Earls, 'Neighborhoods and Violent Crime: A Multilevel Study of Collective Efficacy', *Science*, 277, 1997, pp. 918–24.

20   R.J. Sampson, J.D. Morenoff & T. Gannon-Rowley, 'Assessing Neighbourhood Effects: Social Processes and New Directions in Research', *Annual Review of Sociology*, 28, 2002, pp. 443–78. Collective efficacy 'is the linkage of mutual trust and the shared willingness to intervene for the public good', p. 457.

21   S. Kingwill, 'Isolation: A Key Factor which Affects Australian Families and Their Children: Implications of CONTACT Inc. Initiatives for Commonwealth Policies and Priorities in Education and Child Support', Submission to Employment, Education and Training Reference Committee, 1995, p. 2.

22   G. Zappala, V. Green & B. Parker, *Social Exclusion and Disadvantage in the New Economy*, Working Paper No. 2, The Smith Family, Sydney, 2002, <www.thesmithfamily.com.au/documents/Working_Paper_2_F48AD.pdf>, accessed 2 December 2007.

23   R. Hortulanus & A. Machielse, 'The Issue of Social Isolation', in *Social Isolation in Modern Society*, eds, R. Hortulanus, A. Machielse & L. Meeuwesen, Routledge, Oxford, UK, 2006b, pp. 3–12.

24   S.R. Silburn, S.R. Zubrick, D.M. Lawrence, F.G. Mitrou, J.A. DeMaio, E. Blair, A. Cox, R.B. Dalby, J.A. Griffin, G. Pearson & C. Hayward, 'The Intergenerational Effects of Forced Separation on the Social and Emotional Wellbeing of Aboriginal Children and Young People', *Family Matters*, 75, 2006, pp. 10–17.

25   Daly, 2006; Single fathers with children report the highest levels of loneliness of any group in Australia, see M. Flood, *Mapping Loneliness in Australia*, The Australia Institute Discussion Paper No. 76, The Australia Institute, Canberra, 2005, <www.tai.org.au/documents/downloads/DP76.pdf>, accessed 1 August 2007; J. Hughes & W. Stone, *Family Change and Community Life: Exploring the Links*, Australian Institute of Family Studies Research Paper No. 32, Australian Institute of Family Studies, Melbourne, 2003, <www.aifs.gov.au/institute/pubs/respaper/hughes.html>, accessed 25 July 2007.

26   B. Pocock, *Having a Life: Work, Family, Fairness and Community in 2000*, Centre for Labour Research, Adelaide University, Adelaide, 2000, p. 8, <www.barbarapocock.com.au/documents/havingalife.pdf>, accessed 2 August 2007.

27   Australian Bureau of Statistics, *Australian Demographic Statistics, Dec 2002: Australians on the Move*, catalogue no. 3101.0, Australian Government Publishing Service, 2003e, <www.abs.gov.au/Ausstats/abs@.nsf/94713ad445ff1425ca25682000192af2/812343b3e6694d5dca256d3c0001f4c9!-OpenDocument>, accessed 24 March 2008; Pocock, 2000.

28   Biddulph et al., 2003; R. Henderson, 'Student Mobility: Moving Beyond Deficit Views', *Australian Journal of Guidance and Counselling*, 11, 2001, pp. 121–9; R. Henderson, 'Educational Issues for Children of Itinerant Seasonal Farm Workers: A Case Study in an Australian Context', *International Journal of Inclusive Education*, 8, 2004, pp. 293–310.

29   Australian Bureau of Statistics, *Housing Arrangements: Homelessness*, catalogue no. 4102.0, Australian Government Publishing Service, Canberra, 2004b, <www.abs.gov.au/Ausstats/abs%40.nsf/94713ad445ff1425ca25682000192af2/DDC8DC3787E2D9FCCA256E9E0028F91E?opendocument>, accessed 23 August 2007.

30   G. Melsom, *The Changing Face of Homelessness*, Australian Federation of Homelessness Organisations, Dickson, ACT, 2007, <www.afho.org.au/documents/ThechangingFaceofHomelessness_Op_ed.pdf>, accessed 23 August 2007.

31   Australian Parliament Senate Community Affairs Reference Committee, *A Hand Up Not a Hand Out: Renewing the Fight Against Poverty*, Report on Poverty and Financial Hardship, Senate Printing Unit, Parliament House, Canberra, March 2004, p. 204, <www.aph.gov.au/senate/committee/clac_ctte/completed_inquiries/2002-04/poverty/report/>, accessed 8 August 2007.

32   Vinson, 2007.

33   Cox, 1995.

34   R.A. Findlay, 'Interventions to Reduce Social Isolation Amongst Older People: Where is the Evidence?', *Ageing and Society*, 23, 2003, pp. 647–58.

35   M. Alston & J. Kent, *The Impact of Drought on Secondary Education Access in Australia's Rural and Remote Areas*, Report for the Department of Education, Science and Training (DEST) and the Rural Education Program of the Foundation for Rural and Regional Renewal, Charles Sturt University, Wagga Wagga, 2006.

36   R. Hortulanus, 'Towards a New Policy Vision on Social Isolation', in *Social Isolation in Modern Society*, eds, R. Hortulanus, A. Machielse & L. Meeuwesen, Routledge, Oxford, 2006, pp. 246–57.

37   I. Watson, J. Buchanan, I. Campbell & C. Briggs, *Fragmented Futures: New Challenges in Working Life*, The Federation Press, Sydney, 2004.

38   D. Johnson, B. Headey & B. Jensen, *Communities, Social Capital and Public Policy: A Literature Review*, Department of Family and Community Services Policy Research Paper No. 26, Australian Government, Canberra, 2005.

39   Alston & Kent, 2006.

40   Alston & Kent, 2006.

41   Alston & Kent, 2006.

42   Alston & Kent, 2006.

43   L. Lee & A. Wilks, 'Documenting the Early Literacy and Numeracy Practices of Home Tutors in Distance and Isolated Education in Australia', *Australian Journal of Early Childhood*, 32, 2, 2007, pp. 28–36.

44   Department of Transport Regional Services, *Drought Impacts Beyond the Farm Gate: Two Regional Case Studies*, Farmsafe Australia, Moree, 2004.

45   J.B. Horrigan & L. Rainie, 'Online Communities: Networks that Nurture Long-distance Relationships and Local Ties', Pew Internet and American Life Project, Washington DC, 2001, <www.pewinternet.org/pdfs/PIP_Communities_Report.pdf>, accessed 18 July 2007.

46   S. Willis & A. Tranter, 'Beyond the "Digital Divide": Internet Diffusion and Inequality in Australia', *Journal of Sociology*, 42, 1, 2006, pp. 43–59.

47   NSW Child Death Review Team, *Annual Report 2005*, NSW Commission for Children and Young People, Sydney, 2006, <www.kids.nsw.gov.au/uploads/documents/cdrt2005_full.pdf>, accessed 26 June 2007.

48   J. Garbarino & A. Crouter, 'Defining the Community Context for Parent-child Relations: The Correlations of Child Maltreatment', *Child Development*, 49, 1978, pp. 604–16.

49   Vinson, 2007, p. ix.

50   Sampson et al., 2002.

51   C.J. Coulton, J.E. Korbin, M. Su & J. Chow, 'Community Level Factors and Child Maltreatment Rates', *Child Development*, 66, 1995, pp. 1262–76; V.C. McLoyd, N.L. Aikens & L.M. Burton, 'Child Poverty, Policy and Practice', in *Handbook of Child Psychology*, eds, W. Damon & R.M. Lerner, John Wiley & Sons, Hoboken, NJ, 2006, pp. 700–75.

52   T. Vinson, E. Baldry & J. Hargreaves, 'Neighbourhoods, Networks, and Child Abuse', *British Journal of Social Work*, 26, 1996, pp. 523–43.

53   D. Lievore, *Non-reporting and Hidden Recording of Sexual Assault: An International Literature Review*, Commonwealth Office for the Status of Women, Barton, ACT, 2003, <www.aic.gov.au/publications/reports/2003-06-review.html>, accessed 2 August 2007.

54   J. Hornosty, 'Wife Abuse in Rural Regions: Structural Problems in Leaving Abusive Relationships—A Case Study in Canada', in *With a Rural Focus: An Edited and Refereed Collection of Papers with a Rural Focus presented to the Annual Conference of the Australian Sociological Association Inc.*, ed., F. Vanclay, Deakin University, Melbourne, 1994, pp. 21–34.

55   Alston & Kent, 2006.

56   A. Fleet, R. Kitson, B. Cassady & R. Hughes, 'University-qualified Indigenous Early Childhood Teachers', *Australian Journal of Early Childhood*, 32, 3, 2007, pp. 17–25.

57   Alston & Kent, 2006, p. 67.

58   See <www.familiesfirst.nsw.gov.au>.

59   M. Burchill, D. Higgins, L. Ramsamy & S. Taylor, 'Workin' Together: Indigenous Perspectives on Community Development', *Family Matters*, 51, 2006, pp. 50–9.

60   See Department of Families, Housing, Community Services and Indigenous Affairs (FaHCSIA), <www.facsia.gov.au>.

61   Burchill et al., 2006.

62   R. Cohen, 'Eighty-seven and Still Going Strong', *Bernard van Leer Foundation Newsletter*, 87, October 1997, p. 36.

9

Refugees in Australian Society

Ailsa Burns[1]

It has been said that all wars are fought against non-combatants: civilians young and old who lose their homes, their loved ones, their means of survival, maybe their country, maybe their lives. This is truer than ever today, when the world is awash with devastating weapons that allow warlords to massacre their opponents, and military aircraft to reduce cities to rubble and sow cluster bombs that continue to kill and maim long after the planes have departed. In this chapter we look at the experience of those victims of war who become refugees, in particular those who seek refuge in Australia.

Contexts

The United Nations High Commission for Refugees (UNHCR)[2] estimated that by June 2007 the world would contain over thirty-two million refugees, asylum seekers and internally displaced persons (IDPs) who were being protected or assisted by the UNHCR. Of this number, an estimated one-quarter were men, one-quarter women and one-half children aged under eighteen years.[3] The largest single group (38.9 per cent) were IDPs living in camps or other arrangements in their country of origin, particularly in Africa and the Middle East. Another 30 per cent were refugees, defined as people living outside their country of origin, and unwilling or unable to return because of a 'well-founded fear of persecution for reasons of race, religion, nationality, membership of particular social group or political opinion'. The greatest number of these were living in countries adjacent to their native land—particularly Pakistan, Iran, Syria, Jordan and some African states—many with the hope of returning home when conditions there improved. Substantial numbers were also living in the USA and Western European countries, Germany in particular. A much smaller group were asylum seekers who had arrived in a foreign country—mainly the USA, South Africa or Western Europe—and sought refugee status. A further group were 'stateless persons' who had fled a country where they had lived—maybe for some generations—without being granted citizenship (for example, Palestinians who fled to neighbouring countries after the wars with Israel in the late 1960s and early 1970s). In 2007 0.19 per cent of asylum seekers worldwide were living in Australia or its off-shore detention centres, along with 0.7 per cent of all the refugees in the world.

The United Nations Convention Relating to the Status of Refugees was promulgated in 1951, a time when refugees were understood to be people who had been caught up in World War II, and who had no safe homes to return to. Considerable numbers of European displaced persons (DPs) were offered homes by non-European nations, including Australia, that were eager to expand their economies and their populations. Despite their wartime experiences and the shock of adjusting to 1950s Australia, most of the new arrivals prospered, and many have given illuminating accounts of their experience. Raymond Gaita's *Romulus My Father*[4] provides an especially touching story of his Yugoslav father's hard and lonely life making do and caring for his young son in an isolated cottage near Maryborough, and of that son's later achievements.

A United Nations 1967 Protocol extended the reach of the 1951 Convention to cover people fleeing persecution from situations other than World War II. This introduced an issue that has since faced governments in Australia and elsewhere: the possibility that more people will arrive seeking asylum than the population is prepared to accept. A second concern is the management of relations with foreign states whose nationals seek asylum on the grounds of a 'well-founded fear of persecution' in their homeland. Understandably, the homeland state is likely to treat the grant of asylum as an affront.[5]

How do refugees get here?

Australia currently has a two-track system for refugees: off-shore and on-shore. The off-shore track is the most used one, and the one favoured by government. It offers homes to people selected from UN-supported refugee camps around the world. Australia is one of the few (currently around twenty) countries that have established quotas for the resettlement of such refugees. Camp residents who have been assessed—by the UN in consultation with Australian representatives—as having a strong need of resettlement are offered a place within the quota. Those selected include subgroups such as 'women at risk'. The off-shore track also includes a special humanitarian program, under which people with some connection to Australia, and who have experienced 'substantial discrimination amounting to gross violations of human rights' can be sponsored by Australian citizens or permanent residents (including former refugees). Around half of those approved under the humanitarian program between 2001 and 2005 were aged under twenty years.[6] Permanent resident status and settlement assistance are provided to all off-shore arrivals, and after a waiting period those who can demonstrate adequate English and knowledge of Australian culture can apply for citizenship. Australia has a refugee intake quota of 13,000 a year, of whom around 90 per cent are currently selected from off-shore, in recent years mostly from Africa, the Middle East and Asia.[7]

Ailsa Burns

Thirteen thousand is of course only a tiny fraction of the number of displaced persons around the world, and there are consequently many more applications under this track than places available.

It is no surprise then that many individuals who consider themselves refugees decide to travel directly to those countries where they seek asylum. This 'on-shore' track is the controversial one. In Australia, with its lack of land borders, it comprises people who arrive by sea or air. Most famous are the 'boat people' who first made media headlines in 1976 when a young Vietnamese man sailed a small and worse-for-wear fishing boat from Vietnam to Darwin (navigating reputedly by means of a page torn from a school atlas) and announced to the immigration officials who came on board:

> 'Welcome my boat. My name is Lam Binh and these are my friends from south
> Vietnam and we would like permission to stay in Australia'.[8]

Lam Binh and his crew were Australia's first so-called boat people. They were accepted as refugees. Over the next six years, small and often barely seaworthy boats brought a further 2000 men, women and children. This was only a very small minority of the estimated two million people who fled Vietnam and Cambodia at the end of the Vietnam war, most of whom ended up in camps in Hong Kong and South-East Asia. Contemporary records show, however, that despite the small numbers, many Australians were fearful that the country would be 'swamped' by these uninvited arrivals. The Federal Government nevertheless granted asylum to all, and by 1981 the boats had virtually stopped coming. This was in large part due to an international mass resettlement program in Western countries, in which Australia played a major role.[9]

Boat arrivals started again in late 1989, at first mainly bringing Cambodians, but increasingly refugees from other parts of the world. In 1991 the Australian Government established a number of detention centres, with the aim of deterring these arrivals. However, the numbers continued to increase, peaking in 2000–02. While the government of the time pursued a deterrence policy—fearful perhaps of backlash from voters hostile to the boat people—many private citizens believed that the asylum seekers were being unfairly treated, and organised to defend their rights. Legally, the situation was equivocal, because while the 1951 UN Convention gives people the right to claim asylum in a foreign country, it does not obligate receiving countries to admit them through their borders, to resettle them or to keep them on its territory, even if they have been assessed as meeting the 'well-founded fear of persecution' requirement. Legal, political and media battles followed between government on one side and asylum seekers and their supporters on the other.

During this conflict an early government strategy was to legislate in 1992 to detain all boat people—adults and children—indefinitely in isolated outback centres. The detention orders were not generally subject to judicial review and the centres were off limits to the media. Some other signatories to the 1951 UN Convention also detain asylum seekers for periods of time, but among Western countries Australia's treatment of asylum seekers has been uniquely harsh.[10] Assessment of claims can take a long time, due to lengthy security and medical checks and other procedures. Even after gaining refugee status people can be held in continuing detention while officials search for another country willing to accept them, or indefinitely if no other country can be found to take them. There has been much criticism of this policy, but its legal validity was upheld by the High Court.[11] Alternative arrangements to continue living in Australia have since been made for most of the long-term detainees.[12]

Originally government-run, the detention camps were handed over to a USA-based prison-management company in 1997. Despite the camps' isolation, newspaper reports and some television footage of harsh and humiliating treatment were soon circulating. These reports were inadvertently supported by several government ministers who stated quite explicitly (and in contravention of the 1951 UN Convention) that the purpose of the rough conditions was to deter would-be asylum seekers from arrival.[13]

A new chapter started with the *Tampa* episode on 27 August 2001. The *Tampa* was a Norwegian container ship that was sailing from Perth to Singapore when it rescued 433 asylum seekers from a crowded wooden ferry that was breaking up in the Indian Ocean. The *Tampa* detoured to take the rescued passengers to the Australian territory of Christmas Island. But when it arrived, the *Tampa* was refused permission to enter the harbour. In the previous six days, three boats carrying almost a thousand people had arrived there. If those aboard the *Tampa* had been allowed to disembark, the total for August would have been a record, and the detention centres were already full. A federal election was coming up, and the polls showed that many people continued to be hostile to the asylum seekers, who were portrayed in the media and elsewhere as 'illegals' and 'queue-jumpers'. The government had accordingly decided that no more were to be allowed to land.[14]

The *Tampa* remained off Christmas Island for a week, while its captain, increasingly anxious about the health and mental state of the 433 people on his open deck, sent appeals for help. After frenzied diplomatic and legal negotiations, the government of Nauru—a tiny, poor and isolated island republic close to the Equator—agreed to a deal. In exchange for generous financial aid from Australia, most of the *Tampa* passengers could be accommodated in two camps in the centre of the island, which had previously been mined out for its phosphate deposits. The Australian navy was instructed to deter future boats from arriving, if necessary towing them back out to sea and sending them in the direction of Indonesia. Some medical help was provided to the *Tampa* passengers, and they were moved to a naval vessel for transfer to Nauru.

This was the start of the 'Pacific Solution'. Nauru subsequently agreed to accept some later arrivals rescued from small boats that broke up at sea, and a further camp was opened on Manus Island, off Papua New Guinea. As in Australia, the camps were off limits to the media and most other would-be visitors. A further step in the Pacific Solution was legislation 'excising' Christmas Island and some other islands from Australia. This meant that asylum seekers who reached these areas did not count as having reached Australia proper. Some other moves to restrict numbers were introduced, including the Temporary Protection Visa (TPV), under which those who gained refugee status through 'on-shore' means were to have their cases reconsidered after three years, with the threat of forced return if they could not demonstrate a continued likelihood of persecution in their homeland, no right of return should they leave Australia temporarily, and no right of entry for other family members, including children.

Ailsa Burns

Fifteen days after the *Tampa* rescue, terrorists flew hijacked passenger planes into the Twin Towers in New York and the Pentagon in Washington. In the aftermath, some senior politicians and media figures suggested that as well as being illegals and queue-jumpers, the boat people could include terrorists planning to set up cells in Australia.[15] (Ironically, they especially instanced the Afghanis among them, refugees who were in fact fleeing the Taliban.) The government's 'strong' response proved enormously popular. One MP commented in Parliament that, in all his eighteen-year political career, he had never had an issue that had made 'so many people come up to me in the street, without any urging whatever, and say "Don't back away"'. In the federal election that followed shortly after, the incumbent government was swept back into office. Despite the restriction on public and media access to the detention centres, the whole episode had received vast publicity. One perhaps unexpected consequence was the birth of many volunteer groups that took up the asylum seekers' cause, campaigned for their rights and mounted legal challenges on their behalf.

Through the rest of 2001 the naval blockade turned back a number of boats. One boat sank, drowning over 350. After that the boats virtually stopped. Processing of asylum claims proceeded, and by mid 2006, the Nauru and Manus Island camps were largely empty, several of the mainland detention centres had been closed and many TPVs had been made permanent. However, other groups of asylum seekers—including people who arrived by plane, overstayed their visas and then requested asylum—continued to be detained in the city-based centres and/or placed on 'bridging' visas that forbade them entering employment or receiving any kind of benefits while their case was under consideration. (Holders of bridging visas are mostly supported by church and voluntary agencies, and by private individuals.) Then in late 2006 and 2007, new boatloads of refugees from Burma and Sri Lanka were intercepted and their passengers transferred to Nauru.

Along with adult arrivals, significant numbers of children and unaccompanied minors have spent time in the detention centres, both on the mainland and on the islands: twenty months on average, and five-and-a-half years in the case of one boy who along with his mother was eventually granted refugee status.[16] The children were of all ages and included infants who had spent a large part of their lives in a detention centre, where a UN investigation found that they were at risk of being 'seriously traumatised and severely affected by a culture of self-harm'.[17]

Consequences

Refugees living in Australia today are a diverse population. They come from many different regions of the world, hold different cultural beliefs, speak many different languages and observe different religions. Some are highly educated, some non-literate in any language. Most have overcome major difficulties to cope very well in their new homes, and there are many stories of notable achievements.

OVERCOMING OBSTACLES

Isha, aged eighteen, was in 2007 one of twenty young people who received a scholarship funded by a voluntary agency that provides aid for disadvantaged youths. Isha is an athlete from Sierra Leone who fled the 2006 Commonwealth Games in Melbourne and sought asylum. Her parents and other family members were killed during the civil war. Despite her isolation here, and despite obstacles such as the threat of homelessness, she has set herself the goal of running for Australia in the 2010 Commonwealth Games, and has worked hard to improve her English and literacy. When Isha was presented with her scholarship, she made a speech in front of around five hundred guests, and afterwards swapped contact details with the other young people who received awards: achievements that a volunteer worker described as 'not bad for someone who could hardly make eye contact when I first met her nearly a year ago, and who seemed to find it extremely hard to form relationships'.[18]

Despite all their differences, there are some challenges that are common to most or all refugees resettled in host countries. A first obstacle is overcoming the trauma of past horrific events. Researchers in a number of countries have asked how and under what conditions refugees are able (or unable) to recover from their experiences. The research finds that two factors consistently predict recovery: first, the nature of the past traumatic events; and second, the degree of stress that refugees suffer after arrival in their host country. We look at these two factors separately.

Pre-arrival trauma

Experiences of brutal attack, injury, capture, loss of family members, malnourishment, imprisonment and torture are common among refugees. Physical care and rehabilitation are generally available in Western host nations, but psychological injuries can be harder to deal with. Post-traumatic stress disorder (PTSD)—characterised by traumatic flashbacks, hypervigilance and emotional numbing—is the most common psychological problem among refugees; depression and anxiety are also common. One study[19] investigated the mental health problems of a very large sample of adult refugees—7000—who had taken part in twenty different surveys in seven Western host countries. Despite differences in survey procedures, there was agreement in results: 8–10 per cent were diagnosed with PTSD, a prevalence that is about ten times higher than that of the age-matched USA population. Major depression was diagnosed in 4–6 per cent, and generalised anxiety disorder in 4 per cent. Many people had more than one of these disorders. A further five studies comprising 260 refugee children now living in three host countries found that an average 11 per cent suffered PTSD. Other studies report even higher rates, especially among refugee children and unaccompanied minors.[20] Certain experiences were associated with particular symptoms; for example, traumatic events to the person were associated with PTSD and somatisation symptoms, while trauma to family members was predictive of depression and anxiety.[21]

Ailsa Burns

What discriminates those who suffer continuing distress from those who do not? Degree of trauma and number of events are important. Several Australian studies found that even ten years after resettlement, those who reported three or more trauma events were up to eight times as likely, and those reporting one or two events twice as likely, to suffer a mental health illness when compared to similar-origin refugees who reported no such events.[22] The events most commonly reported were being separated from family, experiencing violence, witnessing murder of family or friends and being deprived of basic needs. People in families that had been able to stay together, or at least with some other family members, had fewer mental health problems, while unaccompanied minors were particularly vulnerable. Refugees from countries that have experienced particularly violent conflicts were most at risk of having suffered multiple trauma.[23] For example, a Queensland study of arrivals from Sudan noted that they could be considered 'an extreme group in terms of pre-migration traumas', Sudan having been in civil war nearly continuously since independence from Britain in 1956.[24]

Some research finds that refugee women are more at risk of mental health problems than men, probably because of their greater vulnerability to rape and sexual abuse; however, not all studies find gender differences. There is evidence that traumatic events exert a long-term sensitisation effect, such that people who have coped well over a long period of time are especially vulnerable to the effects of subsequent disturbing events. The most detailed studies of such events have come from studies of Holocaust survivors in Israel. For example, Holocaust survivors were more likely to experience PTSD when exposed to Scud missiles during the Gulf War. The Israeli studies also indicate that sensitisation effects operate across generations. Children of parents with PTSD were more likely to have the same problem, even where they themselves had not been exposed to traumatic events. They were also more likely to develop symptoms in stressful times: for example, the Israeli soldier children of Holocaust survivors developed more PTSD symptoms after military combat than did soldiers whose parents were not exposed to the Holocaust.[25]

It is commonly reported that uncertainty about the fate of a disappeared family member causes more distress to adults and children than does certain knowledge of their death. There is also evidence that adult survivors who believed in the cause for which they had been fighting had better well-being than those who had no such commitment or had lost commitment.[26] This held true also for the children of these families.[27] One author explained these and other effects by proposing that trauma disrupts five crucial aspects of people's lives: their sense of personal safety, their interpersonal attachments, their sense of justice, their identity or role and their sense of the meaning of existence.[28]

REGAINING A SENSE OF PERSONAL SAFETY

Joseph was a shopkeeper in a Sudanese town. One day militia forces from the north rode in, burning houses and shooting people as they fled. Joseph, his pregnant wife Ayam and two children managed to escape, but they lost contact with other family members, including their third child, a two-year-old who was staying with a relative at the time. They walked virtually across Africa, suffering many hardships, including an injury to Joseph when they encountered a hostile armed group. Ayam's baby was born on the way. They eventually reached a UN camp, and in time were selected for resettlement in Australia. Joseph is learning English and is eager to get a job and support his family, but his health limits him. He is gradually regaining his sense of personal safety, but the loss of his child and other family members is a constant sadness, as is the loss of his job and his health. He doubts that there will be any justice in Sudan for a long time to come. However, he, Ayam and their young children are a very strong family unit, and they receive good help and advice from their local church.

A number of studies have asked whether PTSD and other mental health problems remit over time. Their results are mixed. A ten-year follow-up of South-East Asian refugees in Canada revealed marked improvement in symptoms over time, to the point that the refugees had a lower rate of illness than Canadian-born citizens. Similar improvement was found in a study of Hmong refugees in the USA, and among Vietnamese refugees in Australia. The Vietnamese were doing particularly well: after an average eleven years in Australia, their mental health status was twice as good as that of the general Australian population.[29] On the other hand, the mental health difficulties of Sudanese refugees in Queensland increased over time.[30] These differences could result from many factors, including different pre-arrival experiences, cultural group effects and methodological factors. But one obvious source of differences was the life that refugees had after arrival in the host country.

Post-arrival experience

Research in a number of countries has identified a set of supportive and stressful factors that influence adaptation after resettlement.

Family support is always a major predictor of well-being. Most refugees in Australia come from cultures that are strongly organised around extended families. Having family support in the new country is consequently critical to coping with all the challenges that arise in the new country. This holds for children as well as adults. One study of Vietnamese refugees living in difficult circumstances in the Philippines found that young children accompanied by family members were far less distressed than those who were unaccompanied. Those without the emotional and practical support provided by families were especially vulnerable to anxiety and depression. Unaccompanied minors were the most vulnerable of all.[31]

Support from the ethnic group community is also a predictor of well-being, and is a major reason why new arrivals settle in areas where a local community is already established. This provides neighbours who speak the same language[32] and can tell arrivals how to go about getting the things they need; as well as church and other groups that bring people together, offer services in various languages and give all kinds of practical supports. It also means that refugees living in the major cities are concentrated in a few areas. Affordable rental housing in these areas is increasingly hard to find, especially for large families. This generates difficulties for everyone, but particularly for new arrivals still finding their feet in a strange culture. A longer-term problem with congregating in particular areas is one known to all expatriates: social opportunities may be reduced if you stick to your own community and especially if you can get by without learning much of the local language.

Refugees with permanent residency in Australia receive the welfare payments, medical benefits and educational opportunities available to the rest of the population, along with government assistance with English classes, job-search assistance and some other benefits. Church and community agencies provide other services and opportunities. Those arrivals who are able fairly speedily to acquire enough English and/or skills to get a job have better well-being, but this can be a daunting task, especially for those who have had little education in their country of origin.

Child arrivals with limited or no previous schooling have special problems. They have to acquire not only everyday English but the formal English used in lessons. They are also faced with curricula that assume cultural understandings that are second nature to Australian-born students. One teenage refugee student, for example, described her despair at being asked to write a short essay on 'The Legend of Gallipoli'. School routines and expectations can also present mysteries to those who have never been inside a classroom before.

Provision for English-as-a-Second-Language (ESL) students in Australia varies from state to state, but in general younger children enter the local primary school while those over a certain age attend special English instruction colleges for six to twelve months before transferring to their local school. These older students include those who previously attended a regular school in another language, those who had limited schooling in detention camps and elsewhere, and those who have reached their teens with no schooling and no literacy. Similar-length programs for new arrivals are common in other Western countries. However, it is estimated that in optimum circumstances it takes three to five years to develop oral proficiency in English and four to seven years to gain academic English proficiency—substantially longer when circumstances are not optimal. One-year programs have accordingly been described by some experts as 'wildly unrealistic', especially for the pre-literate.[33]

How do our refugee students get on at school? Anecdotal evidence is that some do marvellously well, and others find it all too hard and drop out. Important factors are the age at arrival and the level of previous education. A small amount of research has looked at what helps refugee students to settle and achieve in school. One British study found that students identified three key themes: the presence of specialist teachers, support from friends and whether the 'whole-school' attitude to refugee children gave them the confidence to identify themselves as refugees, without fear of being bullied.[34]

A qualitative study of Sudanese students in Victorian secondary schools identified the same issues along with some extra ones. While English of all kinds presented problems, the specialist vocabulary in subject areas presented even more. Social studies was a special problem, because many of the topics studied assumed background knowledge of Australian culture and history that these students lacked. Some teaching techniques also presented difficulties, such as the use of videos that they were instructed to watch while taking notes of significant points. The authors comment that:

In order to complete such a task successfully, students must be able to listen and understand, interpret visuals, identify and record key points while continuing to process incoming information. This is a task of overwhelming difficulty for students who lack fluency in general and subject specific language and who are also struggling with literacy.[35]

The use of teacher-prepared worksheets instead of textbooks was also an issue. Students yearned for a textbook that they could always refer to. And small-group work was a particular bane of students who had no previous experience of it, did not know the other group members well or at all, and did not want to risk making mistakes in front of them.

> I don't like when the teacher told me to do it in group. I just go and sit, sit and watch them. I don't like to do that because I don't know it [and] … because I don't know them.[36]

In the face of these difficulties, all the students confessed to some bad moments:

> Sometimes you feel like you don't want to come to class because everyone is ahead of you and you don't know anything. Sometimes it feels like you hate yourself, like why am I not like them? Or why did I come to this country? They already know everything and I know nothing. You are thinking a lot of things so you feel bad.[37]

At the same time, they had high aspirations for their futures, and many concrete suggestions for improvements: in particular for more teachers, more help with English in mainstream subjects, peer support from 'someone from your own culture' and 'time to learn more before you come to high school'.

Post-arrival experiences of the boat people

This relatively small minority had a very different post-arrival experience from that of other refugees. As noted above, most of those who arrived after the first boatloads were isolated for extended periods in remote detention centres, at first in Australia, later as part of the Pacific Solution. The conditions were bleak and prison-like, despite the large number of family groups present. Even small children, for example, were addressed by number, and expected to answer to their numbers. At the same time, the detainees were regularly demonised in the media and elsewhere as undesirable illegals and queue-jumpers. In fact the 1951 UN Convention gave them the legal right to seek asylum in a foreign country, and the countries from which they came had no agencies at which to queue.

An Australian-based study of Tamil asylum seekers compared those held in detention with compatriots applying for refugee status while living in the community.[38] The detained group reported greater exposure to torture and other forms of persecution in their home country, and had much higher levels of depression, panic, PTSD, somatic distress and suicidal urges than the community group. This study also compared the relative effects of pre- and post-arrival experiences on mental health. The finding was that while most post-traumatic stress symptoms originated in trauma suffered in the home country, around a third resulted from difficulties since arrival. There was also evidence that people with the most traumatic pre-arrival experiences also experienced greater post-arrival difficulties. This could be partly because (as noted earlier) horrific pre-arrival events render the victim more vulnerable to later stresses, but also because asylum seekers who face extreme threats are the subgroup most likely to leave the homelands in haste and without documentation, hence placing themselves at greater risk of being detained at the point of entry to a Western country. The authors comment that:

> The cruel irony is that instead of providing special care for the most traumatised indi-
> viduals fleeing persecution, western countries may be subjecting them to the very
> conditions that are likely to hinder psychosocial recovery.[39]

Reports on the detention centres made by the UN Regional Advisor and the Australian Human Rights and Equal Opportunity Commission[40] make distressing reading. The latter report notes that from July 2001 to June 2002 there were 760 major incidents involving 3030 detainees across all detention centres. These included 116 alleged, attempted or actual assaults (sixteen involving children), and 248 self-harm incidents (thirty-five involving children).

A detainee parent told the Australian Human Rights and Equal Opportunity Commission Inquiry:

> Unfortunately the environment is not very healthy because every day they are wit-
> nessing people who are going on top of the tree, who are suiciding or just cutting
> their body by blade or jumping, shouting, doing everything violent and they are wit-
> nessing and they think this is a game that have to participate on it. It's a very danger-
> ous situation and we cannot have any control of it.[41]

And a professional report on twenty children who had been detained for an average of twenty-eight months found that:

> All but one child received a diagnosis of major depressive disorder and all were diag-
> nosed with PTSD. The symptoms of PTSD experienced by the children were almost
> exclusively related to experience of trauma in detention. Children described night-
> mares … and many would scream in their sleep or wake up shouting.[42]

Some detainees were deported to their country of origin, or somewhere nearby, but most were eventually recognised as refugees and granted Temporary Protection Visas. These provide limited rights compared to permanent protection visas, suggesting that the holders are not really wanted in Australia, and forcing them to live under threat of deportation to the country of feared persecution at some time in the future. The TPVs also had some unexpected effects: for example, one teenage boy attending a high school with a substantial population of overseas-born students was bullied by other refugee boys because he was 'only a TPV'.

Identity

Other than the issues already discussed, are there some continuing experiences that distinguish resettled refugees—or at least some resettled refugees—from other overseas-born residents (see Chapter 4)? By late 2007, the Federal Government had decided that there were such differences, when it announced a major reduction in refugees from Africa (Sudan in particular, from where the majority of African arrivals have come), on the grounds that they were 'not integrating properly'. Making the announcement, the Immigration Minister referred to submissions to his Department complaining that the Africans presented 'unique challenges' because compared to other refugee groups they had spent more time in overseas detention camps, had less previous education, had worse English, were more likely to drop out of Australian schools, engaged in more family in-fighting and formed criminal gangs of young males. He did not make public his evidence for these claims, on the grounds that the relevant material had been presented to the Federal Cabinet, and was therefore 'cabinet in confidence'.[43] Nor did he specify how the Africans already settled here were to be assisted to improve their allegedly inadequate integration.

SECURING OUR EXISTENCE

Alice Pung's[44] account of her Cambodian family's life in Australia provides an illuminating example of how arrivals from extremely deprived and dangerous areas have blended their own backgrounds into Australian culture and cultural preoccupations. On first arrival, Alice's family stay at a migrant hostel, where:

> The refugees .... horde packets of sugar, jam and honey from the breakfast table. So used to everything being finite, irrevocably gone if one does not grab it fast enough, they are bewildered when new packets appear on the breakfast table the next day. So they fill their pockets with these too, just in case. Weeks later, the packets still appear. The new refugees learn to eat more slowly, that their food will not be taken from them or their bowls kicked away. They learn that here, no one dies of starvation.

Years later, when Alice is grown up and a lawyer, her father urges her to share his enthusiasm for investment property.

> In Pol Pot's Cambodia [he] once took the belt from his waist and buried it where no one would find it. He then watched as the people around him died of starvation. He was responsible for burying the bodies ... One day, when he felt as if soon he too might be one of those bodies, he dug up his belt, cut it into small strips and boiled it for hours in secret. Then he called his mother and sister over, and they ate it. In this way, they stayed alive.

> [He] will tell you that you don't want to live a life of in-the-moment hedonism like a lot of Australians, always spending what they have and often what they don't have ... to save your family you have to save things. And that is why the idea of the investment property looms so large in the migrant version of the Great Australian Dream. It secures our existence.

Ailsa Burns

The issue of community attitudes

Many people have wondered why the tiny number of boat people who have reached our shores have been regarded as such a threat, and treated so harshly. One senior parliamentarian, for example, has described the Pacific Solution as an 'astronomically expensive and inhumane solution to a non-existent problem'.[45]

It is worth remembering that asylum seekers are not the only group who enter a country uninvited. Prosperous countries, especially those with land borders, receive much larger numbers of so-called 'economic refugees', people from poor countries hoping for a better life. Under international law, economic refugees have no legal right to remain, and many are promptly deported; but others evade detection and stay on for long periods of time. By 2007, for example, the USA held an estimated seven million illegal workers.[46]

One reason the boat people have been harshly treated may be their frequent depiction as really economic refugees: queue-jumping, prosperity-seeking invaders who are trying to cheat the system by pretending to be 'real' refugees. Evolutionary theory holds that humankind has evolved a set of basic instincts that are finely tuned to respond to particular triggers, like fear of strangers, righteous anger and resentment of suspected cheats.[47] These instincts can be readily aroused, and modern communications provide multiple platforms for arousing them. The boat people then can be seen as the unlucky victims of a fear and anger epidemic. Something of this is implicit in the comments by the then Prime Minister, John Howard, at the time of the *Tampa* incident that the unfortunate passengers were trying to 'intimidate us with our own decency'; but that Australians would not be intimidated because 'We will decide who comes to this country and the circumstances in which they come'.

STUDENT EXERCISES

1   How do you think refugee children (including teenagers) with little or no previous education can best be assisted in school?
2   Why do you think some refugee groups have been welcomed into Australia, while others are treated as unwelcome?
3   Environmental scientists tell us that global warming may create a large number of 'environmental refugees' from low-lying parts of the world, including islands near Australia. Consider how Australia could respond to this.
4   Alice Pung's *Unpolished Gem* provides many examples of a refugee family adapting to Australian culture. Interview a refugee who came to Australia as a child about the adaptations made by their family and/or friends.

Notes

1   Many thanks for contributions and advice to Emma Pearson, Zachary Steel and Paul White.
2   United Nations High Commission for Refugees (UNHCR), *Global Trends: Refugees Asylum-seekers, Returnees, Internally Displaced and Stateless Persons 2006* (revised 16.07.07), UNHCR, Geneva, 2007.

3   United Nations High Commission for Refugees (UNHCR), *Statistical Yearbook 2003*, UNHCR, Geneva, 2003.
4   R. Gaita, *Romulus My Father*, Text Publishing, Melbourne, 1998.
5   K. Neumann, 'Been There, Done That?', in *Yearning to Breathe Free*, eds, D. Lusher & N. Haslam, Federation Press, Sydney, 2007, pp. 21–34.
6   S. Gifford, C. Bakopanos, I. Kaplan & I. Correa-Velez, 'Meaning or Measurement? Researching the Social Contexts of Health and Settlement among Newly-arrived Refugee Youth in Melbourne, Australia', *Journal of Refugee Studies*, 20, 2007, pp. 414–40.
7   Department of Immigration and Citizenship, *Report on Performance 2006: Output 1–2: Refugee and Humanitarian Entry and Stay*, Department of Immigration and Citizenship, Canberra, 2006.
8   B. Grant, *The Boat People: An Age Investigation*, Penguin, Melbourne, 1979 as cited in P. Mares, *Borderline*, UNSW Press, Sydney, 2002, p. 66.
9   Mares, 2002; D. Marr & M. Wilkinson, *Dark Victory*, Allen & Unwin, Sydney, 2003.
10   D. Silove, Z. Steel & R. Mollica, 'Detention of Asylum Seekers: Assault on Health, Human Rights and Social Development', *The Lancet*, 357, 2001, pp. 1436–7; Human Rights and Equal Opportunity Commission, *A Last Resort: A Summary Guide to the National Inquiry into Children in Immigration Detention*, HREOC, Sydney, 2004, <www.hreoc.gov.au/human_rights/children_detention_report/index.html>, accessed 28 April 2008.
11   High Court of Australia, '*Al-Kateb vs Godwin & Ors*, HCA 37, 219 CLR 562; 208 ALR 124', High Court of Australia, Canberra.
12   D. Marr, 'Escape From a Life in Limbo', *Sydney Morning Herald*, October 27–28, 2007, p. 298.
13   Gerry Hand and Nick Bolkus, cited in P. Mares, 2002, p. 90.
14   Mares, 2002, p. 123.
15   Peter Reith, Alan Jones and John Howard in Mares, 2002, p. 134.
16   HREOC, 2004.
17   P.N. Bhagwati, *Human Rights and Immigration Detention in Australia: Report of the Regional Advisor for Asia and the Pacific of the UNHCR*, UNHCR, Geneva, 2002, p. 16.
18   *Mercy Refugee Service Newsletter*, 29 September 2007.
19   M. Fazel, J. Wheeler & J. Danesh, 'Prevalence of Serious Mental Disorder in 7000 Refugees Resettled in Western Countries: A Systematic Review', *The Lancet*, 365, 2005, pp. 1309–14.
20   M. Hodes, 'Psychologically Distressed Refugee Children in the United Kingdom', *Child Psychology & Psychiatry Review*, 5, 2000, pp. 57–68.
21   R. Schweitzer, F. Melville, Z. Steel & P. Lacherez, 'Trauma, Post-migration Living Difficulties, and Social Support as Predictors of Psychological Adjustment in Resettled Sudanese Refugees', *Australian and New Zealand Journal of Psychiatry*, 40, 2006, pp. 179–87.
22   Z. Steel, D. Silove, T. Phan & A. Bauman, 'Long-term Effect of Psychological Trauma on the Mental Health of Vietnamese Refugees Resettled in Australia: A Population Based Study', *The Lancet*, 360, 2002, pp. 1056–62; Schweitzer et al., 2006.
23   R. McKelvey & J. Webb, 'Unaccompanied Status as a Risk Factor in Vietnamese Amerasians', *Social Sciences and Medicine*, 41, 1995, pp. 261–96; R. McKelvey & J. Webb, 'A Prospective Study of Psychological Distress Related to Refugee Camp Experience', *Australian & New Zealand Journal of Psychiatry*, 31, 1997, pp. 549–54.
24   Schweitzer et al., 2002.
25   Z. Solomon, M. Kotler & M. Mikulincer, 'Combat-related Posttraumatic Stress Disorder among Second-generation Holocaust Survivors: Preliminary Findings', *American Journal of Psychiatry*, 145, 1988, pp. 865–8.
26   D. Silove, 'The Psychosocial Effects of Torture, Mass Human Rights Violations and Refugee Trauma: Towards an Integrated Conceptual Framework', *Journal of Nervous and Mental Disease*, 187, 1999, pp. 200–7.
27   R. Punamäki, 'Can Ideological Commitment Protect Children's Psychosocial Well-being in Situations of Political Violence?', *Child Development*, 67, 1996, pp. 55–69; M. Basoglu & M. Paker, 'Severity of Trauma as a Predictor of Long-term Psychological Status in Survivors of Torture', *Journal of Anxiety Disorders*, 9, 1995, pp. 339–50.
28   Silove, 1999.
29   Steel et al., 2002.
30   Schweitzer et al., 2006; D. Silove & S. Ekblad, 'How Well do Refugees Adapt after Resettlement in Western Countries?', *Acta Psychiatrica Scandinavica*, 106, 6, 2002, pp. 401–2.
31   Steel et al., 1999.

Ailsa Burns

32 Canadian Task Force on Mental Health Issues Affecting Immigrants and Refugees, *After the Door Had Been Opened: Report of the Canadian Task Force on Mental Health Issues affecting Immigrants and Refugees*, Health and Welfare Canada, Ottawa, 1988.

33 K. Hakuta, Y.G. Butler & D. Witt, *How Long Does it Take English Learners to Attain Proficiency? Policy Report 2000–01*, University of California Linguistic Minority Research Institute, Santa Barbara.

34 R. Hek, 'The Role of Education in the Settlement of Young Refugees in the UK: The Experiences of Young Refugees', *Practice*, 17, 2005, pp. 157–71.

35 J. Brown, J. Miller & J. Mitchell, 'Interrupted Schooling and the Acquisition of Literacy: Experiences of Sudanese Refugees in Victorian Secondary Schools', *Australian Journal of Language and Literacy*, 29, 2006, pp. 150–62.

36 Brown et al., 2006, p. 158.

37 Brown et al., 2006, pp. 159–60.

38 Z. Steel, D. Silove, K. Bird, P. McGorry & O. Mohan, 'Pathways from War Trauma to Posttraumatic Stress Symptoms among Tamil Asylum Seekers, Refugees and Immigrants', *Journal of Traumatic Stress*, 12, 1999, pp. 421–35; M. Thompson, P. McGorry, D. Silove & Z. Steel, 'Maribyrnong Detention Centre Tamil Survey', in *The Mental Health and Well-being of On-shore Asylum Seekers in Australia*, eds, D. Silove & Z. Steel, Psychiatry Research and Teaching Unit, Sydney, 1998, pp. 27–30.

39 Silove et al., 2001, p. 1437.

40 Bhagwati, 2002; HREOC, 2004.

41 HREOC, 2004, *Summary Guide, Safety in Detention Centres*, p. 1.

42 HREOC, 2004, *Summary Guide, Mental Health*, p. 3.

43 *The Australian*, 4 October 2007, pp. 3, 15; Interview with Kevin Andrews, Minister for Immigration and Citizenship, Radio National Breakfast Program, 5 October 2007.

44 A. Pung, *Unpolished Gem*, Penguin, Melbourne, 2006, p. 9; A. Pung, 'Caveat Emptor', *The Monthly*, 17–20 October 2007, <www.themonthly.com.au/tm/node/67>, accessed 19 March 2008. See also K. Huynh, *Where the Sea Takes Us: A Vietnamese-Australian Story*, Harper Collins, Sydney, 2007.

45 L. Allison, 'Introduction to Part 2', in *Yearning to Breathe Free*, eds, D. Lusher & N. Haslam, Federation Press, Sydney, 2007, p. 50.

46 C. Jencks, 'The Immigration Charade', *New York Review of Books*, 54, 14, 2007, pp. 49–52.

47 S. Pinker, *How the Mind Works*, Penguin, Harmondsworth, UK, 1998.

Part D

Beyond Face-to-face: Policy 'in the Best Interests' of Children

10

Child Protection and Out-of-home Care: The Responsibility of Families, Community and State

Judy Cashmore

One of the main areas of contention involving children, families and the state—in Australia and other common law countries—is the extent to which the state is seen as having a legitimate interest in exercising control over the upbringing and education of children, and in intervening in the private domain of the family. While child rearing is regarded as primarily the responsibility of families, ensuring the safety and welfare of children is now generally accepted as a responsibility of the state. This is because the state has a vested interest in children's development and in their capacity to participate in and contribute to society, and because the state is increasingly seen as having a role in protecting and upholding children's rights.

The role of the state in most Western societies now includes providing education for all school-age children (unless they and their parents choose non-government schooling), offering cash income support and other forms of assistance to families with children, and directly intervening when the family is not able to or fails to provide adequate care and protection for children.[1] Where families do not properly meet their responsibilities, a range of responses from the state may follow. These include deducting funds from parents' wages to provide maintenance for their children; initiating investigations and court action to establish the need for, and to secure, orders to protect the child; and, as a last resort, removing children from the care of their parents. The main focuses of this chapter are on these latter responses, the context in which the state intervenes to protect children in Australia, the approach that is taken, and the consequences for children when this happens.

Contexts

Parental/state responsibility for children

The general acceptance that the state has some responsibility for children marks a significant change over the last hundred years in common law countries, from a laissez-faire, minimalist view of the role of the state and the former common law notion that children were the 'property' of their fathers.[2] In particular, over the last decade or so, changes in family law and child welfare law in common law countries have signalled a clear shift from a narrow definition of parental rights over children to a broader definition emphasising parents' duties and responsibilities to their children.[3] As Coady explains, a 'parental right' is the right to look after the rights of the child, and in that way is more like a duty than a right.[4] It does, however, give the parent the power to make certain decisions for those children who are not able to make decisions for themselves. But this is not an unqualified power. For if parents consistently act in a way that clearly harms the child, the right is forfeited.[5]

Evidence of the increasing recognition of the state's responsibility for children and its duty of care towards them is made explicit in the United Nations Convention on the Rights of the Child and in recently revised child welfare legislation.[6] By ratifying the Convention, Australia[7] and other countries, with the exception of the USA, have committed to recognising and implementing the provisions of the Convention, and in particular the three Ps: provision, protection and participation. As Durrant puts it, this means that 'children's basic needs must be met, children must be protected from violence and exploitation, and children must have the opportunity to express their views and influence decision making' that concerns them.[8] The Convention formalises what children might expect from the state, while still recognising the primacy of children's relationships with their parents and their family.

Significantly, children are generally not regarded as 'citizens' in common law countries,[9] in contrast to the approach and underlying philosophy in continental European countries. In Sweden, for example, 'children are considered to be full citizens and are entitled, therefore, to provision from, protection by, and participation in the government's policy decisions.'[10] In addition, children's rights are firmly expressed in policy and practice in relation to universal entitlement to services and more commitment to engaging with families. 'Rather than blaming and punishing individual parents in crisis, the Swedish system emphasises the collective responsibility of *all* citizens to care for and support children.'[11] This is in contrast to the more adversarial approach to the state as an external regulator in English-speaking common law countries. There is, however, evidence of increasing interest in children's citizenship and all that entails in various countries including Australia and New Zealand.[12]

Defining abuse and neglect

Although there may now be general acceptance of the state's responsibility in relation to the safety, welfare and well-being of children, views vary markedly on the particular circumstances in which state intervention is seen to be warranted. While there is likely to be agreement about the need to intervene when children are sexually abused, deliberately burnt, severely beaten or neglected to the point where their health and development are jeopardised, there is little agreement about less extreme forms of parental behaviour, and when these cross the line to become abusive, harmful or 'not good enough'. When does constant belittling become emotionally abusive, minimal supervision become neglectful, and bodily punishment physically abusive rather than 'reasonable chastisement'? How is the state to know and assess poor versus abusive or neglectful parenting? What form of intervention is warranted? Under what circumstances?[13]

These are necessarily subjective judgments that are 'defined within the context of the normative and deviant child rearing behaviour of the time'.[14] Awareness and concern about child abuse have increased markedly since the late 1960s, and definitions and interpretations of what is abusive have broadened from the 'battered babies' described by Kempe 'to the physical abuse of children of all ages, to failure to thrive, neglect, psychological and emotional abuse, and sexual abuse'.[15] More recently, definitions of abuse have been extended to include exposure to domestic violence as concern and understanding about its effects on children's psychosocial and emotional development have increased.[16]

While beliefs about what constitutes acceptable and abusive behaviour towards children have changed over time, they are also culturally determined, and may vary across sub-groups within a culture (for example, social class). This can create some difficulties for a multicultural society such as Australia, a dilemma clearly articulated by Korbin:

> Failure to allow for a cultural perspective in defining child abuse and neglect pro-motes an ethnocentric position in which one's own set of cultural beliefs and prac-tices are presumed to be preferable to others. On the other hand, a stance of extreme cultural relativism, in which all judgements of humane treatment of children are sus-pended, may be used to justify a lesser standard of care for some children.[17]

Korbin identified three levels at which definitions of abuse may be formulated to provide some direction in resolving the definitional difficulties that are exacerbated when these levels are confounded. The first level includes 'practices which are viewed as acceptable in the culture in which they occur, but as abusive or neglectful by out-siders'.[18] This is where cultural conflict is most likely. It is useful for those of us who are members of Western cultures and apt to regard our own values as superior to be reminded that many Western child-rearing behaviours (such as leaving babies and infants to sleep alone in separate rooms and the use of 'controlled crying') are regarded by the members of some other cultures as abusive.

The second level involves 'idiosyncratic abuse or neglect', which includes those behaviours that 'fall outside the range of acceptability' for that society. Although cultures vary in what they deem acceptable, cross-cultural conflict is less likely at this level. For example, while some societies accept fondling of infants' genitals as a means of soothing the child, fondling older children or fondling for adult sexual gratification falls outside the boundaries of acceptable behaviour across cultures.

The third level concerns societal conditions such as poverty, homelessness and lack of health care that are beyond the control of individual parents. While societies vary in the extent to which they tolerate these conditions, and in their capacity to change them, it is clear that the same tolerance level does not apply uniformly within societies. For example, while such conditions would not be condoned for mainstream culture, they are endemic among particular minority groups, such as the Australian Aboriginal population. At the same time, there is increasing concern that 'cultural relativism' and fear of 'over-intervention' are doing just what Korbin warned against—justifying a lesser standard of care for some groups of children, such as Aboriginal children.

It is clear then, as Korbin[19] and others have pointed out, that 'there is no universal standard for optimal child care nor for child abuse and neglect' across or within cultures. In practice, however, child abuse and neglect are operationally defined by the decisions people make in referring suspected abuse and neglect to child protection services, and by the responses of those agencies to the referrals.[20] Different definitions may apply at different stages of the process, depending on the purpose, the expected consequences, and the perceived responsibility and degree of harm involved. The result is that cases may take different routes through the system, with more or less intervention, depending on the skills and the type of professional making the decision, their understanding of the legislative, policy and practice guidelines they are expected to follow, the information available to them, and their perceptions of the harm caused to the child and the assessed responsibility of the perpetrator for that harm.[21]

Incidence of reported child abuse and neglect

What do the available figures tell us about the prevalence of child abuse and neglect in Australia? How many children are reported as abused and neglected? How reliable are the figures? Are child abuse and neglect increasing?

There are no reliable figures on the *prevalence* of child abuse and neglect—the number of children who have experienced child abuse and neglect—in Australia.[22] We therefore have to rely on statistics about the incidence of abuse and neglect that are reported to the various statutory departments in each state and territory.[23] The most reliable figures of reported child abuse and neglect are collated by the Australian Institute of Health and Welfare, based on information supplied by the states and territories, using an agreed general definition of abuse and neglect to take into account the significant differences between the states in relation to their legislation, policy and practice.[24] In the year 2006–07, there were 309,517 'notifications of child abuse and neglect' recorded nationally by state and territory departments. About one in five (58,563 or 18.9 per cent) of these notifications were 'substantiated', meaning that the statutory department investigated the report and concluded that 'the child has been, is being or is likely to be abused, neglected or otherwise harmed'.[25]

The number of notifications of abuse and neglect to the statutory authorities in Australia, the United Kingdom, Canada and the USA has shown a massive increase over the last thirty years or so. In the last decade, the number of reports across Australia has increased two-and-a-half times—from 91,734 in 1995–96 to 309,517 in 2006–07.[26] The number of substantiations has also increased, but to a lesser extent—from 29,833 in 1995–06 to 58,563 in 2006–07.

The interpretation of these figures, and particularly the recent escalation in the figures, is subject to considerable debate and speculation. Like most complex issues, there is no simple answer, but there are several reasons why the number of reports and the number of substantiated reports have increased so markedly. These explanations relate to the changing definitions of child abuse and neglect, the changes in reporting requirements and practices, changed recording procedures by departments, and increased awareness of the harm to children from abusive and neglectful parenting.

First, the definitions of abuse and neglect have been widened to encompass forms of parental and caregiver behaviour that would previously not have been considered 'abusive'. These include forms of physical punishment that were relatively common in schools and homes several decades ago but are now clearly accepted as excessive and abusive (for example, the use of straps, belts and canes) and, more recently, children's exposure to 'domestic violence' as a form of emotional abuse as our understanding of the effects on children's development has grown.[27]

Second, the threshold for reporting has been 'lowered' in most jurisdictions here and in other Anglo-American models to include ('significant') 'risk of harm'. Third, mandatory reporting has been expanded in all Australian states except Western Australia to encompass most professionals working with children.[28] In addition, various jurisdictions have introduced centralised call centres that record all calls, whereas previously reports taken at local offices may not all have been recorded or treated as notifications.[29]

Fourth, there is evidence that the increase in both reports and substantiated cases reflects an increasing incidence of and awareness of parental substance abuse, domestic violence and parental mental illness or disability.[30] In a recent review of drug use in the family, for example, it was noted that international and local studies suggest that 'at least half of the families identified by child and protective services have a profile that includes parental substance misuse', often in combination with family violence, psychiatric disability, intellectual disability, physical disability and financial stress.[31] Cultural background and family type,[32] with underlying poverty in both cases, are also significant factors that affect the rate of reported child abuse and neglect, with Aboriginal and Torres Strait Islander children, and children from single-parent families, both overrepresented. Depending on the state or territory, Aboriginal children were from five to ten times more likely than other children to be the subject of a substantiated notification, particularly for neglect.[33]

Finally, there is evidence that Western societies are increasingly risk averse and are demanding 'higher levels of risk assurance', and are hypercritical of child protection services when children are injured or die as a result of abuse or neglect. A recent New Zealand study has shown that increased media attention was followed by increased reporting, adding to the demand on already burdened systems.[34]

Judy Cashmore

'Causes' of child abuse and neglect

The overrepresentation of Aboriginal children and children from female-headed single-parent families highlights a number of the recognised risk factors for physical and emotional abuse and neglect: poverty, unemployment, lack of resources, social stress and isolation. These factors do not directly *cause* child abuse and neglect but, together with other factors associated with the carer, the child and the family, they clearly increase the risk of abuse and neglect, especially when they are not counteracted by protective factors such as social and community support.[35]

Physical and emotional abuse and neglect

At the individual carer level, some of the main risk factors for physical and emotional abuse and neglect are a history of being abused or neglected as a child, depression, substance abuse, poor impulse control and low self-esteem. There is also evidence that abusive carers are more likely to have unrealistic expectations of the child's behaviour (for example, to expect that toddlers can be toilet-trained without 'accidents'), and to attribute negative explanations to the child ('he's just crying to get at me').[36] While most parents who were abused or neglected as children do not go on to abuse their own children, there is some evidence to suggest that those who do so are more likely to be hypersensitive and negatively reactive to babies' crying, and to stressful and non-stressful mother–child interactions,[37] and that a history of abuse may indeed result in exaggerated stress responses or hyperreactivity.[38]

At the child's level, a number of factors have been found to increase the risk of abuse and neglect. These include the child's developmental stage, temperament, health status, disability and behaviour. Younger children are both more vulnerable to the harm caused by abuse and neglect[39] and more likely to be abused and neglected than older children, but adolescents are also at greater risk than pre-adolescent children. As Belsky points out, young children may be at greater risk of maltreatment for several reasons.[40] They spend more time with their carers and are more physically and emotionally dependent on them. They have more difficulty in regulating their emotions than older children, and if physical force is used to control them it is potentially more damaging to a younger child. Both toddlers and adolescents also display oppositional behaviour in asserting their independence, and it seems likely that this behaviour increases their risk of maltreatment.[41] Children who put a strain on family resources in other ways by having a disability, being in poor health, being unwanted or too closely spaced are also more likely to be at increased risk of maltreatment, not just within Western industrialised societies, but cross-culturally.[42]

Children's behaviour as a risk factor is less clear-cut. While a mismatch between the parent's and the child's temperament may increase the risk of maltreatment, the evidence seems to point to children's behavioural problems being more likely to be a consequence of maltreatment than a cause of it.[43] In fact, it seems likely that it is the parent's responses and attributions about the child's behaviour that explain or predict their abusive response rather than the child's behaviour. Abusive parents tend to report more problem behaviours by their children than are reported by outside 'observers', and they are also more likely than non-abusive parents to rely on physical punishment, and less likely to support and reward children's positive behaviours.[44] Although maltreated infants and toddlers may display behaviour problems that make them difficult to manage, interventions to increase mothers' sensitivity and knowledge about children's development and behaviour management strategies have shown some success.[45]

It is clear that child maltreatment can have many causes, with a number of risk factors at the level of the individual carer and child, the family environment, the community context, and even at the societal level in determining the value of children and the tolerance of violence. According to this developmental–ecological approach, maltreatment and maladaptive parenting occur when 'stressors outweigh supports and risks are greater than protective factors'.[46] There are therefore multiple pathways to physical and emotional abuse and neglect.[47]

Sexual abuse

The preceding discussion of 'causes' focused on physical and emotional abuse and neglect and excluded sexual abuse. This is because the causes of child sexual abuse are recognised as being significantly different from the causes of other forms of child maltreatment, although they are still insufficiently understood.[48] While personal and/or socio-economic disadvantages are recognised as risk factors for physical and emotional abuse and neglect, their association with child sexual abuse is much weaker. 'Unlike neglect (which is often seen as a function of poverty) and physical abuse which is often related to a range of stresses, sexual abuse cuts across the whole socioeconomic spectrum. It exists in all types of communities and at all socioeconomic levels.'[49] The best predictor of sexual abuse is still gender: the vast majority of sexual abuse perpetrators are male and the majority of the children in *reported* cases are female.

Consequences

There is a substantial literature on the consequences or the effects of abuse and neglect on children's behaviour and socio-emotional development.[50] The adverse outcomes that have been associated with abuse and neglect include problems in attachment and trust, poor self-esteem and self-regulation, aggressive behaviour and depression. More recently, there has been significant attention to the effects on young children's brain development and the underlying neurobiological processes that are thought to mediate the longer-term outcomes.[51] This has galvanised the focus of a range of professionals who are presenting this as evidence for the need for early intervention to prevent difficult-to-reverse adverse outcomes.

It is also important to note that many of the social and familial factors known to increase the risk of child maltreatment are also significant predictors of other social problems concerning children. Poverty, social isolation, harsh and inconsistent parenting, parental rejection, family conflict and violence have also been identified as risk factors

Judy Cashmore

for juvenile offending, youth suicide and homelessness. Furthermore, there is evidence that young children who are abused and neglected are at increased risk of being aggressive and involved in criminal behaviour as adolescents.[52] Working to decrease the risk factors and increase the protective factors early in children's lives is therefore likely to have additional pay-offs, not just in preventing child abuse and neglect, but also in tackling juvenile crime, homelessness and mental health problems.

Responding to child abuse and neglect

The origins of child maltreatment lie at several different levels, and correspondingly the response needs to occur at different levels, and to take both a short- and a long-term perspective.[53] Unfortunately, the main focus of the response to child abuse and neglect has generally been *after* maltreatment has occurred and been identified, and it is also usually directed at the individual level—to the particular child and family involved. It has tended to be reactive rather than proactive, preventive and community-based, although increasingly there are programs such as maternal nurse home visiting, play and parental support groups and other early intervention programs that aim to prevent child abuse and neglect by developing family and community supports.[54]

Over the last decade, however, there has been increasing concern in the USA, the United Kingdom and Australia about the capacity of the system to respond to and provide appropriate services for the ever-increasing numbers of child protection reports that concern families and children *in need* rather than reports of children *being harmed*. Concerns about the focus, the effectiveness and the efficacy of the statutory investigative response were clearly articulated in the 1990s in both the United Kingdom and the USA,[55] and increasingly in these countries and in Australia,[56] New Zealand[57] and Canada.[58] The common increasingly urgent concern is the capacity of child protection systems based on the Anglo–American model to manage the ever-increasing numbers of reports. These systems have become largely absorbed by receiving, recording and 'investigating' reports, relying on risk-assessment methodologies to triage the flow of reports, and with few resources to help or support children and families that come to their attention. Indeed, the Dartington research in the United Kingdom indicated that families were often less receptive and less likely to receive services after being reported to the child protection authority than before it.[59] As Scott[60] and Melton[61] and others have argued, in these systems the focus is on 'What happened?', not 'How is the child?' and 'What can we do to help?'

In contrast, continental European models in Sweden, Norway and France, for example, have a far greater focus on universal services for children and supporting families, with child protection services embedded within the overall child welfare and public health system.[62] Their child homicide rates are very low compared with English-speaking common law countries, as also are the rates of injury, asthma and mental health problems among children.[63] Clearly, social policy does matter but the relationships between the children, families, the community and the state are very complex and culturally embedded. The challenge is to build a child welfare system—rather than a child protection system—that encourages early intervention and prevention so that fewer children in future need to be subjected to the more intrusive end of statutory intervention.

Children in out-of-home care

Removing children from their family in a transfer of guardianship to the state is the most serious form of intervention the state can take, and is increasingly a measure of 'last resort'. There are several reasons for this: a recognition of the need for connection with their families of origin for most children, and the evidence that many children return there even after some years in care; an acknowledgment that being in care does not ensure positive outcomes for children; and a severe shortage of carers. Only a small proportion of children who are the subject of a substantiated allegation of child abuse or neglect are found to be 'in need of care and protection', necessitating a court order, and even fewer are removed from their homes or have guardianship transferred from their parents. In 2006–07, for example, 32,585 children were the subject of a substantiated report in Australia, most commonly for emotional abuse or neglect. Just under 40 per cent of those for whom there was a substantiated report were admitted to care and protection orders and entered care in that year, two thirds for the first time. The highest rates of entry in all states and territories were for children under five years, and especially those under twelve months of age. There were 28,441 children in out-of-home care in Australia on 30 June 2007, representing 5.8 children per 1000 aged 0–17 years in the population.[64] This rate has nearly doubled over the last decade from 3 per 1000 in 1997 to 5.8 per 1000 in 2007. Once again, Indigenous children were heavily overrepresented, with 36.1 children per 1000 in care, making Indigenous children 8.3 times more likely to be in care than non-Indigenous children.[65]

PLACEMENT OF CHILDREN IN OUT-OF-HOME CARE

The most common placement for children in Australia who enter care is foster care (49.5 per cent in 2006–07), followed by relative or kinship care (43.9 per cent) with the exception of New South Wales, where relative care placements are now more prevalent than non-relative foster carers. The reasons for the increase in the numbers of children placed with relatives are both ideological and pragmatic. Relative care fits with notions of family preservation and the importance of children maintaining connections with their families. It is also cost-effective and practical because of the shortage of foster carers and the difficulty of finding suitable placements for children in need of care. It also has particular advantages for Indigenous children and is consistent with traditional practices of caring for children within their kinship groups. While some research points to positive benefits for children in relative care, especially in terms of stability and continuity of family contact, much of the research is descriptive and limited in relation to outcome measures for children.[66] There are also concerns about the lack of proper assessment and support for relative carers. Many relative carers are grandmothers who are older, single and have minimal economic resources, and who are called on to care for young children with little financial and practical support.

Another feature of out-of-home care in Australia is the attempt to increase the placement options for older children and troubled adolescents for whom foster placements are not appropriate. The difficult and challenging behaviours of some young people put considerable serious strain on an out-of-home care system which does not have the specialist services to meet their needs. The radical shift from residential care to family-based placements in the 1970s and 1980s occurred across the Western world, 'fuelled by cost considerations, abuse enquiries, research about children's development and attachment needs, notions of "normalisation" and "least restrictive environments" and a belief in the importance of families for children'.[67] It has, however, been more exaggerated in Australia so that a much lower proportion of children and young people in out-of-home care are now in residential care than in other countries such as the United Kingdom (15 per cent in 1999) and the USA (approximately 20 per cent). In 2005–06, only 4.9 per cent of children and young people in care in Australia were in residential care.[68] In 1961, the figure was closer to 46 per cent.[69] There is, however, renewed and increasing interest in Australia in the development of a range of therapeutic models of care for these young people, following overseas examples of specialist services, to try to meet their mental health, educational and safety needs.

PERMANENCY PLANNING

For many children who enter care, their stay in care is short-lived and intended to be so. In line with the now generally accepted principle that children should so far as possible remain within their families, the preferred option for permanency in most jurisdictions is for children to return to their families as soon as circumstances have changed to allow them to return safely and to be cared for adequately.

The national figures for Australia indicate that in 2006–07 around a quarter of the children in out-of-home care had been in care for less than twelve months (ranging from 20 per cent to 50 per cent in different jurisdictions); about one in five (ranging from 10 per cent to 30 per cent) had been in care for five years or longer.[70] The most obvious interpretation of these cross-sectional point-in-time figures is positive—that children are able to return home within relatively short periods. The problem revealed by the only Australian longitudinal study of children entering care is that most (69 per cent) of the 129 children who were entering care had already been in care before the entry into care that brought them into this study.[71] Similarly, other studies overseas have found that a significant proportion of children returned home re-enter care within twelve to twenty-four months.[72] This means that a significant number of children are 'oscillators', cycling in and out of care.[73] The concern is that current policies, intended to overcome the earlier problem of children drifting *in* care without proper planning and moving through multiple changes of placements, are now moving *in and out* of care or are remaining at home in unsafe and inadequate care for too long. Their 'recycling' or delayed entry to care means that when they do come into care they do so with significant levels of disturbance and attachment difficulties, increasing the likelihood of further placement breakdowns and 'corroding the very core of the capacity of a child to develop trust'.[74]

One of the most contentious issues in child welfare policy and practice is how and when to draw the line and ensure some certainty and permanence in the lives of children in (or *in and out of*) out-of-home care. Most jurisdictions have attempted to implement policies and practices, backed by changes in legislation, to promote timely, long-term decision making for children in care. The reality is that such certainty, permanence and security for children continue to be difficult to achieve.[75]

One reason is that children are often returned home with insufficient preparation and very little support. There is a multitude of factors associated with or predicting a safe, timely and successful return home, but Marianne Berry's work in the USA indicates that engagement with the family is crucial and that re-abuse rates and re-entry to care for children are less likely the more time and help families receive in their own homes.[76] These families often need help with retaining housing, managing debt and financial stress, overcoming substance abuse problems, dealing with mental health issues and engaging with the community.

Where returning children to live with their parents or within the extended family is not a realistic option, the other options for permanency and the order of choice tend to vary across countries. In the USA, the *Adoption and Safe Families Act* of 1997 actively promotes adoption as the preferred option for children who cannot return home and prescribes strict time limits within which a decision must be made and parental rights terminated. Official funding policy also penalises states that do not meet their targets for adoption from foster care.[77] The intention is to try to force decision makers to make the hard decision to terminate parental responsibility, but such policies have been strongly criticised for being unduly harsh and unfair when few resources are provided to help parents make the required changes, particularly in relation to drug rehabilitation. Further, the concern is that such policies cause workers and judges to make decisions to return children home too quickly in order to avoid having to terminate parental rights, a move that may jeopardise the child's safety and well-being.[78]

Adoption is also encouraged in the United Kingdom but the stance is not so 'tough', and long-term foster care is still accepted as a reasonable option.[79] In Australia, adoption by carers is much less common and arguably under-used, with only twenty-one children being adopted by their carers in the year 2005–06. There appear to be a number of reasons for the very low adoption rate for children from care in Australia. Again these are both ideological and pragmatic. The ideological objections relate to the severing of legal ties with the biological family and the cultural inappropriateness of the concept of adoption within Indigenous communities, especially given the history of the 'stolen generations'. Legislative provisions in most states 'allow for adoptions by carers or relatives other than stepparents only in exceptional circumstances, that is, when a guardianship or custody order would not adequately provide for the welfare of the child'.[80] Practically, many carers cannot afford to lose the carer allowance for the children, and many workers do not have the time and the skills to process the adoption, especially if the parents are not contactable or not willing or able to give consent. In many cases, children are also in the care of relatives and adoption by a relative is neither necessary nor appropriate when the child remains in the same extended family.

Perhaps one reason that this area has been so difficult and contentious is that there are few midway options. The choice is often a binary one: to leave/return children home or to place them in foster/kinship care. Other options that are beginning to be considered include 'shared care', extended respite care with professional foster carers and 'boarding school'/residential care arrangements, all of which provide support to the whole family and care for the child on a shared basis.[81] The alternative legal option is a permanent care order. 'Unlike adoption orders, permanent care orders do not change the legal status of the child and they expire when the child turns 18 or marries.'[82]

Judy Cashmore

CHILDREN'S EXPERIENCE IN CARE

The difficulties facing children in care, and in particular children who drift in and out of care, are well documented. While some children experience a series of 'broken' placements—numerous workers, changes of school, and little contact with their parents, siblings and other relatives—a number of children in care do well in stable, long-term foster care. When compared with children in the community who are not in care, however, children in care are generally significantly behind in their school performance and educational achievements, and their emotional well-being and physical and mental health are often significantly poorer. They often have difficulty forming and maintaining intimate relationships, and may display asocial or antisocial behaviours.[83]

The reasons why children in care do more poorly than other children are complex and, as some recent studies and reviews show, relate to their early adverse environment and pre-care experiences, and to some extent to their in-care experience and lack of emotional security in care.[84] There is increasing evidence that children who come into care later have higher levels of disturbance (and lower chances of remediation) than those who enter care early. This is in line with the earlier discussion about the effects of abuse and neglect on children's early brain development, and the 'damage' caused to children who 'oscillate' or cycle in and out of care.

UNSTABLE CARE

Shane first came to the notice of the Department when he was two years old. He was placed with his aunt when he was three and lived there until he was twelve. He was assessed as being temperamentally difficult and emotionally insecure. He was suspended from school and his aunt could no longer cope with his behaviour. A series of temporary respite care and refuge placements followed, then a number of attempts to restore him to his mother, then his father, then his aunt. He became a ward when he was thirteen, and had several stints in residential care and a detention centre.

Shane was discharged from the care of the state at sixteen because the Department said there was nothing more they could do for him. He did not complete Year 9, and has had a series of casual jobs. He has a history of problematic relationships with housemates and family members who he feels have rejected him. He has been homeless and stayed in refuges on a number of occasions before and after leaving care. Shane says he has had problems with substance abuse and had attempted suicide on at least one occasion, and felt that no one really loved or cared about him.[85]

It is important, however, to recognise that the findings of various comparative studies depend on the study design. While point-in-time comparisons of children in care with children not in care in the general population generally indicate poorer outcomes for children in care, longitudinal studies of children in care have shown that children's cognitive performance and their social and emotional adjustment generally improve over time in care, especially in the context of stable care.[86] Furthermore, children who remained in care were 'better off' in terms of their behavioural and emotional adjustment and 'quality of life' than those who were returned home or whose entry into care was delayed.[87]

The critical role of stability of placement in care and, more importantly, children's perceived emotional security, is evident in several overseas studies and recently in a longitudinal study of young people leaving care in Australia.[88] Cashmore and Paxman found that young people who had spent at least 75 per cent of their time in care in one long-term placement were better off than those who had not, even if they were not living in that placement when they were discharged from wardship. They attended fewer schools, were happier, were more likely to have completed at least Year 10 at school, to report being able to 'make ends meet', to be satisfied with what the Department had done for them, to be less likely to say they missed out on affection and 'things other kids had', and were less likely to have thought about or attempted suicide.

Perceived emotional security was, however, a more powerful predictor of positive outcomes, and young people who indicated that they had felt secure and that they were loved while they were in care were also doing significantly better five years after leaving care than those who had never felt there was someone who loved and cared about them. Young people who reported that they could call upon a range of other people (family members, former carers, networks) for social and emotional support, and for financial support, were faring significantly better four to five years after leaving care than those whose level of perceived support was less. This was also related to the level of 'felt security' in care; young people who had felt more secure in care also felt they had more supports available to them after leaving care.[89]

STABLE CARE

Jade became a ward when she was fourteen after being sexually abused by her father and rejected by her mother and sisters. By her choice, she was placed in a non-government children's home for the whole time she was in care rather than in foster care. She developed a very positive and supportive relationship with one of the home's workers and had a committed departmental caseworker who made repeated, and finally successful, applications for her to take an exchange trip overseas and to take up semi-independent living on her return in a transition house within the same agency. She had an extensive support network that included members of her church, her former worker and other friends, but she had no contact with her family. As a young adult, Jade had had a variety of work experiences working in rural areas, and was planning to do a child care course. She had had no problems in relation to substance use or criminal involvement, and she had never attempted or thought about suicide. She had never been homeless and had been either working or studying throughout her time in care and after leaving care. [90]

LEAVING CARE

The risks for children and young people in out-of-home care continue beyond childhood and their time in care. Young people who may have had little continuity or stability

Judy Cashmore

in out-of-home care are often discharged from care at the age of sixteen or eighteen, with little financial and social support, and with poor prospects for employment and good stable accommodation. By contrast, many young people in the general population living with their parents now often remain at home until they are in their early to middle twenties, and they may leave and return several times before they finally live independently. While increasing expectations of government suggest that parents be responsible for their children's post-secondary education fees and living expenses into their twenties, there is minimal support from governments to assist the young people for whom the state has assumed guardianship to make their transition to independent adulthood. Research has consistently shown that young people leaving care have low levels of educational attainment and high rates of unemployment, mobility, homelessness, financial difficulty, loneliness and physical and mental health problems.[91]

Although the state clearly has a duty to continue providing support, this responsibility has been recognised only recently.[92] The concept of 'corporate parenting', increasingly recognised in the United Kingdom and elsewhere, is a term that has not yet achieved much currency in Australia.[93] Priority access to services for children in care and after leaving care is not well established in practice here, despite some of the rhetoric and the development of a Charter for Children in Care.

Improving the response to child abuse and neglect

While there have been some significant advances over the past thirty years or so in the recognition of child abuse and neglect, and in the acceptance of some communal responsibility for child protection and for the care of children who can no longer live with their families, there are some very big challenges ahead. There are at least three areas for making some inroads. These include proper resourcing and shared responsibility, early intervention and prevention, and participation by children and families in the decisions that affect their lives.

PROPER RESOURCING AND SHARED RESPONSIBILITY

The lack of resources in child protection and out-of-home care, especially in terms of professionally qualified, well-supervised and supported workers, is not new and in many areas is getting worse. Indeed, there is increasing concern about the continuing sustainability of the child protection and out-of-home care systems based on the Anglo-American model.[94] Doing more of the same and doing it more efficiently is not the solution. Engaging in more prevention and early intervention measures, engaging more with families and calling upon services beyond the statutory departments, need to be part of a rethinking of the model. Population health research has clearly shown that many of the determinants of 'health' and well-being lie in housing, employment and income support, and social support.[95]

Pressures on child welfare services have been increased by the inadequacy of other services, particularly in relation to mental health problems and substance abuse, and by a philosophy that sees the responsibility for children as sitting more squarely with the family than one that is shared by the state and the community.[96] Working out the balance and what measures and approaches are effective with what children and families in what circumstances, and how to scale up and implement those approaches, are critical.

EARLY INTERVENTION AND PREVENTION

The aim of early intervention and prevention is, of course, to forestall abuse and neglect and to promote children's development and well-being. This means taking action before problems develop to the point where full-scale protective intervention is necessary—action that must often be early in the life of the child, or when there are early indications of problems such as emotional disturbance or behaviour problems in the child. The need for more services and coordinated early intervention in relation to children with behavioural problems is pressing, because these are the children who may not get the help they need from the available services and are often then suspended or expelled from the school or even pre-school system, and may be later involved in the care or juvenile justice system.

Early intervention programs can be universal (available, say, to all parents or all first-time parents), or more specifically focused or targeted to particular social or demographic groups (for example, young single mothers, teenage mothers or parents experiencing stress and isolation as a result of poverty or other problems). The aim of a number of existing community-based programs and services such as family (or child and family) support programs, early intervention programs and home visiting programs is specifically to intervene early to prevent child abuse and neglect. They do so by providing a range of information, advice and support services to families at the neighbourhood/community level. Unfortunately, many are being forced to give priority to families already in crisis—a demand that usually denies them the 'luxury' of focusing on prevention. There is, however, increasing recognition of the need to support and coordinate a range of services for children and families, and to integrate and use other universal services, including good quality child care in a more effective way, to assist vulnerable children and their families.

PARTICIPATION OF CHILDREN AND FAMILIES

One important potential driver for change in the child protection and out-of-home care systems lies in greater participation in advocacy and decision making by children and their families, including members of the extended family. Associations such as CREATE, formerly the Australian Association of Young People in Care, are playing an increasingly influential role as advocates for children in care.

In many ways, children involved in the child protection system and their families both face similar difficulties in having their voices heard, and for similar reasons. Probably the biggest barriers are attitudinal. Children and young people tend to be treated as 'objects of concern', who either lack the capacity or competence to participate or who should not be burdened with the responsibility. Similarly, their parents tend to be seen as the cause of the concern relating to the child, and to lack the capacity to be involved—or perhaps even to have forfeited that right. Underlying these attitudes is also the issue of control, and the unwillingness of some workers to give up control to families.

Judy Cashmore

Other more structural reasons for this lack of involvement are the absence of guidance or requirements for workers to involve children and families in this way, a dearth of training for workers, and families' and children's ignorance of the processes. Even when some participatory processes do occur, they are likely to be mere tokens if there is no adequate preparation for the family and workers have no real commitment to it. For example, despite the requirements for working together and partnership with parents in the United Kingdom's *Children Act* 1989 and 2004, British research indicates that fewer than half of the parents who were asked about their involvement in child protection cases said that they had contributed to the plans, and only about a third said they took part in the decision making.[97] A number of studies asking children and young people for their views on and experience in taking part in decision making about their lives, have indicated significant difficulties for them being heard but positive benefits when they are.[98]

The positive signs are that there is now increasing acknowledgment of the participation rights of children and families in decision-making processes that affect them in the child protection and out-of-home care systems, and greater recognition of the value of such engagement. There are new models that encourage participation (for example, family group conferences) and there is evidence of the benefits of participation. These include improved practice, better outcomes for children and their families and greater commitment and compliance with decisions by families.[99] As pointed out in *Messages from Research*, 'A great deal of social work research shows that clients will co-operate even if it is against their obvious personal interests as long as they see the process as "just"'.[100]

Turning such rhetoric into reality and establishing a whole-of-government commitment to children and to participation is a real challenge. It requires some rethinking of the underlying philosophy and the more adversarial approach to child welfare and family and state responsibility compared with that in the continental European systems. Children are a community responsibility, and the price of not providing adequate care for them will be paid by the community in the long term.

STUDENT EXERCISES

1   To what extent do you think that child protection is a community responsibility? What do you think are the barriers to community responsibility in this area?

2   Why is it difficult to provide clear definitions of child abuse and neglect?

3   What are some of the risk factors for child abuse and neglect? How do you think they operate to increase the likelihood of children being abused or neglected?

4   How do you think a child welfare system might operate more effectively to protect children and promote their development and well-being?

5   Compare the two case studies presented in boxes in this chapter and discuss the factors that contribute to the best possible outcomes for children who are placed in out-of-home care.

Notes

1   Australian Law Reform Commission/Human Rights and Equal Opportunity Commission, *Seen and Heard: Priority for Children in the Legal Process*, Report no. 84, Australian Law Reform Commission, 1997.

2   Fox Harding, *Perspectives in Child Care Policy*, Longman, London, 1991.

3   R. Dingwall, J. Eekelaar & T. Murray, *The Protection of Children: State Intervention and Family Life* (2nd edn), Avebury, Aldershot, 1995.

4   M.M. Coady, 'Reflections on Children's Rights', in *Citizen Child: Australian Laws and Children's Rights*, ed., K. Funder, Australian Institute of Family Studies, Melbourne, 1996, p. 22.

5   There is still some way to go before children's rights are recognised in the same way as are there of adults. For example, children are still the only group in our society who may still legally be hit. J. Cashmore & N. de Haas, *Legal and Social Aspects of the Physical Punishment of Children*, Commonwealth Department of Human Services and Health, Canberra, 1995.

6   Fox Harding, 1991. For example, the *Children's Act* UK 1989, 2004 and the *NSW Children and Young Person's (Care and Protection) Act 1998*.

7   One assessment of how Australia measured up is outlined in The National Children's and Youth Law Centre and Defence for Children International (Australia), *The Non-Government Report on the Implementation of the Convention on the Rights of the Child in Australia*, May 2005, and more importantly in the UN Committee's Concluding Observations.

8   J. Durrant, 'From Mopping Up the Damage to Preventing the Flood: The Role of Social Policy in Preventing Violence Against Children', *Social Policy Journal of New Zealand*, 28, 2006, <www.msd.govt.nz/documents/publications/msd/journal/issue28/28-pages-1-17.pdf>, accessed 24 March 2008.

9   J. Cashmore, 'Children: Non-contractual Persons?', in *The New Contractualism?*, eds, G. Davis, B. Sullivan & A. Yeatman, Macmillan, Melbourne, 1997, pp. 57–70.

10   Durrant, 2006, pp. 7–8.

11   Durrant, 2006, p. 7.

12   C. Waldegrave, 'Contrasting National and Welfare Responses to Violence to Children', *Social Policy Journal of New Zealand*, 27, 2006, pp. 57–76.

13   Fox Harding, 1991, pp. 1–3.

14   D. Scott & S. Swain, *Confronting Cruelty: Historical Perspectives on Child Protection in Australia*, Melbourne University Press, Melbourne, 2002, p. xii.

15   Kempe, 1978, cited in D. Gough, 'Defining the Problem', *Child Abuse and Neglect*, 20, 1996, p. 994.

16   P. Jaffe, D. Wolfe & S. Wilson, *Children of Battered Women*, Sage, Newbury Park, CA, 1990; C. Humphreys & N. Stanley, eds, *Domestic Violence and Child Protection: Directions for Good Practice*, Jessica Kingsley Publishers, London, 2006.

17   J.E. Korbin, 'Cross-cultural Perspectives and Research Directions for the 21st Century', *Child Abuse & Neglect*, 15, Supplement 1, 1991, p. 68.

18   Korbin, 1991, p. 68.

19   Korbin, 1991.

20   D. Gough, 1996.

21   H. Dubowitz, M. Black, R.H. Starr & S. Zuravin, 'A Conceptual Definition of Child Neglect', *Criminal Justice and Behavior*, 20, 1993, pp. 8–26; Gough, 1996; S.J. Rose & W. Meezan, 'Defining Child Neglect: Evolution, Influences and Issues', *Social Service Review*, 67, 1997, pp. 279–93.

22   National Child Protection Clearinghouse, *Child Abuse Statistics*, Child Abuse Prevention Resource Sheet No. 1, Australian Institute of Family Studies, Melbourne, 2004.

23   Clearly these reports or notifications include concerns about children that do not meet the criteria for abuse and neglect, and on the other hand, it is also clear that not all abuse and neglect is reported. There is therefore an unknown 'dark figure'— the number of children who have been abused and/or neglected but not *recorded* or not *substantiated* as being so.

24   L. Bromfield & D. Higgins, *National Comparison of Child Protection Systems: National Child Protection Clearing House Child Abuse Prevention Issues Paper no. 22*, Australian Institute of Family Studies, Melbourne, 2005; Australian Institute of Health and Welfare (AIHW), *Child Protection Australia 2006–07*, AIHW catalogue no. CWS 31 (Child Welfare Series no. 43), Canberra, 2008.

25   Australian Institute of Health and Welfare, 2008, p. 3.

26   Changes in the definition of what constitutes reportable 'abuse and neglect' and changes in the reporting, recording and response to child abuse and neglect mean that any comparisons over time and across jurisdictions using recorded child maltreatment figures are problematic.

Judy Cashmore

27 Victorian Department of Human Services, *Child Protection and Family Violence: Guidance for Child Protection Practitioners*, Department of Human Services, Melbourne, 2005, <www.office-for-children.vic.gov.au/child_protection/library/publications/protection/guidance>, accessed 20 March 2008.

28 In New South Wales, the new legislation [*Children and Young Persons (Care and Protection) Act 1998*] also introduced a substantial penalty ($22,000) for failure to report as a mandatory reporter, which is likely to have increased the tendency to 'defensive reporting'.

29 See J. Mansell, 'The Underlying Instability in Statutory Child Protection: Understanding the System Dynamics Driving Risk Assurance Levels', *Social Policy Journal of New Zealand*, 28, 2006, pp. 97–132.

30 See A. Tomison, *Child Maltreatment and Substance Abuse, National Child Protection Clearing House Discussion Paper no. 2*, Australian Institute of Family Studies, Melbourne, 1996a; A. Tomison, *Child Maltreatment and Mental Disorder, National Child Protection Clearing House Discussion Paper no. 3*, Australian Institute of Family Studies, Melbourne, 1996b; A. Tomison, 'Exploring Family Violence: Links Between Child Maltreatment and Domestic Violence', *Issues in Child Abuse Prevention, no. 13*, Australian Institute of Family Studies, Melbourne, 2000; NSW Child Death Review Team, *Second Annual Report 1996–1997*, NSW Commission for Children & Young People, Sydney, 1998.

31 S. Dawe, *Drug Use in the Family: Impacts and Implications for Children*, Australian National Council on Drugs, Canberra, 2007.

32 Australian Bureau of Statistics, *Social Trends 2003*, catalogue no. 4102.0, Australian Government Publishing Service, Canberra, 2003c, <www.abs.gov.au/AUSSTATS/abs@.nsf/Latestproducts/F4B15709EC89CB1ECA25732C002079B2?opendocument>, accessed 10 December 2007.

33 Australian Institute of Health and Welfare, 2008, pp. 27, 29.

34 Mansell, 2007, pp. 107–9.

35 J. Belsky, 'Etiology of Child Maltreatment: A Developmental–ecological Analysis', *Psychological Bulletin*, 114, 1993, pp. 413–34. See also J. Garbarino & D. Sherman, 'High Risk Neighbourhoods and High Risk Families: The Human Ecology of Child Maltreatment', *Child Development*, 51, 1980, pp. 188–98; J. Garbarino & K. Kostelny, 'Neighborhood-based Programs', in *Protecting Children from Abuse and Neglect: Foundations for a New National Strategy*, eds, G.B. Melton & F.D. Barry, The Guilford Press, New York, 1994, pp. 304–52; D. Weatherburn & B. Lind, *Social and Economic Stress, Child Neglect and Juvenile Delinquency*, NSW Bureau of Crime Statistics and Research, Sydney, 1997.

36 Belsky, 1993.

37 A.M. Frodi & M.E. Lamb, 'Child Abusers' Responses to Infant Smiles and Cries', *Child Development*, 51, 1980, pp. 238–41; D.A. Wolfe, 'Child-abusive Parents: An Empirical Review and Analysis', *Psychological Bulletin*, 97, 1985, pp. 462–82.

38 D. Cicchetti, 'Child Maltreatment: Implications for Developmental Theory and Research', *Human Development*, 39, 1996, pp. 18–39; D.B. Bugental, D.H. Olster & G.A. Martorell, 'A Developmental Neuroscience Perspective on the Dynamics of Parenting', in *Handbook of Dynamics in Parent-Child Relations*, ed., L. Kuczynski, Sage, Thousand Oaks, CA, 2003, pp. 25–48.

39 Child death statistics indicate that the majority of children who have died as a result of abuse, neglect or in suspicious circumstances were under five New South Wales Ombudsman, *Report of Reviewable Deaths in 2006 Volume 2: Child Deaths*, NSW Ombudsman, Sydney, 2007.

40 Belsky, 1993.

41 M.A. Straus, R.J. Gelles & S.K. Steinmetz, *Behind Closed Doors: Violence in the American Family*, Anchor Books, Garden City, NJ, 1980.

42 Korbin, 1991.

43 Belsky, 1993.

44 Belsky, 1993; E.E. Whipple & C. Webster-Stratton, 'The Role of Parental Stress in Physically Abusive Families', *Child Abuse and Neglect*, 15, 1991, pp. 279–91.

45 J. Brooks-Gunn, L.J. Berlin & A.S. Fuligini, 'Early Childhood Intervention Programs: What About the Family?', in *Handbook of Early Childhood Intervention* (2nd edn), eds, J.P. Shonkoff & S.J. Meisels, Cambridge University Press, Cambridge, 2000, pp. 549–88; C. Goddard, *Child Abuse and Child Protection*, Churchill Livingstone, Melbourne, 1996.

46 J.D. Osofsky & M.D. Thompson, 'Adaptive and Maladaptive Parenting: Perspectives on Risk and Protective Factors', in *Handbook of Early Childhood Intervention* (2nd edn), eds, J.P. Shonkoff & S.J. Meisels, Cambridge University Press, Cambridge, 2000, pp. 54–75.

47 Belsky, 1993, p. 427.

48 D. Daro, *Confronting Child Abuse: Research for Effective Program Design*, The Free Press, New York, 1988; J. Kaufman & K. Zigler, 'The Prevention of Child Maltreatment: Programming, Research,

and Policy', in *Prevention of Child Maltreatment: Developmental and Ecological Perspectives*, eds, D. J. Willis, E. W. Holden & M. Rosenberg, Wiley & Sons, New York, 1992, pp. 269–95.

49 Daro, 1988, p. 110.

50 See, for example, D. Cicchetti, S. L. Toth & A. Maughan, 'An Ecological-Transactional Model of Child Maltreatment', in *Handbook of Developmental Psychopathology* (2nd edn), eds, A. J. Sameroff & M. Lewis, Kluwer Academic Publishers, Dordrecht, Netherlands, 2000, pp. 689–722; B. Egeland, T. Yates, K. Appleyard & M. van Dulmen, 'The Long-Term Consequences of Maltreatment in the Early Years: A Developmental Pathway Model to Antisocial Behavior', *Children's Services: Social Policy, Research, & Practice*, 5, 4, 2002, pp. 249–60; F. W. Putnam, 'Ten-Year Research Update Review: Child Sexual Abuse', *Journal of the American Academy of Child & Adolescent Psychiatry*, 42, 2003, pp. 269–78.

51 D. Glaser, 'Child Abuse and Neglect and the Brain—A Review', *Journal of Child Psychology and Psychiatry*, 41, 2000, pp. 97–116.

52 National Crime Prevention, *Pathways to Prevention: Developmental and Early Intervention Approaches to Crime in Australia*, National Anti-Crime Strategy, Canberra, 1999; P. Salmelainen, 'Child Neglect: Its Causes and its Role in Delinquency', *Crime and Justice Bulletin: Contemporary Issues in Crime and Justice*, 33, <http://search.informit.com.au/documentSummary;dn=916542316157238;res= E-LIBRARY>, accessed 9 January 2008; C. Smith & T. P. Thornberry, 'The Relationship between Childhood Maltreatment and Adolescent Involvement in Delinquency', *Criminology*, 33, 1995, pp. 451–81.

53 J. A. Durlak, 'Common Risk and Protective Factors in Successful Prevention Programs', *American Journal of Orthopsychiatry*, 68, 1998, pp. 512–20; J. Cashmore, 'Family, Early Development and the Life Course: Common Risk and Protective Factors in Pathways to Prevention', in *The Social Origins of Health and Well-Being: From the Planetary to the Molecular*, eds, R. Eckersley, J. Dixon & B. Douglas, Cambridge University Press, Melbourne, 2001a.

54 See Chapters 7 and 11.

55 See *Child Protection: Messages from Research* publications in the United Kingdom and the report by the US Advisory Board on Child Abuse and Neglect (1990) which proclaimed a national emergency in relation to the child protection crisis in the USA; and, more recently, J. Waldfogel, 'Welfare Reform and the Child Welfare System', *Children and Youth Services Review*, 26, 2004, pp. 919–39.

56 M. Harries, B. Lonne & J. Thompson, 'Beyond Buzzwords—Principles and Themes for Reforming Child Protection Practice: Challenging Practices', paper presented at the Third Conference on International Research Perspectives on Child and Family Welfare, Mackay, Queensland, 2005. This paper is available on the CROCCS website, <www.croccs.org.au/downloads/2005_conf_papers/ HarriesLonneThomsonCROCCSpaper.pdf >, accessed 14 December 2007; D. Scott, 'Sowing the Seeds of Innovation in Child Protection', keynote presentation at the 10th Australasian Conference on Child Abuse and Neglect, Wellington, New Zealand, 15 February, 2006; P. Testro & C. Peltola, *Rethinking Child Protection: A New Paradigm?*, PeakCare Qld Inc., Brisbane, 2007.

57 Mansell, 2007.

58 K. Barter, 'Renegotiating Relationships to Build Community Capacity for the Health and Well-Being of Children: A Time For Action', paper presented at the CROCCS 4th International Conference on Working Together for Families, Mackay, Queensland, 4–6 August 2006; Child Welfare League of Canada, *The Welfare of Canadian Children: It's Our Business: A Collection of Resource Papers for a Healthy Future for Canadian Children and Families*, Centre of Excellence for Child Welfare, 2007, <www.cwlc.ca/policy/welfare_e.htm>, accessed 13 December 2007.

59 H. Cleaver & P. Freeman, *Parental perspectives in cases of suspected child abuse*, London, HMSO, 1995.

60 D. Scott, 'A Vision for Family Services: Support and Prevention that Works for Families at Risk', keynote presentation at the forum on A Vision for Family Services and Prevention that Works for Families at Risk, Sydney, 30 April 2003a.

61 G. B. Melton, 'Chronic Neglect of Family Violence: More than a Decade of Reports to Guide US Policy', *Child Abuse and Neglect*, 26, 2002, pp. 569–86.

62 Durrant, 2006; Waldegrove, 2006.

63 Durrant, 2006; S. Phipps, *Does Policy Affect Outcomes for Young Children? An Analysis with International Microdata*, Applied Research Branch Strategic Policy, Human Resources Development, Quebec, Canada, August 1999.

64 While overall approximately 88 per cent of children in out-of-home care are on a care and protection order, some children (some of whom have a disability) are placed in care on a 'voluntary' basis by their parents when they are unable to provide adequate care.

65 Australian Institute of Health and Welfare (AIHW), 2008, pp. 61–2.

Judy Cashmore

66 F. Ainsworth & A.N. Maluccio, 'Kinship Care: False Dawn or New Hope?', *Australian Social Work*, 51, 4, 1998, pp. 3–8.

67 C.M. Sultmann & P. Testro, *Directions in Out of Home Care: Challenges and Opportunities*, PeakCare Qld Inc., Paddington, Qld, 2001, p. 10.

68 Australian Institute of Health and Welfare, 2008, p. 57.

69 D. Scott, 'Opening Comments', presented at the CAFWAA Symposium on When Care is Not Enough, Canberra, 17 September 2003b.

70 Australian Institute of Health and Welfare, 2008, p. 60; calculations excluding Queensland because there were no available figures for Queensland.

71 P.H. Delfabbro, J.G. Barber & L. Cooper, 'Placement Disruption and Dislocation in South Australian Substitute Care', *Children Australia*, 25, 2, 2000, pp. 16–20; P.H. Delfabbro, J.G. Barber & L.L. Cooper, 'Predictors of Short-Term Reunification in South Australian Substitute Care', *Child Welfare*, 82, 2002, pp. 27–51.

72 R. Bullock, M. Little & S. Millham, 'Going Home: The Return of Children Separated from their Families', Dartmouth, Aldershot, 1993; B. Minty, 'A Review of the Effects of Living Long-term in Substitute Care in the Context of a Discussion of Outcome Criteria', *Social Work & Social Sciences Review*, 8, 2000, pp. 169–93.

73 Bullock, Little & Millham, 1993.

74 Scott, 2003.

75 G. Schofield, J. Thoburn, D. Howell & J. Dickens, 'The Search for Stability and Permanence: Modelling the Pathways of Long-stay Looked After Children', *British Journal of Social Work*, 37, 2007, pp. 619–42.

76 M. Berry, K. McCauley & T. Lansing, 'Permanency through Group Work: A Pilot Intensive Reunification Program', *Child and Adolescent Social Work Journal*, 24, 2007, pp. 477–93.

77 J. Cashmore, 'What Can We Learn from the US Experience on Permanency Planning?', *Australian Journal of Family Law*, 15, 2001b, 215–29.

78 H.N. Taussig, R.B. Clyman & J. Landsverk, 'Children Who Return Home from Foster Care: A 6-Year Prospective Study of Behavioural Health Outcomes in Adolescence', *Pediatrics*, 108, 2001, pp. 1–7.

79 The 'official hierarchy of desirable placement options' in the United Kingdom, according to Minty, 2000, is reunification, fostering by relatives, adoption, foster care with approved non-relatives and residential care.

80 Australian Institute of Health and Welfare (AIHW), *Adoptions Australia 2004–05*, AIHW catalogue no. CWS 25 (Child Welfare Series no. 37), Canberra, 2005b, p. 20.

81 J. Doyle, 'Boys Town Engadine', paper presented to the ACWA Reunification Forum, Sydney, 6 December 2007.

82 Australian Institute of Health and Welfare (AIHW), 2005b, p. 24.

83 E. Fernandez, 'How Children Experience Fostering Outcomes: Participatory Research With Children', *Child and Family Social Work*, 11, 2006, pp. 1–10; A. Rushton, J. Treseder & D. Quinton, 'An Eight-Year Prospective Study of Older Boys Placed in Permanent Substitute Families', *Journal of Child Psychology and Psychiatry*, 17, 1995, pp. 39–45.

84 J. Cashmore & M. Paxman, 'Predicting Outcomes for Young People after Leaving Care: The Importance of "Felt" Security', *Child and Family Social Work: Special Issue on Leaving Care*, 11, 2006a, pp. 232–41; Minty, 2000.

85 Case study adapted from J. Cashmore & M. Paxman, *Wards Leaving Care: Four to Five Years On*, Social Policy Research Centre, University of New South Wales and NSW Department of Community Services, Sydney, 2006b, pp. 115–16.

86 D. Fanshel & F.B. Shinn, *Children in Foster Care: A Longitudinal Study*, Columbia University Press, New York, 1978; J.G. Barber, P.H. Delfabbro & L.L. Cooper, 'Placement Stability and the Psychosocial Wellbeing of Children in Foster Care', *Research on Social Work Practice*, 13, 2003, pp. 409–25.

87 B. Davidson-Arad, D. Englechin-Segal & Y. Wozner, 'Short-Term Follow-Up of Children at Risk: Comparison of the Quality of Life of Children Removed from Home and Children Remaining at Home', *Child Abuse & Neglect*, 27, 2003, pp. 733–50; L. St Clair & A.F. Osborne, 'The Ability and Behaviour of Children Who Have Been in Care or Separated from their Parents', *Early Childhood Development and Care, Special Issue*, 28, 1987, p. 3.

88 G. Schofield, *Part of the Family: Pathways Through Foster Care*, British Agencies for Adoption and Fostering, London, 2003; J. Cashmore & M. Paxman, *Wards Leaving Care: A Longitudinal Study*, NSW Department of Community Services, Sydney, 1996; J. Cashmore & M. Paxman, 'Wards Leaving Care: Follow Up Five Years On', *Children Australia*, 31, 2006c, pp. 18–25.

89   Cashmore & Paxman, 2006c, p. 22.

90   Case study adapted from J. Cashmore & M. Paxman, 2006b.

91   N. Biehal, J. Clayden, M. Stein & J. Wade, *Moving On: Young People and Leaving Care Schemes*, HMSO, London, 1995; B. Broad, *Improving the Health and Well Being of Young People Leaving Care*, Russell House Publishing, Lyme Regis, UK, 2005; M.E. Courtney, A. Dworsky, G. Ruth, T. Keller, J. Havlicek & N. Bost, *Midwest Evaluation of the Adult Functioning of Former Foster Youth: Outcomes at Age 19*, Chapin Hall Working Paper, Chapin Hall Center for Children at the University of Chicago, Chicago, 2005; K. Kufeldt & B. McKenzie, eds, *Child Welfare: Connecting Research, Policy and Practice*, Wilfrid Laurier University Press, Waterloo, Ontario, 2003; D. Maunders, M. Liddell, M. Liddell & S. Green, *Young People Leaving Care and Protection*, Australian Clearinghouse for Youth Studies, Hobart, Tasmania, 1999; P. Mendes & B. Moslehuddin, 'From Dependence to Interdependence: Towards Better Outcomes for Young People Leaving State Care', *Child Abuse Review*, 15, 2006, pp. 110–26; M. Stein, *Overcoming the Odds: Resilience and Young People Leaving Care*, Joseph Rowntree Foundation, London, 2005.

92   Broad, 2005; Cashmore & Paxman, 2006; Stein 2004.

93   R. Bullock, M. Courtney, R. Parker, I. Sinclair & J. Thoburn, 'Can the Corporate State Parent?', *Children and Youth Services Review*, 28, 2006, pp. 1344–58; J. Cashmore, 'Child Protection— Integrating Research Policy Practice: The Potential and the Limits of Corporate Parenting', paper presented at the Child Safety Research Conference, Brisbane, 14–15 November 2006.

94   Testro & Peltola, 2007. The Wood Commission of Inquiry in New South Wales was set up in late 2007 specifically to address these concerns.

95   Child Welfare League of Canada, 2007; Coulton et al., 2007; Scott, 2003, 2005.

96   Barter, 2006; Durrant, 2006.

97   J. Thoburn, A. Lewis & D. Shemmings, *Paternalism or Partnership: Family Involvement in the Child Protection Process*, HMSO, London, 1995.

98   J. Cashmore, 'Facilitating the Participation of Children and Young People in Care', *Child Abuse and Neglect*, 26, 8, 2002, pp. 837–47; Fernandez, 2007.

99   Department of Health, *Child Protection: Messages from Research*, HMSO, London, 1995.

100 Department of Health, 1995, p. 47.

Judy Cashmore

11

Strong State Intervention: The Stolen Generations

Ailsa Burns, Kate Burns and Karen Menzies

Sixteen children, all related one way or another, were removed from the mission on a day Julia has never forgotten ... The assembled children were loaded onto the truck very suddenly and their things thrown in hastily after them. The suddenness and the suppressed air of tension shocked the mothers and the children and they realised something was seriously wrong ... children began to cry and the mothers to wail and cut themselves ... The tailgate was slammed shut and bolted and the truck screeched off with things still hanging over the back and mothers and other children running after it crying and wailing.[1]

The National Inquiry into the Separation of Aboriginal and Torres Strait Islander Children from their Families concluded that over the period 1910–70 between one in three and one in ten children were forcibly removed from their families and communities and, in some places and at some times, this was a much higher proportion. The Inquiry further concluded that 'not one Indigenous family escaped the effects of forcible removal',[2] with many affected over a number of generations. Why and how did the Australian authorities take this extreme action, and what were the outcomes? In this chapter we consider these questions, drawing extensively on the findings of the National Inquiry.

Contexts

Child removal: early events and beliefs

In line with their belief that education of the children in European ways was best for Indigenous populations, the Australian colonial authorities made early efforts to school Aboriginal children. Aboriginal families were initially willing to let their children attend, but by 1833 the only Aboriginal school operating in New South Wales had just four pupils.[3] A 'problem' noted by government authorities was the strength and attraction of the Indigenous lifestyle: 'We had an institution here, in Governor Macquarie's time, where the native children were educated, and turned out of it at the age of puberty good readers and writers; but being all associated together, and their native instincts and ideas still remaining paramount, they took to their old ideas again as soon as freed from thraldom'.[4]

To overcome this problem of 'reversion' to Aboriginal ways, the separation of Indigenous children from their families and communities became an entrenched aspect of colonial protection policy. On the reserves and missions children were housed in dormitories, and contact with their families was strictly limited. In some states the Chief Protector of Aborigines was made the legal guardian of all Indigenous children, overruling the rights of parents.

By the late nineteenth century it had become apparent that while the full-descent Aboriginal population was diminishing, the mixed-descent population was increasing. The colonial authorities had been prepared to supply basic food and shelter to the dwindling full-descent population, but the growth in the mixed-descent numbers raised other issues.

First, there were genetic considerations. In accordance with the Darwinist ideas of the day, 'half-castes' were regarded as potentially undesirable characters who needed to be carefully controlled, since they were likely to inherit 'the worst traits of both races'. In the Northern Territory, where white settlers were few, they were considered to be positively dangerous.[5] But they were also regarded as having greater developmental potential. James Isdell, for example, an early Protector in Western Australia, argued, 'The half-caste is intellectually above the aborigine, and it is the duty of the State they be given a chance to lead a better life than their mothers'.[6]

Second, the existence of the mixed-descent children raised humanitarian and religious issues. Many of the mothers were without any form of support from the white fathers of the children and unable to provide for them, and some children were rejected by their communities because of their parentage. Without help, their futures were bleak. In addition, the missionaries wished to convert them to Christianity. An alternative to removal would have been to provide the mothers with some support, but this option was ruled out by the belief that children of mixed descent should be merged into white society.

Third, the increasing mixed-descent population raised financial and labour-force issues. Governments were not prepared to support this expanding population as 'dependents'. Moreover, the Australian economy needed labour if it was to develop. The approach taken by state governments in collaboration with missionaries was to step up efforts to separate Aboriginal children from their families at an early age, remove them to institutions for basic education plus religious and vocational training, and send them to work as domestics, farmhands or labourers as soon as they reached their early teens.

Comparisons with the state's approach to non-Indigenous children

In some ways the removal policy was consistent with the state's approach to white children whose parents were regarded as exerting a bad influence. For these children,

Ailsa Burns, Kate Burns & Karen Menzies

too, institutionalisation was seen as removing children from 'the irregular and immoral habits of the Parents' and educating them in 'religious as well as industrious habits'.[7]

However, there were critical differences between the approaches of the state to Indigenous and to white children. Aboriginal culture was regarded by the state as both degenerate and seductive, so that it was especially important to remove children at an early age, before strong ties could be formed. There were different opinions as to what age was best. One official argued that children should be taken away as soon as they were born, because 'if they are in the wurley for a week it is bad for them'.[8] Other authorities favoured removal when children were two or four years old, thereby avoiding the costs involved in caring for babies, but before their Aboriginal identity was too strongly forged. The male administrators emphasised that though separation might be painful at the time, it was for their own good: 'In some cases, when the child is very young, it must of necessity be accompanied by its mother, but in other cases, even though it may seem cruel to separate the mother and child, it is better to do so, when the mother is living, as is usually the case, in a native camp'.[9]

To combat the influence of Aboriginal culture, the authorities made special efforts to sever family ties. A woman missionary explained how it was done:

> The Mission desired to give the half-caste children such a training as would help
> them to merge into the white population. They were unable to do so as long as the
> Home was in close proximity to an aboriginal camp. Some of the little ones had rela-
> tives in the Oodnadatta camp, and it was not possible to segregate them from their
> own people. The only way to do this was by taking them away where they could
> no longer see the natives or hear the sounds of corroboree … After much prayer for
> guidance, it was decided to remove the children to a place further south, where there
> were no aborigines.[10]

Other strategies used to detach the children from Aboriginal culture included not allowing the parents to see their children, giving them new names, not telling them who their family were (this included separating children from siblings who were also in state custody: 'splitting the litter'), telling them that their parents were dead or had rejected them, intercepting and destroying correspondence, forbidding the use of Aboriginal languages, not telling (lighter-skinned) children that they were Aboriginal, and telling them that Aborigines were inferior, and should be avoided.[11]

A second difference between the state's approaches to Aboriginal children and to white children lay in their different legislative treatment. In a number of states, the Chief Protector was the guardian of all Aboriginal children from the moment they were born. This allowed him or his delegate to remove children without the need to prove that removal was in the interests of the child, as was the case with white children. In Queensland and Western Australia the Chief Protectors were able to use their powers to force all Indigenous people onto large, highly regulated settlements and missions, to remove children from their mothers around the age of four and place them in dormitories and training schools, and then to send them off the missions and settlements to work.

Many personal accounts describe the experience of those who were removed. For example, one woman who herself had been taken away at birth, who had been brought up in four different institutions, and subsequently had her own three children taken, described four generations of removal, starting with a tribal grandmother, and extending over three states:

> My grandmother was taken from up Tennant Creek … they brought her down to The Bungalow [an institution at Alice Springs]. Then she had Uncle Billy [at age 14] and my Mum [at age 15] to an Aboriginal Protection Officer. She had not much say in that from what I can gather … When she was 15 and a half they took her to Hermannsburg and married her up to an Aranda man … When Mum was 3, they [took her] from Hermannsburg, putting her in The Bungalow until she was 11. And then they sent her to Mulgoa mission in NSW. From there they sent her to Carlingford Girls' Home [New South Wales] to be a maid. She couldn't get back to the Territory, and she'd had a little baby … In the end [they told her] 'We'll pay your fare back on the condition that you leave the baby here'. So she left her baby behind and came back to the Territory, and then she had me and my brother and another two brothers and a sister and we were all taken away as soon as we were born.[12]

Although government policy targeted mixed-descent children, and the legislation expressed this policy in terms of amount of 'Aboriginal blood', in practice skin colour was the deciding factor. Officials who visited the camps and settlements to remove the mixed-descent children selected those of light colour, while the parents tried to hide or camouflage them by blackening their skins.

HIDING CHILDREN

One submission to the National Inquiry described how parents tried to hide their children from authorities:

> Every morning our people would crush charcoal and mix that with animal fat and smother that all over us, so that when the police came they could only see black children in the distance. We were told always to be on the alert, and, if white people came, to run into the bush or run and stand behind the trees as stiff as a poker, or else hide behind logs or run into culverts and hide. Often the white people … would come into our camps. And if the Aboriginal group was taken unawares, they would stuff us into flour bags and pretend we weren't there. We were told not to sneeze. We knew if we sneezed and they knew that we were in there bundled up, we'd be taken off and away from the area … During the raids on the camps it was not unusual for people to be shot … You can understand the terror that we lived in …[13]

The development of government policy during the twentieth century

Up until 1937 the various state governments acted independently on Aboriginal issues, although their philosophies were quite similar. In that year the first national conference was held, and it concluded with an agreement that all states (except Tasmania, which did not attend) would adopt consistent policies aimed at 'assimilation'. 'Assimilation' differed from the previous policy of 'merging' or 'biological absorption' in that it presumed a much more intensive intervention by the state. It also often involved the idea that Aboriginality would in time be 'bred out' through intermarriage with the white population.[14] In line with the assimilationist view that Aboriginal communities were 'just like groups of poor whites',[15] over the next thirty years responsibility shifted from the Aboriginal protection authorities to state child welfare departments. The legislation permitting the removal of Aboriginal children on the ground of their 'blood' was repealed, and they now came under the same child welfare laws as white children, and could be removed if they were found by a court to be 'neglected', 'destitute' or 'uncontrollable'.

Despite this change, the procedures were much the same: the same police and other officials who previously removed children on the basis of race now utilised the neglect and destitution provisions of the child welfare legislation to remove even larger numbers. Destitution was easy to prove as most Aboriginal families were very poor; neglect was used to characterise Aboriginal mores such as frequent travelling and sharing child-rearing across the extended family; and children who resisted schooling or indeed were excluded from school could be classed as uncontrollable.

Many witnesses to the 1997 National Inquiry described their bitterness regarding the 'neglected' and 'uncontrollable' tags that resulted in their removal from happy homes to strange, regimented and poorly resourced institutions, where food could be short and discipline harsh.[16]

The increasing numbers of Indigenous children being removed put considerable pressure on state welfare budgets and charitable agencies. From the late 1940s, fostering with white families rather than institutionalisation became more common: it was cheaper and it found support in child development theory, which increasingly stressed the importance of children's relationship with a primary caregiver. Adoption of Aboriginal children by white families was also promoted: for the state it had the advantage of transferring the cost and responsibility onto the adopting parents. What was overlooked was that for Aboriginal children the experience of being separated not only from family and community, but from other Aboriginal children, was intensely isolating and distressing.

Assimilation through education was another form of removal. In the more remote communities and the Northern Territory, Aboriginal parents were persuaded or coerced into allowing their children to be taken to cities to live in hostels or with white families while attending school. In line with this policy, governments gradually removed the rights of schools authorities to refuse to enrol Aboriginal children, but European parents (and their children) made their dislike of Aboriginal children known.

By the later 1960s it had become clear that despite the high level of state intervention, Aboriginal people were not being assimilated. They were resisting attempts to break up their families and communities and seeking each other out after being forcibly separated. At the same time, the white population was continuing to discriminate against them in employment, housing and social security rights. Instead of becoming respectable working members of white society, these Aboriginal children were moving into the criminal justice system or having their own children taken from them. By this time, also, Bowlby's writings[17] on the destructive effects of maternal deprivation were well accepted in respect of non-Aboriginal children, and the discrepancy between policies for black and for white children was becoming more obvious.

In 1967 the Commonwealth acquired joint responsibility for Aboriginal affairs. The policies of the Whitlam Government, elected in 1972, included support for Aboriginal self-determination, and the new government provided funding for Indigenous groups to challenge the removal policy. There was an immediate decline in the numbers being removed, and a sympathetic response from welfare agencies. The traumatic nature of removal, and the lifelong problems that stemmed from it, began to be appreciated among some welfare staff. After extensive lobbying, the National Inquiry was set up to investigate the effects of child removal, and its report was made public in 1997.

Child removal: the practice

The program was carried out with minimal resources. Australia was not a wealthy country, the state governments had limited budgets and staff, and they had many other commitments to which they gave higher priority. In addition, the economic depressions of the 1890s and 1930s were very severe in many parts of the country. Thus, while the aims of the removal policy were ambitious, the practice was sparsely funded and heavily reliant on the services of local police, missionaries, and the kind of staff prepared to work for low pay in often overcrowded children's institutions.

The institutions differed in size, in whether they were close to or separate from adult settlements and camps, and in operating style, religious affiliation and relationship to the wider community. What they had in common was limited funds and staff, which meant limited food (and in some cases water), limited space, limited protection from the weather and limited adult attention. Illness and child mortality rates were often high. On Groote Eylandt almost 50 per cent of one generation of mixed descent suffered from leprosy, owing, according to the Chief Protector, to 'low resistance following years of improper feeding'.[18] In addition, inadequate staffing meant that harsh methods of management and control were often resorted to, including severe physical punishment, denial of food, forced standing and kneeling for long periods, heavy work assignments, head-shaving and every kind of shaming. A Queensland woman recalled that: 'We were called the dormitory girls. But the kids who slept out on the verandah … they were the pee-the-beds … Maybe you'd pee the bed [just] one night, but you were transferred from your bed out onto the verandah. You slept on a mattress on the floor and all you were called was pee-the-beds … "Tell the pee-the-beds it's time to get up." No identity at all. Absolutely nothing'.[19]

Conditions in some Northern Territory institutions were particularly harsh, and further exacerbated in the 1920s by the severe drought that devastated central Australia at that time. At the Half-caste Home outside Darwin, by 1928 there were seventy-six inmates living in a 'house large enough for only one family'.[20] At The Bungalow, which comprised three corrugated-iron sheds on land opposite the police station, there were about fifty children and ten adults, and rations were scarce. One submission by a man removed from his mother at the age of three described his experience at The Bungalow:

> There's where food was scarce again. Hardly anything … night time we used to cry with hunger, y'know, lice, no food. And we used to go out there to the town dump … we had to come and scrounge at the dump, y'know, eating old bread and smashing tomato sauce bottles and licking them. Half of the time our food we got from the rubbish dump. Always hungry there …
>
> That's another thing—culture was really lost there, too. Because religion was drummed into us, y'know, when we'd be out there and we'd have knuckle-up and that, we were that religious we'd kneel down in prayer … We had to pray every time you swear or anything, you'd go down on your hands and knees … they pumped that religion into us.[21]

Despite the emphasis on religious and moral training, sexual abuse was a problem, both within the institutions and when girls were sent out to domestic service, often returning pregnant. Archbishop Donaldson, visiting Barambah settlement in 1915, noted that of the girls sent out to service 'over 90 per cent come back pregnant to a white man'.[22] The baby would then be removed in its turn, creating a cycle that could continue for generations. A particularly hated feature of places like Barambah was the dormitory system, whereby mothers and siblings were housed in the same institution, but in different dormitories, with contact prevented.

Of all the children's homes, Colebrook in South Australia has been most commonly cited as a success story. A number of its alumni became leading figures in Aboriginal affairs, and others made successful careers in teaching, nursing and administration. Colebrook had the advantage of being staffed over the period 1927–52 by two exceptional women, who are described with respect and affection in alumni memoirs. As well as themselves acting as consistent parent figures, Matron Hyde and Sister Rutter supported their children's emotional needs by encouraging attachments between the older girls and younger children: 'When you were in Colebrook the older kids … sort of took the young ones under their care. So you got your love in a different way. Matron couldn't give everybody hugs and loves and kisses, but that minder was more like my mother … she took that place as that warm caring person and each one had their older one looking after them'.[23]

Even so, Colebrook children shared with those in other institutions the problems of scarce resources, staff turnover and loss of cultural identity, as many memoirs make clear: 'Colebrook started with Sister Hyde and Sister Rutter. They *were* Colebrook … What we had was constant love and attention from the two ladies, although often we were short on food … Those kids went through hell on earth after they had gone'.[24]

As a source of income, the institutions sent their children out on work assignments, as servants and labourers, sometimes from an early age. A common complaint of those sent out was that they 'never saw' any of the money they earned, which was paid to the institutions and, in theory, kept in trust for them.[25] In 1941 Commonwealth child endowment was extended to Aboriginal children, and this money came to the institutions rather than to the parents, providing another source of funding. Nevertheless, income usually remained inadequate, and there were constant reports of poor conditions and overcrowding in the children's homes. One solution, especially after 1940, was to move children into welfare homes for non-Aboriginal children and, if they had been declared 'uncontrollable', into juvenile justice institutions. A 1980 report noted that in New South Wales '17.2 per cent of children in corrective institutions are Aboriginal … [of whom] 81 per cent … are not in their home regions [and] 34 per cent had no contact with either parents or relatives … 10.2 per cent of [all] children in non-government children's homes are Aboriginal [and] 15.5 per cent of children in foster care are Aboriginal'.[26] The Aboriginal population of New South Wales at the time was about 1 per cent of the total.

FOSTERING AND ADOPTION

Besides institutionalisation, fostering and adoption were the options for removed children. From early on, some children were taken into non-Aboriginal homes in this way. It was also common for children to experience a mix of placements, moving from institution to foster home and then back again to the institution—perhaps a number of times. Among removed people making submissions to the National Inquiry, one-quarter had spent their entire time in a single institution, 14 per cent had lived for the whole period with a non-Aboriginal family and 54 per cent had spent time in both. The proportion of children who were fostered or adopted increased in the 1950s and 1960s, when the institutions could no longer cope with the large numbers involved, and child welfare thinking had come to the view that institutions were less desirable than family rearing. Placement in white families was preferred, as this was seen as helping children to assimilate more quickly. The arrangements made were often very casual. The Victorian government noted that:

> An informal placement takes place when some person … considers that there are
> Aboriginal children in the area who are at risk. Contact is then made with some
> resource person who may have contact with a group of people who will accept care
> and responsibility for these children at a minute's notice … the children are placed
> informally with various other people and as has happened on many occasions, when
> parents request the return of their children, some cannot be traced … It is often diffi-
> cult to identify these children as it is not uncommon for the 'foster parents' to change
> the name of the child.[27]

One consequence of this uncontrolled approach was that a very mixed group of people were able to foster or adopt children. Some adoptive parents were 'fantastic', and strong attachments were formed. Other removed children described foster parents who were mentally ill, cruel, sexually predatory, exploitative of the child's labour or just insufficiently caring.

Ailsa Burns, Kate Burns & Karen Menzies

Renegotiating identity

Waters, who interviewed a number of those removed and subsequently adopted or fostered, noted that:

> things seem to have gone quite well until they got into the teenage years. Then they started to become more aware … that they were different … It was the impact of what peers were doing and saying which seemed to be most distressing to them. And sometimes their families didn't deal with that very well. They were dismissive. 'Look, the best thing to do is just forget you were ever Aboriginal' or 'Tell them that you came from Southern Europe' … But in none of those families was there a sense that one way to manage this situation was to recapture your sense of Aboriginality. There seemed to be no honour and dignity in being an Aboriginal, even if you'd been brought up by a family.[28]

Even the most sensitive of adoptive parents often knew little of the child's background, which meant that it could be very hard to trace the biological parents. In some cases there were no records. In other cases the birth records, when found, showed the name of the adoptive mother or some other person rather than that of the birth mother. Adopting parents themselves described being deceived: being told, for example, that their adopted child was an orphan, and later finding the child had been removed from a mother who continued to seek it.[29]

As the adoption stories illustrate, a terrible weakness in the removal philosophy was its failure to prepare the white community for 'merging' or 'assimilation'. The removed children ran into discrimination, prejudice and racism at school, in their peer groups, in the workforce and on the streets. Some were racist themselves, having been told from an early age that Aboriginal people were undesirables, and to be avoided ('Our instructions were quite explicit: run across the park, don't talk to the natives'.).[30] The individualist philosophy underlying assimilation—that 'given a chance', each individual should be able to make his or her own way in mainstream society—also overlooked (or, more accurately, denied) the developmental importance of a sense of cultural identity, except where the culture was that of the assimilationists.

Consequences

Child removal: the outcomes

As we have seen, implementation of the removal policy varied with time and place, and there was no attempt to conduct an ongoing evaluation of the effects. However, the 1994 national survey of Indigenous people[31] conducted by the Australian Bureau of Statistics provides one means of assaying the effects of the policy. It compared those who had or had not been taken away on a number of measures of life success. These can be compared with the stated aims of the policy, which, as we have seen, included 'rescuing' children from their family situation, and providing them with a higher level of education than they would have otherwise received, a greater commitment to the workforce, better earning potential, improved health, a more law-abiding lifestyle and more personal stability and morality.

The findings were of failure on all these counts: there was either no difference between the groups, or those taken away fared worse. (It should be remembered that the survey was conducted in the 1990s, so that most removals would have occurred after 1940, rather than in earlier times.) In educational achievement and employment status there were no significant differences between the two groups, although those not taken away were a little more likely to be employed (see Table 1).

TABLE 1: POST-SCHOOL QUALIFICATIONS AND EMPLOYMENT STATUS OF INDIGENOUS ADULTS TWENTY YEARS AND ABOVE[32]

QUALIFICATION	TAKEN AWAY	NOT TAKEN AWAY
Higher education	1.9%	2.0%
TAFE	1.9%	1.8%
Other	0.6%	1.0%
None	95.6%	94.8%
Not stated	—	0.3%
EMPLOYMENT STATUS		
Employed non-Community Development Employment Program	22.8%	25.0%
Employed CDEP	8.2%	8.5%
Unemployed	22.2%	20.0%
Not in labour force	39.2%	38.3%
Not applicable	7.6%	8.2%

Income in both groups was very low, with under 6 per cent from either group earning more than $30,000 per annum. More of those taken away had incomes in the $8000–$16,000 range (39.9 per cent compared with 16.7 per cent), while those not removed were more likely to be in the $0–$3000 range (21.5 per cent compared with 13.3 per cent). Social security payments available at the time fell in the $8000–$16,000 range, suggesting that the group taken away were likely to be living in more settled areas and receiving social security, while those not taken were more likely to be living in remote communities and not doing so. The policy's aim of cutting government costs had thus also failed.

The figures also show that the policy had negative effects on health and crime. Those taken away in childhood were twice as likely to have been arrested more than once

Ailsa Burns, Kate Burns & Karen Menzies

in the past five years (22 per cent as against 11 per cent).[33] Self-reported health status (which has been shown to be a good measure of subsequent morbidity and mortality) was worse in the removed group, 29 per cent of whom described their health as only fair or poor, compared with 15 per cent of the non-removed.

A smaller-scale longitudinal study comparing those removed or not in childhood found psychological distress to be very high in both groups.[34] Overall, two-thirds of all participants were described as distressed throughout the three years of the study, with depression the most common diagnosis. However, distress was far higher in the removed (90 per cent) than the non-removed group (45 per cent). Factors that offered protection against the development of depression and other psychiatric problems included a strong Aboriginal identity, frequent contact with one's extended family and acknowledgment of Aboriginal culture—all of which were much weaker in the removed group. The removed group was also found to have a lower level of education, less stable living arrangements and weaker social relationships. And these people were twice as likely to have been arrested by police and convicted of an offence, three times more likely to have been in jail and twice as likely to use illicit substances, including intravenously. Later studies reported similar results. A national study in 2002 (Table 2)[35] showed that Indigenous people who were removed from their natural families reported poorer health outcomes.

TABLE 2: HEALTH OUTCOMES AMONG INDIGENOUS ADULTS WHO WERE OR WERE NOT REMOVED FROM THEIR FAMILIES AS CHILDREN

HEALTH OUTCOME	TAKEN AWAY	NOT TAKEN AWAY
Excellent or good health	33%	46%
Fair or poor health	40%	22%
Regular smoker	65%	47%
Disability or long-term health condition	54%	35%
Profound/severe core activity limitation	14%	8%
Psychological disability	20%	8%

A 2005 study in Western Australia[36] found that an estimated 2760 (12 per cent) of the state's Aboriginal children aged four to seventeen years had a carer who had been forcibly separated from his or her family. Compared to other Indigenous carers who had not been separated they were more likely to live in households with gambling or alcohol problems, were one-and-a-half times as likely to have had contact with Western Australian mental health services, were less than half as likely to have someone close to them with whom they could discuss their problems, and were almost twice as likely to have been arrested or charged by police. Their children were more than twice as likely to suffer clinically significant emotional and behavioural difficulties, and this remained true after adjusting for age, sex, areal remoteness and whether the carer was the child's birth mother. They were also approximately twice as likely to use alcohol and other drugs.

INTERGENERATIONAL EFFECTS

An important aim of the removal policy was that of 'breaking the cycle' of behaviour seen as undesirable. This is a difficult aspect to evaluate, but the outcome appeared to be the opposite: the institution of a new cycle of ineffective parenting. Topp[37] compared parenting among Aboriginal people in Victoria with that in remote communities in central Australia where there had been few removals:

> In central Australia I never saw any infants with feeding or sleep difficulties and whenever I saw infants who were unsettled it was because they were unwell. Young mothers were clearly well supported and advised by their relatives and they had a strong belief in what they were doing. In contrast in Victoria … I saw many young mothers with very little idea of how to interact with their young infants, how to feed them, how to rear and discipline their older children or how to set limits. Removal of children from their families and from their culture has at the very least resulted in loss of role models for them to learn their parenting skills.

Brady[38] makes a similar distinction regarding petrol sniffing. She found that this addiction was rare in pastoral communities where the pastoralists had not interested themselves in their Aboriginal workers' family life, but more common in settlements where government or mission staff had been more intrusive, and traditional tribal authority undermined.

Kamien's[39] 1972 study in Bourke, New South Wales, adds to this picture. Many of the Aboriginal adults in Bourke had themselves been separated in childhood. Among their children, Kamien found that one-quarter of the boys aged five to fourteen and one-third of the girls had substantial behavioural problems. Kamien commented that nearly all the Bourke children experienced 'inconsistency, unpredictability, and a conflict of values with the dominant white society'.[40] Waters noted in his clinical work with Aboriginal families that:

> Not only has the legacy of impaired interpersonal relationships and poor self-worth rendered them more liable to unplanned parenthood, but they make poor parents and their children in turn have often been taken into care for having been abused or neglected. Such parents are often disorganised, impatient, capricious and ultimately demoralised, feeling unable to provide for their children what they missed out on and often being painfully aware that the experience of childhood they are providing for their children [is] not dissimilar to that which they experienced.[41]

Another expert witness to the National Inquiry noted that the separated children could, as adults, be 'afraid of the dependency of their children' and unable to meet their needs, despite a 'yearning to look after their kids consistently'.[42]

Were there any positive outcomes? There is no ready answer. There was considerable variation across institutions, and at different times, but there is no research relating these variations to outcomes. Some removed children went on to notable achievements; but, as Table 1 shows, their overall education and occupation levels were a little lower than those of the non-removed, who also had access to schooling. It has to be remembered, too, that child mortality in the Aboriginal camps was often high, and some mothers

Ailsa Burns, Kate Burns & Karen Menzies

were unable to keep their children because of destitution and/or community rejection, and surrendered them voluntarily to the missions. Thus removal may have saved some (or many) lives. However, we lack research in these areas.[43]

What developmental processes are important?

How can developmental psychology help us to better understand these outcomes? An obvious issue is that of attachment. In his 1951 report on the effects of institutionalisation, Bowlby[44] described a range of damaging outcomes, including impaired cognitive and language development, inability to form close relationships, hostility, depression, substance abuse and what he termed 'affectionless character': a readiness to delinquent or criminal behaviour associated with absence of feeling for the victims. Bowlby attributed these deficits to 'maternal deprivation', that is, the absence of a stable mothering figure to whom the infant and child would become attached. This primary attachment to the mother formed the template for all later attachments, and without it later attachments would be deficient. The primary attachment also provided the child with a sense of security and well-being, and the presence of the attachment figure gave the child a 'secure base', from which it was able to venture out to explore and enjoy the world. Absence or loss of the mothering person damaged the child's sense of security, hindering all aspects of development and rendering the child prone to passivity, anxiety, rage and despair.

There has been debate over some of Bowlby's ideas: for example whether infants need a *single* primary caregiver (what about fathers?). But his findings were from the beginning extremely influential, and throughout the Western world at least there was a rapid move away from institutionalisation of children and towards fostering, family support and small family-type group homes. At the same time, and in order to describe the nature of maternal deprivation more exactly, a number of researchers studied children living in group homes in different countries. They concluded that young children can generally cope with more than one major caregiver, but that what they need to develop normally are sustained interactions with caring and responsive people. If these conditions are not present, the child risks failing to develop an understanding of their own feelings and aims, or those of others, or a cohesive sense of self.[45]

The many destructive outcomes attributed to maternal deprivation appear to apply only too well to the removed children. Given the general acceptance of Bowlby's views, and the retreat from institutionalisation of non-Aboriginal children, how was it then that Indigenous children continued to be removed into the 1970s? One answer appears to be that those in authority saw these children's situation as different from that of children in general, and believed that they would be worse off if they continued to live in their own communities. The records present many expressions of this view, for example the following: '[The] half-caste, who possesses few of the virtues and nearly all of the vices of whites, grows up to be a mischievous and very immoral subject; it may appear to be a cruel thing to tear an aborigine child from its mother, but it is necessary in some cases to be cruel to be kind'.[46]

Other examples have already been cited. It is of interest that from early on some Aboriginal women appreciated that this perception was the root of the problem, and attributed it in part to the fact that the white authorities were men, who lacked understanding of the feelings of women and children:

> In many things the white people mean well, but they have so little understanding. My experience has convinced me that, sociologically, the Native Department is working on wrong lines ... The same law that applies to the white race should apply to the native races in that particular ... Our native mothers have all the natural feeling of mothers the world over, and to many of them the administration of the Native Department by men only, is stark tragedy.[47]

A second question concerns the operating style of the children's homes. Given the increased understanding of developmental needs after Bowlby's classic work, why were they permitted to operate in such unsatisfactory ways? The answer here is lack of resources, and the difficulty of recruiting and keeping suitable staff. Inexperienced staff often held responsibilities beyond their capacities, and 'the burdens placed on [them] and the stresses and frustrations they experienced, were no doubt responsible for the brutal punishments that often occurred'.[48] The National Inquiry also documents many instances of sexual abuse, and given the known tendency of institutions to draw paedophiles, this comes as no surprise.

Emotional abuse is another form of abuse, harder to define, but generally considered to include bullying, terrorising, shaming, humiliation, denigration and discrimination. Stories told to the National Inquiry and elsewhere[49] demonstrated a distressing variety of such abuse, including many particular incidents that had remained vivid in the victims' memories over decades.

To 'maternal deprivation', then, we must add the effect of physical, sexual and emotional abuse in some cases. The detrimental effects of physical abuse are by now well documented, and include low self-esteem, anxiety, anger, depression, lack of empathy with the sufferings of others, substance abuse and increased likelihood of oneself becoming a child abuser.[50] In the case of sexual abuse, confusion over sexual identity and sexual norms, dissociation, emotional numbing and guilt are also reported, and parenting problems are again a feature.[51] As with other forms of abuse, emotional abuse is linked with low self-esteem and poor mental health in adulthood.

Running through all of these aspects is a third theme that is central to personality development: that of identity, in this case ethnic/cultural identity. It is well documented that the achievement of a coherent sense of identity is an important developmental task, with adolescence usually a critical time.[52] Occupational and sexual identity has generally been seen as the core of personal identity, with ethnic/cultural identity a more peripheral aspect. This seems a fair description of the experience of members of the mainstream culture. For example, at the time of writing, one of the authors was involved in a survey that asked respondents to nominate their 'cultural group'. Most of the Anglo-Australians bypassed this question, or gave joke answers such as WASP and SNAG. For them, cultural identity was a non-issue. However, as Chapter 4 notes, minority-group individuals often find themselves categorised by others in terms of their group rather than as individuals. For them, in consequence, coming to terms with this attributed group membership is a central aspect of personal identity. This was the case for the removed children, who were consistently reminded of their ethnicity, usually in a denigratory way.

Ailsa Burns, Kate Burns & Karen Menzies

PORTRAYALS OF ABORIGINALITY

One woman, removed in the 1940s as a baby, told how:

> There was a big poster at the end of the dining room and it used to be pointed
> out to us all the time [in] religious instruction ... They had these Aborigine people
> sitting at the end of this big wide road and they were playing cards, gambling
> and drinking. And it had this slogan ... 'Wide is the road that leads us into
> destruction' which led up into hell. The other side they had these white people,
> all nicely dressed, leading on this narrow road and 'Narrow is the road that leads
> us into the kingdom of life or the Kingdom of God'.[53]

Other stories were sometimes of worse, sometimes of milder identity devaluations, as in the advice from foster parents to 'tell them you came from southern Europe'. In each case, however, it sooner or later became clear that 'merging' or 'assimilation' was not the ready option envisaged by the policy makers because, even if Indigenous people wished to merge, the European population was not prepared to accept and absorb them simply as individuals. The developmental task of achieving coherent and positive identity development thus involved achieving a cultural identity. Personal stories describe many ways in which it was sought, and many failures. An insightful account was given by a man removed from his family in the 1950s and placed in an Anglican boys' home.

> When they took us away, we could only talk Aboriginal, we only knew one language,
> and when we went down there, well we had to communicate somehow. Anyway,
> when I come back I couldn't even speak my own language. And that really buggered
> my identity up. It took me 40 odd years before I became a man in my own people's
> eyes, through Aboriginal law. Whereas I should've went through that when I was
> about 12 years of age.[54]

Legislation, policy and saying 'sorry'

In 1980 the Aboriginal family tracing and reunion agency Link–Up was established in New South Wales, since when it has extended across the country. Subsequently the Aboriginal Child Placement Principle—that when Aboriginal or Torres Strait Islander children are to be placed in substitute care, they should wherever possible be placed within their own culture and community—was introduced. Today it is recognised in all Australian jurisdictions, either in legislation or in policy, although its implementation remains problematic.

Responses at the state and territory level to other recommendations made in the report have varied, reflecting the priorities of the governments that have been in office. These recommendations included the setting up of a national compensation fund for people affected by forcible removal, and that all Australian parliaments acknowledge and formally apologise for their role in the policy. Throughout the years of the Howard Government no compensation fund was created, the Howard Government taking the view that 'there is no practical or appropriate way to address [the issue].'[55] All states and territories had officially apologised to the stolen generations. However, the Federal Government had refused to do so, instead expressing 'regret that indigenous Australians suffered injustices under the practices of past generations.'[56]

At the same time, the Federal Government spent over $10 million in court costs defending against individual claims for compensation. Two claimants (Lorna Cubillo and Peter Gunner) lost their court case when the High Court supported earlier rulings that the events in question were so long ago that key witnesses had either died or were unable to give evidence.[57] Another claimant (Joy Williams, who sued the State of New South Wales) lost her case on similar and other legal grounds. However, in a later case (August 2007) in which clearer evidence was available, the South Australian Supreme Court found that Bruce Trevorrow (aged fifty in 2007) had been 'falsely imprisoned and unlawfully treated' by the State when he was removed from his mother's care and handed over to a white family in 1957, aged thirteen months. The Court ordered that compensation of $525,000 be paid.

In November 2006 the Tasmanian Government passed legislation to financially compensate Tasmanian Aborigines forcibly removed from their families. All political parties supported the bill. The legislation mandated the appointment of an independent Stolen Generations Assessor to consider claims and make payments to an estimated 150 surviving members of the Tasmanian Stolen Generation, and eighty children of deceased victims. The Premier stated that by this action the Tasmanian Government was 'setting the standard' for other states by recognising the wrongs of the past. To date, none of the mainland states has followed Tasmania's lead, although several states have provided financial grants.

Figures from the 2006 Census[58] and from the Productivity Commission[59] show that the Indigenous population in general has made some gains—for example, the number of Indigenous students attending university or TAFE increased by 21 per cent between 1996 and 2006, and Indigenous home ownership also rose substantially. But Aboriginal health and welfare continue to lag behind that of other Australians. Life expectancy is seventeen years lower than for Australians overall, and infant mortality three times greater than for all Australian babies. These differences are much greater than those between the indigenous and general populations of New Zealand, Canada and the USA, where there have been significant improvements. Virtually all indicators show Aboriginal children at a major disadvantage; for example, the death rate from 'external causes and preventable disease' is five times that of other Australian children, and juveniles are twenty-three times more likely to be in detention.

In June 2007 the Northern Territory Government released *Little Children are Sacred*,[60] a report that describes shocking (although previously well-documented) levels of violence and abuse of Aboriginal children throughout the Territory. The report makes ninety-seven recommendations that include major reforms in education, health, service delivery and housing. When copies of this report reached the Federal Government, it declared a state of national emergency and announced that teams of police, military and government staff would be sent into some seventy Aboriginal communities in the Territory, starting immediately. Bans on alcohol and other substances would be introduced, and welfare legislation changed to ensure that money was spent on food and other essentials. Medical and nursing staff would undertake physical examination of all children and associated treatment. The permit-only system for entry into these communities would be revoked, so that government officials could enter without gaining permission, and a manager would be appointed to each community.[61] This drastic and abruptly introduced plan brought applause from some Australians and condemnation from others; and to some Indigenous communities it brought fear that children were once again to be removed from their families.

On 13 February 2008, at the opening of the forty-second Federal Parliament, and in the presence of many stolen generation members invited to Canberra for the occasion, the newly elected Prime Minister Kevin Rudd moved a formal motion of apology for the nation's past treatment of Indigenous Australians. The motion received unanimous support from members of Parliament, and strong support from the public. The new government resisted calls for compensation payments to stolen generation members, stating that it preferred to spend money on reducing the gap between the living standards of Indigenous and non-Indigenous Australians. However, in March 2008 a federal Senate Inquiry was set up to consider the compensation issue. Readers may wish to explore the outcomes so far.

STUDENT EXERCISES

1   The 'stolen generations' themselves suffered greatly from being removed from their families. What do you see as the 'ripple effect' of these policies and practices? Discuss the impact of these events on succeeding generations and on Aboriginal communities.

2   At different historical times, and even during the same era, the interpretation of the words 'in the best interests of the children' has differed markedly. Why was removal of Aboriginal children from their families seen as being in their best interests? Discuss how this differs from policies and practices concerning Aboriginal children and their families today. Compare this interpretation of the 'best interests' policy with policies and practices concerning non-Indigenous children at the same time (for example, the sending from England to Australia of children from disadvantaged backgrounds; adoption laws and practices).

3   The report of the National Inquiry into the Separation of Aboriginal and Torres Strait Islander Children from their Families, *Bringing them Home*, suggested that the policies and practices documented in the report amounted to genocide, or the deliberate destruction of a race of people. Do you agree that this was a case of genocide?

4   How can Bowlby's theories about the detrimental effect of maternal deprivation be reconciled with the 'best interests of children' presented as a defence for the policies that led to removal of Aboriginal children from their families?

5   Explore what has happened with the Federal Government's (2007) intervention into Indigenous communities in the Northern Territory. Do you think this intervention has anything in common with the stolen generations interventions?

6   Investigate the impact of the Rudd Government's apology and the changes made to government policy since February 2008.

Notes

1   Human Rights and Equal Opportunity Commission (HREOC), *Bringing Them Home: Report of the National Inquiry into the Separation of Aboriginal & Torres Strait Islander Children from their Families*, HREOC, Sydney, 1997, p. 142.
2   HREOC, 1997, p. 37.
3   C. Rowley, *The Destruction of Aboriginal Society*, Penguin, Ringwood, 1970.
4   Rowley, 1970, p. 92.
5   See B. Cummings, *Take This Child*, Aboriginal Studies Centre, Canberra, 1990.
6   HREOC, 1997, p. 104.
7   *Historical Records of Australia, Additional Instructions to Governor Bligh*, 20.11.1805, HRA Series I, Vol VI, Government Printer, Sydney, 1915, pp. 18–19.
8   Secretary of the SA State Children's Council, quoted in C. Mattingley & K. Hampton, *Survival in Our Own Land*, Hodder & Stoughton, Sydney, 1992, p. 160.
9   Chief Protector Spencer of the Northern Territory, quoted in Cummings, 1990, p. 17.
10 Violet Turner, quoted in Mattingley & Hampton, 1992, p. 213.
11 HREOC, 1997, Chapter 10; R. van Krieken, *Children and the State*, Allen & Unwin, Sydney, 1991.
12 HREOC, 1997, pp. 147–9.
13 HREOC, 1997, p. 27.
14 HREOC, 1997, pp. 30–2; Public submission by James Miller to the National Inquiry. See also R. Manne, 'The Stolen Generation', *Quadrant*, January/February 1998, pp. 53–63.
15 J. Bell, 'Assimilation in NSW', in *Aborigines Now: New Perspectives in the Study of Aboriginal Communities*, ed., M. Reay, Angus & Robertson, London, 1964, p. 68.
16 See, for example, HREOC, 1997, Chapter 10.
17 J. Bowlby, *Maternal Care and Mental Health*, World Health Organization, Geneva, 1951.
18 A. Markus, *Governing Savages*, Allen & Unwin, Sydney, 1990, p. 87.
19 HREOC, 1997, p. 84.
20 Cummings, 1990, p. 20.
21 HREOC, 1997, p. 134.
22 Quoted in R. Kidd, 'You Can Trust Me, I'm With the Government', paper presented at One Family, Many Histories Conference, 13–15 September 1994, Brisbane.
23 Faith Thomas, quoted in Mattingley & Hampton, 1992, pp. 215–18.
24 Faith Thomas, quoted in Mattingley & Hampton, 1992, pp. 215–18.
25 See for instance HREOC, 1997, pp. 171–2.
26 NSW Parliament, *Report of the NSW Aboriginal Children's Research Project to the Select Committee of the Legislative Assembly upon Aborigines*, NSW Government Printer, Sydney, 1981, p. 292.
27 HREOC, 1997, p. 67.
28 B. Waters, in HREOC, 1997, p. 158.
29 HREOC, 1997, p. 66.
30 HREOC, 1997, p. 174.
31 Australian Bureau of Statistics, *National Aboriginal and Torres Strait Islander Survey*, catalogue no. 4155.0, Australian Government Publishing Service, Canberra, 1994.
32 Australian Bureau of Statistics, *National Survey of Indigenous People*, 1994, cited in HREOC, 1997, p. 14.
33 Australian Bureau of Statistics, 1994, p. 58.
34 J. McKendrick, in HREOC, 1997, p. 22.
35 Australian Bureau of Statistics, *National Aboriginal and Torres Strait Islander Social Survey, Western Australia*, catalogue no. 4714.5.55.001, Australian Government Publishing Service, Canberra, 2002b.
36 S. Zubrick, S. Silburn, C. Haywood & F. Pearson, *Western Australian Aboriginal Health Survey Child Mental Health Survey*, Telethon Institute for Child Health Research, Perth, 2005.
37 J. Topp, in HREOC, 1997, pp. 225–6.
38 M. Brady, *Heavy Metal*, Aboriginal Studies Press, Canberra, 1992, pp. 183–90.
39 M. Kamien, *The Dark People of Bourke*, 1972, cited in HREOC, 1997, p. 225.
40 Kamien, 1972, quoted in HREOC, 1997, p. 225.
41 B. Waters, in HREOC, 1997, p. 222.
42 Public Submission by N. Kowalenko to the National Inquiry.
43 G. Seagrim & R. London, *Furnishing the Mind: A Comparative Study of Cognitive Development in Central Australian Aborigines*, Academic Press, Sydney, 1980, provides an interesting comparison of removed and non-removed children on cognitive tasks.

44 Bowlby, 1951. See also Bowlby's *Attachment and Loss*, vols 1, 2 & 3, Basic Books, New York, 1969–80.

45 See, for example, S. Provence & R. Lipton, *Infants in Institutions*, International Universities Press, New York, 1962; M. Rutter, *Maternal Deprivation Re-assessed*, Penguin, New York, 1981; B. Tizard, *Adoption: A Second Chance*, Open Books, London, 1977; L. Robins & M. Rutter, eds, *Straight and Devious Pathways from Childhood to Adulthood*, Cambridge University Press, Cambridge, 1990.

46 J.M. Drew, WA Parliamentary Debates, quoted in P. Biskup, *Not Slaves, Not Citizens: The Aboriginal Problem in Western Australia, 1898–1954*, University of Queensland Press, St Lucia, 1973, p. 142.

47 Gladys Prosser, a Noongar mother, quoted in the WA Legislative Council by the Hon. H. Seddon, *Hansard*, 22 November 1938, WA Government Printing Office, Perth, p. 2246.

48 Cited in Cummings, 1990, p. 119.

49 See, for example, Mattingley & Hampton, 1992.

50 S.T. Azar & D.A. Wolfe, 'Child Physical Abuse and Neglect', in *Treatment of Childhood Disorders* (3rd edn), eds, E.J. Marsh & R.A. Barkley, Guilford Press, New York, 2006, pp. 147–54.

51 M.E. Pipe, M.E. Lamb, Y. Orbach & A.C. Cedarborg, eds, *Child Sexual Abuse: Disclosure, Delay and Denial*, Lawrence Erlbaum, Mahwah, NJ, 2007.

52 W.D. Wakefield & C. Hudley, 'Ethnic and Racial Identity and Adolescent Wellbeing', *Theory into Practice*, 46, 2, 2007, pp. 147–54.

53 HREOC, 1997, p. 157.

54 HREOC, 1997, p. 203.

55 Senator John Herron, Minister for Aboriginal and Torres Strait Islander Affairs, 'Bringing Them Home—Commonwealth Initiatives', media release, Canberra, 26 August 1999.

56 Hon. John Howard, *Hansard*, Commonwealth of Australia: House of Representatives, Statement on the Motion of Reconciliation, 26 August 1999.

57 P. O'Brien, 'Are We Helping Them Home?', paper on the Surveys of Progress in the Implementation of the *Bringing Them Home* Recommendations, Parliament House, Canberra, 13 November 2002; A. Buti, 'Unfinished Business: The Australian Stolen Generations', *Murdoch University Electronic Journal of Law*, 7, 4, 2000, <www.murdoch.edu.au/elaw/indices/issue/v7n4.html>, accessed 24 March 2008.

58 Australian Bureau of Statistics, *Census 2006*, Australian Government Publishing Service, Canberra, 2007i.

59 Steering Committee for the Review of Government Service Provision (Productivity Commission), *Overcoming Indigenous Disadvantage*, Attorney-General's Department, Canberra, 2007.

60 Board of Inquiry into the Protection of Aboriginal Children from Sexual Abuse, *Little Children are Sacred*, Northern Territory Government, Darwin, 2007.

61 See <www.facsia.gov.au/internet/Minister3.nsf/content/phaseone_26jun07.htm>, accessed 25 August 2007.

12

Child Care and Australian Social Policy

Deborah Brennan

The care and education of children below school age has experienced 'a surge of policy attention' in recent years.[1] At the international level, the Organisation for Economic Cooperation and Development (OECD), the United Nations Children's Emergency Fund (UNICEF) and the World Bank have all expressed interest in policies surrounding the early years and have published reports and made policy recommendations.[2] Many governments, too, have overhauled their approach to educational and social provision for their youngest citizens. Child care is firmly entrenched in the Australian political agenda and is an accepted part of social provision in this country. In the last decade, however, there has been a fundamental transformation in the rationale for the provision of child care and the philosophy underlying service provision. The ideals of the community-based, non-profit child care movement that underpinned Commonwealth policy for decades no longer hold sway; they have been superseded by a more hard-edged, market-driven approach that sees child care as a commodity to be bought and sold. Caring for children below school age is now big business, with major child care corporations listed on the stock exchange and their owners featured in *Business Review Weekly*'s list of Australia's richest individuals.

The rights and needs of children do not play a major part in current Australian policy debates—child care is firmly focused on the needs of adults: parents and employers. As a result of Commonwealth Government policy changes, both Labor and Coalition, the for-profit sector is now the major provider of centre-based long day care in Australia. Total outlays on child care increased under the Howard Government, but this was because of an expansion in out-of-school-hours care. The number of long day care places has grown in the last decade, but not dramatically. Meanwhile, child care costs have risen for most families, especially those who choose to use non-profit services.

This chapter explores the transitions that have taken place in the philosophy underlying child care in Australia since its inception in the 1890s. The emphasis is on services that cater for children from birth to school age and that are open for at least eight hours a day throughout the year. The term 'child care' is used to describe such services even though some authors argue for the more inclusive term 'early childhood education and care'. In this chapter, since pre-schools and kindergartens are beyond the scope of the discussion, the broader term is not appropriate. The central argument of the chapter is that the shift towards the market, justified by reference to 'choice' and 'competition', has not brought the promised benefits to the sector. There has not been a major expansion in the number of places, costs have gone up and in some areas quality has been compromised. Community-based, non-profit services have been sidelined in favour of privately owned businesses. Further, since the beginning of the twenty-first century, the private sector itself has changed as corporate providers have taken over more and more of the formerly independent, private, for-profit services. While profit-driven care operates in many countries, Australia is unique in the extent to which publicly listed corporations, rather than independent owner-operators, dominate the provision of this vital service.

Contexts

Early kindergartens and day nurseries

The earliest group care services for children in Australia were set up by philanthropic organisations such as the various Kindergarten Unions (which were established in all states between 1895 and 1911), the Sydney Day Nursery Association (1905) and the Victorian Day Nurseries Association (1910). The establishment of kindergartens and day nurseries was closely linked with the founding of staff training colleges. In New South Wales, for example, the first free kindergarten was opened in 1896 and students were enrolled in the Kindergarten Training College the following year. Students worked in the kindergartens during the mornings, and undertook the more theoretical aspects of their studies in the afternoons. The close ties between the preparation of staff and the administration of services have long been regarded as a strength of the early childhood field.

The founders of children's services in Australia were not narrowly focused on the provision of kindergartens and day nurseries; they had much broader social goals. Their work included home visits to the families of the children enrolled in their services, and the establishment of supervised playgrounds in the inner suburbs.[3] Considerable effort was put into the preparation of staff to work with children in the early years of school, promoting the idea that 'early childhood' extended beyond the pre-school years into the first part of formal school.

LILLIAN DE LISSA: EARLY ACTIVIST

The work of Lillian de Lissa, a key figure in children's services in South Australia, is an example of the broad social commitment of the early activists' concerns. In her account of efforts to establish kindergartens in Adelaide, de Lissa acknowledged that, at first, the inner-urban families she attempted to work with were quite suspicious. None of them had heard of a kindergarten and they were understandably wary of someone who, for no apparent reason, wanted to take care of their children for the whole morning.

Once the first kindergarten was opened, however, it proved extremely popular, and the mothers who used it decided that they would like to see the idea extended to a neighbouring area. Accordingly, a group of mothers went to a nearby suburb where they spent a week keeping house and caring for the children of women they did not know. They did this to enable the second group of women to spend time observing how kindergartens were run, so that they, in turn, could have such a service set up in their own neighbourhood. De Lissa commented: 'I was more stirred by this than by anything that had happened in my life up to that time, because I saw a vision of a new world; a world in which women, as women, would begin to think about children who were not their own and who would work for them and their well-being though they themselves were getting nothing out of it'.[4]

CHILD CARE ACT 1972 (CTH)

By the 1960s most state governments had begun to provide assistance for pre-school education, but the provision of day care remained in the philanthropic sphere. As the demand for women's labour became more pressing and the women's liberation movement emerged, the Commonwealth Government became the focus of sustained claims for assistance with child care services that would support maternal employment.

The *Child Care Act 1972* (Cth) marked the beginning of the Commonwealth Government's large-scale involvement in funding child care. Introduced by the then Minister for Labour and National Service, the Act was designed to facilitate the labour-force participation of mothers of young children. The scope of the legislation was strictly limited: it authorised the Commonwealth to provide financial assistance only to non-profit, centre-based long day care. In the early 1970s, virtually the only recognised voices in the children's services field were those of the established philanthropic–cum–educational bodies. Feminists were beginning to become active around child care issues, but were still very new players in the field and did not have access to government ministers. The philosophy of the Act reflected the dominance of the traditional organisations and their ethos of professionalism. Thus there was no debate about parent participation in the running of services, for example, as this had never been part of the early childhood tradition. Nevertheless, the legislation had a clear focus on children through its insistence that funded services meet defined quality standards. The original funding formula, established by the Child Care Act, linked funding to the employment of trained staff. The ratios and staff qualifications built into the Act were those laid down by the Australian Pre-school Association (precursor of Early Childhood Australia).

Although it had significant limitations, the *Child Care Act* was extremely important. Its very existence was an acknowledgment that affordable, quality child care was beyond the reach of ordinary families. As one of the government speakers in the parliamentary debate commented, 'child care which is beneficial to the child's overall development is

Deborah Brennan

prohibitively costly for the large body of parents and … the child minding arrangements that most parents could afford fall far short of the quality required in the interests of child welfare …'[5] Further, the Act embodied the idea that it was appropriate for the Commonwealth to assume responsibility in an area traditionally seen as an extension either of child welfare or of education (and therefore the province of the states).

Another development of the 1970s was the emergence of the community child care movement. Participants in this movement called for the provision of free child care centres, available to all parents, regardless of their reasons for use. They saw child care as part of a broad social revolution that would lead to less rigid sex role and generational stereotypes, and provide opportunities for individuals to maximise their choices concerning work, leisure and child rearing, depending upon individual temperament and ability. They cautioned against a narrow, work-related focus, arguing that child care services should not simply be designed to free women to work outside the home during the day at dreary, exhausting labour that left them with the housework to do at night: 'To only want day care on the grounds that it will give us a chance to prove we are as good as men in a man's world is to entirely miss the point of the new feminism.'[6]

Although the legislation enabling the Commonwealth Government to fund child care was passed in the last days of the McMahon Coalition Government, it was under the Whitlam Labor Government (1972–75) that Australian child care policy development and funding really got under way. During the short life of this government early childhood educators, philanthropic organisations and feminists vied with one another to influence government policy and determine expenditure priorities.

The Whitlam era was a turning point in the politics of child care. It was a period when crucial lessons about policy making, policy implementation and bureaucratic politics were learned by feminists.[7] These years were also a period of struggle and uncertainty for the women who had previously dominated the traditional early childhood organisations, and whose role as expert advisers to government on matters pertaining to the care and education of young children had hitherto gone unchallenged.

Within the government itself ministers and bureaucrats clashed over the most desirable direction for child care policy and the most appropriate department (education or social security) for this policy function. From mid 1973 onwards, official Labor policy called for 'a comprehensive child care service [which would] provide support for women to participate more fully in society'.[8] This policy had been devised by feminists within the party, particularly the New South Wales Labor Women's Committee, and was strongly supported by the Prime Minister's Adviser on Women's Affairs, Elizabeth Reid. In mid 1974 the Labor Government announced that it intended to establish a Children's Commission so that by 1980 'all children in Australia [would] have access to services designed to take care of their physical, social and recreational needs'.[9]

Despite this visionary ideal, the Whitlam Government in fact allocated most of its child care funding to sessional pre-schools run by traditional organisations such as the Kindergarten Unions. This happened largely because the government used a model of funding that relied on submissions from the community, and which thus gave the edge to organised groups that were familiar with bureaucratic procedures. It was also the result of sustained opposition to the wider children's services program by state governments and a range of vested interests both inside and outside the bureaucracy.[10]

Following the dismissal of the Whitlam Government in late 1975, uncertainty surrounded the future of Commonwealth-funded child care. The Coalition Government led by Malcolm Fraser was committed to reducing Commonwealth expenditure and to encouraging a greater role for families and the market in responding to social needs such as child care. Despite this, most of the central components of the children's services program survived the Fraser Government (1975–83), although funding was substantially curtailed.

This outcome was the result of the determined efforts of a small number of committed people. A key role was performed by Beryl Beaurepaire, a close friend of the Prime Minister and Vice-President of the Victorian Liberal Party. Beaurepaire was appointed Convenor of the first National Women's Advisory Council in 1976 and used this position to lobby strenuously for a range of women's issues including child care. Senator Margaret Guilfoyle, Minister for Social Security (1975–80) and Minister Assisting the Prime Minister on Child Care Matters (1975–76) was also sympathetic to the need for children's services, especially long day care. Women in the bureaucracy (especially the Women's Affairs Branch) developed economic arguments to support the case for switching priorities to long day care.[11]

In addition to all these 'insider' efforts, the activities of various state-based lobby groups became far more effectively coordinated. These included Community Child Care (which by this time existed in both Victoria and New South Wales), the Women's Trade Union Commission, the Family Day Care Association and the Ethnic Child Care Development Unit. In 1983 the National Association of Community Based Children's Services (NACBCS) was formed. NACBCS aimed to represent the interests of all types of community-based children's services and, in particular, to overcome traditional divisions between home-based and centre-based care.

The Hawke and Keating Labor Governments

The politics of child care under the Hawke and Keating Labor Governments (1983–96) presented a distinct contrast with that of previous administrations and raised new issues and dilemmas. During these years, care policy was shaped by persistent tension between the government's economic and social justice objectives. Labor's economic goals in this period included reducing both public expenditure and the budget deficit. In the context of this climate of fiscal austerity, advocates of expanded child care provision found it necessary to use economic arguments to support their case. The close relationship between the government and the Australian Council of Trade Unions (ACTU), as expressed through the Accord, was also significant here. Under the Accord, the unions agreed to exercise wage restraint in return for increases in the social wage (the latter being broadly understood to include health, social welfare and community services such as child care) and a government commitment to reducing unemployment.

The ACTU took up the child care issue in a number of ways: it pressed for increases in the provision of community-based and work-related services; it urged the government to ensure that fees in subsidised services were kept at reasonable levels; and it helped to coordinate campaigns for improvements to the pay, working conditions and career structures of child care workers. During these years, the ACTU became a far more significant player than feminist groups and community child care advocates. As a result of this, and also because of the government's broader economic agenda, child care provision was increasingly tied to the needs of the labour market.

In the late 1980s a bitter struggle erupted within the government over the very existence of publicly funded child care, and especially over subsidies to middle- and high-income families. In 1991, following a period of sustained lobbying by private operators and pressure from the ACTU, the government extended subsidies to users of private, for-profit child care centres. This represented a profound shift in government policy. The move was vigorously opposed on the grounds that the care of children should be a public responsibility rather than a profit-making activity. Concerns were also voiced about the failure of most private centres to provide care for babies and toddlers. The standard of care offered in some private centres was also an issue. Research conducted by the Australian Bureau of Statistics had shown that commercial centres had fewer qualified staff than community-based services, employed four times as many staff under eighteen years and had fewer ancillary staff.[12] The industrial conditions in commercial centres were also of concern, particularly the propensity of some operators to hire very young staff and dismiss them when they became eligible for adult wages. In response to these concerns, the Labor Government introduced an accreditation system, the Quality Improvement and Assurance System, which covered both private and community-based long day care centres.

Accreditation focuses particularly on the quality of interactions within each centre; it is thus quite separate from the licensing of the premises, which remains a state responsibility. In the words of June Wangmann (a Sydney-based academic and a key player in the accreditation debate): 'Regulations only deal with issues which affect children before they come in the door—the number of toilets, ratio of staff, the qualifications they hold. Accreditation looks at how staff interact with children.'[13] The idea behind accreditation was that public subsidies should only be available to centres that participated in this process, thus ensuring that public monies would not go to services that were in any way substandard. Accreditation has since been extended to family day care and out-of-school-hours care.

During the Labor years the role of the Commonwealth was increasingly defined as that of supporting other players, notably employers, commercial providers and state governments. Budgetary constraints resulted in pressure from Treasury to limit direct capital expenditure by the Commonwealth and to shift responsibility onto private businesses and employers. Further efforts were made to focus child care provision on work-related needs and to limit access by other users such as parents at home. Not long after the extension of subsidies to the private sector, Labor proposed the introduction of a 'two-tier' system of child care assistance (then called fee relief), in which work-related and non-work-related care would attract different rates of subsidy. This proposal was intended to discourage non-employed parents from using child care by requiring them to pay higher fees.[14] Almost all users in this category would have been reliant on a single income, and the suggestion that such families could afford to pay more for their child care than those with two incomes provoked vehement opposition. Particular concern was expressed about the possibility that children at risk of abuse might lose their access to child care. Labor quietly let the proposal drop.

The rapid growth of mothers' participation in the labour force is a key factor behind the increased demand for child care. The Longitudinal Study of Australian Children showed that in 2004 25 per cent of mothers had returned to work before their infants were six months old and 40 per cent were back before their baby's first birthday.[15] (Australia's status as one of only two developed nations where women lack a general entitlement to paid maternity leave is a strong contributing factor in this.) Although parental employment is the single most important reason parents give for using child care, it is not the only one. Many seek child care because they see it as having positive benefits for their children.

Privatisation and the growth of corporate child care

The broad thrust of policy change under the Hawke and Keating Labor Governments, extended and reinforced by the Howard Government, was to subsidise consumer demand, thereby encouraging competition between commercial and non-profit providers. The changes included the extension of child care assistance to users of for-profit centres; the active encouragement of expansion in this sector at the expense of the community sector; and the withdrawal of operational subsidies from long day care centres from July 1997 and out-of-school-hours care services from January 1998.

The winding back, almost to a standstill, of new non-profit services, together with the explosive, unplanned growth of for-profit care, resulted in increasing privatisation of child care and the marginalisation of community-based non-profit care. Less tangibly, it contributed to a government approach to child care that targets the individual family as the recipient of services and ignores the community and social purposes of such care. Thus, despite significant levels of government funding, child care is increasingly constructed as a 'private' problem, which individual families can 'solve' by choosing to use a commercial service, a publicly owned service or internal resources such as grandparents, other family members and friends.

The Commonwealth Government does not limit or constrain the growth of commercial care. It supports expansion in any location chosen by private businesses. In order for parents to be able to claim Child Care Benefit, services must be approved by the Commonwealth. This requires them to open for a certain number of hours per day and weeks per year, to be licensed by the relevant state or territory authority and to be registered with the Quality Improvement and Accreditation System. There is no overall planning of the location of new private child care centres—even though the profits of these centres are underwritten by Commonwealth subsidies. Across Australia, two-thirds of all long day centres are operated as private, for-profit businesses, although the proportion varies from almost 80 per cent in Queensland to around 30 per cent in Tasmania.[16]

Child care services in Australia have also been marked by a shift towards *corporate* care, that is, care provided by publicly listed companies whose shares are bought and

Deborah Brennan

sold on the stock exchange. In 2001 a Queensland company, ABC Learning Centres (or 'ABC Learning'), became the first publicly listed child care corporation in Australia. Several other companies followed suit. By listing on the stock exchange, these companies gained access to significant amounts of capital, enabling them to expand more rapidly and to invest in physical improvements to the services they acquired.

THE BUSINESS OF CARE

ABC Learning adopted a rapid expansion strategy, taking over some centres run by community-based, non-profit groups and others owned by individual owner-operators. Many of these formerly independent centres are now franchises of ABC Learning. Within a few years, ABC Learning had absorbed most of its corporate rivals, as well as hundreds of individual centres, and had become the dominant player in Australian long day care. ABC Learning now controls around 30 per cent of all Australian long day care.[17] In 2006, at the height of his financial involvement in the business the CEO of ABC Learning, Eddy Groves, was named Australia's richest person under forty; his personal wealth at that time was estimated at $272 million.[18]

The character of Australian child care has thus changed in two separate, but related, ways: the community based, non-profit component has been marginalised politically and also in terms of numerical significance, and the private sector is increasingly dominated by corporate interests rather than independent operators.

As yet, there are no major studies of the impact of this transformation of Australian child care, although some important work has been done to map out the scope of the issues raised. Jennifer Sumsion has outlined an 'ethical audit and research agenda',[19] for example, while Frances Press and Christine Woodrow have looked at ways in which notions of corporatisation and marketisation are beginning to shape the policy and service context of young children in Australia.[20] Joy Goodfellow has written persuasively of the growing gap between a market or property view of the child, and the more humanistic approaches that have traditionally been associated with early childhood education.[21]

Most writers in this area caution against the assumption that private, for-profit care is necessarily bad or inferior to the care provided under non-profit auspices. They are also keen to avoid lumping all for-profit services together. The private child care sector comprises many providers with diverse philosophies, aspirations and motives. Many owner-operators are experienced professionals, committed to the well-being of the children in their care. It would be inaccurate to depict all private providers, whether owner-operators or corporations, as unscrupulous profit seekers, and equally inaccurate to suggest that all non-profit care meets some superior standard.

There is, however, evidence of emerging disparities between the sectors. In a recent report on staff perceptions of quality in child care, the Australia Institute made a useful distinction between three types of providers: community-based, non-profit providers (including all centres run by 'community groups, religious organizations, charities, local governments and by or in state government premises'[22]); independent private providers (owner-operated small businesses that usually own a single centre); and corporate chains listed on the stock exchange. Based on a stratified random sample of long day care staff, the Australia Institute found many similarities between community-based providers and independent private providers. On many indices of quality, the results from staff in these two categories clustered together, with markedly different results from staff employed in corporate chains. On the critical issue of whether staff have time to form relationships with children, 54 per cent of staff in community-based centres and 49 per cent in independent centres agreed that they did, whereas only 25 per cent of staff in corporate chains held this view.[23] Similarly, 80 per cent of staff in community centres and 75 per cent in independent private centres said there was 'always' enough food for children, but only 54 per cent of staff employed in corporate chains had this view.[24] When asked whether they would be happy to enrol a child of their own (if they had one) in the centre in which they worked, or one of a similar quality, 21 per cent of staff in corporate chains said they would not be happy to do so, because of quality concerns; by contrast, only 4 per cent of staff in community-based and 6 per cent in independent private centres expressed this view.[25]

It would be problematic to generalise from these findings alone; however, international research also suggests an association between high-quality care and non-profit status. Economist Michael Krashinsky has shown that public centres are superior to private ones in Canada on a range of measures of quality.[26] This finding has been reinforced in recent work by another Canadian economist, Gordon Cleveland, who worked with a team of scholars to investigate the role of the non-profit sector in providing early childhood education and care. Cleveland and his colleagues found significant differences, on average, between non-profit and for-profit child care. Reviewing the evidence from four large data sets they found a 'remarkably uniform' pattern:

> Everywhere, nonprofits produce a higher quality of care in child care centres, whether measured by the Early Childhood Environments Rating Scale and the Infant Toddler Environments Rating Scale, or by the special scale developed to measure the quality of 'educational' child care in Quebec, or by the measures used by the City of Toronto. Although there are good quality nonprofits and poor quality nonprofits, nonprofit centres are overrepresented at higher levels of quality and underrepresented at lower levels of quality. Although the frequency distributions of quality in nonprofit and in for-profit care overlap, the nonprofit distribution is shifted towards higher quality levels.[27]

Corporate child care has expanded markedly in the twenty-first century: ABC Learning is now the biggest child care company in the world; as well as dominating the Australian market, it is the largest provider of child care in the United Kingdom[28] and the second largest provider in the USA.[29] Interestingly, though, the proportion of services owned by ABC Learning in these countries is far smaller than its share of Australian child care.

For some observers and analysts, particularly early childhood educators, both the privatisation of child care and the rise of corporate services raise troubling questions. Press and Woodrow point out that private sector domination 'has tended to shift policy deliberation away from children's needs to issues of profitability'.[30] Historically, the

Deborah Brennan

non-profit sector has urged strengthened regulations and improved pay and conditions for early childhood professionals, and these have been opposed by the private sector.

In New South Wales, private providers have twice defeated efforts to strengthen the regulations governing child care, particularly the ratio of staff to babies and toddlers. Existing regulations in the state require one staff member to be employed for every five children in attendance. This is a lower standard than that which applies in some other states (for example, the 1:4 ratio that is current in Western Australia and Queensland) and well below the 1:3 ratio recommended by respected international bodies such as the National Association for the Education of Young Children and the American Academy of Pediatrics. In 2006, a government-appointed taskforce recommended the phasing in of a 1:4 ratio in New South Wales. After receiving the report, the government rejected the taskforce's recommendation, favouring instead a minority report submitted by taskforce members representing the private sector.[31] This was the second time within a short period that lobby groups representing for-profit providers had opposed efforts to bring New South Wales regulations into line with international recommendations. The argument is that changing the ratios will result in additional costs, thus raising prices for families and/or reducing the profits of providers. It is unclear where the needs and interests of children fit into this analysis.

Equally concerning is the emerging evidence that some service providers are unable to comply with even the minimal regulations that currently operate in New South Wales, either due to staff shortages or because qualified workers are 'voting with their feet' and seeking employment elsewhere. Research conducted by the Social Policy Research Centre (SPRC) has shown that private operators are more likely than community-based services to seek exemptions from the state government regulation requiring the employment of university-qualified teachers in centres with more than twenty-nine children present. They do this on the grounds that they cannot find teachers to work in their services.[32] The research has revealed a disturbingly high rate of complaints about for-profit services that have gained such exemptions, although, interestingly, there were relatively few complaints against non-profit services that have had exemptions from employing trained teachers. In the period reviewed by the SPRC researchers, fifty-seven complaints were made to the New South Wales Department of Community Services about centres with exemptions, including fifty-two against private centres compared to five against non-profit services.[33] Even allowing for the fact that more private centres than non-profit centres had obtained exemptions, the skewed nature of the complaints is of concern.

Another concern about the growth of private child care is that policies geared towards gender equality and intended to have beneficial effects for mothers and babies—paid maternity leave, for example—could be seen as antithetical to the business interests of private child care providers. In the midst of an intense public debate about the possibility of introducing such a scheme in Australia, the 'Money' section of the *Weekend Australian* reported: 'The main area which could affect private child care companies is the proposal to introduce some form of paid maternity leave, which would affect demand for child care services as more women stayed at home longer after giving birth.'[34]

The other major issue facing users of Australian children's services is cost. In 2000 the Commonwealth introduced the Child Care Benefit, amalgamating 'child care assistance' and the 'child care rebate'. In response to sustained community pressure concerning the gap between Commonwealth assistance and the actual fees charged, the maximum amount of Child Care Benefit was increased by $7.50 per week. Initially these changes had a real impact in increasing the affordability of child care, but these gains have since been eroded as child care fees have risen faster than both inflation and average earnings.[35] Many families now struggle to find decent child care that they can afford. Barbara Pocock's research into work and family issues in Australia has shown that in a range of occupations and industries—including call centres, factories, hospitals and offices—parents work different shifts in order to avoid the costs and stresses associated with finding child care.[36]

Many families are caught in a difficult bind: both parents need to work, but the cost of child care combined with the loss of benefits such as rental subsidies and family tax benefits that result from increased incomes, means they are in a no-win situation.[37] Research by the National Centre for Economic Modelling has shown that low-income families can sometimes be worse off if the mother increases her hours of work. This happens because as the family receives more income, family benefits are withdrawn, child care costs go up, more tax is taken and the rent charged for public housing rises. These effects are particularly sharp for low-income women with several children. A low-income woman with three children loses at least 60 per cent of her hourly wages once tax, reduced family assistance and increased child care costs are factored in.[38]

Consequences

Implications of policy for children and families

When considering the issues that will shape the future for children, their families and communities, it is essential to take a broad view of the relevant policy arenas. Many policies—including employment, industrial relations, taxation, social security and immigration—can be considered as 'family policies' since all have a significant impact upon the resources, opportunities, constraints and choices available to family members. Thus it does not make good sense for children's advocates to restrict their involvement in public policy debates to those issues that are *directly* about children and families. Participation in a range of debates including taxation, social security, employment and the appropriate division of Commonwealth–state responsibilities is vital.

Industrial relations is an example of an area where early childhood students, teachers and advocates need to be informed about debates and policy changes beyond those that are directly relevant to their professional concern as educators. Patterns of employment and unemployment in Australia have changed considerably since the early 1970s. Many of the changes are structural (long-term changes in production patterns, for example), while others are political. Changes to the industrial relations environment were a key element of the policy agenda of the Howard Government. Since the introduction of the *Workplace Relations Act 1996* (Cth) in its first year in office, the government increasingly shifted responsibility for industrial relations to the workplace level, rather than leaving it

Deborah Brennan

to decisions made at a central level by the Australian Industrial Relations Commission. *WorkChoices* legislation, introduced in 2006, took this process a step further by accelerating the shift away from collective bargaining towards individual contracts. *WorkChoices* has been repealed by the Rudd Government since it took power late in 2007.

Evidence is now beginning to show that the restructuring of industrial relations (and especially the emphasis on establishing a flexible labour market) has had profound impacts upon parents and thus, indirectly, upon children. The main features of the changing nature of work in Australia include a substantial increase in part-time and casual work (almost a quarter of the Australian workforce is now employed part-time, compared with only 10 per cent in the 1970s); far greater reliance on 'non-standard' forms of employment such as contract, seasonal and 'on call' work; substantial increases in overtime; more jobs requiring employees to do split shifts, twelve-hour shifts and weekend work; and a reduction in the proportion of jobs with fixed starting and finishing times. Less than half the workforce now works Monday to Friday, and one-quarter works at least part of the weekend. By the late 1990s 'only 7 per cent of workers work[ed] all their weekday hours between 9 am and 5 pm'.[39]

The new world of work requires that children, as well as their parents, 'adjust' to non-standard hours of employment. For example, given the growth in work patterns outlined above, many children have to contend with unpredictability in their parents' schedules, not knowing when they will be collected from the centre or family day care premises and not having their parents at home in the evenings or on weekends. It is indeed ironic that a government professing to be strongly in favour of 'traditional family values' was encouraging employers to adopt patterns of work that had the potential to disrupt stable family life for many Australian workers. It remains to be seen whether these patterns will change under the Rudd Labor Government.

The 'flexibility' of the new world of work can be a two-edged sword. Working hours and patterns of employment that enable employees to meet both the routine and the unexpected demands of family life are desired by working parents. However, if flexibility essentially means an increase in the amount of insecure part-time work, or if it means that more workers are required to work long hours or extra days at short notice, then major problems will arise, such as accessing quality child care during the required working hours.

The community-based child care movement that once provided the spirit and philosophy behind Australian children's services policy has been radically downgraded since the mid 1990s. Community-based, non-profit care and its antecedents—the nursery school and free kindergarten movements—were born out of a public vision of the well-being of children and families. The establishment of neighbourhood links, the building of support networks and the task of working together in a common enterprise were features of the community-based child care movement that simply cannot be sustained in an environment where the great majority of services are built for the purpose of private profit.

The winding-down of community-managed services in which parents have a stake—not only because of their own needs, but also because of their concern for the needs of their fellow citizens—is a major loss. At the same time significant changes in society, such as the transformation of patterns of work and unemployment, are creating pressures on children, families and communities. There is an urgent need, as we move further into the new millennium, to reinvigorate public debate about the links between children, parents and communities, and to reformulate the arguments for public support for child care.

STUDENT EXERCISES

1 Discuss how the relationship between group care services and parents has changed since the establishment of the first day nurseries and kindergartens in Australia.

2 For what reasons did the Commonwealth Government become involved in policy and funding of children's services? Did these reasons affect the types of services provided to families and to children? What are the processes by which policy translates into effects on individual children and families?

3 How has the provision of children's services in Australia been influenced by the political actions of parents? Give some examples of parental involvement and discuss favourable and unfavourable contexts for change from the 'bottom up' (rather than from the 'top down').

4 How will changing patterns of work in Australian society affect families and, particularly, children? How can detrimental impacts on children and families be avoided?

5 What are the implications of the growth of 'corporate child care' in Australia?

Notes

1   OECD, *Starting Strong—Early Childhood Education and Care*, OECD, Paris, 2001, p. 7.

2   OECD, 2001; OECD, *Starting Strong II: Early Childhood Education and Care*, OECD, 2006; World Bank, *Early Child Development: From Measurement to Action—A Priority for Growth and Equity*, The World Bank, Washington, D.C., 2007; UNICEF, *The State of the World's Children*, UNICEF, New York, 2007.

3   P. Spearritt, 'The Kindergarten Movement: Tradition and Change', in *Social Change in Australia: Readings in Sociology*, ed., D. Edgar, Cheshire, Melbourne, 1974, pp. 583–96.

4   L. de Lissa, *Talks Given at the Golden Jubilee of the Kindergarten Union of South Australia*, Kindergarten Union of South Australia, Adelaide, 1955.

5   Commonwealth, *Parliamentary Debates*, House of Representatives, vol. 81, 10 October 1972, p. 2289.

6   W. McCaughey, 'Day Care—Liberating Who for What?', *Dissent*, 28, Winter, 1972, p. 7.

7   S. Dowse, 'The Women's Movement's Fandango with the State: The Movement's Role in Public Policy since 1972', in *Women, Social Welfare and the State* (2nd edn), eds, C.V. Baldock & B. Cass, Allen & Unwin, Sydney, 1988, pp. 205–26.

8   Australian Labor Party, *Platform, Constitution and Rules*, Canberra, 1973, p. 17.

9   Quoted in D. Brennan, *The Politics of Australian Child Care: From Philanthropy to Feminism*, Cambridge University Press, Cambridge, 1994, p. 90.

10   Brennan, 1994, pp. 92–5; Dowse, 1988.

11   M. Sawer & A. Groves, *Working from the Inside: Twenty Years of the Office of the Status of Women*, Australian Government Publishing Service, Canberra, 1994.

12   Australian Bureau of Statistics, *Commercial Long Day Child Care Australia*, catalogue no. 4414.0, Australian Government Publishing Service, Canberra, 1989.

13   *Sydney Morning Herald*, 4 March 1993.

Deborah Brennan

14   J. Gifford, *Child Care Funding Reassessed: Operational Subsidies, Fee Relief and Taxation Measures*, Australian Early Childhood Association and National Association of Community Based Children's Services, Canberra, 1992, p. 36.

15   Australian Institute of Family Studies, *Growing Up in Australia: The Longitudinal Study of Australian Children*, 2004 Annual Report, AIFS, Melbourne, 2005a.

16   Department of Family and Community Services, *2004 Census of Child Care Services, Summary Booklet*, Australian Government, Canberra, 2005, p. 21.

17   FACSIA, personal communication with the author.

18   F. Farouque, 'The Other Eddy Everywhere', *The Age*, 8 April 2006, <www.theage.com.au/news/in-depth/the-other-eddy-everywhere/2006/04/07/1143916718012.html>, accessed 17 August 2007.

19   J. Sumsion, 'The Corporatization of Australian Childcare', *Journal of Early Childhood Research*, 4, 2, 2006, pp. 99–120.

20   F. Press & C. Woodrow, 'Commodification, Corporatisation and Children's Spaces', *Australian Journal of Education*, 49, 3, 2005, pp. 278–91.

21   J. Goodfellow, 'Market Childcare: Preliminary Considerations of a "Property View" of the Child', *Contemporary Issues in Early Childhood*, 6, 1, 2005, pp. 54–65.

22   E. Rush, *Child Care Quality in Australia*, Discussion Paper No. 84, Australia Institute, Canberra, 2006, p. 2.

23   Rush, 2006.

24   Rush, 2006.

25   Rush, 2006.

26   M. Krashinsky, 'Does Auspice Matter?: The Case of Day Care for Children in Canada', in *Private Action and the Public Good*, eds, W.W. Powell & E.S. Clemens, Yale University Press, New Haven, CO, 1999, pp. 114–23.

27   G. Cleveland, B. Forer, D. Hyatt, C. Japel & M. Krashinsky, 'An Economic Perspective on the Current and Future Role of Nonprofit Provision of Early Learning and Child Care Services in Canada: Final Project Report', University of Toronto, University of British Columbia & Université du Québec, 2007, p. 14.

28   *Financial Times*, 14 August 2007.

29   ABC Learning Centres, *Annual Report*, ABC Learning Centres Limited, 2006.

30   Press & Woodrow, 2005, p. 284.

31   A. Horin, 'Taskforce on Child Care Rejected', *Sydney Morning Herald*, 1 January 2007.

32   C. Purcal & K. Fisher, *Review of the Early Childhood Teachers Shortage Interim Policy*, Final Report for the NSW Department of Community Services, Office of Child Care, SPRC Report 5/04, University of New South Wales, 2004.

33   Purcal Fisher, 2004, p. 12.

34   A. Summers, 'Making Profits out of Preschoolers', *Sydney Morning Herald*, 11 November 2002, p. 15.

35   Australian Institute of Health and Welfare, *Trends in the Affordability of Child Care Services 1991–2004*, Bulletin, Issue No. 35, April 2006.

36   B. Pocock, *The Work/Life Collision*, Federation Press, Annandale, 2003, p. 202.

37   D. Brennan, 'The ABC of Child Care Politics', *Australian Journal of Social Issues*, 42, 2, 2007, pp. 213–25.

38   M. Toohey & G. Beer, 'Is it Worth Working Now? Financial Incentives for Working Mothers Under Australia's New Tax System', paper presented at the Australian Social Policy Conference, Sydney, July 2003.

39   I. Watson, J. Buchanan, I. Campbell & C. Briggs, *Fragmented Futures: New Challenges in Working Life*, Federation Press, Annandale, 2003.

| 13 |

Children, Families and Communities: Looking Forward

Jennifer Bowes, Alan Hayes and Rebekah Grace

This chapter takes the theoretical framework explored in the preceding chapters and examines its application to future challenges for children, families and communities in Australia. It explores the range of prevention and intervention programs developed to support children, families and communities and the need for interventions and wider policy support for children and families.

Contexts

A review of the issues

The chapters in this book have embraced an ecological approach and argued that people always exist within a context. People are active in engaging with their environment. They adapt and make accommodations in response to the cultural and economic forces around them. In turn, the environment will change because of the people who are part of it. The process of accommodation is dynamic and bidirectional. However, people vary in the extent to which they are able to adapt, and in their power to modify the larger environment. There are some environments that are more flexible than others, and allow greater scope for the development of personal characteristics that are necessary for engendering change. As evidenced in earlier chapters, and discussed further in this chapter, there is a great deal of activity currently focused on modifying contexts in a variety of ways to benefit children and families.

It is clear from the examples provided earlier that there is considerable variation in the contexts of development for Australia's children, families and communities. We have argued that to understand development it is necessary to consider not only the individual, but also the context in which their development is taking place. This is a considerable shift from earlier approaches to the study of development that focused on individual development without a central concern for context.

A second focus of the book has been on the pathways to developmental outcomes. The consequences of shifts in the wider social contexts that surround children have been demonstrated in examples related to Australian policies and practices. These examples show the consequences that flow from contexts, including those close to children's everyday lives and those that are more distant.

A third, and related, focus has been on the importance of time, or the extent to which people and contexts change, both in the short term and over the longer sweep of historical time. Change of one element (person or context) tends to change the other, to a varying degree. As argued in the first chapter, contexts also vary according to whether their impact is direct (via processes of direct interaction) or indirect (through consequences that flow from changes at the level of government or society to communities or families, and on to children).

Direct and indirect influences function to increase or constrain resources, services and opportunities for children and families, and in this way alter the developmental consequences for all family members. Contexts can be differentiated by the degree to which they provide protective factors that reduce the impact of negative influences on children's development. Contexts can also be categorised in terms of the extent to which they operate to increase or reduce children's resilience in response to adversity. Abusive, neglectful or substance-abusing parents can, for example, dramatically elevate the risks to their children, as can some social policies and practices that, for example, place children in detention centres. By contrast, policies that support families and strengthen their communities may act in a protective way even in settings of multiple risks.

It may be difficult to determine in individual instances which children will be affected adversely by negative factors in their lives, although we know that the greater the number of risk factors in a child's life, the greater the chances of negative developmental consequences.[1] Some children, due to their own personal characteristics or protective aspects in the relationships that surround them, will be remarkably resilient, while others will show vulnerability when confronted by similar disadvantage or challenges. For children and families, the balance between the challenges facing them and the resources they have to meet those challenges is a key concept when considering effective ways to provide support or timely intervention.

Impetus for change in Australia

As we have seen in previous chapters, there is a need in both policy and practice to consider how Australian society might best support its children. This need is additionally evident in the light of advances in child development research and recent changes in Australian society that have affected the well-being of children. The current renewed focus on the importance of the early years of human development stems from wider public awareness of research on brain development.

Research within the field of developmental neurology provides strong evidence to support the claim that 'there is no more important period in human development than conception through early childhood in maximizing the potential for living fully'.[3] Stimulation during the early years is essential to brain development as the young brain is more malleable and is constructed by experience. So many brain systems are 'use-dependent', and rely on exposure to stimulation during the sensitive periods of early development. For example, if an infant is deprived of early visual experiences he or she will permanently lose vision. We know from animal studies that visual deprivation leads to deterioration in the connections between the nerve cells in the visual cortex.[4] The first two years of life are the most rapid period of brain development, with later childhood development more concerned with shedding and ordering the brain cells developed over the first two years of life.[5] Exposure of the young child to the richness of experiences that day-to-day life has to offer ensures the best possible start. Healthy early brain development also relies on the establishment of a warm and nurturing relationship with a carer.[6] Children who are not exposed to a stimulating environment or who experience abuse do not develop the same sophistication in the connections within their brain.[7] Although recovery is possible at any time in the life span, the research on early positive and adverse effects of experience on the neural structure of the brain does highlight the importance of the early years of life in establishing a good foundation for children's later development.

The health and well-being of children in Australian society is another factor in the need for policy intervention. Despite the country's wealth, there is a growing perception of substantial threats to the health and well-being of children, a situation common to market-driven modern economies and referred to by Keating and Hertzman as 'modernity's paradox'.[8] These threats include increases in the rates of health problems, including obesity, as well as unacceptable rates of child abuse and neglect, and youth suicide.[9] There is accumulating evidence of threats to the contexts in which children are growing up, with signs of growing disadvantage, social exclusion and vulnerability in some communities with implications for the cost of public services.[10]

A major demographic change in Australia has been a rise in the proportion of children in one-parent families, most of which are headed by mothers.[11] One-parent families are more likely to be in the bottom quartile of income and struggling to provide basic health and care for their children.[12] The patterns are complex, however, with many individuals protected if their family is well-functioning and community supports are available.

The extent of perturbation of relationships is clear in the data on divorce and remarriage. Marriage breakdown is another reality of family life in Australia. The Australian Bureau of Statistics has estimated that, at current rates, 33 per cent of marriages will end in divorce.[13] In 2006 alone divorce affected the lives of 1 per cent of children, or 48,396 young Australians. Second marriages are at higher risk of breakdown.

The complex and at times rapid succession of relationships experienced by many children clearly contributes to their risk of later behavioural adjustment and relationship disorders. In Australia, approximately one in four children under the age of eighteen has a parent who lives elsewhere.[14] Thirty per cent of Australian children are involved in one-parent, step or blended families. Behavioural problems are more common in children living in such circumstances, particularly for boys.[15] Children in one-parent, step or blended families are also at increased risk of abuse and neglect.[16] Abuse is likely to be a significant predictor of mental illness risk and relationship difficulties.[17] Mental health problems also show a disturbing prevalence in the Australian community. Sawyer estimates that 14 per cent of all children aged from four to sixteen, or 522,000 children, have a mental health problem.[18] Again, mental health problems are likely to be strongly related to difficulties in forming secure attachments and stable relationships.

Developmental risks are higher for children in particular Australian communities. Vinson has shown that there are ghettos of disadvantage in Australia in low-income communities that are characterised by high levels of unemployment, substance abuse and crime.[19] Indigenous communities often have these characteristics with the added continuing distress of children having been separated from their families over several generations, with direct family members affected in over a third of Indigenous families in the Western Australian Aboriginal Child Health Survey.[20]

Consequences

In response to these indications of social risk for children in Australia, policy makers have taken a range of initiatives including the implementation of programs to intervene in the lives of children, families and communities seen to be at risk. Intervention programs are often referred to as 'early intervention'. Early intervention has been defined by Hayes as 'planned and organised attempts to alter the behaviour or development of individuals who show the early signs of an identified problem and/or who are considered at high risk of developing that problem'.[21] The term 'early intervention' has been used for many years, and continues to be used, to refer specifically to programs of therapeutic intervention for children with disabilities. More recently, it has also been widely used in a more general sense to refer to intervention in the first years of life. This second kind of intervention has gained much political and popular appeal through its linking with research on brain development.

It is important to remember, however, that intervention can be successful at other ages and all is not lost if children experience a disadvantaged start to life. Important interventions turning children away from a pathway to crime, for example, have been effective in the early adolescent years.[22] Several researchers and commentators have warned against seeing early intervention as some kind of magic bullet that does away with the need for any other programs or interventions in later parts of life.[23] In fact, research into the long-term effects on children of intervention programs suggest that unless support similar to that in early intervention programs continues beyond the early years, effects of early intervention may be diminished or may disappear entirely.[24] This conclusion is supported by the continuing positive effects for children found in the few programs that provide quality education in the pre-school and into early school years such as the Chicago Child Parent Centers.[25]

'Early intervention', it has been argued, needs to be used in a wider sense to refer to intervention early in pathways.[26] Life trajectories are never in straight lines set at birth. Circumstances and choices can change a pathway at any time during the life course. If young people have 'got in with the wrong crowd', for example, intervention is far more likely to be effective if it is attempted early rather than later in the pathway to crime and this could occur in middle childhood, in adolescence or even in early adulthood.

Modifying contexts to strengthen children, families and communities

The social ecological model has provided policy makers and program designers with a broader perspective on ways to support children and their families. A focus on individual 'problem' children and families with a predominantly case approach to treatment and intervention has been broadened to a consideration of children and families in context and the important role of communities in supporting all children and families. This change in focus has been accompanied by a shift in approach by welfare agencies from crisis intervention to preventative intervention. A proliferation of intervention programs influenced by the social ecological approach has been developed over the last thirty years. This has occurred mainly in the USA with other countries, including Australia, adopting and adapting programs from overseas or developing their own programs.[27]

The idea behind these programs has been to enhance the health, development and well-being of children by reducing the number and severity of risk factors in their lives and by strengthening the protective factors in their environment. This has involved attempts to increase the social capital of the communities in which children live so that more resources are available to support them and their families. Attention has been given to strengthening families as a key context for children's development and to the development of quality early childhood education for children. The programs found to be most effective incorporate intervention at several levels.[28]

APPROACHES TO INTERVENTION

Some have argued that early childhood education, because it works directly with children, offers the most effective approach to conferring benefits to children.[29] Even though it is undisputed that families exert a more powerful influence on children's development than any other setting with which children are involved, including early childhood education,[30] early childhood education can nevertheless confer measurable benefits for children's learning and social development.[31] The assumption that parenting education on its own will flow on to benefit children has not always been borne out in research on more parent-focused interventions, even though it has been found to influence aspects of parenting.[32] Associated family support programs or partnerships with parents in early childhood education, however, have been shown to increase the effectiveness of early childhood education for children.[33]

INTERVENTION: A SUCCESSFUL CASE STUDY FROM THE USA

An example of an intervention in the USA based on early childhood education is the High/Scope Perry Preschool Project.[34] The program itself took place over five years during the 1960s and participants have been followed into adulthood. Participants were pre-school-aged African-American children living in poverty and at risk of school failure. The central intervention was high-quality pre-school education for the children, with a program that encouraged learning of cognitive as well as social-emotional skills. Parents were supported to become partners in their children's education but were not the focus of the intervention.

This is a program often cited for the educational and social benefits for the children involved, benefits evident into adulthood through follow-up studies of participants twenty-two years after their pre-school experience. The program is also well known for its calculation of the cost-effectiveness of high-quality early childhood education in helping to prevent the later educational and social costs associated with such high-risk groups. The most recent cost-benefit analysis of the program concluded that US$1 spent on high-quality early childhood education saves US$17.07 in later costs to the educational, welfare and criminal justice systems.[35]

In her review of research on the effectiveness of intervention programs for children and families, Brooks-Gunn[36] included the two-generation approach as one of three features needed for effective programs. The other two features were high quality and comprehensiveness (involving services from a range of agencies such as health, education and housing).

In Australia, there has been an increasing interest in providing comprehensive services for children and families and in integrating those services through use of a coordinating agency, even if the services are provided by a range of government and non-government groups. An example is the Brighter Futures strategy in New South Wales in which a lead agency, generally a non-government welfare or early childhood education group, coordinates services for children and young families in the area that are funded through the state government's Brighter Futures program.[37] Pilot programs that provide child care, health and family support programs on the same site for communities are being trialled throughout Australia by government and non-government groups and evaluation of these programs is under way.

COMMUNITIES FOR CHILDREN: AN AUSTRALIAN INITIATIVE

Communities for Children[38] is an Australian Government initiative, part of the Strengthening Families and Communities Strategy. It is a community-based intervention designed to strengthen communities so that they are better places to bring up children. The idea is that community improvements in services will flow on as benefits to families and children. The program builds on the work of government and non-government agencies already working with families in thirty-five disadvantaged areas across Australia. A non-government agency is always the lead agency. For example, The Smith Family, a national non-profit community service organisation, leads a project in an area of western Sydney. Among other aims, workers are trying to make the local park more attractive and safer for families so that is has more community use, and they are bringing speech therapy services to children and families in an informal way through a range of services in the community such as child care and playgroups.

A number of challenges remain in successful and effective implementation of intervention programs. In relation to comprehensive programs such as Communities for Children, Powell observed in USA programs a common 'struggle with the availability, integration and quality of existing services provided by different agencies and with different assumptions about how best to support families'.[39] Another important issue is staffing of programs. In Australia there is a need for more specialised education and professional development that includes child development, family functioning and interdisciplinary-environment working skills for staff working in comprehensive services for children and families.

Another major challenge is to determine the best way to 'roll out' approaches to intervention that have been found through research to be effective in pilot or demonstration projects such as the Perry Preschool Project or the David Olds' Nurse Home Visitation Program.[40] This is a key consideration for government or non-government agencies that have been charged with implementing programs for families on a large scale, and involves concerns about balancing program fidelity with modifications to match the needs of different communities.[41]

SHIFTS IN APPROACH TO INTERVENTION PROGRAMS

There are several notable shifts in focus in early intervention programs in the USA that are not yet widespread in Australia. One is an increased concern for developing social support networks for families.[42] Often intervention programs focus on the children and families within the program and the benefits that the program can give them without considering sufficiently the longer-term support available through neighbours and friends that can assist families long after an intervention program has ceased to operate (such programs often have short-term funding). Some Australian research on new mothers' groups set up through health departments suggests that the support provided to one another by mothers with children born at around the same time can be considerable and can extend over many years.[43]

Another trend in programs in the USA has been to involve families to a greater extent in programs.[44] This refers not to token involvement but to family involvement in program decisions and actions. In this way, programs are seen as agents for families and as responsive to families in a way that is evident in very few Australian programs. As Powell notes, however, in the USA there is a gap between principles and practice in family involvement.[45]

A third shift in focus has been from attention to risk factors in the design of interventions to attention to promotive factors.[46] Several writers have argued that traditional notions of risk factors are too restrictive. Sameroff argues that '… a focus on individual characteristics of individuals or families, such as gender, race, resourcefulness or income, can never explain more than a small proportion of variance in behavioral development. To truly appreciate the determinants of competency requires attention to a broad constellation of ecological factors in which these individuals and families are embedded'.[47] In his critique of the traditional concept of risk factors in relation to Indigenous children and families, Homel made a similar point. He argued in addition that 'instead of a catalogue of statistical risk factors that mostly refer to deficiencies in

Jennifer Bowes, Alan Hayes and Rebekah Grace

children and in their families, we need to think in terms of the resources needed for parents and their communities to overcome the barriers or solve the problems that they face on a daily basis in their child-rearing efforts'.[48]

Promoting a better fit between the daily problems faced by families and the knowledge, skills and resources they have available to deal with their problems represents a more strengths-based approach to working with families. Such a promotive approach can operate through intervention programs or through strengthening the services and institutions available to families in general. It has been argued that if the gains made by intervention are to be sustained in the long term, there needs to be more attention given to sustaining systems that include fundamental societal institutions as well as families.[49] The quality of institutions such as the education system or the health system, Homel argues, can offer more benefits to more children than intervention programs that are likely to be available in limited locations and for relatively short periods of time.[50] In addition, as Brennan noted in Chapter 12, a comprehensive policy approach is needed to support children and families as well as the communities in which they live. An example of such a comprehensive approach on a national level is provided in the case of Sweden. In legislative changes such as a law prohibiting physical punishment of children, social provisions such as universal free health and dental care for children, and generous leave provisions and other benefits for parents, Sweden has invested in the future through its commitment to children's right to a safe, non-violent and health-promoting environment. As a result, Sweden has a very low rate of child deaths through abuse and neglect and a low health budget.[51]

The interconnectedness of contexts and consequences

The consequences for children, families and communities at risk do not occur in isolation. The model developed in this book highlights the interconnectedness of contexts and consequences. Within any society, changes in relative affluence, demography, social structures, community resources or government policies have implications for the society as a whole. Despite the rhetoric of improved quality of life for children, strengthening of their families and renewal of their communities, the lived reality can be very different. For too many children, families and communities, life can be indelibly influenced by poverty, diminished resources to cope in the face of increased risks, and limited social cohesion. This chapter has already highlighted changes in family structure, particularly the dramatic growth in one-parent families in Australia, and the effects on children of parental separation and divorce. Other trends also have implications for the nation in the twenty-first century.

The declining fertility rate was perhaps the most marked of the changes that occurred during the last century.[52] At the beginning of the twentieth century, the total fertility rate (TFR)[53] in Australia was close to four babies per woman.[54] During the Great Depression the TFR declined to 2.1 in 1934 and after World War II increased with the improved economic outlook, reaching 3.5 in 1961. It then fell so that since the mid 1970s the TFR has been below replacement level (about 2.1). It stabilised in the late

1970s and the 1980s, at between 1.8 and 1.9, to again fall in small progressive steps in the 1990s. In recent years, however, the TFR has increased slightly, reaching 1.81 in 2006, up from 1.73 in 2001.[55]

Trends in fertility provide rather interesting examples of the links between contexts and consequences. Gray, Qu and Weston[56] have recently examined the relationship between the level of public financial support for families and the fertility rates in OECD countries. They concluded that government policies that reduce the costs of children can facilitate the combining of paid employment and parenting. Earlier work by Weston, Qu, Parker and Alexander[57] on fertility decision making showed that most people want to have children, aspire to have more than the replacement level, but revise their aspirations downwards as they grow older. The reasons for their changes relate to financial, employment and partnership issues. The complex interplay of personal and contextual factors is clear. Another consequence of these trends is that family formation is increasingly delayed.

Both female and male life expectancy has also increased considerably over the last hundred years. Of greater concern, however, is the marked bulge in the distribution of the population by age as the 'baby boomer' generation gets older.[58] An increasingly smaller proportion of young people in the Australian population will carry responsibility in their adult years for the health and aged care of the predominantly older citizens of the nation. Accordingly, the health and well-being of the current generation of children is all the more crucial in economic and social terms for the future of Australian society. At the same time, however, there is some sign of a lack of sympathy for families with children. There seems to be a growing divide between families with and without children, and children are often regarded in public discourse as a burden rather than as an asset to society.

The trends in population and disadvantage converge when one considers the nation's children. Birth rates differ considerably by social class, with women who have high levels of education and employment having significantly fewer children than women who do not.[59] Disadvantage also influences the rates of infant mortality and morbidity (the occurrence of health and developmental problems). The numerous risk factors that lead to problems in childhood tend to be related, though not exclusively, to social class. The interplay of child, family and community factors is also seen in the areas of abuse and neglect, school failure and criminality, among others. These areas of social concern reflect similar sets of risk factors related to poverty, limited parental education, family problems, unemployment and lack of connectedness to community. The impact on the health and well-being of children in disadvantaged communities is widespread.

A considerable body of evidence is accumulating on a phenomenon called the 'social gradient'.[60] The term refers to the linear increase, or decrease, in some aspect of development, health or well-being in direct relation to social status. The measures of social status may include education, income or occupation, among others. Keating and Hertzman have provided compelling evidence of such gradients in many aspects of development, health and well-being. Among these they include data on the pre- and perinatal status of infants, child health, cognitive development, behavioural development, academic performance including literacy and numeracy outcomes, criminality and outcomes in adult life.[61] As social status increases, outcomes across the range of

Jennifer Bowes, Alan Hayes and Rebekah Grace

areas of development, health and well-being are higher. These are of course population measures and there will be individual variation in outcomes within any social status group. The message is clear, however, that social status is a powerful indicator of outcomes, both within a development period and across life.

Of greater interest, however, are the cross-national comparisons that have been undertaken analysing gradients from a range of countries as well as exploring gradients from areas within a country. Here the overwhelming message is that the flatter the gradient (the less the difference between social groups), the higher the personal, social and economic capital of a society, and the lower the social problems.[62] Starkly, socially differentiated nations, while having some high achievers, will adversely influence the life chances of those who are socially disadvantaged to an extent that has impacts on the overall development, health and well-being of the entire population.

The solution to the current problems will require commitment to prevention and a willingness to invest in preventive services such as child care, education, family support and community capacity building. Such services have been found to be the most cost-effective ways of reducing social and developmental risk and preventing their negative consequences, such as crime, educational underachievement and problems of health and well-being.[63]

The focus of social policy has turned to social exclusion, a term that inherently captures the sense of detachment from context, or rather the absence of many of the opportunities that connect us to the key contexts in which we develop and contribute to the development of others. Influenced by developments in the United Kingdom, the European Union and the USA, the positive counterpart, social inclusion is a matter of providing access to opportunity for all members of a society.[64] This policy frame has systematically been applied within Australia at the state level by the South Australian Government.[65] The establishment of the Social Inclusion Board and the Social Inclusion Unit within the Department of the Premier and Cabinet represents an innovative approach to ensuring policy integration and development of new solutions to complex problems including homelessness, school retention and mental health services.[66] The availability of an accurate, up-to-date evidence base underpins the approach taken in South Australia. At the national level, the recently elected (2007) Australian Government has expressed a similar commitment to social inclusion.

It is vital to acknowledge the complexity of the issues that these social inclusion initiatives address and the need for community involvement in, and ownership of, the solutions. This entails rejection of simplistic approaches. Complex social issues cannot be dealt with merely by interventions with children or by strengthening families. As has been argued in this book, the evidence is that intervention and policy will need to be focused on all three elements: children, families and communities.

STUDENT EXERCISES

1 Think about the issues in your local community for children and families: What are the factors that would need to be considered in the design of an intervention

program aimed at reducing the incidence of nominated problems? Some questions that you might consider are:

a) How could a strength-based approach be used in planning the approach to intervention?

b) What features would the program need to have to strengthen the children concerned, their families and the local community?

c) Would the program be universal or targeted at particular groups?

2 Like many other developed countries, Australia has a fertility rate that is below replacement level. What are the future implications for children, families and communities in Australia of a continuing decline in the fertility rate? In particular, how will parenting be affected by the resulting demographic shift to a society with a higher proportion of elderly people and a lower proportion of children? What are the implications for social policy?

Notes

1   A. Sameroff, 'Identifying Risk and Protective Factors for Healthy Child Development', in *Families Count: Effects on Child and Adolescent Development*, eds, A. Clarke-Stewart & J. Dunn, Cambridge University Press, Cambridge, 2006, pp. 53–76.

2   A report developed by the Ontario Government, Canada, was instrumental in this awareness: M. McCain & J.F. Mustard, *Reversing the Real Brain Drain: Early Years Study, Final Report*, Ontario Children's Secretariat, Toronto, 1999.

3   J.A. Blackman, 'Early Intervention: A Global Perspective', *Infants and Young Children*, 15, 2002, pp. 11–19, p. 11.

4   D.H. Hubel & T.N. Wiesel, 'The Period of Susceptibility to the Physiologic Effects of Unilateral Eye Closure in Kittens', *Journal of Physiology*, 206, 1970, pp. 419–36.

5   J.P. Shonkoff & D.A. Phillips, *From Neurons to Neighbourhoods: The Science of Early Childhood Development*, National Academy Press, Washington, 2000.

6   P. Champion, 'Infant/Maternal Interactive Social/Emotional Learning Where the Infant Has a Disability or Is at Risk for a Disability', *Infants and Young Children*, 12, 2000, pp. 10–16.

7   Shonkoff & Phillips, 2000.

8   D.P. Keating & C. Hertzman, *Developmental Health and the Wealth of Nations*, The Guilford Press, New York, 1999, p. 1.

9   F. Stanley, S. Richardson & M.R. Prior, *Children of the Lucky Country?: How Australian Society has Turned its Back on Children and Why Children Matter*, Pan Macmillan Australia, Sydney, 2005.

10   T. Vinson, *Dropping off the Edge: Mapping the Distribution of Disadvantage in Australia*, Jesuit Social Services and Catholic Social Services Australia, Canberra, 2007; Australian Bureau of Statistics, *Australian Social Trends, 2006*, catalogue no. 4102.0, Australian Government Publishing Service, Canberra, 2007h.

11   Australian Bureau of Statistics, 2007h.

12   J.R. Bray, 'Hardship in Australia: An Analysis of Financial Stress Indicators', in the *1998–99 Australian Bureau of Statistics Household Expenditure Survey*, Occasional Paper no. 4, Department of Family and Community Services, Canberra, 2001; J. Pryor & B. Rodgers, *Children in Changing Families: Life After Parental Separation*, Academy of the Social Sciences in Australia, Canberra, 2002.

13   Australian Bureau of Statistics, 2007h.

14   Pryor & Rodgers, 2002.

15   Y. Racine & M.H. Boyle, 'Family Functioning and Children's Behaviour Problems', in *Vulnerable Children*, ed., J.D. Willms, University of Alberta Press, Alberta, 2002, pp. 199–209; P.S. Malone, J.E. Lansford, D.R. Castellino, L.J. Berlin, K.A. Dodge, J.E. Bates & G.S. Petit, 'Divorce and Child Behavior Problems: Applying Latent Change Score Models to Life Event Data', *Structural Equation Modeling*, 11, 2004, pp. 401–23; P.R. Amato & D.D. DeBoer, 'The Transmission of Marital Instability across Generations: Relationship Skills or Commitment to Marriage?', *Journal of Marriage and Family*, 63, 2001, pp. 1038–51.

Jennifer Bowes, Alan Hayes and Rebekah Grace

16   L.M. Berger, 'Income, Family Characteristics and Physical Violence Toward Children', *Child Abuse and Neglect*, 29, 2005, pp. 107–33.

17   Racine & Boyle, 2002.

18   M. Sawyer, 'Child and Adolescent Mental Health Issues: Future Directions', in *Investing in Our Children: Developing a Research Agenda*, ed., M. Prior, Academy of the Social Sciences in Australia, Canberra, 2002, pp. 83–94.

19   Vinson, 2007.

20   See S.R. Silburn, S.R. Zubrick, D.M. Lawrence, F.G. Mitrou, J.A. DeMaio, E. Blair, A. Cox, R.B. Dalby, J.A. Griffin, G. Pearson & C. Hayward, 'The Intergenerational Effects of Forced Separation on the Social and Emotional Wellbeing of Aboriginal Children and Young People', *Family Matters*, 75, 2006, pp. 10–17; R. Homel, C. Lamb & K. Freiberg, 'Working With the Indigenous Community in the Pathways to Prevention Project', *Family Matters*, 75, 2006, pp. 18–23.

21   A. Hayes, 'Why Early in Life is Not Enough: Timing and Sustainability in Prevention and Early Intervention', in *Pathways and Crime Prevention: Theory, Policy and Practice*, eds, A. France & R. Homel, Willan Publishing, Uffculme, UK, 2007, pp. 202–25, p. 205.

22   J.J. Goodnow, 'Second Looks at Views of Development, Families, and Communities, and at Translations into Practice', in *Families Count: Effects on Child and Adolescent Development*, eds, A. Clarke-Stewart & J. Dunn, Cambridge University Press, Cambridge, 2006, pp. 337–60.

23   J. Brooks-Gunn, 'Do You Believe in Magic? What We Can Expect from Early Childhood Intervention Programs', *Social Policy Report of the Society for Research in Child Development*, 17, 2003, pp. 3–14.

24   D.R. Powell, 'Families and Early Childhood Interventions', in *Handbook of Child Psychology*, vol. 4, eds, W. Damon & R.M. Lerner, John Wiley & Sons, Hoboken, NJ, 2006, pp. 548–91.

25   A.J. Reynolds, *Success in Early Intervention: Chicago Child Parent Centers*, University of Nebraska Press, Lincoln, NA, 2000.

26   Brooks-Gunn, 2003; Goodnow, 2006; Hayes, 2007.

27   For examples of programs, see Powell, 2006 and S. Wise, L. Da Silva, E. Webster & A. Sanson, *The Efficacy of Early Childhood Interventions, Research Report no. 14*, Australian Institute of Family Studies, Commonwealth of Australia, Melbourne, 2005.

28   Powell, 2006.

29   J. Brooks-Gunn, 'Families and Policies Matter: How to Enhance the Well-being of Children in Poverty', presented at the Australian Social Policy Conference, Sydney, July 2007.

30   M. Hyson, C. Copple & J. Jones, 'Early Childhood Development and Education', in *Handbook of Child Psychology*, eds, W. Damon & R.M. Lerner, John Wiley & Sons, Hoboken, NJ, 2006, pp. 3–47.

31   Powell, 2006.

32   S. Wise, B. Edwards, J. Bowes, A. Sanson, J. Ungerer, L. Harrison & T. Simpson, 'The Relation of Multiple and Changeable Childcare Arrangements to Early Communication Skills', presented at the 9th Australian Institute of Family Studies Conference, Melbourne, February 2005, <www.aifs.gov.au/institute/afrc9/wise1.html>, accessed 8 January 2008.

33   Wise et al., 2005.

34   D.P. Weikart & L.J. Schweinhart, 'High/Scope Preschool Program Outcomes', in *Preventing Antisocial Behavior: Interventions from Birth through Adolescence*, eds, J. McCord & R.E. Tremblay, The Guilford Press, New York, 1992, pp. 67–88; L.J. Schweinhart, H.V. Barnes & D.P. Weikart, *Significant Benefits: The High/Scope Perry Preschool Study through Age 27*, High/Scope Press, Ypsilant, MI, 1993.

35   See Hayes, 2007.

36   Brooks-Gunn, 2003.

37   See: <www.community.nsw.gov.au/docswr/_assets/main/documents/brighter_futures_ fact.pdf>, accessed 24 January 2008.

38   Australian Institute of Family Studies, 'Communities for Children Initiative', *Stronger Families Learning Exchange*, Bulletin no. 7, pp. 3–5, 2005b, <www.aifs.gov.au/sf/pubs/bull7/communities.pdf>, accessed 28 January 2008.

39   Powell, 2006, p. 552.

40   H. Kitzman, D.L. Olds, C.R. Henderson, R. Tatelbaum, K.M. McConnochie, K. Sidora, D.W. Luckey, D. Shaver, K. Engelhardt, D. James & K. Barnard, 'Effect of Prenatal and Infancy Home Visitation by Nurses on Pregnancy Outcomes, Childhood Injuries, and Repeated Childbearing', *Journal of the American Medical Association*, 278, 1997, pp. 644–52; D.L. Olds, J. Eckenrode, C.R. Henderson, H. Kitzman, J. Powers, R. Cole, K. Sidora, P. Morris, L.M. Petitt & D. Luckey, 'Long-term Effects of Home Visitation on Maternal Life Course and Child Abuse and Neglect', *Journal of the American Medical Association*, 278, 1997, pp. 637–43.

41   M. Salveron, F. Arney & D. Scott, 'Sowing the Seeds of Innovation: Ideas for Child and Family Services', *Family Matters*, 73, 2006, pp. 38–45.

42   V.C. McLoyd, N.L. Aikens & L.M. Burton, 'Child Poverty, Policy and Practice', in *Handbook of Child Psychology*, eds, W. Damon & R.M. Lerner, John Wiley & Sons, Hoboken, NJ, 2006, pp. 700–75; Powell, 2006.

43   D. Scott, 'Embracing What Works: Building Communities that Strengthen Families', *Children Australia*, 25, 2000, pp. 4–9; D. Scott, S. Brady & P. Glynn, 'New Mothers Groups as a Social Network Intervention: Consumer and Maternal Child Health Nurse Perspectives', *Australian Journal of Advanced Nursing*, 18, 4, 2001, pp. 23–9.

44   Powell, 2006.

45   Powell, 2006.

46   Powell, 2006.

47   Sameroff, 2006, pp. 69–70.

48   Homel et al., 2006, p. 23.

49   McLoyd et al., 2006.

50   R. Homel, 'Forum on Building Family and Community Capacities: Policies that Make a Difference for Children and Families Facing Economic Adversity', *Australian Social Policy Conference*, Sydney, July 2007.

51   J.E. Durrant, 'Trends in Youth Crime and Well-being Since the Abolition of Corporal Punishment in Sweden', *Youth and Society*, 31, 4, 2000, pp. 437–55; J.E. Durrant & G.M. Olsen, 'Parenting and Public Policy: Contextualising the Swedish Corporal Punishment Ban', *Journal of Social Welfare and Family Law*, 19, 4, 1997, pp. 443–61; UNICEF, *Official Summary: The State of the World's Children*, UNICEF, New York, 2003.

52   P. McDonald, 'Low Fertility in Australia: Evidence, Causes and Policy Responses', *People and Place*, 8, 2000, pp. 6–21.

53   TFR is a synthetic measure that refers to the number of children a woman would have if she experiences the current age-specific fertility rate at each age of her reproductive life.

54   G. Hugo, *Yearbook Australia 2001: A Century of Population Change in Australia*, catalogue no. 1301.0, Australian Bureau of Statistics, Canberra, 2001.

55   Australian Bureau of Statistics, *Births Australia 2006*, catalogue no. 3301.0, Australian Government Publishing Service, Canberra, 2007e.

56   M. Gray, L. Qu & R. Weston, *Fertility and Family Policy in Australia*, Australian Institute of Family Studies, Melbourne, 2008, <www.aifs.gov.au/institute/pubs/rp41/rp41.pdf>, acccessed 19 March 2008.

57   R. Weston, L. Qu, R. Parker & M. Alexander, *It's Not for Lack of Wanting Kids, Research Report no. 11*, report on the Fertility Decision Making Project, Melbourne, Australian Institute of Family Studies, 2004.

58   Australian Bureau of Statistics, *Australian Social Trends 2003*, catalogue no. 4102.0, Australian Government Publishing Service, Canberra, 2003c.

59   L. Risse, 'Does Maternity Leave Encourage High Birth Rates?: Analysis of the Australian Labour Force', *Australian Journal of Labour Economics*, 9, 2006, pp. 343–70.

60   G. Jack, 'Ecological Influences on Parenting and Child Development', *British Journal of Social Work*, 30, 2000, pp. 703–20; Keating & Hertzman, 1999; E. Sloat & J.D. Willms, 'A Gradient Approach to the Study of Childhood Vulnerability', in *Vulnerable Children*, ed., J.D. Willms, University of Alberta Press, Alberta, 2002, pp. 23–44.

61   Australian National Crime Prevention National Anti-crime Strategy, Pathways to Prevention: Developmental and Early Intervention Approaches to Crime in Australia, National Crime Prevention, Attorney General's Department, Barton, ACT, 1999.

62   Keating & Hertzman, 1999; Jack, 2000.

63   P.W. Greenwood, K.E. Model, C.P. Rydell & J. Chiesa, *Diverting Children From a Life of Crime: Measuring Costs and Benefits*, RAND Corporation, Santa Monica, CA, 1996.

64   Social Inclusion Unit, *Evaluation: The Social Inclusion Initiative Big Picture, Roundtables, Background Discussion Paper Two, Social Inclusion Initiative Indicators*, Department of the Premier and Cabinet, South Australia, <www.socialinclusion.sa.gov.au/files/RR_SIIEPFebRTSIIndicators.pdf>, accessed 21 January 2008.

65   D. Cappo, *Australia's Welfare 2007 Conference: Disadvantage and Diversity*, keynote address to the Australian Institute of Health and Welfare, 6 December 2007, <www.socialinclusion.sa.gov.au/files/AIHW%20Speech%206%20Dec%2007%20FINAL.pdf>, accessed 21 January 2008.

66   Cappo, 2007.

Bibliography

ABC Learning Centres, *Annual Report*, ABC Learning Centres Limited, 2006.

Abbeduto, L., Seltzer, M.M., Shattuck, P., Krauss, M.W., Orsmond, G. & Murphy, M.M., 'Psychological Well-being and Coping in Mothers of Youths with Autism, Down Syndrome, or Fragile X Syndrome', *American Journal on Mental Retardation*, 109, 2004, pp. 237–54.

Aboud, F.E., *Children and Prejudice*, Blackwell, Oxford, 1988.

Ahnert, L. & Lamb, M.E., 'Shared Care: Establishing a Balance Between Home and Child Care Settings', *Child Development*, 74, 2003, pp. 1044–9.

Ainsworth, F. & Maluccio, A.N., 'Kinship Care: False Dawn or New Hope?', *Australian Social Work*, 51, 4, 1998, pp. 3–8.

Ainsworth, M.S., Blehar, M., Waters, E. & Wall, S., *Patterns of Attachment*, Erlbaum, Hillsdale, NJ, 1978.

Aldridge, J., 'The Experiences of Children Living with and Caring for Parents with Mental Illness', *Child Abuse Review*, 15, 2006, pp. 79–88.

Allison, L., 'Introduction to Part 2', in *Yearning to Breathe Free*, eds, D. Lusher & N. Haslam, Federation Press, Sydney, 2007, pp. 49–51.

Alston, M. & Kent, J., *The Impact of Drought on Secondary Education Access in Australia's Rural and Remote Areas*, Report for the Department of Education, Science and Training (DEST) and the Rural Education Program of the Foundation for Rural and Regional Renewal, Charles Sturt University, Wagga Wagga, 2006.

Amato, P.A., 'More than Money? Men's Contributions to their Children's Lives', in *Men in Families*, eds, A. Booth & A.C. Crouter, Lawrence Erlbaum, Mahwah, NJ, 1998, pp. 241–78.

Amato, P.R. & DeBoer, D.D., 'The Transmission of Marital Instability across Generations: Relationship Skills or Commitment to Marriage?', *Journal of Marriage and Family*, 63, 2001, pp. 1038–51.

American Academy of Pediatrics, 'Prevention of Pediatric Overweight and Obesity Committee on Nutrition (Policy Statement)', *Pediatrics*, 112, 2, 2003, pp. 424–9.

Andersson, B., 'Effects of Day-care on Cognitive and Socioemotional Competence of Thirteen-year-old Swedish School Children', *Child Development*, 63, 1992, pp. 20–36.

Arnett, J., 'Care-givers in Day-care Centers: Does Training Matter?', *Journal of Applied Developmental Psychology*, 10, 1989, pp. 541–52.

Australian Bureau of Statistics, *Commercial Long Day Child Care Australia*, catalogue no. 4414.0, Australian Government Publishing Service, Canberra, 1989.

Australian Bureau of Statistics, *National Aboriginal and Torres Strait Islander Survey*, catalogue no. 4155.0, Australian Government Publishing Service, Canberra, 1994.

Australian Bureau of Statistics, *Special Article: Casual Employment*, Australian Government Publishing Service, Canberra, 2002a.

Australian Bureau of Statistics, *National Aboriginal and Torres Strait Islander Social Survey, Western Australia*, catalogue no. 4714.5.55.001, Australian Government Publishing Service, Canberra, 2002b.

Australian Bureau of Statistics, *Disability, Ageing and Carers: Summary of Findings*, catalogue no. 4430.0, Australian Government Publishing Service, Canberra, 2003a.

Australian Bureau of Statistics, *Population Characteristics: People Living in Institutions*, catalogue no. 4102.0, Australian Government Publishing Service, Canberra, 2003b, <www.abs.gov.au/AUSSTATS/abs@.nsf/7d12b0f6763c78caca257061001cc588/9c1dc93dd9a137daca2570eb0082e463!OpenDocument>, accessed 5 February 2008.

Australian Bureau of Statistics, *Australian Social Trends 2003*, catalogue no. 4102.0, Australian Government Publishing Service, Canberra, 2003c, <www.abs.gov.au/AUSSTATS/abs@.nsf/46d1bc47ac9d0c7bca256c470025ff87/12a1c7480a30c138ca256d39001bc331!OpenDocument>, accessed 19 March 2008.

Australian Bureau of Statistics, *Marriages and Divorces, Australia, 2002*, catalogue no. 3310.0, Australian Government Publishing Service, Canberra, 2003d, <www.abs.gov.au/AUSSTATS/abs@.nsf/ProductsbyCatalogue/893C1288678FD232CA2568A90013939C?OpenDocument>, accessed 5 February 2008.

Australian Bureau of Statistics, *Australian Demographic Statistics, Dec 2002: Australians on the Move*, catalogue no. 3101.0, Australian Government Publishing Service, 2003e, <www.abs.gov.au/Ausstats/abs@.nsf/94713ad445ff1425ca25682000192af2/812343b3e6694d5dca256d3c0001f4c9!OpenDocument>, accessed 24 March 2008.

Australian Bureau of Statistics, *Family Characteristics, Australia, 2003*, catalogue no. 4442.0, Australian Government Publishing Service, Canberra, 2004a.

Australian Bureau of Statistics, *Housing Arrangements: Homelessness*, catalogue no. 4102.0, Australian Government Publishing Service, Canberra, 2004b, <www.abs.gov.au/Ausstats/abs%40.nsf/94713ad445ff1425ca25682000192af2/DDC8DC3787E2D9FCCA256E9E0028F91E?opendocument>, accessed 23 August 2007.

Australian Bureau of Statistics, *Family, Household and Income Unit Variables*, catalogue no. 1286, Australian Government Publishing Service, Canberra, 2005.

Australian Bureau of Statistics, *Schools, Australia, 2006*, catalogue no. 4221.0, Australian Government Publishing Service, Canberra, 2006, <www.ausstats.abs.gov.au/ausstats/subscriber.nsf/0/9DDA83611950C66FCA25728B000CFC92/$File/42210_2006.pdf>, accessed 5 February 2008.

Australian Bureau of Statistics, *Year Book Australia, 2006*, catalogue no. 3101.0, Australian Government Publishing Service, Canberra, 2007a, <www.abs.gov.au/ausstats/abs@.nsf/Previousproducts/1301.0Feature%20Article92006?opendocument&tabname=Summary&prodno=1301.0&issue=2006&num=&view=>, accessed 5 February 2008.

Australian Bureau of Statistics, *Australian Social Trends, 2007*, catalogue no. 4102.0, Australian Government Publishing Service, Canberra, 2007b.

Australian Bureau of Statistics, *2006 Census QuickStats: Australia*, Australian Government Publishing Service, 2007c, <www.censusdata.abs.gov.au/ABSNavigation/prenav/ViewData?subaction=1&producttype=QuickStats&areacode=0&action=401&collection=Census&textversion=false&breadcrumb=PL&period=2006&javascript=true&navmapdisplayed=true&>, accessed 4 February 2008.

Australian Bureau of Statistics, *Population Distribution: Aboriginal and Torres Strait Islander Australians*, catalogue no. 4705, Australian Government Publishing Service, Canberra, 2007d.

Australian Bureau of Statistics, *Births Australia 2006*, catalogue no. 3301, Australian Government Publishing Service, Canberra, 2007e.

Australian Bureau of Statistics, *Australian Social Trends, 2007: Lifetime Marriage and Divorce Trends*, catalogue no. 4102.0, Australian Government Publishing Service, Canberra, 2007f, <www.abs.gov.au/AUSSTATS/abs@.nsf/Latestproducts/26D94B4C9A4769E6CA25732 C00207644?opendocument>, accessed 5 February 2008.

Australian Bureau of Statistics, *Trends in Women's Employment 2006*, catalogue no. 4201.0, Australian Government Publishing Service, Canberra, 2007g.

Australian Bureau of Statistics, *Australian Social Trends, 2006*, catalogue no. 4102.0, Australian Government Publishing Service, Canberra, 2007h.

Australian Bureau of Statistics, *Census 2006*, Australian Government Publishing Service, Canberra, 2007i.

Australian Department of Communications, Infotech and the Arts, *The Role of ICT in Building Communities and Social Capital: A Discussion Paper*, Australian Department of Communications, Infotech and the Arts, Canberra, 2005, <www.dbcde.gov.au/ communications_for_consumers/funding_programs__and__support/community_ connectivity/the_role_of_ict_in_building_communities_and_social_capital_a_discussion_ paper>, accessed 24 March 2008.

Australian Government Task Force on Child Development, Health and Wellbeing, *Towards the Development of a National Agenda for Early Childhood: Consultation Paper*, Commonwealth of Australia, Canberra, 2003.

Australian Institute of Family Studies, *Growing Up in Australia: The Longitudinal Study of Australian Children, 2004 Annual Report*, AIFS, Melbourne, 2005a.

Australian Institute of Family Studies, 'Communities for Children Initiative', *Stronger Families Learning Exchange*, bulletin no. 7, 2005b, pp. 3–5, <www.aifs.gov.au/sf/pubs/bull7/ communities.pdf>, accessed 28 January 2008.

Australian Institute of Family Studies, *A Snapshot of How Australian Families Spend Their Time*, AIFS, Canberra, 2007, <www.aifs.gov.au/institute/pubs/snapshots/familytime.html>, accessed 9 January 2008.

Australian Institute of Health and Welfare, *Australia's Welfare*, AIHW catalogue no. AUS 65, AIHW, Canberra, 2005a.

Australian Institute of Health and Welfare, *Adoptions Australia 2004–05*, AIHW catalogue no. CWS 25 (Child Welfare Series no. 37), AIHW, Canberra, 2005b, p. 20.

Australian Institute of Health and Welfare, *Trends in the Affordability of Child Care Services 1991–2004*, Bulletin, issue no. 35, April 2006.

Australian Institute of Health and Welfare (AIHW), *Child Protection Australia 2006–07*, AIHW catalogue no. CWS 31 (Child Welfare Series no. 43), AIHW, Canberra, 2008.

Australian Labor Party, *Platform, Constitution and Rules*, Canberra, 1973.

Australian Law Reform Commission/Human Rights and Equal Opportunity Commission, *Seen and Heard: Priority for Children in the Legal Process*, Report no. 84, 1997.

Australian National Crime Prevention National Anti-Crime Strategy (Australia), *Pathways to Prevention: Developmental and Early Intervention Approaches to Crime in Australia*, National Crime Prevention, Attorney General's Department, Barton, ACT, 1999.

Australian Parents Council, *Children's Learning: The Parent Factor*, Australian Government Publishing Service, Canberra, 1996.

Australian Parliament Senate Community Affairs Reference Committee, *A Hand Up Not a Hand Out: Renewing the Fight Against Poverty (Report on Poverty and Financial Hardship)*, Senate Printing Unit, Parliament House, Canberra, March 2004, p. 204, <www.aph.gov.au/senate/committee/ clac_ctte/completed_inquiries/2002-04/poverty/report/>, accessed 8 August 2007.

Aylward, G.P., Gustafson, N., Verhulst, S.J. & Colliver, J.A., 'Consistency in the Diagnosis of Cognitive, Motor and Neurologic Function over the First Three Years', *Journal of Pediatric Psychology*, 12, 1987, pp. 77–98.

Azar, M. & Badr, L.K., 'The Adaptation of Mothers of Children with Intellectual Disability in Lebanon', *Journal of Transcultural Nursing*, 17, 2006, pp. 375–80.

Azar, S.T. & Wolfe, D.A., 'Child Physical Abuse and Neglect', in *Treatment of Childhood Disorders* (3rd edn), eds, E.J. Marsh & R.A. Barkley, Guilford Press, New York, 2006, pp. 147–54.

Bågenholm, A. & Gillberg, C., 'Psychosocial Effects on Siblings of Children with Autism and Mental Retardation: A Population-based Study', *Journal of Mental Deficiency Research*, 35, 1991, pp. 291–307.

Barber, J.G., Delfabbro, P.H. & Cooper, L.L., 'Placement Stability and the Psychosocial Wellbeing of Children in Foster Care', *Research on Social Work Practice*, 13, 2003, pp. 409–25.

Barnard, K.E. & Martell, L.K., 'Mothering', in *Handbook of Parenting*, ed., M.H. Bornstein, Lawrence Erlbaum, Mahwah, NJ, 1995, pp. 3–26.

Barnett, L.A., 'Playfulness: Definition, Design, and Measurement', *Play & Culture*, 3, 1990, pp. 319–36.

Barnett, L.A., 'Characterizing Playfulness: Correlates with Individual Attributes and Personality Traits', *Play & Culture*, 4, 4, 1991, pp. 371–93.

Barnett, W.S., 'Long-term Effects of Early Childhood Programs on Cognitive and School Outcomes', *The Future of Children*, 5, 1995, pp. 25–50.

Barter, K., 'Renegotiating Relationships to Build Community Capacity for the Health and Well-Being of Children: A Time For Action', paper presented at the CROCCS 4th International Conference on Working Together for Families, Mackay, Queensland, 4–6 August 2006.

Bateson, G., 'The Message, "This is Play"', in *Child's Play*, eds, R.E. Herron & B. Sutton-Smith, Wiley & Sons, New York, pp. 261–9; Skard & Bundy, in press.

Baumrind, D., 'Child Care Practices Anteceding Three Patterns of Preschool Behavior', *Genetic Psychology Monographs*, 75, 1967, pp. 43–88.

Baumrind, D., 'Current Patterns of Parental Authority', *Developmental Psychology Monographs, Part 2*, 4, 1, 1971.

Baxter, J., Gray, M., Alexander, M., Strazdins, L. & Bittman, M., 'Mothers and Fathers with Young Children: Paid Employment, Caring and Well Being', Social Policy Research Paper no. 30, Department of Families, Community Services and Indigenous Affairs, Canberra, 2007.

Bee, H., *The Developing Child*, Harper Collins, New York, 1992.

Bell, J., 'Assimilation in NSW', in *Aborigines Now: New Perspectives in the Study of Aboriginal Communities*, ed., M. Reay, Angus & Robertson, London, 1964.

Belsky, J., 'Two Waves of Day-care Research: Developmental Effects and Conditions of Quality', in *The Child and Day-care Setting*, ed., R. Ainslie, Praeger, New York, 1984, pp. 1–34.

Belsky, J., 'Parental and Nonparental Child Care and Children's Socioemotional Development: A Decade in Review', *Journal of Marriage and the Family*, 52, 1990, pp. 885–903.

Belsky, J., 'Etiology of Child Maltreatment: A Developmental–ecological Analysis', *Psychological Bulletin*, 114, 1993, pp. 413–34.

Belsky, J., 'Developmental Risks (still) Associated with Early Child Care', *Journal of Child Psychology and Psychiatry*, 42, 2001, pp. 845–59.

Belsky, J., Lowe Vandell, D., Burchinal, M., Clarke-Stewart, K.A., McCartney, K. & Tresch Owen, M. & NICHD Early Child Care Research Network, 'Are there Long-term Effects of Early Child Care?', *Child Development*, 78, 2007, pp. 681–701.

Belsky, J. & Steinberg, L., 'The Effects of Day Care: A Critical Review', *Child Development*, 49, 1978, pp. 929–49.

Bengston, V.L., 'Beyond the Nuclear Family: The Increasing Importance of Multigenerational Bonds', *Journal of Marriage and the Family*, 63, 2001, pp. 1–16.

Berger, L.M., 'Income, Family Characteristics and Physical Violence Toward Children', *Child Abuse and Neglect*, 29, 2005, pp. 107–33.

Bernard, B., *Fostering Resilience in Children*, ERIC Clearinghouse on Elementary and Early Childhood Education, EDO-PS-95-9, Illinois, 1995.

Bernheimer, L.P. & Weisner, T.S., 'Family Life is More Than Managing a Crisis: Broadening the Agenda of Research on Families Adapting to Childhood Disability', in *Developmental*

Perspectives on Children with High Incidence Disabilities, eds, R. Gallimore, L.P. Bernheimer, D. MacMillan, D. Spence & S. Vaughn, Lawrence Erlbaum, Mahwah, NJ, 1999, pp. 40–80.

Berrueta-Clement, J.R., Schweinhart, L.J., Barnett, W.S., Epstein, A.S. & Weikart, D.P., 'Changed Lives: The Effects of the Perry Preschool Program on Youths through Age 19', in *Monographs of the High/Scope Educational Research Foundation*, 8, 1984.

Berry, M., McCauley, K. & Lansing, T., 'Permanency through Group Work: A Pilot Intensive Reunification Program', *Child and Adolescent Social Work Journal*, 24, 2007, pp. 477–93.

Bhagwati, P.N., *Human Rights and Immigration in Australia: Report of the Regional Advisor for Asia and the Pacific of the UNHCR*, UNHCR, Geneva, 2002.

Biddulph, F. , Biddulph, J. & Biddulph, C., *The Complexity of Community and Family Influences on Children's Achievement in New Zealand*, New Zealand Ministry of Education, Wellington, New Zealand, 2003.

Biehal, N., Clayden, J., Stein, M. & Wade, J., *Moving on: Young People and Leaving Care Schemes*, HMSO, London, 1995.

Bigby, C., *Moving on Without Parents. Planning, Transitions, and Sources of Support for Middleaged and Older Adults with Intellectual Disability*, MacLennan & Petty, Sydney, 2000.

Bigby, C. & Ozanne, E., 'Shifts in the Model of Service Delivery in Intellectual Disability in Victoria', *Journal of Intellectual & Developmental Disability*, 26, 2001, pp. 177–90.

Birenbaum, A., 'Poverty, Welfare Reform, and Disproportionate Rates of Disability Among Children', *Mental Retardation*, 40, 2002, pp. 212–18.

Birrell, R., 'Ethnic Concentrations: The Vietnamese Experience', *People and Place*, 1, 1993, pp. 26–32.

Biskup, P., *Not Slaves, Not Citizens*, University of Queensland Press, Brisbane, 1973.

Bittles, A.H., Petterson, B.A., Sullivan, S.G., Hussain, R., Glasson, E.J. & Montgomery, P.D., 'The Influence of Intellectual Disability on Life Expectancy', *Journal of Gerontology: Series A: Biological Sciences and Medical Sciences*, 57A, M470–M472, 2002.

Bittman, M., Hoffman, S. & Thompson, D., *Men's Uptake of Family Friendly Employment Provisions*, Social Policy Research Centre, University of New South Wales, Sydney, 2002.

Blackman, J.A., 'Early Intervention: A Global Perspective', *Infants and Young Children*, 15, 2002, pp. 11–19, p. 11.

Board of Enquiry into the Protection of Aboriginal Children from Sexual Abuse, *Little Children are Sacred*, Northern Territory Government, Darwin, 2007.

Bonnes, M. & Secchiaroli, G., *Environmental Psychology*, Sage, London, 1995.

Booth, M.J., Oakley, A.D., Denney-Wilson, E., Hardy, L., Yang, B. & Dobbins, T., 'NSW Schools Physical Activity and Nutrition Survey (SPANS) 2004: Summary Report', NSW Department of Health, Sydney, 2006.

Booth, T. & Booth, W., *Parenting Under Pressure: Mothers and Fathers with Learning Difficulties*, Open University Press, Buckingham, 1997.

Boss, P., Edwards, S. & Pitman, S., *Profile of Young Australians: Facts, Figures and Issues*, Churchill Livingstone, Melbourne, 1995.

Bottomley, G., ed., *From Another Place: Migration and the Politics of Culture*, Cambridge University Press, Cambridge, 1992.

Bowes, J., 'Emphasizing the Family in Work—Family Research: A Review of Current Research and Recommendations for Future Directions', in *Work and Family: An International Perspective*, ed., S.A.Y. Poelmans, Lawrence Erlbaum Associates, Mahwah, NJ, 2005, pp. 415–38.

Bowes, J.M., Chen, M-J., Li, Q.S. & Li, Y., 'Reasoning and Negotiation About Child Responsibility in Urban Chinese Families: Reports from Mothers, Fathers and Children', *International Journal of Behavioral Development*, 28, 2004, pp. 48–58.

Bowes, J.M. & Goodnow, J.J., 'Work for Home, School or Labor Force: The Nature and Sources of Children's Understanding', *Psychological Bulletin*, 119, 1996, pp. 300–21.

Bowes, J. & Harrison, L., *Patterns of Care Involving Regulated Childcare Settings: Parent Perspectives*, presented at the Australian Human Development Association Biennial conference, Sydney, July 2007.

Bowes, J., Harrison, L., Wise, S., Sanson, A., Ungerer, J., Watson, J. & Simpson, T., 'Child Care Choices: A Longitudinal Study of Children, Families and Child Care in Partnership with Policy Makers', *The Australian Educational Researcher*, 2004, 31, pp. 69–86.

Bowes, J.M., Wise, S., Harrison, L., Sanson, A., Ungerer, J., Watson, J. & Simpson, T., 'Continuity of Care in the Early Years?: Multiple and Changeable Childcare in Australia', *Family Matters*, 64, 2003, pp. 30–5.

Bowlby, J., *Maternal Care and Mental Health*, World Health Organization, London, 1951.

Bowlby, J., *Attachment and Loss*, vols 1, 2 & 3, Basic Books, New York, 1969–80.

Bowman, D. & Virtue, M., *Public Policy, Private Lives*, Australian Institute of Intellectual Disability, Canberra, 1993.

Bown, K. & Sumsion, J., 'Voices from the Other Side of the Fence: Early Childhood Teachers' Experiences with Mandatory Regulatory Requirements', *Contemporary Issues in Early Childhood*, 8, 1, 2007, pp. 30–49.

Braddock, D., Emerson, E., Felce, D. & Stancliffe, R.J., 'Living Circumstances of Children and Adults with Mental Retardation or Developmental Disabilities in the United States, Canada, England and Wales, and Australia', *Mental Retardation and Developmental Disabilities Research Review*, 7, 2001, pp. 115–21.

Brady, M., *Heavy Metal*, Aboriginal Studies Press, Canberra, 1992.

Bray, J.R., 'Hardship in Australia: An Analysis of Financial Stress Indicators in the 1998–99 Australian Bureau of Statistics Household Expenditure Survey', Occasional Paper no. 4, Department of Family and Community Services, Canberra, 2001.

Brennan, D., *The Politics of Australian Child Care: From Philanthropy to Feminism*, Cambridge University Press, Cambridge, 1994.

Brennan, D., 'The ABC of Child Care Politics', *Australian Journal of Social Issues*, 42, 2, 2007, pp. 213–25.

Broad, B., *Improving the Health and Well Being of Young People Leaving Care*, Russell House Publishing, Lyme Regis, UK, 2005.

Broberg, A.G., Wessels, H., Lamb, M.E. & Hwang, C.P., 'Effects of Child Care on the Development of Cognitive Abilities in 8-year-olds: A Longitudinal Study', *Developmental Psychology*, 33, 1997, pp. 62–9.

Bromfield, L. & Higgins, D., *National Comparison of Child Protection Systems: National Child Protection Clearing House Child Abuse Prevention Issues Paper no. 22*, Australian Institute of Family Studies, Melbourne, 2005.

Bronfenbrenner, U., *The Ecology of Human Development*, Harvard University Press, Cambridge, MA, 1979.

Bronfenbrenner, U., 'Recent Advances in the Research on Human Development', in *Development as Action in Context*, eds, R.K. Silbereisen, K. Eyforth & G. Rudinger, Springer-Verlag, Heidelberg, Germany, 1986, pp. 287–9.

Bronfenbrenner, U., 'Principles for the Healthy Growth and Development of Children', in *Marriage and Family in a Changing Society*, ed., J.M. Henslin, The Free Press, New York, 1989.

Bronfenbrenner, U., 'The Biological Model from a Life Course Perspective: Reflections of a Participant Observer', in *Examining Lives in Context*, eds, P. Moen, G.H. Elder Jr & K. Lüscher, American Psychological Association, Washington, DC, 1995a, pp. 599–618.

Bronfenbrenner, U., 'Developmental Ecology Through Space and Time', in *Examining Lives in Context*, eds, P. Moen, G.H. Elder Jr & K. Lüscher, American Psychological Association, Washington, DC, 1995b, pp. 619–48.

Bronfenbrenner, U., 'Environments in Developmental Perspective: Theoretical and Operational Models', in *Measuring Environment across the Life Span: Emerging Methods and Concepts*, eds, S.L. Friedman & T.D. Wachs, American Psychological Association, Washington, DC, 1999, pp. 3–28.

Brooks-Gunn, J., 'Children in Families in Communities: Risk and Intervention in the Bronfenbrenner Tradition', in *Examining Lives in Context*, eds, P. Moen, G.H. Elder Jr & K. Lüscher, American Psychological Association, Washington, DC, 1995, pp. 467–519.

Brooks-Gunn, J., 'Do You Believe in Magic? What We Can Expect from Early Childhood Intervention Programs', *Social Policy Report of the Society for Research in Child Development*, 17, 2003, pp. 3–14.

Brooks-Gunn, J., 'Families and Policies Matter: How to Enhance the Well-being of Children in Poverty', paper presented at the Australian Social Policy Conference, Sydney, July 2007.

Brooks-Gunn, J., Berlin, L.J. & Fuligini, A.S., 'Early Childhood Intervention Programs: What About the Family?', in *Handbook of Early Childhood Intervention* (2nd edn), eds, J.P. Shonkoff & S.J. Meisels, Cambridge University Press, Cambridge, 2000, pp. 549–88.

Brown, J., Miller, J. & Mitchell, J., 'Interrupted Schooling and the Acquisition of Literacy: Experiences of Sudanese Refugees in Victorian Secondary Schools', *Australian Journal of Language and Literacy*, 29, 2006, pp. 150–62.

Buchanan, C., 'Building Better Playgrounds: A Project for Parents?', *UAB Magazine (University of Alabama)*, 19, 3, 1999, <http://main.uab.edu/show.asp?durki=25353253>, accessed 12 July 2006.

Buchanan, J. & Thornwaite, L., *Paid Work and Parenting: Charting a New Course for Australian Families*, Report prepared for the Chifley Foundation, University of Sydney, Sydney, 2001.

Bugental, D.B., Olster, D.H. & Martorell, G.A., 'A Developmental Neuroscience Perspective on the Dynamics of Parenting', in *Handbook of Dynamics in Parent-Child Relations*, ed., L. Kuczynski, Sage, Thousand Oaks, CA, 2003, pp. 25–48.

Bullock, R., Courtney, M., Parker, R., Sinclair, I. & Thoburn, J., 'Can the Corporate State Parent?', *Children and Youth Services Review*, 28, 2006, pp. 1344–58.

Bullock, R., Little, M. & Millham, S., *Going Home: The Return of Children Separated from their Families*, Dartmouth, Aldershot, 1993.

Bundy, A., Tranter, P., Luckett, T., Naughton, G., Wyver, S., Spies, G. & Ragen, J.A. (in press), 'Playful Interaction: Occupational Therapy for "All" Children on the Playground', *American Journal of Occupational Therapy*.

Burchill, M., Higgins, D., Ramsamy, L. & Taylor, S., 'Workin' Together: Indigenous Perspectives on Community Development', *Family Matters*, 51, 2006, pp. 50–9.

Burns, A. & Goodnow, J.J., *Children and Families in Australia*, Allen & Unwin, Sydney, 1985.

Burr, R. & Montgomery, H., 'Family, Kinship and Beyond', in *Childhoods in Context*, eds, J. Maybin, M. Woodhead, Wiley/Open University Press, Chichester, UK, 2003, pp. 39–80.

Buti, A., 'Unfinished Business: The Australian Stolen Generations', *Murdoch University Electronic Journal of Law*, 7, 4, 2000, <www.murdoch.edu.au/elaw/>, accessed 19 November 2003.

Cadzow, J., 'The Bubble-wrap Generation', *Sydney Morning Herald Good Weekend Magazine*, 17 January 2004, pp. 18–21.

Cairns, R.B. & Cairns, B.D., *Lifelines and Risks: Pathways of Youth in Our Time*, Cambridge University Press, New York, 1994.

Cairns, R.B. & Cairns, B.D., 'Social Ecology Over Time and Space', in *Examining Lives in Context*, eds, P. Moen, G.H. Elder Jr & K. Lüscher, American Psychological Association, Washington, DC, 1995, pp. 397–421.

Campbell, F.A., Pungello, E.P., Miller-Johnson, S., Burchinal, M.R. & Ramey, C., 'The Development of Cognitive and Academic Abilities: Growth Curves from an Early Intervention Educational Experiment', *Developmental Psychology*, 37, 2001, pp. 231–42.

Canadian Task Force on Mental Health Issues Affecting Immigrants and Refugees, *After the Door Had Been Opened: Report of the Canadian Task Force on Mental Health Issues Affecting Immigrants and Refugees*, Health and Welfare Canada, Ottawa, 1988.

Cappo, D., 'Australia's Welfare 2007 Conference: Disadvantage and Diversity', keynote address to the Australian Institute of Health and Welfare, 6 December 2007, <www.socialinclusion.sa.gov.au/files/AIHW%20Speech%206%20Dec%2007%20FINAL.pdf>, accessed 21 January 2008.

Carrington, V., 'The Interethnic Family in 1990s Australia', paper presented at the Australian Family Research Conference, Brisbane, 1996.

Cashmore, J., 'Children: Non-contractual Persons?', in *The New Contractualism?*, eds, G. Davis, B. Sullivan & A. Yeatman, Macmillan, Melbourne, 1997.

Cashmore, J., 'Family, Early Development and the Life Course: Common Risk and Protective Factors in Pathways to Prevention', in *The Social Origins of Health and Well-Being: From the Planetary to the Molecular*, eds, R. Eckersley, J. Dixon & B. Douglas, Cambridge University Press, Melbourne, 2001a, pp. 216–30.

Cashmore, J., 'What Can We Learn from the US Experience on Permanency Planning?', *Australian Journal of Family Law*, 15, 2001b, pp. 215–29.

Cashmore, J., 'Facilitating the Participation of Children and Young People in Care', *Child Abuse & Neglect*, 26, 8, 2002, pp. 837–47.

Cashmore, J., 'Child Protection—Integrating Research Policy Practice: The Potential and the Limits of Corporate Parenting', paper presented at the Child Safety Research Conference, Brisbane, 14–15 November 2006.

Cashmore, J. & de Haas, N., *Legal and Social Aspects of the Physical Punishment of Children*, Commonwealth Department of Human Services and Health, Canberra, 1995.

Cashmore, J. & Paxman, M., *Wards Leaving Care: A Longitudinal Study*, NSW Department of Community Services, Sydney, 1996.

Cashmore, J. & Paxman, M., 'Predicting Outcomes for Young People after Leaving Care: The Importance of "Felt" Security', *Child and Family Social Work: Special Issue on Leaving Care*, 11, 2006a, pp. 232–41.

Cashmore, J. & Paxman, M., *Wards Leaving Care: Four to Five Years On*, Social Policy Research Centre, University of New South Wales and NSW Department of Community Services, Sydney, 2006b, pp. 115–16.

Cashmore, J. & Paxman, M., 'Wards Leaving Care: Follow Up Five Years On', *Children Australia*, 31, 2006c, pp. 18–25.

Caughy, M.O., DiPietro, J. & Strobino, M., 'Day-care Participation as a Protective Factor in the Cognitive Development of Low-income Children', *Child Development*, 65, 1994, pp. 457–71.

Champion, P., 'Infant/Maternal Interactive Social/Emotional Learning Where the Infant Has a Disability or Is at Risk for a Disability', *Infants and Young Children*, 12, 2000, pp. 10–16.

Chan, J.B. & Sigafoos, J., 'A Review of Child and Family Characteristics Related to the Use of Respite Care in Developmental Disability Services', *Child & Youth Care Forum*, 29, 2000, pp. 27–37.

Child Welfare League of Canada, 'The Welfare of Canadian Children: It's Our Business: A Collection of Resource Papers for a Healthy Future for Canadian Children and Families', Centre of Excellence for Child Welfare, 2007, <www.cwlc.ca/policy/welfare_e.htm>, accessed 13 December 2007.

Children's Play Council, *Managing Risk in Play Provision: A Position Statement*, National Children's Bureau, London, 2002, <www.childfriendlycities.org/cgi-bin/cfc/main.sql?file=search_simple_result.sql&lunga=Yes&ProductID=426>, accessed 11 April 2006.

Christie, J.K. & Roskos, K.A., 'Standards, Science and the Role of Play in Early Literacy Education', in *Play = Learning: How Play Motivates and Enhances Children's Cognitive and Social-emotional Growth*, eds, D.G. Singer, R.M. Golinkoff & K. Hirsh-Pasek, Oxford University Press, Oxford, 2006, pp. 57–73.

Cicchetti, D., 'Child Maltreatment: Implications for Developmental Theory and Research', *Human Development*, 39, 1996, pp. 18–39.

Cicchetti, D., Toth, S.L. & Maughan, A., 'An Ecological-Transactional Model of Child Maltreatment', in *Handbook of Developmental Psychopathology* (2nd edn), eds, A.J. Sameroff & M. Lewis, Kluwer Academic Publishers, Dordrecht, Netherlands, 2000, pp. 689–722.

Clarke, A.B.D. & Clarke, A.M., 'The Historical Context', in *New Approaches to Down Syndrome*, eds, B. Stratford & P. Gunn, Cassell, London, 1996, pp. 12–22.

Cleveland, G., Forer, B., Hyatt, D., Japel, C. & Krashinsky, M., 'An Economic Perspective on the Current and Future Role of Nonprofit Provision of Early Learning and Child Care Services in Canada: Final Project Report', University of Toronto, University of British Columbia & Université du Québec, 2007.

Coady, M.M., 'Reflections on Children's Rights', in *Citizen Child: Australian Laws and Children's Rights*, ed., K. Funder, Australian Institute of Family Studies, Melbourne, 1996, pp. 11–33.

Cohen, R., 'Eighty-seven and Still Going Strong', *Bernard van Leer Foundation Newsletter*, 87, October 1997.

Cole, M., 'The Supra-individual Envelope of Development: Activity and Practice, Situation and Context', in *New Directions for Child Development*, no. 67, eds, J.J. Goodnow, P.J. Miller & F. Kessel, Jossey-Bass, San Francisco, 1995, pp. 105–18.

Coleman, J.S., 'Social Capital in the Creation of Human Capital', *American Journal of Sociology*, 94, 1988, pp. 94–120.

Colwell, M., Petit, G., Meece, D., Bates, J.E. & Dodge, K.A., 'Cumulative Risk and Continuity in Nonparental Care from Infancy to Early Adolescence', *Merrill-Palmer Quarterly*, 47, 2001, pp. 207–34.

Commonwealth, *Parliamentary Debates*, House of Representatives, vol. 81, 10 October 1972.

Commonwealth Department of Education, Science and Training, *Higher Education: Report for 2003 to 2005 Triennium*, Commonwealth Government Publishing, Canberra, 2003.

Consortium Advisory Group, *Introducing the Longitudinal Study of Australian Children*, LSAC Discussion Paper no. 1, Australian Institute of Family Studies, Melbourne, Australia, 2002, p. x.

Cooke, P. & Standen, P.J., 'Abuse and Disabled Children: Hidden Need…?', *Child Abuse Review*, 11, 2002, pp. 1–18.

Cooley, C.H., *Human Nature and the Social Order*, Scribners, New York, 1902.

Cotton, S. & Richdale, A., 'Brief Report: Parental Descriptions of Sleep Problems in Children with Autism, Down Syndrome, and Prader-Willi Syndrome', *Research in Developmental Disorders*, 27, 2006, pp. 151–61.

Coulton, C.J., Korbin, J.E., Su, M. & Chow, J., 'Community Level Factors and Child Maltreatment Rates', *Child Development*, 66, 1995, pp. 1262–76.

Courtney, M.E., Dworsky, A., Ruth, G., Keller, T., Havlicek, J. & Bost, N., *Midwest Evaluation of the Adult Functioning of Former Foster Youth: Outcomes at Age 19*, Chapin Hall Working Paper, Chapin Hall Center for Children at the University of Chicago, Chicago, 2005.

Cowan, P.A., Cowan, C.P. & Schulz, M.S., 'Thinking about Risk and Resilience in Families', in *Stress, Coping and Resiliency in Children and Families*, eds, E.M. Hetherington & E.A. Blechman, Lawrence Erlbaum, Mahwah, NJ, 1996, pp. 1–38.

Cox, E., *A Truly Civil Society: 1995 Boyer Lectures*, ABC Books, Sydney, 1995.

Craig, L., 'Caring Differently: A Time Use Analysis of the Type and Social Context of Child Care Performed by Fathers and Mothers', Discussion Paper no. 116, Social Policy Research Centre, University of New South Wales, Sydney, 2002.

Craig, L., *How Do They Do It?: A Time-diary Analysis of How Working Mothers Find Time for the Kids*, Social Policy Research Centre, UNSW, Sydney, 2005.

Crockenberg, S.C., 'Rescuing the Baby from the Bathwater: How Gender and Temperament (may) Influence how Child Care Affects Child Development', *Child Development*, 74, 2003, pp. 1034–8.

Crocker, A.C., 'Introduction: The Happiness in All Our Lives', *American Journal on Mental Retardation*, 105, 2002, pp. 319–25.

Cummings, B., *Take This Child*, Aboriginal Studies Centre, Canberra, 1990.

Cummings, E.M. & Davies, P., *Children and Marital Conflict: The Impact of Family Dispute and Resolution*, The Guilford Press, New York, 1994.

Cunningham, A. & Knoester, C., 'Marital Status, Gender, and Parents' Psychological Well-being', *Sociological Inquiry*, 77, 2007, pp. 264–87.

Cunningham, C. & Glenn, S., 'Self-awareness in Young Adults with Down Syndrome: I. Awareness of Down Syndrome and Disability', *International Journal of Disability, Development and Education*, 51, 2004, pp. 335–62.

Cunningham, C., Jones, M. & Barlow, M., *Town Planning and Children: A Case Study of Lismore, New South Wales, Australia*, Department of Geography and Planning, University of New England, Armidale, 1996.

Cunningham, C., Jones, M. & Taylor, N., 'The Child-friendly Neighbourhood: Some Questions and Tentative Answers from Australian Research', *International Play Journal*, 2, 1994, pp. 79–95.

Cuskelly, M., 'Adjustment of Siblings of Children with a Disability: Methodological Issues', *International Journal for the Advancement of Counselling*, 21, 1999, pp. 111–24.

Cuskelly, M. & Gunn, P., 'Sibling Relationships of Children with Down Syndrome: Perspectives of Mothers, Fathers and Siblings', *American Journal on Mental Retardation*, 108, 2003, pp. 234–44.

Daly, A., 'Social Inclusion and Exclusion Among Australia's Children: A Review of the Literature', National Centre for Social and Economic Modelling Discussion Paper No. 62, National Centre for Social and Economic Modelling, University of Canberra, Canberra, 2006.

D'Andrade, R.G. & Strauss, C., eds, *Human Motivation and Cultural Models*, Cambridge University Press, New York, 1992.

Daro, D., *Confronting Child Abuse: Research for Effective Program Design*, The Free Press, New York, 1988.

Davidson-Arad, B., Englechin-Segal, D. & Wozner, Y., 'Short-term Follow-up of Children at Risk: Comparison of the Quality of Life of Children Removed from Home and Children Remaining at Home', *Child Abuse & Neglect*, 27, 2003, pp. 733–50.

Davies, A., 'Classroom Revolution As Schools Connected to the World', *Sydney Morning Herald*, 17 March 2007, <www.smh.com.au/news/schools/classroom-revolution-as-schools-connected-to-world/2007/03/16/1173722745511.html>, accessed 31 January 2008.

Davies, P.T., Harold, G.T., Goeke-Morey, M.C. & Cummings, E.M., 'Child Emotional Security and Interparental Conflict', *Monographs of the Society for Research in Child Development*, Serial no. 270, 67, 3, 2002.

Dawe, S., *Drug Use in the Family: Impacts and Implications for Children*, Australian National Council on Drugs, Canberra, 2007.

Deater-Deckard, K. & Dunn, J., 'Multiple Risks and Adjustments of Young Children Growing Up in Different Family Settings', in *Coping with Divorce, Single Parenthood and Remarriage: A Risk and Resiliency Perspective*, ed., E.M. Hetherington, Lawrence Erlbaum, Mahwah, NJ, 1999, pp. 47–64.

Deater-Deckard, K., Ivy, L. & Smith, J., 'Resilience in Gene-environment Transactions', in *Handbook of Resilience in Childhood*, eds, S. Goldstein & R.B. Brooks, Springer, New York, 2006, pp. 49–63.

Deater-Deckard, K., Pinkerton, R. & Scarr, S., 'Child Care Quality and Children's Behavioral Adjustment: A Four-year Longitudinal Study', *Journal of Child Psychology and Psychiatry*, 37, 1996, pp. 937–48.

Deaux, K., *To Be An Immigrant*, Russell Sage Foundation, New York, 2006.

Delfabbro, P.H., Barber, J.G. & Cooper, L.L, 'Placement Disruption and Dislocation in South Australian Substitute Care', *Children Australia*, 25, 2, 2000, pp. 16–20.

Delfabbro, P.H., Barber, J.G. & Cooper, L.L., 'Predictors of Short-term Reunification in South Australian Substitute Care', *Child Welfare*, 82, 2002, pp. 27–51.

de Lissa, L., *Talks Given at the Golden Jubilee of the Kindergarten Union of South Australia*, Adelaide, Kindergarten Union of South Australia, 1955.

Department of Family and Community Services, *2004 Census of Child Care Services, Summary Booklet*, Australian Government, Canberra, 2005.

Department of Health, *Child Protection: Messages from Research*, HMSO, London, 1995.

Department of Immigration and Citizenship, *Report on Performance 2006: Output 1–2: Refugee and Humanitarian Entry and Stay*, Department of Immigration and Citizenship, Canberra, 2006.

Department of Transport Regional Services, *Drought Impacts Beyond the Farm Gate: Two Regional Case Studies*, Farmsafe Australia, Moree, 2004.

de Vaus, D., Qu, L. & Weston, R., 'Changing Patterns of Partnering', *Family Matters*, 64, 2003, pp. 10–15.

de Vaus, D. & Wolcott, I., *Australian Family Profiles: Social and Demographic Patterns*, Australian Institute of Family Studies, Melbourne, 1997.

Dingwall, R., Eekelaar, J. & Murray, T., *The Protection of Children: State Intervention and Family Life* (2nd edn), Avebury, Aldershot, 1995.

Dowse, S., 'The Women's Movement's Fandango with the State: The Movement's Role in Public Policy Since 1972', in *Women, Social Welfare and the State* (2nd edn), eds, C.V. Baldock & B. Cass, Allen & Unwin, Sydney, 1988, pp. 205–26.

Doyle, J., 'Boys Town Engadine', paper presented to the ACWA Reunification Forum, Sydney, 6 December 2007.

Dubowitz, H., Black, M., Starr, R.H. & Zuravin, S., 'A Conceptual Definition of Child Neglect', *Criminal Justice and Behavior*, 20, 1993, pp. 8–26.

Duchesne, S., *Parental Beliefs and Behaviours in Relation to Schooling*, unpublished PhD thesis, Macquarie University, 1996.

Dunlop, A-W., 'Bridging Early Educational Transitions in Learning Through Children's Agency', in *Transitions, European Early Childhood Education Research Journal Themed Monograph Series no. 1*, 2003, pp. 67–86.

Dunlop, R., 'Family Processes: Towards a Theoretical Framework', in *Images of Australian Families*, ed., K. Funder, Longman Cheshire, Melbourne, 1991, pp. 122–35.

Dunn, J., *The Beginnings of Social Understanding*, Harvard University Press, Cambridge, MA, 1988.

Dunn, L. & Dunn, L., *Peabody Picture Vocabulary Test-Revised*, American Guidance Service, Circle Pines, MN, 1981.

Dunst, C.J. & Dempsey, I., 'Family-professional Partnerships and Parenting Competence, Confidence, and Enjoyment', *International Journal of Disability, Development and Education*, 54, 3, 2007, pp. 305–18.

Dunst, C., Trivette, C. & Deal, A., *Supporting and Strengthening Families: Methods, Strategies and Practices*, Brookline Books, Cambridge, MA, 1994.

Durkin, K., *Developmental Social Psychology*, Blackwell, Oxford, 1995.

Durlak, J.A., 'Common Risk and Protective Factors in Successful Prevention Programs', *American Journal of Orthopsychiatry*, 68, 1998, pp. 512–20.

Durrant, J.E., 'Trends in Youth Crime and Well-being Since the Abolition of Corporal Punishment in Sweden', *Youth and Society*, 31, 4, 2000, pp. 437–55.

Durrant, J., 'From Mopping Up the Damage to Preventing the Flood: The Role of Social Policy in Preventing Violence Against Children', *Social Policy Journal of New Zealand*, 28, 2006, <www.msd.govt.nz/documents/publications/msd/journal/issue28/28-pages-1-17.pdf>, accessed 24 March 2008.

Durrant, J.E. & Olsen, G.M., 'Parenting and Public Policy: Contextualising the Swedish Corporal Punishment Ban', *Journal of Social Welfare and Family Law*, 19, 4, 1997, pp. 443–61.

Earle, J., 'Family-friendly Workplaces: A Tale of Two Sectors', *Family Matters*, 61, 2002, pp. 12–17.

Edwards, B., 'Does It Take a Village? An Investigation of Neighbourhood Effects on Australian Children's Development', *Family Matters*, 72, 2005, pp. 36–43.

Edwards, R.W., *Measuring Social Capital: An Australian Framework and Indicators*, Australian Bureau of Statistics, Canberra, 2004, <www.ausstats.abs.gov.au/ausstats/free.nsf/Lookup/13C0688F6B98DD45CA256E360077D526/$File/13780_2004.pdf>, accessed 14 August 2007.

Edwards, R.W. & Madden, R., *The Health and Welfare of Australia's Aboriginal and Torres Strait Islander Peoples 2001*, catalogue no. 4704.0, ABS, Canberra, 2001.

Egeland, B., Yates, T., Appleyard, K. & van Dulmen, M., 'The Long-term Consequences of Maltreatment in the Early Years: A Developmental Pathway Model to Antisocial Behavior', *Children's Services: Social Policy, Research, & Practice*, 5, 4, 2002, pp. 249–60.

Einam, M. & Cuskelly, M., 'Paid Employment of Mothers and Fathers of an Adult Child with Multiple Disabilities', *Journal of Intellectual Disability Research*, 46, 2002, pp. 158–67.

Emerson, E., Hatton, C., Llewellyn, G., Blacher, J. & Graham, H., 'Socio-economic Position, Household Composition, Health Status and Indicators of the Well-Being of Mothers of Children with and without Intellectual Disabilities', *Journal of Intellectual Disability Research*, 50, 2006, pp. 862–73.

Encel, S. & Strudecki, H., *Partnership: A Review*, University of NSW Social Policy Research Centre, Sydney, 2000.

Essex, E.L., 'Mothers and Fathers of Adults with Mental Retardation: Feelings of Intergenerational Closeness', *Family Relations*, 51, 2002, pp. 156–65.

Fanshel, D. & Shinn, F.B., *Children in Foster Care: A Longitudinal Study*, Columbia University Press, New York, 1978.

Farouque, F., 'The Other Eddy Everywhere', *The Age*, 8 April 2006, <www.theage.com.au/news/in-depth/the-other-eddy-everywhere/2006/04/07/1143916718012.html>, accessed 17 August 2007.

Fazel, M., Wheeler, J. & Danesh, J., 'Prevalence of Serious Mental Disorder in 7000 Refugees Resettled in Western Countries: A Systematic Review', *The Lancet*, 365, 2005, pp. 1309–14.

Fenech, M., 'The Impact of Regulatory Environments on Early Childhood Professional Practice and Job Satisfaction: A Review of Conflicting Discourses', *Australian Journal of Early Childhood*, 31, 2, 2006, pp. 49–52.

Fenech, M., Sumsion, J. & Goodfellow, J., 'The Regulatory Environment in Long Day Care: A "Double Edged Sword" for Early Childhood Professional Practice', *Australian Journal of Early Childhood*, 31, 3, 2006, pp. 49–56.

Fergusson, D.M., Horwood, L.J. & Lynskey, M.T., 'A Longitudinal Study of Early Childhood Education and Subsequent Academic Achievement', *Australian Psychologist*, July 1994, pp. 110–15.

Fergusson, D.M. & Horwood, L.J., 'Resilience to Childhood Adversity: Results of a 21-Year Study', in *Resilience and Vulnerability: Adaptation in the Context of Childhood Adversities*, ed., S.S. Luthar, Cambridge University Press, Cambridge, 2003, pp. 130–55.

Fernandez, E., 'How Children Experience Fostering Outcomes: Participatory Research With Children', *Child and Family Social Work*, 11, 2006, pp. 1–10.

Findlay, R.A., 'Interventions to Reduce Social Isolation Amongst Older People: Where is the Evidence?', *Ageing and Society*, 23, 2003, pp. 647–58.

Flanagan, C., 'Families and Schools in Hard Times', in *New Directions for Child Development*, no. 46, eds, V.C. McLoyd & C.A. Flanagan, Jossey-Bass, San Francisco, 1990, pp. 7–26.

Fleet, A., Kitson, R., Cassady, B. & Hughes, R., 'University-qualified Indigenous Early Childhood Teachers', *Australian Journal of Early Childhood*, 32, 3, 2007, pp. 17–25.

Flood, M., *Mapping Loneliness in Australia*, The Australia Institute Discussion Paper No. 76, The Australia Institute, Canberra, 2005, <www.tai.org.au/documents/downloads/DP76.pdf>, accessed 1 August 2007.

Foley, G.M., 'The Loss-Grief Cycle: Coming to Terms with the Birth of a Child with a Disability', in *Mental Health in Early Intervention: Achieving Unity in Principles and Practice*, eds, G.M. Foley & J.D. Hochman, Paul H Brookes, Baltimore, MD, 2006, pp. 227–43.

Fox Harding, L., *Perspectives in Child Care Policy*, Longman, London, 1991.

Franks, A., *Indigenous Services in the Northern Rivers Region of NSW*, NSW Health, Sydney, 2001.

Frodi, A.M. & Lamb, M.E., 'Child Abusers' Responses to Infant Smiles and Cries', *Child Development*, 51, 1980, pp. 238–41.

Gaita, R., *Romulus My Father*, Text Publishing, Melbourne, 1998.

Gallimore, R., Weisner, T.S., Bernheimer, L.P., Guthrie, D. & Nihira, K., 'Family Responses to Young Children with Developmental Delays: Accommodation Activity in Ecological and Cultural Context', *American Journal on Mental Retardation*, 98, 1993, pp. 185–206.

Gallimore, R., Weisner, T.S., Kaufman, S.Z. & Bernheimer, L.P., 'The Social Construction of Ecocultural Niches: Family Accommodation of Developmentally Delayed Children', *American Journal on Mental Retardation*, 94, 1989, pp. 216–30.

Garbarino, J., *Raising Children in a Socially Toxic Environment*, Jossey-Bass, San Francisco, 1995.

Garbarino, J. & Crouter, A., 'Defining the Community Context for Parent–child Relations: The Correlates of Child Maltreatment', *Child Development*, 49, 1978, pp. 604–16.

Garbarino, J. & Sherman, D., 'High Risk Neighbourhoods and High Risk Families: The Human Ecology of Child Maltreatment', *Child Development*, 51, 1980, pp. 188–98.

Gath, A. & Gumley, D., 'Family Background of Children with Down's Syndrome and of Children with a Similar Degree of Mental Retardation', *British Journal of Psychiatry*, 149, 1986, pp. 161–71.

Gibbons, S., Green, A., Gregg, P. & Machin, S., *Is Britain Pulling Apart? Area Disparities in Employment, Education and Crime*, University of Bristol Working Paper No. 05/120, The Centre for Market and Public Organisation, University of Bristol, Bristol, UK, 2005, <www.bris.ac.uk/Depts/CMPO/workingpapers/wp120.pdf>, accessed 2 December 2007.

Gifford, J., *Child Care Funding Re-assessed: Operational Subsidies, Fee Relief and Taxation Measures*, Australian Early Childhood Association and National Association of Community Based Children's Services, Canberra, 1992.

Gifford, S., Bakopanos, C., Kaplan, I. & Correa-Velez, I., 'Meaning or Measurement? Researching the Social Contexts of Health and Settlement among Newly-arrived Refugee Youth in Melbourne, Australia', *Journal of Refugee Studies*, 20, 2007, pp. 414–40.

Gilbert, R. & O'Brien, C., *Child- and Youth-friendly Land-use and Transport Planning Guidelines*, The Centre for Sustainable Transportation, Toronto, 2005; P.J. Tranter, 'Overcoming Social Traps: A Key to Creating Child Friendly Cities', in *Creating Child Friendly Cities: Reinstating Kids in the City*, eds, B. Gleeson & N. Sipe, Routledge, New York, 2006, pp. 121–35.

Giles, H., Coupland, N. & Coupland, J., 'Accommodation Theory: Communication, Context and Consequence', in *Contexts of Accommodation*, eds, H. Giles, N. Coupland & J. Coupland, Cambridge University Press, Cambridge, 1991, pp. 1–68.

Gittins, D., *The Family Question* (2nd edn), Macmillan, London, 1993.

Glaser, D., 'Child Abuse and Neglect and the Brain—A Review', *Journal of Child Psychology and Psychiatry*, 41, 2000, pp. 97–116.

Glasson, E.J., Sullivan, S.G., Patterson, B.A., Montgomery, P.D. & Bittles, A.H., 'The Changing Survival Profile of People with Down's Syndrome: Implications for Genetic Counselling', *Clinical Genetics*, 62, 2002, pp. 390–3.

Glenn, S. & Cunningham, C., 'Self-awareness in Young Adults with Down Syndrome: II. Self-understanding', *International Journal of Disability, Development and Education*, 51, 2004, pp. 363–82.

Goddard, C., *Child Abuse and Child Protection*, Churchill Livingstone, Melbourne, 1996.

Goffman, E., *Stigma*, Penguin, Harmondsworth, 1963.

Golinkoff, R.M., Hirsh-Pasek, K. & Singer, D.G., 'Play = Learning: A Challenge for Parents and Educators', in *Play = Learning: How Play Motivates and Enhances Children's Cognitive and Social-emotional Growth*, eds, D.G. Singer, R.M. Golinkoff & K. Hirsh-Pasek, Oxford University Press, Oxford, 2006, pp. 3–20.

Gomby, D.S., Larner, M.B., Stevenson, C.S., Lewitt, E.M. & Behrman, R.E., 'Long-term Outcomes of Early Childhood Programs: Analysis and Recommendations', *The Future of Children*, 5, 1995, pp. 6–24.

Goodfellow, J., 'Multicare Arrangement Patchworks: The Multiple Use of Formal and Informal Childcare in NSW', report for the NSW Department of Community Services, Office of Child Care, Sydney, 1999.

Goodfellow, J., 'Grandparents as Regular Child Care Providers: Unrecognised, Under-valued and Under-resourced', *Australian Journal of Early Childhood*, 28, 2003, pp. 7–17.

Goodnow, J.J., 'Acceptable Disagreement Across Generations', in *Beliefs About Parenting*, ed., J.G. Smetana, Jossey-Bass, San Francisco, 1995a, pp. 51–64.

Goodnow, J.J., 'Differentiating Among Social Contexts: By Spatial Features, Forms of Participation, and Social Contracts', in *Examining Lives in Context*, eds, P. Moen, G.H. Elder Jr & K. Lüscher, American Psychological Association, Washington, DC, 1995b, pp. 269–301.

Goodnow, J.J., 'Parenting and the "Transmission" and "Internalization" of Values: From Social–cultural Perspectives to Within-family Analyses', in *Parenting Strategies and Children's Internalization of Values: A Handbook of Theoretical and Research Proposals*, eds, J. Grusec & L. Kuczynski, Wiley, New York, 1997, pp. 333–61.

Goodnow, J.J., 'Contexts, Diversity, Pathways: Advances and Next Steps' in *Developmental Pathways Through Middle Childhood: Rethinking Contexts and Diversity as Resources*, eds, C.R. Cooper, G. Coll, T. Bartko, H. Davis & C. Chatman, Lawrence Erlbaum, Mahwah, NJ, 2005, pp. 295–312.

Goodnow, J.J., 'Second Looks at Views of Development, Families, and Communities, and at Translations into Practice', in *Families Count: Effects on Child and Adolescent Development*, eds, A. Clarke-Stewart & J. Dunn, Cambridge University Press, Cambridge, 2006, pp. 337–60.

Gordon, M., Rosenman, L. & Cuskelly, M., 'Maternal Employment: A Comparative Study of Paid Work Levels and the Desire to Work among Mothers with and without Dependent Children with Disabilities', *Journal of Applied Research on Intellectual Disabilities*, 20, 2007, pp. 236–46.

Gottlieb, B., *The Family in the Western World from the Black Death to the Industrial Age*, Oxford University Press, Oxford, 1993.

Gough, D., 'Defining the Problem', *Child Abuse & Neglect*, 20, 1996, pp. 993–1002.

Grant, B., *The Boat People: An Age Investigation*, Penguin, Melbourne, 1979.

Gray, D.E., 'Ten Years On: A Longitudinal Study of Families of Children with Autism', *Journal of Intellectual & Developmental Disability*, 27, 2000, pp. 215–22.

Gray, D.E., 'Gender and Coping: The Parents of Children with High Functioning Autism', *Social Science & Medicine*, 56, 2003, pp. 631–42.

Gray, M., Qu, L. & Weston, R., *Fertility and Family Policy in Australia*, Australian Institute of Family Studies, Melbourne, 2008, <www.aifs.gov.au/institute/pubs/rp41/rp41.pdf>, acccessed 19 March 2008.

Green, S.E., '"We're Tired, Not Sad": Benefits and Burdens of Mothering a Child with a Disability', *Social Science & Medicine*, 64, 2007, pp. 150–63.

Greenwood, P.W., Model, K.E., Rydell, C.P. & Chiesa, J., *Diverting Children From a Life of Crime: Measuring Costs and Benefits*, RAND Corporation, Santa Monica, CA, 1996.

Groce, N.E., *Everybody Here Spoke Sign Language: Hereditary Deafness on Martha's Vineyard*, Harvard University Press, Cambridge, MA, 1985.

Hagekull, B. & Bohlin, G., 'Quality of Care and Problem Behaviors in Early Childhood', paper presented at the Biennial Meeting of the Society for Research in Child Development, New Orleans, LA, 1993.

Hagekull, B. & Bohlin, G., 'Child Care Quality, Family and Child Characteristics and Socioemotional Development', *Early Childhood Research Quarterly*, 10, 1995, pp. 505–26.

Hakuta, K., Butler, Y.G. & Witt, D., *How Long Does it Take English Learners to Attain Proficiency? Policy Report 2000–01*, University of California Linguistic Minority Research Institute, Santa Barbara.

Hallidie-Smith, K.A., 'The Heart', in *New Approaches to Down Syndrome*, eds, B. Stratford & P. Gunn, Cassell, London, 1996, pp. 85–99.

Hand, K. & Lewis, V., 'Fathers' Views on Family Life and Paid Work', *Family Matters*, 61, 2002, pp. 26–9.

Harkness, S. & Super, C., eds, *Parents' Cultural Belief Systems*, The Guilford Press, New York, 1996.

Harland, P. & Cuskelly, M., 'Patterns of Involvement: The Responsibilities and Concerns of Young Adult Siblings in Relation to their Brother/Sister with Vision and Hearing Disabilities', *International Journal of Development, Disability and Education*, 47, 2000, pp. 293–307.

Harms, T., Clifford, M. & Cryer, D., *Early Childhood Environment Rating Scale, Revised Edition (ECERS-R)*, Teachers College Press, New York, 1998.

Harries, M., Lonne, B. & Thompson, J., 'Beyond Buzzwords—Principles and Themes for Reforming Child Protection Practice: Challenging Practices', paper presented at the Third Conference on International Research Perspectives on Child and Family Welfare, Mackay, Queensland, 2005, <www.croccs.org.au/downloads/2005_conf_papers/HarriesLonneThomsonCROCCSpaper.pdf>, accessed 14 December 2007.

Harrison, A.O., Wilson, M.N., Pine, C.J., Chan, S.Q. & Buriel, R., 'Family Ecologies of Ethnic Minority Children', *Child Development*, 61, 1990, pp. 347–62.

Harrison, L.J. & Ungerer, J.A., 'The Sydney Family Development Project: Family and Child Care Predictors at Age Six', paper presented in the symposium, Longitudinal Studies of Early Childhood in Australia, J. Bowes (Chair), at the Australian Association for Research in Education Conference, Brisbane, December 2002.

Harrison, L.J. & Ungerer, J.A., 'What Can the Longitudinal Study of Australian Children Tell Us about Infants and 4 to 5 Year Olds' Experiences of Early Childhood Education and Care?', *Family Matters*, 2006, 72, pp. 26–35.

Harrison, L.J., Ungerer, J.A., Smith, G.J., Zubrick, S.R. & Wise, S. with Press, F., Waniganayake, M. & the LSAC Research Consortium, *Child Care in Australia: The Longitudinal Study of Australian Children, Wave 1 Thematic Paper*, Australian Government Department of Families, Community Services and Indigenous Affairs, Canberra, Australia, 2007.

Hartley, R., ed., *Families and Cultural Diversity in Australia*, Australian Institute of Family Studies, Melbourne, 1995.

Hastings, R.P., Kovshoff, H., Ward, N.J., degli Espinosa, F., Brown, T. & Remington, B., 'Systems Analysis of Stress and Positive Perceptions in Mothers and Fathers of Pre-school Children with Autism', *Journal of Autism and Developmental Disorders*, 35, 2005, pp. 635–44.

Hastings, R.P. & Taunt, H.M., 'Positive Perception in Families of Children with Developmental Disabilities', *American Journal on Mental Retardation*, 107, 2002, pp. 116–27.

Hayes, A., 'Why Early in Life is Not Enough: Timing and Sustainability in Prevention and Early Intervention', in *Pathways and Crime Prevention: Theory, Policy and Practice*, eds, A. France & R. Homel, Willan Publishing, Uffculme, UK, 2007, pp. 202–25, p. 205.

Hayes, C.D., Palmer, J.L. & Zaslow, M.J., *Who Cares for America's Children? Child Care Policy for the 1990s*, National Academy Press, Washington, DC, 1990.

Hedov, G., Anneren, G. & Wikblad, K., 'Swedish Parents of Children with Down's Syndrome', *Scandinavian Journal of Caring Sciences*, 16, 2002, pp. 424–30.

Hek, R., 'The Role of Education in the Settlement of Young Refugees in the UK: The Experiences of Young Refugees', *Practice*, 17, 2005, pp. 157–71.

Helburn, S., ed., *Cost, Quality and Child Outcomes in Child Care Centers*, University of Colorado, Denver, CO, 1995.

Henderson, R., 'Student Mobility: Moving Beyond Deficit Views', *Australian Journal of Guidance and Counselling*, 11, 2001, pp. 121–9.

Henderson, R., 'Educational Issues for Children of Itinerant Seasonal Farm Workers: A Case Study in an Australian Context', *International Journal of Inclusive Education*, 8, 2004, pp. 293–310.

Herrara, C. & Dunn, J., 'Early Experiences with Family Conflict: Implications for Arguments with a Close Friend', *Development Psychology*, 33, 5, 1997, pp. 869–81.

Herron, J., Minister for Aboriginal and Torres Strait Islander Affairs, 'Bringing Them Home—Commonwealth Initiatives', media release, Canberra, 26 August 1999.

Hess, L. & Bundy, A.C., 'The Association Between Playfulness and Coping Adolescents', *Physical and Occupational Therapy in Pediatrics*, 23, 1, 2003, pp. 5–17.

Higgins, D., *Early Learnings: Indigenous Community Development Projects*, vol. 2, Telstra Foundation Research Report, Australian Institute of Family Studies, Melbourne, 2005.

High Court of Australia, '*Al-Kateb vs Godwin & Ors*, HCA 37, 219 CLR 562; 208 ALR 124', High Court of Australia, Canberra.

Hirschfield, L.A., *Race in the Making: The Child's Construction of Human Kinds*, MIT Press, Cambridge, MA, 1996.

Historical Records of Australia, Additional Instructions to Governor Bligh, 20.11.1805, HRA Series I, Vol VI, Government Printer, Sydney, 1915, pp. 18–19.

Ho, H.M. & Keiley, M.K., 'Dealing with Denial: A Systems Approach for Family Professionals Working with Parents of Individuals with Multiple Disabilities', *The Family Journal*, 11, 2003, pp. 239–47.

Hodes, M., 'Psychologically Distressed Refugee Children in the United Kingdom', *Child Psychology & Psychiatry Review*, 5, 2000, pp. 57–68.

Homel, R., 'Forum on Building Family and Community Capacities: Policies that Make a Difference for Children and Families Facing Economic Adversity', Australian Social Policy Conference, Sydney, July 2007.

Homel, R., Lamb, C. & Freiberg, K., 'Working with the Indigenous Community in the Pathways to Prevention Program', *Family Matters*, 75, 2006, pp. 18–53.

Honore, C., *In Praise of Slow: How a Worldwide Movement is Challenging the Cult of Speed*, Orion, London, 2004.

Horin, A., 'Taskforce on Child Care Rejected', *Sydney Morning Herald*, 1 January 2007.

Hornosty, J., 'Wife Abuse in Rural Regions: Structural Problems in Leaving Abusive Relationships—A Case Study in Canada', in *With a Rural Focus: An Edited and Refereed Collection of Papers with a Rural Focus presented to the Annual Conference of the Australian Sociological Association Inc.*, ed., F. Vanclay, Deakin University, 1994, pp. 21–34.

Horrigan, J.B. & Rainie, L., *Online Communities: Networks that Nurture Long-distance Relationships and Local Ties*, Pew Internet and American Life Project, Washington, DC, 2001, <www.pewinternet.org/pdfs/PIP_Communities_Report.pdf>, accessed 18 July 2007.

Hortulanus, R., 'Social Environment and Social Isolation', in *Social Isolation in Modern Society*, eds, R. Hortulanus, A. Machielse & L. Meeuwesen, Routledge, Oxford, UK, 2006a, pp. 156–75.

Hortulanus, R., 'Towards a New Policy Vision on Social Isolation', in *Social Isolation in Modern Society*, eds, R. Hortulanus, A. Machielse & L. Meeuwesen, Routledge, Oxford, 2006b, pp. 246–57.

Hortulanus, R. & Machielse, A., 'The Issue of Social Isolation', in *Social Isolation in Modern Society*, eds, R. Hortulanus, A. Machielse & L. Meeuwesen, Routledge, Oxford, UK, 2006, pp. 3–12.

Howard, J., *Hansard*, Commonwealth of Australia: House of Representatives, Statement on the Motion of Reconciliation, 26 August 1999.

Howes, C., 'Relations Between Early Child Care and Schooling', *Developmental Psychology*, 24, 1988, pp. 53–7.

Howes, C., 'The Earliest Friendships', in *The Company they Keep*, eds, W.M. Bukowski, A.F. Newcomb & W.W. Hartup, Cambridge University Press, New York, 1996, pp. 66–86.

Howes, C., Rodning, C., Galluzzo, D.C. & Myers, L., 'Attachment and Child Care: Relationships with Mother and Caregiver', *Early Childhood Research Quarterly*, 3, 1988, pp. 403–16.

Hubel, D.H. & Wiesel, T.N., 'The Period of Susceptibility to the Physiologic Effects of Unilateral Eye Closure in Kittens', *Journal of Physiology*, 206, 1970, pp. 419–36.

Hughes, D. & Chen, L., 'When and What Parents Tell Their Children About Race: An Examination of Race-related Socialization in African-American Families', *Applied Development Sciences*, 1, 1997, pp. 200–14.

Hughes, J. & Stone, W., *Family Change and Community Life: Exploring the Links*, Australian Institute of Family Studies Research Paper No. 32, Australian Institute of Family Studies, Melbourne, 2003, <www.aifs.gov.au/institute/pubs/respaper/hughes.html>, accessed 25 July 2007.

Hugo, G., *Yearbook Australia 2001: A Century of Population Change in Australia*, catalogue no. 1301.0, Australian Bureau of Statistics, Canberra, 2001.

Human Rights and Equal Opportunity Commission (HREOC), *Bringing Them Home: Report of the National Inquiry into the Separation of Aboriginal and Torres Strait Islander Children from their Families*, HREOC, Sydney, 1997.

Human Rights and Equal Opportunity Commission (HREOC), *A Last Resort: A Summary Guide to the National Inquiry into Children in Immigration Detention*, HREOC, Sydney, 2004.

Humphreys, C. & Stanley, N., eds, *Domestic Violence and Child Protection: Directions for Good Practice*, Jessica Kingsley Publishers, London, 2006.

Hunter, B.H., 'Trends in Neighbourhood Inequality of Australian, Canadian and US Cities Since the 1970s', *The Australian Economic History Review*, 43, 2003, pp. 22–44.

Hunter, B. & Gray, M., 'Family and Social Factors Underlying the Labour Force Status of Indigenous Australians', *Family Matters*, 62, 2002, pp. 18–25.

Huynh, K., *Where the Sea Takes Us: A Vietnamese-Australian Story*, Harper Collins, Sydney, 2007.

Hyson, M., Copple, C. & Jones, J., 'Early Childhood Development and Education', in *Handbook of Child Psychology*, eds, W. Damon & R.M. Lerner, John Wiley & Sons, Hoboken, NJ, 2006, pp. 3–47.

International Center for Technology Assessment, *In-car Air Pollution*, CTA, 2000, <www.icta.org/doc/In-car%20pollution%20report.pdf>, accessed 19 March 2008.

Jack, G., 'Ecological Influences on Parenting and Child Development', *British Journal of Social Work*, 30, 2000, pp. 703–20.

Jaffe, P., Wolfe, D. & Wilson, S., *Children of Battered Women*, Sage, Newbury Park, CA, 1990.

Janicki, M.P., Dalton, A.J., Henderson, C.M. & Davidson, P.W., 'Mortality and Morbidity among Older Adults with Intellectual Disability: Health Service Considerations', *Disability and Rehabilitation*, 21, 1999, pp. 284–94.

Jencks, C., 'The Immigration Charade', *New York Review of Books*, 54, 14, 2007, pp. 49–52.

Jobling, A. & Cuskelly, M., 'Life Styles of Adults with Down Syndrome Living at Home', in *Down Syndrome Across the Life Span*, eds, M. Cuskelly, A. Jobling & S. Buckley, Whurr Publishers, London, 2002, pp. 109–20.

Johnson, D., Headey, B. & Jensen, B., *Communities, Social Capital and Public Policy: A Literature Review*, Department of Family and Community Services Policy Research Paper no. 26, Australian Government, Canberra, 2005.

Johnson, H.McB., 'My Right to Life', *Weekend Australian Magazine*, 3–4 May 2003, p. 21.

Kamien, M., *The Dark People of Bourke*, Australian Institute of Aboriginal Studies, Canberra, 1978.

Katz, R.T., 'Life Expectancy for Children with Cerebral Palsy and Mental Retardation: Implications for Life Care Planning', *NeuroRehabilitation*, 18, 3, 2003, pp. 261–70.

Kaufman, J. & Zigler, E., 'The Prevention of Child Maltreatment: Programming, Research, and Policy', in *Prevention of Child Maltreatment: Developmental and Ecological Perspectives*, eds, D.J. Willis, E.W. Holden & M. Rosenberg, Wiley, New York, 1992, pp. 269–95.

Kazdin, A.E., 'Conduct Disorder Across the Life-span', in *Developmental Psychopathology: Perspectives on Adjustment, Risk and Disorder*, eds, S.S. Luthar, J.A. Burack, D. Cicchetti & J.R. Weisz, Cambridge University Press, Cambridge, 1997, pp. 248–72.

Kearns, R.A., Collins, D.C.A. & Neuwelt, P.M., 'The Walking School Bus: Extending Children's Geographies?', *Area*, 35, 3, 2003, pp. 285–92.

Keating, D.P. & Hertzman, C., *Developmental Health and the Wealth of Nations*, The Guilford Press, New York, 1999.

Kidd, R., 'You Can Trust Me, I'm With the Government', paper presented at One Family, Many Histories Conference, Brisbane, September 1994.

Kilmartin, C., 'Working Mothers Throughout the Decade', *Family Matters*, 26, 1990, p. 49.

Kim, H.W., Greenberg, J.S., Seltzer, M.M., & Krauss, M.W., 'The Role of Coping in Maintaining the Psychological Well-being of Mothers of Adults with Intellectual Disability and Mental Illness', *Journal of Intellectual Disability Research*, 47, 2003, pp. 313–27.

King, G.A., Zwaigenbaum, L., King, S., Baxter, D., Rosenbaum, P. & Bates, A., 'A Qualitative Investigation of Changes in the Belief Systems of Families of Children with Autism or Down Syndrome', *Child: Care, Health & Development*, 32, 2006, pp. 353–69.

Kingwill, S., 'Isolation: A Key Factor which Affects Australian Families and Their Children: Implications of CONTACT Inc. Initiatives for Commonwealth Policies and Priorities in Education and Child Support', Submission to Employment, Education and Training Reference Committee, Canberra, 1995.

Kitzman, H., Olds, D.L., Henderson, C.R., Tatelbaum, R., McConnochie, K.M., Sidora, K., Luckey, D.W., Shaver, D., Engelhardt, K., James, D. & Barnard, K., 'Effect of Prenatal and Infancy Home Visitation by Nurses on Pregnancy Outcomes, Childhood Injuries, and Repeated Childbearing', *Journal of the American Medical Association*, 278, 1997, pp. 644–52.

Korbin, J., 'Cross-cultural Perspectives and Research Directions for the 21st Century', *Child Abuse & Neglect*, 15, Supplement 1, 1991, pp. 66–77.

Krashinksy, M., 'Does Auspice Matter?: The Case of Day Care for Children in Canada', in *Private Action and the Public Good*, eds, W.W. Powell & E.S. Clemens, Yale University Press, New Haven, CO, 1999, pp. 114–23.

Krishbaum, M., 'A Disability Culture Perspective on Early Intervention with Parents with Physical or Cognitive Disabilities and their Infants', *Infants and Young Children*, 13, 2, 2000, pp. 9–20.

Kufeldt, K. & McKenzie, B., eds, *Child Welfare: Connecting Research, Policy and Practice*, Wilfrid Laurier University Press, Waterloo, Ontario, 2003.

Ladd, G., 'Peer Relationships and Social Competence During Early and Middle Childhood', *Annual Review of Psychology*, 50, 1999, pp. 333–59.

Lamb, M.E., 'Fathers and Child Development: An Introductory Overview and Guide', in *The Role of the Father in Child Development*, ed., M.E. Lamb, John Wiley & Sons, New York, 1997, pp. 1–18.

Laszloffy, T.A., 'Rethinking Family Development Theory: Teaching with the Systemic Family Development (SFD) Model', *Family Relations*, 51, 2002, pp. 206–14.

La Valle, I., Arthur, S., Millward, C., Scott, J. & Clayden, M., *Happy Families?: Atypical Work and Its Influence on Family Life*, The Policy Press, Bristol, UK, 2002.

Lave, J. & Wenger, E., *Situated Learning: Legitimate Peripheral Participation*, Cambridge University Press, Cambridge, 1999.

Laverty, J., 'The Experience of Grandparents Providing Regular Child Care for their Grandchildren', unpublished MEd (Hons) thesis, University of Western Sydney, 2003.

Lavin, K.E., McGuire, B.E. & Hogan, M.J., 'Age at Death of People with an Intellectual Disability in Ireland', *Journal of Intellectual Disability*, 10, 2006, pp. 155–64.

Laws, G. & Kelly, E., 'The Attitudes and Friendship Intentions of Children in United Kingdom Mainstream Schools Towards Peers with Physical or Intellectual Disabilities', *International Journal of Disability, Development and Education*, 52, 2005, pp. 79–99.

Lee, L. & Wilks, A., 'Documenting the Early Literacy and Numeracy Practices of Home Tutors in Distance and Isolated Education in Australia', *Australian Journal of Early Childhood*, 32, 2, 2007, pp. 28–36.

Lerner, M., Gunnarsson, L., Cochran, M. & Haggund, S., 'The Peer Relations of Children Reared in Child Care Centers or Home Settings: A Longitudinal Analysis', paper presented to the Biennial Meeting of the Society for Research in Child Development, Kansas City, MO, 1989.

Leventhal, T. & Brooks-Gunn, J., 'The Neighbourhoods They Live In: The Effects of Neighbourhood Residence Upon Child and Adolescent Outcomes', *Psychological Bulletin*, 126, 2000, pp. 309–37.

Leventhal, T. & Brooks-Gunn, J., 'Children and Youth in Neighbourhood Contexts', *Current Directions in Psychological Science*, 12, 2003, pp. 27–31.

Leventhal, T. & Brooks-Gunn, J., 'A Randomized Study of Neighbourhood Effects on Low-Income Children's Educational Outcomes', *Developmental Psychology*, 40, 2004, pp. 488–507.

Lewis, P. & Ker, S., *The Relationship Between Australian Transport Systems and Public Health*, proceedings of the 28th Australasian Transport Research Forum, Sydney, 28–30 September 2005, <www.patrec.org/atrf/papers/2005/Lewis%20&%20Ker%20S%20 (2005).pdf>, accessed 21 December 2007.

Lewis, V., *Development and Disability*, Blackwell Publishing, Malden, Mass., 2003.

Lievore, D., *Non-reporting and Hidden Recording of Sexual Assault: An International Literature Review*, Commonwealth Office for the Status of Women, Barton, ACT, 2003, <www.aic.gov.au/publications/reports/2003-06-review.html>, accessed 2 August 2007.

Linville, P.W., Salovey, P. & Fischer, G.W., 'Stereotyping and Perceived Distributions of Social Characteristics: An Application of Ingroup–outgroup Perception', in *Prejudice, Discrimination, and Racism*, eds, J.F. Davidio & S.L. Gaertner, Academic Press, San Diego, CA, 1986, pp. 165–208.

Little, H., 'Children's Risk-taking Behaviour: Implications for Early Childhood Policy and Practice', *International Journal of Early Years Education*, 14, 2, 2006, pp. 141–54.

Little, L., 'Differences in Stress and Coping for Mothers and Fathers of Children with Asperger's Syndrome and Nonverbal Learning Disorders', *Pediatric Nursing*, 28, 2002, pp. 565–70.

Llewellyn, G., Dunn, P., Fante, M., Turnbull, L. & Grace, R., 'Family Factors Influencing Out-of-home Placement Decisions', *Journal of Intellectual Disability Research*, 43, 3, 1999, pp. 219–41.

Llewellyn, G., Gething, L., Kenndig, H. & Cant, R., 'Older Parent Caregivers' Engagement with the Service System', *American Journal on Mental Retardation*, 109, 2004, pp. 379–96.

Llewellyn, G. & McConnell, D., 'Mothers With Learning Difficulties and Their Support Networks', *Journal of Intellectual Disability Research*, 46, 1, 2002, pp. 17–34.

Love, J.M., Harrison, L., Sagi-Schwartz, A., van Ijzendoorn, M.H., Ross, C., Ungerer, J.A., Raikes, H., Brady-Smith, C., Boller, K., Brooks-Gunn, J., Constantine, J., Kisker, E.E., Paulsell, D. & Chazan-Cohen, R., 'Child Care Quality Matters: How Conclusions May Vary with Context', *Child Development*, 74, 2003, pp. 1021–33.

Lustig, D.C., 'Family Coping in Families with a Child with a Disability', *Education and Training in Mental Retardation and Developmental Disabilities*, 37, 2002, pp. 14–22.

Luthar, S., Suniya, S. & Cicchetti, D., 'The Construct of Resilience: A Critical Evaluation and Guidelines for Future Work', *Child Development*, 71, 2000, p. 543–62.

Luthar, S. & Zelazo, L., 'Research on Resilience: An Integrative Review', in *Resilience and Vulnerability: Adaptation in the Context of Childhood Adversities*, ed., S. Luthar, Cambridge University Press, Cambridge, 2003, pp. 510–49.

MacQueen, K.M., McLellan, E., Metzger, D.S., Kegeles, S., Strauss, R.P., Scotti, R., Blanchard, L. & Trotter, R.T., 'What is Community? An Evidence-based Definition for Participatory Public Health', *American Journal of Public Health*, 91, 2001, pp. 1929–38.

Magaña, S. & Smith, M.J., 'Health Outcomes of Midlife and Older Latina and Black American Mothers of Children with Developmental Disabilities', *Mental Retardation*, 44, 2006, pp. 224–34.

Malone, P.S., Lansford, J.E., Castellino, D.R., Berlin, L.J., Dodge, K.A., Bates, J.E & Petit, G.S., 'Divorce and Child Behavior Problems: Applying Latent Change Score Models to Life Event Data', *Structural Equation Modeling*, 11, 2004, pp. 401–23.

Mandleco, B., Olsen, S.F., Dyches, T. & Marshall, E., 'The Relationship Between Family and Sibling Functioning in Families Raising a Child with a Disability', *Journal of Family Nursing*, 9, 4, 2003, pp. 365–96.

Manne, R., 'The Stolen Generation', *Quadrant*, January/February 1998, pp. 53–63.

Mansell, J., 'The Underlying Instability in Statutory Child Protection: Understanding the System Dynamics Driving Risk Assurance Levels', *Social Policy Journal of New Zealand*, 28, 2006, pp. 97–132.

Manuel, J.C., Balkrishnan, R., Camacho, F., Smith, B.P. & Koman, L.A., 'Factors Associated with Self-esteem in Pre-Adolescents and Adolescents with Cerebral Palsy', *Journal of Adolescent Health*, 32, 2003, pp. 456–8.

Manuel, J., Naughton, M.J., Balkrishnan, M.R., Smith, B.P. & Koman, L.A., 'Stress and Adaptation in Mothers of Children with Cerebral Palsy', *Journal of Pediatric Psychology*, 28, 2003, pp. 197–201.

Mares, P., *Borderline*, UNSW Press, Sydney, 2001.

Markus, A., *Governing Savages*, Allen & Unwin, Sydney, 1990.

Marr, D., 'Escape From a Life in Limbo', *Sydney Morning Herald*, October 27–28, 2007, p. 298.

Marr, D. & Wilkinson, M., *Dark Victory: The Military Campaign to Re-elect the Prime Minister*, Allen & Unwin, Sydney, 2003.

Martin, J.I., *The Migrant Presence*, Allen & Unwin, Sydney, 1979.

Mason, M.A., 'The Modern American Stepfamily: Problems and Possibilities', in *Family in Transition* (14th edn), eds, A. Skolnick & J. Solnick, 2007, pp. 201–23.

Masten, A. & Powell, J., 'A Resilience Framework for Research, Policy and Practice', in *Resilience and Vulnerability: Adaptation in the Context of Childhood Adversities*, ed., S. Luthar, Cambridge University Press, Cambridge, 2003, pp. 2–25.

Mattingley, C. & Hampton, K., *Survival in Our Own Land*, Hodder & Stoughton, Sydney, 1992.

Maunders, D., Liddell, M., Liddell, M. & Green, S., *Young People Leaving Care and Protection*, Australian Clearinghouse for Youth Studies, Hobart, Tasmania, 1999.

McCain, M. & Mustard, J.F., *Reversing the Real Brain Drain: Early Years Study, Final Report*, Ontario Children's Secretariat, Toronto, 1999.

McCarthy, A., Cuskelly, M., van Kraayenoord, C. & Cohen, J., 'Predictors of Stress in Mothers and Fathers of Children with Fragile X Syndrome', *Research in Developmental Disabilities*, 27, 2006, pp. 688–704.

McCaughey, W., 'Day Care—Liberating Who for What?', *Dissent*, 28, Winter 1972, pp. 3–8.

McCollough, A. & Joshi, H., *Neighbourhood and Family Influences on the Cognitive Ability of Children in the British National Child Development Study*, Institute for Social and Economic Research, University of Essex, Colchester, 2000, <www.iser.essex.ac.uk/pubs/workpaps/pdf/2000-24.pdf>, accessed 25 July 2007.

McConnell, D. & Llewellyn, G., 'Stereotypes, Parents with Intellectual Disability and Child Protection', *Journal of Social Welfare and Family Law*, 24, 3, 2002, pp. 1–21.

McDonald, P., 'Low Fertility in Australia: Evidence, Causes and Policy Responses', *People and Place*, 8, 2000, pp. 6–21.

McGurk, H., Caplan, M., Hennessy, E. & Moss, P., 'Controversy, Theory and Social Context in Contemporary Child Care Research', *Journal of Child Psychology and Psychiatry*, 34, 1993, pp. 3–23.

McKelvey, R. & Webb, J., 'Unaccompanied Status as a Risk Factor in Vietnamese Amerasians', *Social Sciences and Medicine*, 41, 1995, pp. 261–96.

McKelvey, R. & Webb, J., 'A Prospective Study of Psychological Distress Related to Refugee Camp Experience', *Australian & New Zealand Journal of Psychiatry*, 31, 1997, pp. 549–54.

McKie, L. & Cunningham-Burley, S., eds, *Families and Relationships: Families in Society, Boundaries and Relationships*, Policy Press, Bristol, 2005.

McLaren, P., *Life in Schools*, Longman, White Plains, NY, 1989.

McLoyd, V.C., Aikens, N.L. & Burton, L.M., 'Child Poverty, Policy and Practice', in *Handbook of Child Psychology*, eds, W. Damon & R.M. Lerner, John Wiley & Sons, Hoboken, NJ, 2006, pp. 700–75.

Meadows, S., *Parenting Behaviour and Children's Cognitive Development*, Psychology Press, Hove, 1996.

Mekertichian, L.K. & Bowes, J.M., 'Does Parenting Matter? The Challenge of the Behaviour Geneticists', *Journal of Family Studies*, 2, 1996, pp. 131–45.

Melsom, G., *The Changing Face of Homelessness*, Australian Federation of Homelessness Organisations, Dickson, ACT, 2007, <www.afho.org.au/documents/ ThechangingFaceofHomelessness_Op_ed.pdf>, accessed 23 August 2007.

Melton, G.B., 'Chronic Neglect of Family Violence: More than a Decade of Reports to Guide US Policy', *Child Abuse & Neglect*, 26, 2002, pp. 569–86.

Mendes, P. & Moslehuddin, B., 'From Dependence to Interdependence: Towards Better Outcomes for Young People Leaving State Care', *Child Abuse Review*, 15, 2006, pp. 110–26.

Mercer, J., *Labelling the Mentally Retarded*, University of California Press, Berkeley, 1973.

Merkes, M., 'Is Social Capital Moving Online?', *Opinion Online*, posted 15 January 2002, <www.onlineopinion.com.au/view.asp?article=1471>, accessed 15 July 2007.

Micklewright, J., 'Child Poverty in English-Speaking Countries: Innocenti Working Paper no. 94', UNICEF Innocenti Research Centre, Florence, 2003.

Miller, N.B., Cowan, P.A., Cowan, C.P., Hetherington, E.M. & Clingempeel, G., 'Externalising in Preschoolers and Early Adolescents: A Cross-study Replication of a Family Model', *Developmental Psychology*, 29, 1993, pp. 3–18.

Miller, P.J. & Goodnow, J.J., 'Cultural Practices: Toward an Integration of Culture and Development', in *New Directions for Child Development*, no. 67, eds, J.J. Goodnow, P.J. Miller & F. Kessel, Jossey-Bass, San Francisco, 1995, pp. 5–16.

Millward, C., 'Intergenerational Family Support', *Family Matters*, 39, 1994, pp. 10–13.

Minty, B., 'A Review of the Effects of Living Long-term in Substitute Care in the Context of a Discussion of Outcome Criteria', *Social Work & Social Sciences Review*, 8, 2000, pp. 169–93.

Mitchell, W., 'Research Review: The Role of Grandparents in Intergenerational Support for Families with Disabled Children: A Review of the Literature', *Child and Family Social Work*, 12, 2007, pp. 94–101.

Moore, L.L., Gao, D., Bradlee, M.L., Cupples, L.A., Sundarajan-Ramamurti, A. & Proctor, M.H., 'Does Early Physical Activity Predict Body Fat Change Throughout Childhood?', *Preventative Medicine*, 37, 2003, pp. 10–17.

Moore, M. & Russ, S.W., 'Pretend Play as a Resource for Children: Implications for Pediatricians and Health Professionals', *Developmental and Behavioral Pediatrics*, 27, 3, 2006, pp. 237–48.

Morgan, S., *My Place*, Fremantle Arts Centre Press, Fremantle, 1987.

Mrug, S. & Wallander, J.L., 'Self-concept of Young People with Physical Disabilities: Does Integration Play a Role?', *International Journal of Disability, Development and Education*, 49, 2002, pp. 267–80.

Muirhead, S., 'An Appreciative Inquiry About Adults with Down Syndrome', in *Down Syndrome Across the Life Span*, eds, M. Cuskelly, A. Jobling & S. Buckley, Whurr Publishers, London, 2002, pp. 149–58.

National Child Protection Clearinghouse, *Child Abuse Statistics*, Child Abuse Prevention Resource Sheet no. 1, Australian Institute of Family Studies, Melbourne, 2004.

National Crime Prevention, *Pathways to Prevention: Developmental and Early Intervention Approaches to Crime in Australia*, National Anti-Crime Strategy, Canberra, 1999; P. Salmelainen, 'Child Neglect: Its Causes and its Role in Delinquency', *Crime and Justice Bulletin: Contemporary Issues in Crime and Justice*, 33, <http://search.informit.com.au/ documentSummary;dn=916542316157238;res=E-LIBRARY>, accessed 9 January 2008.

National Institute of Child Health and Human Development (NICHD), 'Early Child Care and Children's Development Prior to School Entry: Results from the NICHD Study of Early Child Care', *American Educational Research Journal*, 39, 2002, pp.133–64.

National Institute of Child Health and Human Development (NICHD) Early Child Care Research Network, 'Child Care and Child Development: The NICHD Study of Early

Child Care', in *Developmental Follow-up: Concepts, Domains, and Methods*, eds, S.L. Friedman & H.C. Haywood, Academic Press, San Diego, CA, 1994, pp. 377–96.

National Institute of Child Health and Human Development (NICHD) Early Child Care Research Network, 'Characteristics of Infant Childcare: Factors Contributing to Positive Caregiving', *Early Childhood Research Quarterly*, 11, 1996, pp. 267–306.

National Institute of Child Health and Human Development (NICHD) Early Child Care Research Network, 'The Effects of Infant Child Care on Infant–Mother Attachment Security: Results of the NICHD Study of Early Child Care', *Child Development*, 68, 1997, pp. 860–79.

National Institute of Child Health and Human Development (NICHD) Early Child Care Research Network, 'Childcare and Mother–child Interaction in the First 3 years of Life', *Developmental Psychology*, 35, 1999, pp. 1399–413.

National Institute of Child Health and Human Development (NICHD) Early Child Care Research Network, 'Child Care and Child Development, Childcare and Family Predictors of Preschool Attachment and Stability from Infancy', *Developmental Psychology*, 37, 2001, pp. 847–62.

National Institute of Child Health and Human Development (NICHD) Early Child Care Research Network, 'Child-care Structure Process Outcome: Direct and Indirect Effects of Child Care Quality on Young Children's Development', *Psychological Science*, 13, 2002a, pp. 199–206.

National Institute of Child Health and Human Development (NICHD) Early Child Care Research Network, 'Early Child Care and Children's Development Prior to School Entry: Results from the NICHD Study of Early Child Care', *American Educational Research Journal*, 39, 2002b, pp. 367–87.

National Institute of Child Health and Human Development (NICHD) Early Child Care Research Network, 'Families Matter—Even for Kids in Child Care', *Journal of Developmental and Behavioural Pediatrics*, 24, 2003, pp. 58–62.

National Institute of Child Health and Human Development (NICHD) Early Child Care Research Network, eds, *Child Care and Child Development: Results from the NICHD Study of Early Child Care and Youth Development*, Guilford Press, New York, 2005a.

National Institute of Child Health and Human Development (NICHD) Early Child Care Research Network, 'Early Child Care and Children's Development in the Primary Grades: Results from the NICHD Study of Early Child Care', *American Educational Research Journal*, 43, 2005b, pp. 537–70.

National Institute of Child Health and Human Development (NICHD) Early Child Care Research Network, 'Child Care Effect Sizes for the NICHD Study of Early Child Care and Youth Development', *American Psychologist*, 61, 2006, pp. 99–116.

Neilsen-Hewett, C.M., 'Children's Peer Relations and School Adjustment: Looking Beyond the Classroom Walls', unpublished PhD thesis, Macquarie University, 2001.

Neumann, E.A., *The Elements of Play*, MSS Information, New York, 1971.

Neumann, K., 'Been There, Done That?', in *Yearning to Breathe Free*, eds, D. Lusher & N. Haslam, Federation Press, Sydney, 2007, pp. 21–34.

Nguyen, V. & Ho, M., 'Vietnamese–Australian Families', in *Families and Cultural Diversity in Australia*, ed., R. Hartley, Australian Institute of Family Studies, Melbourne, 1995, pp. 216–40.

Nicholas, D.B., McNeill, T., Montgomery, G., Stapleford, C. & McClure, M., 'Communication Features in an Online Group for Fathers of Children with Spina Bifida: Considerations for Group Development Among Men', *Social Work with Groups*, 26, 2, 2003, pp. 65–80.

Noonan, B.M., Gallor, S.M., Hensler-McGinnis, N.F., Fassinger, R.E., Wang, S. & Goodman, J., 'Challenge and Success: A Qualitative Study of the Career Development of Highly Achieving Women with Physical and Sensory Disabilities', *Journal of Counselling Psychology*, 51, 2004, pp. 68–80.

Nowicki, E.A., 'A Cross-Sectional Multivariate Analysis of Children's Attitudes towards Disabilities', *Journal of Intellectual Disability Research*, 50, 2006, pp. 335–48.

NSW Aboriginal Education Consultative Group and New South Wales Department of
    Education and Training, *The Report of the Review of Aboriginal Education*, NSW Department
    of Education and Training, Darlinghurst, 2004.

NSW Child Death Review Team, *Second Annual Report 1996–1997*, NSW Commission for
    Children & Young People, Sydney, 1998.

NSW Child Death Review Team, *Annual Report 2005*, NSW Commission for Children and
    Young People, Sydney, 2006, <www.kids.nsw.gov.au/uploads/documents/cdrt2005_full.pdf>,
    accessed 26 June 2007.

NSW Ombudsman, *Report of Reviewable Deaths in 2006 Volume 2: Child Deaths*, NSW
    Ombudsman, Sydney, 2007.

NSW Parliament, *Report of the NSW Aboriginal Children's Research Project to the Select
    Committee of the Legislative Assembly upon Aborigines*, NSW Government Printer, Sydney,
    1981.

Oakley, A., 'Women and Children First and Last: Parallels and Differences Between Children's
    and Women's Studies', in *Children's Childhoods: Observed and Experienced*, ed., B. Mayall,
    Falmer Press, London, 1994, pp. 13–32.

O'Brien, C., 'Transportation that's Actually Good for the Soul', *National Center for Bicycling
    and Walking (NCBW) Forum (Canada)*, 54, 2003, pp. 1–13.

O'Brien, P., 'Are We Helping Them Home?', a paper on the surveys of progress in the
    implementation of the *Bringing Them Home* Recommendations, Responses by the
    Government and Opposition Main Committee Room, Parliament House, Canberra,
    13 November 2002.

Ochiltree, G., *Effects of Child Care on Young Children: Forty Years of Research*, AIFS Early
    Childhood Study, paper no. 5, Australian Institute of Family Studies, Melbourne, 1994.

Olds, D.L., Eckenrode, J., Henderson, C.R., Kitzman, H., Powers, J., Cole, R., Sidora, K.,
    Morris, P., Petitt, L.M. & Luckey, D., 'Long-term Effects of Home Visitation on Maternal
    Life Course and Child Abuse and Neglect', *Journal of the American Medical Association*, 278,
    1997, pp. 637–43.

Olson, D.H., 'Circumplex Model of Marital and Family Systems: Assessing Family
    Functioning', in *Normal Family Processes*, ed., F. Walsh, The Guilford Press, New York, 1993.

Olsson, M.B. & Hwang, P.C., 'Influence of Macrostructure of Society on the Life Situation
    of Families with a Child with Intellectual Disability: Sweden as an Example', *Journal of
    Intellectual Disability Research*, 47, 2003, pp. 328–41.

Organisation for Economic Co-operation and Development (OECD), *Starting Strong—Early
    Childhood Education and Care*, OECD, Paris, 2001.

Organisation for Economic Co-operation and Development (OECD), *Starting Strong II: Early
    Childhood Education and Care*, OECD, Washington, DC, 2006.

Osofsky, J.D. & Thompson, M.D., 'Adaptive and Maladaptive Parenting: Perspectives on
    Risk and Protective Factors', in *Handbook of Early Childhood Intervention* (2nd edn), eds,
    J.P. Shonkoff & S.J. Meisels, Cambridge University Press, Cambridge, 2000, pp. 54–75.

Ouyang, L., Grosse, S.D., Armour, B.S. & Waitzman, N.J., 'Health Care Expenditures of
    Children and Adults with Spina Bifida in a Privately Insured U.S. Population', *Birth
    Defects Research Part A: Clinical and Molecular Teratology*, 79, 2007, pp. 552–8.

Paquette, D., 'Theorizing the Father-Child Relationship: Mechanisms and Developmental
    Outcomes', *Human Development*, 47, 2004, pp. 193–219.

Parens, E. & Ach, A., 'Disability Rights Critique of Parental Genetic Testing: Reflections and
    Recommendations', *Mental Retardation and Developmental Disabilities Research Reviews*, 9,
    2003, pp. 40–7.

Park, J., Turnbull, A.P. & Turnbull, H.R. III., 'Impact of Poverty on Quality of Life in Families
    of Children with Disabilities', *Exceptional Children*, 68, 2002, pp. 151–71.

Parke, R.D., 'Fathers and Families', in *Handbook of Parenting*, vol. 3, ed., M.H. Bornstein,
    Lawrence Erlbaum, Mahwah, NJ, 1995, pp. 27–63.

Parke, R.D. & Buriel, R., 'Socialization in the Family: Ethnic and Ecological Perspectives', in
    Handbook of Child Psychology, ed., N. Eisenberg, Wiley, New York, 1997, pp. 463–552.

Patterson, J.M., 'Understanding Family Resilience', *Journal of Clinical Psychology*, 58, 2002, pp. 233–46.

Peisner-Feinberg, E.S., Burchinal, M.R., Clifford, R.M., Culkin, M.L., Howes, C., Kagan, S.L. & Yazejian, N., 'The Relation of Preschool Child-Care Quality to Children's Cognitive and Social Developmental Trajectories through Second Grade', *Child Development*, 72, 2001, pp. 1534–53.

Pelchat, D. & Lefebvre, H., 'A Holistic Intervention Programme for Families with a Child with a Disability', *Journal of Advanced Nursing*, 48, 2004, pp. 124–31.

Pellegrini, A.D. & Bjorklund, D.F., 'The Ontogeny and Phylogeny of Children's Object and Fantasy Play', *Human Nature*, 15, 1, 2004, pp. 23–43.

Pellegrini, A.D. & Smith, P.K., 'Physical Activity Play: The Nature and Function of a Neglected Aspect of Play', *Child Development*, 69, 3, 1998, pp. 577–98.

Phillips, D. & Howes, C., 'Indicators of Quality in Child Care: Review of Research', in *Quality in Child Care: What Does Research Tell Us?*, ed., D. Phillips, National Association for the Education of Young Children, Washington, DC, 1987, pp. 1–19.

Phillips, D.A., McCartney, K. & Scarr, S., 'Child Care Quality and Children's Social Development', *Developmental Psychology*, 23, 1987, pp. 537–43.

Phipps, S., *Does Policy Affect Outcomes for Young Children? An Analysis with International Microdata*, Applied Research Branch Strategic Policy, Human Resources Development, Quebec, Canada, August 1999.

Pinker, S., *How the Mind Works*, Penguin, Harmondsworth, UK, 1998.

Pipe, M.E., Lamb, M.E., Orbach, Y. & Cedarborg, A.C., eds, *Child Sexual Abuse: Disclosure, Delay and Denial*, Lawrence Erlbaum, Mahwah, NJ, 2007.

Pocock, B., *Having a Life: Work, Family, Fairness and Community in 2000*, Centre for Labour Research, Adelaide University, Adelaide, 2000, p. 8, <www.barbarapocock.com.au/documents/havingalife.pdf>, accessed 2 August 2007.

Pocock, B., *The Work/Life Collision*, Federation Press, Annandale, 2003.

Pottie, C. & Sumarah, J., 'Friendships Between Persons with and without Developmental Disabilities', *Mental Retardation*, 42, 2004, pp. 55–66.

Powell, D.R., 'Families and Early Childhood Interventions', in *Handbook of Child Psychology*, vol. 4, eds, W. Damon & R.M. Lerner, John Wiley & Sons, Hoboken, NJ, 2006, pp. 548–91.

Press, F., *What about the Kids?: Policy Directions for Improving the Experiences of Infants and Young Children in a Changing World*, NSW Commission for Children & Young People, QLD Commission for Children and Young People and Child Guardian, National Investment for the Early Years (NIFTeY), Sydney, 2007.

Press, F. & Woodrow, C., 'Commodification, Corporatisation and Children's Spaces', *Australian Journal of Education*, 49, 3, 2005, pp. 278–91.

Preston, N. & Symes, C., *Schools and Classrooms: A Cultural Studies Analysis of Education*, Longman, Melbourne, 1997.

Price, C., 'Ethnic Intermixture in Australia', *People and Place*, 2, 1993, pp. 8–10.

Provence, S. & Lipton, R., *Infants in Institutions*, International Universities Press, New York, 1962.

Punamäki, R., 'Can Ideological Commitment Protect Children's Psychosocial Well-being in Situations of Political Violence?', *Child Development*, 67, 1996, pp. 55–69.

Pung, A., 'Caveat Emptor', *The Monthly*, 17–20 October 2007, <www.themonthly.com.au/tm/node/67>, accessed 19 March 2008.

Pung, A., *Unpolished Gem*, Penguin, Melbourne, 2006.

Purcal, C. & Fisher, K., *Review of the Early Childhood Teachers Shortage Interim Policy*, Final Report for the NSW Department of Community Services, Office of Child Care, SPRC Report 5/04, University of New South Wales, 2004.

Putnam, F.W., 'Ten-year Research Update Review: Child Sexual Abuse', *Journal of the American Academy of Child & Adolescent Psychiatry*, 42, 2003, pp. 269–78.

Racine, Y. & Boyle, M.H., 'Family Functioning and Children's Behaviour Problems', in *Vulnerable Children*, ed., J.D. Willms, University of Alberta Press, Alberta, 2002, pp. 199–209.

Radke-Yarrow, M., Richters, J. & Wilson, W.E., 'Child Development in a Network of Relationships', in *Relationships Within Families: Mutual Influences*, eds, R.A. Hinde & J. Stevenson-Hinde, Clarendon, Oxford, 1988, p. 56.

Rank, J., Folke, J. & Jespersen, P.H., 'Differences in Cyclists and Car Drivers Exposure to Air Pollution from Traffic in the City of Copenhagen', *The Science of the Total Environment*, 279, 2001, pp. 131–6.

Reynolds, A.J., *Success in Early Intervention: Chicago Child Parent Centers*, University of Nebraska Press, Lincoln, NA, 2000.

Rheingold, H., *The Virtual Community: Homesteading on the Electronic Frontier*, MIT Press, Cambridge, MA, 2000, p. 5.

Rice, A. & Press, F., *Early Childhood Education in New South Wales: A Comparative Report*, report for the NSW Department of Education and Training commissioned by the Strategic Research Directorate, 2003.

Richters, J.E. & Zahn-Waxler, C., 'The Infant Day Care Controversy: Current Status and Future Directions', *Early Childhood Research Quarterly*, 3, 1988, pp. 319–36.

Rillotta, F. & Nettelbeck, T., 'Effects of an Awareness Program on Attitudes of Students without an Intellectual Disability towards Persons with an Intellectual Disability', *Journal of Intellectual & Developmental Disability*, 32, 2007, pp. 19–27.

Risse, L., 'Does Maternity Leave Encourage High Birth Rates?: Analysis of the Australian Labour Force', *Australian Journal of Labour Economics*, 9, 2006, pp. 343–70.

Robins, L. & Rutter, M., eds, *Straight and Devious Pathways from Childhood to Adulthood*, Cambridge University Press, Cambridge, 1990.

Rogoff, B., *Apprenticeship in Thinking: Cognitive Development in a Social Context*, Oxford University Press, New York, 1990.

Rogoff, B., *The Cultural Nature of Human Development*, Oxford University Press, New York, 2003.

Rooney, M., '"Oh You're Just up the Street!" Discovering Community as an Agent of Change', BA Honours Thesis, Human Ecology Program, School of Resources, Environment and Society, The Australian National University, Canberra, 2006.

Rosen, M., Clark, G. & Kivitz, M., *The History of Mental Retardation: Collected Papers*, vols 1 & 2, University Park Press, Baltimore, 1976.

Rowland, D.T., 'Family Diversity and the Life Cycle', *Journal of Comparative Family Studies*, 12, 1991, pp. 1–14.

Rowley, C., *The Destruction of Aboriginal Society*, Penguin, Ringwood, 1970.

Royal Children's Hospital, *Parenting Young Children*, Policy Brief no. 9, Centre for Community Child Health, Royal Children's Hospital, Melbourne, 2007.

Ruopp, R., Travers, J., Glantz, F. & Coelen, C., *Children at the Centre: Final Report of the National Day Care Study*, Abt Associates, Cambridge, MA, 1979.

Rush, E., *Child Care Quality in Australia*, Discussion Paper no. 84, Australia Institute, Canberra, 2006.

Rushton, A., Treseder, J. & Quinton, D., 'An Eight-Year Prospective Study of Older Boys Placed in Permanent Substitute Families', *Journal of Child Psychology and Psychiatry*, 17, 1995, pp. 39–45.

Russell, G., 'Sharing the Pleasures and Pain of Family Life', *Family Matters*, 37, 1994, pp. 13–19.

Rutter, M., *Maternal Deprivation Re-assessed*, Penguin, New York, 1981.

Rutter, M., 'Resilience Reconsidered: Conceptual Considerations, Empirical Findings, and Policy Considerations', in *Handbook of Early Childhood Intervention*, eds, J.A. Shonkoff & S.J. Meisels, Cambridge University Press, Cambridge, 2000, pp. 651–82.

Salmelainen, P., 'Child Neglect: Its Causes and its Role in Delinquency', *Crime and Justice Bulletin*, 33, 1996.

Salveron, M., Arney, F. & Scott, D., 'Sowing the Seeds of Innovation: Ideas for Child and Family Services', *Family Matters*, 73, 2006, pp. 38–45.

Sameroff, A., 'Identifying Risk and Protective Factors for Healthy Child Development', in *Families Count: Effects on Child and Adolescent Development*, eds, A. Clarke-Stewart & J. Dunn, Cambridge University Press, Cambridge, 2006, pp. 53–76.

Sammons, P., Sylva, K., Melhuish, E.C., Siraj-Blatchford, I., Taggart, B. & Grabbe, Y., *The Effective Provision of Pre-School and Primary Education 3-11 Project (EPPE 3-11): Influences on Children's Attainment and Progress in Key Stage 2: Cognitive Outcomes in Year 5. Full Report*, London: DfES/Institute of Education, University of London, 2007, <www.ioe.ac.uk/schools/ecpe/eppe/eppe3-11/eppe3-11%20pdfs/eppepapers/Tier%202%20full%20report%20-%20Final.pdf>, accessed 24 March 2008.

Sampson, R.J., Morenoff, J.D. & Gannon-Rowley, T., 'Assessing Neighbourhood Effects: Social Processes and New Directions in Research', *Annual Review of Sociology*, 28, 2002, pp. 443–78.

Sampson, R.J., Raudenbush, S.W. & Earls, F., 'Neighborhoods and Violent Crime: A Multilevel Study of Collective Efficacy', *Science*, 277, 1997, pp. 918–24.

Sanson, A., Nicholson, J., Ungerer, J., Zubrick, S., Wilson, K., Ainley, J., Berthelsen, D., Bittman, M., Broom, D., Harrison, L., Rodgers, B., Sawyer, M., Silburn, S., Strazdins, L., Vimpani, G. & Wake, M., *Introducing the Longitudinal Study of Australian Children, LSAC Discussion Paper no. 1*, Australian Institute of Family Studies, Melbourne, 2002.

Sawer, M. & Groves, A., *Working from the Inside: Twenty Years of the Office of the Status of Women*, Australian Government Publishing Service, Canberra, 1994.

Sawyer, M., 'Child and Adolescent Mental Health Issues: Future Directions', in *Investing in Our Children: Developing a Research Agenda*, ed., M. Prior, Academy of the Social Sciences in Australia, Canberra, 2002, pp. 83–94.

Scarr, S., *Mother Care/Other Care*, Basic Books, New York, 1984.

Schofield, G., *Part of the Family: Pathways Through Foster Care*, British Agencies for Adoption and Fostering, London, 2003.

Schofield, G., Thoburn, J., Howell, D. & Dickens, J., 'The Search for Stability and Permanence: Modelling the Pathways of Long-stay Looked After Children', *British Journal of Social Work*, 37, 2007, pp. 619–42.

Schweinhart, L.J., Barnes, H.V. & Weikart, D.P., *Significant Benefits: The High/Scope Perry Preschool Study through Age 27*, High/Scope Press, Ypsilant, MI, 1993.

Schweinhart, L.J. & Weikart, D.P., 'A Summary of Significant Benefits: The High/Scope Perry Pre-school Study through Age 27', in *Start Right: The Importance of Early Learning*, ed., C. Ball, Royal Society for the Encouragement of Arts, Manufacture & Commerce, London, 1994, pp. 97–102.

Schweitzer, R., Melville, F., Steel, Z. & Lacherez, P., 'Trauma, Post-migration Living Difficulties, and Social Support as Predictors of Psychological Adjustment in Resettled Sudanese Refugees', *Australian and New Zealand Journal of Psychiatry*, 40, 2006, pp. 179–87.

Scott, D., 'Embracing What Works: Building Communities that Strengthen Families', *Children Australia*, 25, 2000, pp. 4–9.

Scott, D., 'A Vision for Family Services: Support and Prevention that Works for Families at Risk', keynote presentation at Forum, A Vision for Family Services and Prevention that Works for Families at Risk, Sydney, 30 April 2003a.

Scott, D., 'Opening Comments', presented at CAFWAA Symposium, When Care is Not Enough, Canberra, 17 September 2003b.

Scott, D., 'Sowing the Seeds of Innovation in Child Protection', keynote presentation at the 10th Australasian Conference on Child Abuse and Neglect, Wellington, New Zealand, 15 February 2006.

Scott, D., Brady, S. & Glynn, P., 'New Mothers Groups as a Social Network Intervention: Consumer and Maternal Child Health Nurse Perspectives', *Australian Journal of Advanced Nursing*, 18, 4, 2001, pp. 23–9.

Scott, D. & Swain, S., *Confronting Cruelty: Historical Perspectives on Child Protection in Australia*, Melbourne University Press, Melbourne, 2002, p. xii.

Seagrim, G. & London, R., *Furnishing the Mind: A Comparative Study of Cognitive Development in Central Australian Aborigines*, Academic Press, Sydney, 1980.

Seddon, H., *Hansard*, WA Government Printing Office, Perth, 1938.

Seltzer, M.M., Greenberg, J.S., Orsmond, G.I. & Lounds, J., 'Life Course Studies of Siblings of Individuals with Developmental Disabilities', *Mental Retardation*, 43, 2005, pp. 354–9.

Senate Community Affairs References Committee, *A Hand Up Not a Hand Out: Renewing the Fight against Poverty*, Report on Poverty and Financial Hardship, Senate Printing Unit, Parliament House, Canberra, 2004.

Servais, L., 'Sexual Health Care in Persons with Intellectual Disabilities', *Mental Retardation and Developmental Disabilities Research Reviews*, 12, 1, 2006, pp. 48–56.

Shin, J.Y., 'Social Support for Families of Children with Mental Retardation: Comparison Between Korea and the United States', *Mental Retardation*, 40, 2002, pp. 103–18.

Shonkoff, J. & Phillips, D., *From Neurons to Neighbourhoods: The Science of Early Childhood Development*, National Academy Press, Washington DC, 2000.

Silburn, S.R., Zubrick, S.R., Lawrence, D.M., Mitrou, F.G., DeMaio, J.A., Blair, E., Cox, A., Dalby, R.B., Griffin, J.A., Pearson, G. & Hayward, C., 'The Intergenerational Effects of Forced Separation on the Social and Emotional Wellbeing of Aboriginal Children and Young People', *Family Matters*, 75, 2006, pp. 10–17.

Silove, D., 'The Psychosocial Effects of Torture, Mass Human Rights Violations and Refugee Trauma: Towards an Integrated Conceptual Framework', *Journal of Nervous and Mental Disease*, 187, 1999, pp. 200–7.

Silove, D. & Ekblad, S., 'How Well do Refugees Adapt after Resettlement in Western Countries?', *Acta Psychiatrica Scandinavica*, 106, 6, 2002, pp. 401–2.

Silove, D., Steel, Z. & Mollica, R., 'Detention of Asylum Seekers: Assault on Health, Human Rights and Social Development', *The Lancet*, 357, 2001, pp. 1436–7.

Silverstein, I., 'Transforming the Debate About Child Care and Maternal Employment', *American Psychologist*, 46, 1991, pp. 1025–32.

Simeonsson, R.J., McMillen, J.S. & Huntington, G.S., 'Secondary Conditions in Children with Disabilities: Spina Bifida as a Case Example', *Mental Retardation and Developmental Disabilities Research Reviews*, 8, 2002, pp. 198–205.

Sims, M. & Hutchins, T., 'The Many Faces of Child Care: Roles and Functions', *Australian Journal of Early Childhood*, 21, 1996, pp. 21–46.

Siraj-Blatchford, I., Sylva, K., Muttock, S., Gilden, R. & Bell, D., *Research Report no. 356, Researching Effective Pedagogy in the Early Years*, University of London, Institute of Education/Department for Education and Skills, London, 2002.

Skard, G. & Bundy, A.C., 'Play and Playfulness: What to Look For', in *Play in Occupational Therapy for Children* (2nd edn), eds, L.D. Parham & L.S. Fazio, Mosby, St Louis, in press.

Sloat, E. & Willms, J.D., 'A Gradient Approach to the Study of Childhood Vulnerability', in *Vulnerable Children*, ed., J.D. Willms, University of Alberta Press, Alberta, 2002, pp. 23–44.

Smith, C. & Thornberry, T.P., 'The Relationship Between Childhood Maltreatment and Adolescent Involvement in Delinquency', *Criminology*, 33, 1995, pp. 451–81.

Smith, P.K. & Drew, L.M., 'Grandparenthood', in *Handbook on Parenting: Becoming a Parent*, vol. 3, ed., M.H. Bornstein, Lawrence Erlbaum, Mahwah, NJ, 2002, pp. 141–73.

Social Inclusion Unit, *Evaluation: The Social Inclusion Initiative Big Picture, Roundtables, Background Discussion Paper Two, Social Inclusion Initiative Indicators*, Department of the Premier and Cabinet, South Australia, <www.socialinclusion.sa.gov.au/files/RR_SIIEPFebRTSIIndicators.pdf>, accessed 21 January 2008.

Solomon, Z., Kotler, M. & Mikulincer, M., 'Combat-related Posttraumatic Stress Disorder among Second-generation Holocaust Survivors: Preliminary Findings', *American Journal of Psychiatry*, 145, 1988, pp. 865–8.

Spearritt, P., 'The Kindergarten Movement: Tradition and Change', in *Social Change in Australia: Readings in Sociology*, ed., D. Edgar, Cheshire, Melbourne, 1974, pp. 583–96.

Stainton, T. & Besser, H., 'The Positive Impact of Children with an Intellectual Disability on the Family', *Journal of Intellectual & Developmental Disability*, 23, 1998, pp. 57–70.

Stanley, F., Richardson, S. & Prior, M., *Children of the Lucky Country?: How Australian Society Has Turned its Back on Children and Why Children Matter*, Macmillan, Sydney, 2005.

St Clair, L. & Osborne, A.F., 'The Ability and Behaviour of Children Who Have Been in Care or Separated from their Parents', *Early Childhood Development and Care*, Special Issue, 28, 1987.

Steel, Z., Silove, D., Bird, K., McGorry, P. & Mohan, O., 'Pathways from War Trauma to Posttraumatic Stress Symptoms among Tamil Asylum Seekers, Refugees and Immigrants', *Journal of Traumatic Stress*, 12, 1999, pp. 421–35.

Steel, Z., Silove, D., Phan, T. & Bauman, A., 'Long-term Effect of Psychological Trauma on the Mental Health of Vietnamese Refugees Resettled in Australia: A Population Based Study', *The Lancet*, 360, 2002, pp. 1056–62.

Steering Committee for the Review of Government Service Provision (Productivity Commission), *Overcoming Indigenous Disadvantage*, Attorney-General's Department, Canberra, 2007.

Stein, M., *Overcoming the Odds: Resilience and Young People Leaving Care*, Joseph Rowntree Foundation, London, 2005.

Stephenson, A., 'Physical Risk-taking: Dangerous or Endangered', *Early Years: An International Journal of Research and Development*, 23, 1, 2003, pp. 35–43.

Stratford, B., 'In the Beginning', in *New Approaches to Down Syndrome*, eds, B. Stratford & P. Gunn, Cassell, London, 1996, pp. 3–11.

Straus, M.A., Gelles, R.J. & Steinmetz, S.K., *Behind Closed Doors: Violence in the American Family*, Anchor Books, Garden City, NJ, 1980.

Strauss, C., 'Motives and Models', in *Human Motivation and Cultural Models*, eds, R.G. D'Andrade & C. Strauss, Cambridge University Press, New York, 1992, pp. 1–20.

Strauss, D., Shavelle, R., Reynolds, R., Rosenbloom, L. & Day, S., 'Survival in Cerebral Palsy in the Last 20 Years: Signs of Improvement?', *Developmental Medicine and Child Neurology*, 49, 2, 2007, pp. 86–92.

Strazdins, L., Clements, M.S., Korda, R.J., Broom, D.H. & D'Souza, R.M., 'Unsociable Work?: Non-standard Work Schedules, Family Relationships, and Children's Well-being in a 24-hour Economy', *Journal of Marriage and Family*, 68, 2, 2006, pp. 394–410.

Strike, J. & McConnell, D., 'Parents with Intellectual Disability: Just the Same, Only Different', *Interaction*, 15, 4, 2002, pp. 11–15.

Stubbs, C.O. & Lee, A.J., 'The Obesity Epidemic: Both Energy Intake and Physical Activity Contribute', *Medical Journal of Australia*, 181, 2004, pp. 489–91.

Sullivan, P.M. & Knutson, J.F., 'Maltreatment and Disabilities: A Population-based Epidemiological Study', *Child Abuse and Neglect*, 24, 2000, pp. 1257–73.

Sultmann, C.M. & Testro, P., *Directions in Out of Home Care: Challenges and Opportunities*, PeakCare Qld Inc., Paddington, Qld, 2001.

Summers, A., 'Making Profits out of Preschoolers', *Sydney Morning Herald*, 11 November 2002, p. 15.

Sumsion, J., 'The Corporatization of Australian Childcare', *Journal of Early Childhood Research*, 4, 2, 2006, pp. 99–120.

Sylva, K., Melhuish, E., Sammons, P., Siraj-Blatchford, I. & Taggart, B., *Technical Paper 12, The Final Report: Effective Pre-School Education*, University of London, Institute of Education, London, 2004.

Sylva, K., Melhuish, E., Sammons, P., Siraj-Blatchford, I., Taggart, B. & Elliot, K., *The Effective Provision of Pre-School Education (EPPE) Project: Findings from the Pre-school Period*, University of London, Institute of Education, London, 2003, pp. 3–4.

Sylva, K., Siraj-Blatchford, I. & Taggart, B., *The Early Childhood Environmental Rating Scale: 4 Curricular Subscales*, University of London, Institute of Education, London, 2003.

Sylva, K., Stein, A., Leach, P., Barnes J., Malmberg L-E. & FCCC Team, 'Family and Child Factors Related to the Use of Non-maternal Infant Care: An English Study', *Early Childhood Research Quarterly*, 22, 2007, pp. 118–36.

Taanila, A., Syjälä, L., Kokkonen, J. & Järvelin, M.R., 'Coping of Parents with Physically and/or Mentally Disabled Children', *Child: Care, Health & Development*, 28, 2002, pp. 73–86.

Tajfel, H., *Human Groups and Social Categories*, Cambridge University Press, Cambridge, 1981.

Taussig, H.N., Clyman, R.B. & Landsverk, J., 'Children Who Return Home from Foster Care: A 6-Year Prospective Study of Behavioural Health Outcomes in Adolescence', *Pediatrics*, 108, 2001, pp. 1–7.

Testro, P. & Peltola, C., *Rethinking Child Protection: A New Paradigm?*, PeakCare Qld Inc., Brisbane, 2007.

Thoburn, J., Lewis, A. & Shemmings, D., *Paternalism or Partnership: Family Involvement in the Child Protection Process*, HMSO, London, 1995.

Thomas, D., *The Social Psychology of Childhood Disability*, Methuen, London, 1978.

Thompson, M., McGorry, P., Silove, D. & Steel, Z., 'Maribyrnong Detention Centre Tamil Survey', in *The Mental Health and Well-being of On-shore Asylum Seekers in Australia*, eds, D. Silove & Z. Steel, Psychiatry Research and Teaching Unit, Sydney, 1998, pp. 27–30.

Thornton, M.C., Chatters, L.M., Taylor, R.J. & Allen, W.R., 'Sociodemographic and Environmental Correlates of Racial Socialization by Black Parents', *Child Development*, 61, 1990, pp. 401–9.

Tizard, B., *Adoption: A Second Chance*, Open Books, London, 1977.

Tolstoy, L., *Anna Karenina*, trans. A. & L. Maude, Penguin Books, Harmondsworth, 1954.

Tomison, A., 'Child Maltreatment and Substance Abuse', *National Child Protection Clearing House Discussion Paper no. 2*, Australian Institute of Family Studies, Melbourne, 1996a.

Tomison, A., 'Child Maltreatment and Mental Disorder', *National Child Protection Clearing House Discussion Paper no. 3*, Australian Institute of Family Studies, Melbourne, 1996b.

Tomison, A., 'Exploring Family Violence: Links Between Child Maltreatment and Domestic Violence', *Issues in Child Abuse Prevention*, no. 13, Australian Institute of Family Studies, Melbourne, 2000.

Toohey, M. & Beer, G., 'Is it Worth Working Now? Financial Incentives for Working Mothers Under Australia's New Tax System', paper presented at the Australian Social Policy Conference, Sydney, July 2003.

Townsend, M. & Hassell, J., 'Mainstream Students' Attitudes to Possible Inclusion in Unified Sports with Students Who Have an Intellectual Disability', *Journal of Applied Research in Intellectual Disabilities*, 20, 2007, pp. 265–73.

Traci, M.A., Seekins, T., Szalda-Petree, A. & Ravesloot, C., 'Assessing Secondary Conditioning Among Adults with Developmental Disabilities: A Preliminary Study', *Mental Retardation*, 40, 2002, pp. 119–31.

Tranter, P.J. & Pawson, E., 'Children's Access to Local Environments: A Case-study of Christchurch, New Zealand', *Local Environment*, 6, 1, 2001, pp. 27–48.

Trute, B., 'Grandparents of Children with Developmental Disabilities: Intergenerational Support and Family Well-being. Families in Society', *The Journal of Contemporary Human Services*, 84, 2003, pp. 119–27.

Trute, B., Hiebert-Murphy, D. & Levine, K., 'Parental Appraisal of the Family Impact of Childhood Developmental Disability: Times of Sadness and Times of Joy', *Journal of Intellectual & Developmental Disability*, 32, 2007, pp. 1–9.

UNICEF, *Official Summary: The State of the World's Children*, UNICEF, New York, 2003.

UNICEF, *The State of the World's Children*, UNICEF, New York, 2007.

United Nations High Commission for Refugees (UNHCR), *Statistical Yearbook 2003*, UNHCR, Geneva, 2003.

United Nations High Commission for Refugees (UNHCR), *Global Trends: Refugees Asylum-seekers, Returnees, Internally Displaced and Stateless Persons 2006* (revised 16.07.07), UNHCR, Geneva, 2007.

Valsiner, J., 'Two Alternative Epistemological Frameworks in Psychology: The Typological and Variational Modes of Thinking', *Journal of Mind and Behavior*, 5, 1984, pp. 449–70.

Vandell, D.L., Henderson, V.K. & Wilson, K., 'A Longitudinal Study of Children with Child Care Experiences of Varying Quality', *Child Development*, 59, 1988, pp. 1286–92.

Van Krieken, R., *Children and the State*, Allen & Unwin, Sydney, 1991.

Vash, C.L. & Crewe, N.M., *Psychology of Disability* (2nd edn), Springer Publishing, New York, 2004.

Vaughan, G.M., 'A Social Psychological Model of Ethnic Identity and Development', in *Children's Ethnic Socialization: Pluralism and Development*, eds, J.S. Phinney & M.J. Rotheran, Sage, Newbury Park, CA, 1987, pp. 73–91.

Victorian Department of Human Services, *Child Protection and Family Violence: Guidance for Child Protection Practitioners*, Department of Human Services, Melbourne, <www.office-for-children.vic.gov.au/child_protection/library/publications/protection/guidance>, accessed 20 March 2008.

Vig, S. & Kaminer, R., 'Maltreatment and Developmental Disabilities in Children', *Journal of Developmental and Physical Disabilities*, 14, 2002, pp. 371–86.

Vinson, T., *Reports of the Inquiry into the Provision of Public Education in New South Wales*, NSW Teachers Federation and Federation of P & C Associations of NSW, Sydney, 2002.

Vinson, T., *Dropping Off The Edge: The Distribution of Disadvantage in Australia*, Catholic Social Services Australia, Canberra, 2007.

Vinson, T., Baldry, E. & Hargreaves, J., 'Neighbourhoods, Networks, and Child Abuse', *British Journal of Social Work*, 26, 1996, pp. 523–43.

Vygotsky, L., *Mind in Society: The Development of Higher Psychological Processes*, Harvard University Press, Cambridge, MA, 1978.

Wakefield, W.D. & Hudley, C., 'Ethnic and Racial Identity and Adolescent Wellbeing', *Theory into Practice*, 46, 2, 2007, pp. 147–54.

Waldegrave, C., 'Contrasting National and Welfare Responses to Violence to Children', *Social Policy Journal of New Zealand*, 27, 2006, pp. 57–76.

Waldfogel, J., 'Welfare Reform and the Child Welfare System', *Children and Youth Services Review*, 26, 2004, pp. 919–39.

Walsh, P., 'Fixed Equipment: A Time for Change', *Australian Journal of Early Childhood*, 18, 2, 1993, pp. 23–9.

Warfield, M.E., 'Employment, Parenting, and Well-being Among Mothers of Children with Disabilities', *Mental Retardation*, 39, 2001, pp. 297–309.

Watamura, S.E., Donzella, B., Alwin, J. & Gunnar, M.R., 'Morning-to-afternoon Increases in Cortisol Concentrations for Infants and Toddlers at Child Care: Age Differences and Behavioural Correlates,' *Child Development*, 74, 2003, pp. 1006–20.

Waters, E.B. & Baur, L.A., 'Childhood Obesity: Modernity's Scourge', *Medical Journal of Australia*, 178, 9, 2003, pp. 422–3.

Watson, I., Buchanan, J., Campbell, I. & Briggs, C., *Fragmented Futures: New Challenges in Working Life*, Federation Press, Annandale, 2003.

Watson, J., 'Determined to be Self-determined', paper presented at the Frozen Futures Conference, Sydney, November 2002.

Watson, N., 'Well, I Know This is Going to Sound Very Strange to You, But I Don't See Myself as a Disabled Person: Identity and Disability', *Disability and Society*, 17, 2002, pp. 509–27.

Weatherburn, D. & Lind, B., *Social and Economic Stress, Child Neglect and Juvenile Delinquency*, NSW Bureau of Crime Statistics and Research, Sydney, 1997.

Weikart, D.P. & Schweinhart, L.J., 'High/Scope Preschool Program Outcomes', in *Preventing Antisocial Behavior: Interventions from Birth through Adolescence*, eds, J. McCord & R.E. Tremblay, The Guilford Press, New York, 1992, pp. 67–88.

Weisner, T., 'Ethnographic and Ecocultural Perspectives on Sibling Relationships', in *The Effects of Mental Retardation, Disability, and Illness on Sibling Relationships*, eds, Z. Stoneman & P.W. Berman, Paul H. Brookes Publishing, Baltimore, 1993, pp. 51–83.

Weisner, T.S., 'Ecocultural Understanding of Children's Developmental Pathways', *Human Development*, 45, 2002, pp. 275–81.

Werner, E.E., 'Resilience Research: Past, Present and Future', in *Resilience in Children, Families and Communities: Linking Context to Practice*, eds, R.deV. Peters & R.J. MacMahon, Plenum, New York, 2005, pp. 3–11.

Werner, E.E. & Smith, R.S., *Kauai's Children Come of Age*, University of Hawaii Press, Honolulu, HI, 1977.

Weston, R., Qu, L., Parker, R. & Alexander, M., *It's Not for Lack of Wanting Kids, Research Report no. 11*, report on the Fertility Decision Making Project, Melbourne, Australian Institute of Family Studies, 2004.

Weston, R., Qu, L. & Soriano, G., 'Implications of Men's Extended Work Hours', *Family Matters*, 61, 2002, pp. 18–25.

Whipple, E.E. & Webster-Stratton, C., 'The Role of Parental Stress in Physically Abusive Families', *Child Abuse & Neglect*, 15, 1991, pp. 279–91.

Whitebrook, M., Howes, C. & Phillips, D., *Who Cares? Child Care Teachers and the Quality of Care in America*, final report of the National Child Care Staffing Study, Child Care Employee Project, Oaklands, CA, 1990.

Wicker, A.W., *An Introduction to Ecological Psychology*, Cambridge University Press, Cambridge, 1979.

Wiener, J. & Schneider, B.H., 'A Multisource Exploration of the Friendship Patterns of Children with and without Learning Disabilities', *Journal of Abnormal Child Psychology*, 30, 2002, pp. 127–41.

Williams, J., Wake, M., Hesketh, K., Maher, E. & Waters, E., 'Health-related Quality of Life of Overweight and Obese Children—A Population Study', *Journal of the American Medical Association*, 293, 1, 2005, pp. 70–6.

Willis, S. & Tranter, A., 'Beyond the "Digital Divide": Internet Diffusion and Inequality in Australia', *Journal of Sociology*, 42, 1, 2006, pp. 43–59.

Wise, S., Edwards, B., Bowes, J., Sanson, A., Ungerer, J., Harrison, L. & Simpson, T., 'The Relation of Multiple and Changeable Childcare Arrangements to Early Communication Skills', presented at the 9th Australian Institute of Family Studies Conference, Melbourne, February 2005, <www.aifs.gov.au/institute/afrc9/wise1.html>, accessed 8 January 2008.

World Bank, *Early Child Development: From Measurement to Action—A Priority for Growth and Equity*, 2007, <web.worldbank.org/WBSITE/EXTERNAL/TOPICS/EXTCY/EXTECD/0,,contentMDK:21304601~pagePK:210058~piPK:210062~theSitePK:344939,00.html>, accessed 20 March 2008.

World Health Organization, 'International Classification of Functioning, Disability and Health', WHO, Geneva, 2001.

Wylie, C., Thompson, J. & Hendricks, A.K., *Competent Children at 5: Families and Early Education*, NZCER, Wellington, 1997.

YWCA, *Walking School Bus Output and Performance Report*, YWCA, Canberra, 2006.

Zimmerman, M.A. & Arunkumar, R., 'Resiliency Research: Implications for Schools and Policy', Social Policy Report, VIII, no. 4, Society for Research in Child Development, Ann Arbor, MI, 1994.

Zubrick, S., Silburn, S., Haywood, C. & Pearson, F., *Western Australian Aboriginal Health Survey Child Mental Health Survey*, Telethon Institute for Child Health Research, Perth, 2005.

Zuo, Y., Norberg, M., Wen, L.M. & Risel, C., 'Estimates of Overweight and Obesity among Samples of Preschool-aged Children in Melbourne and Sydney', *Nutrition & Dietetics*, 63, 2006, pp. 179–82.

Index